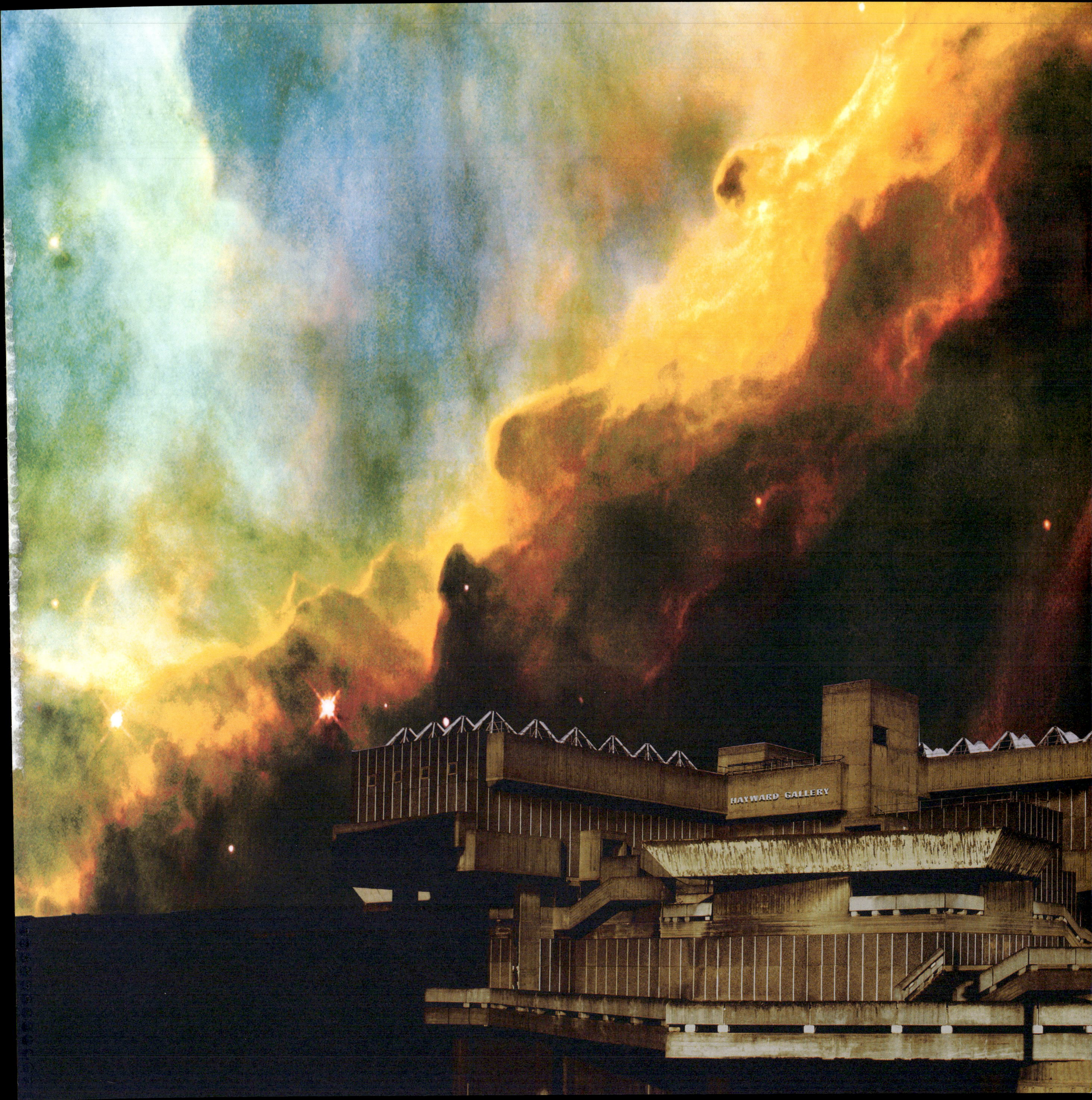
HAYWARD GALLERY

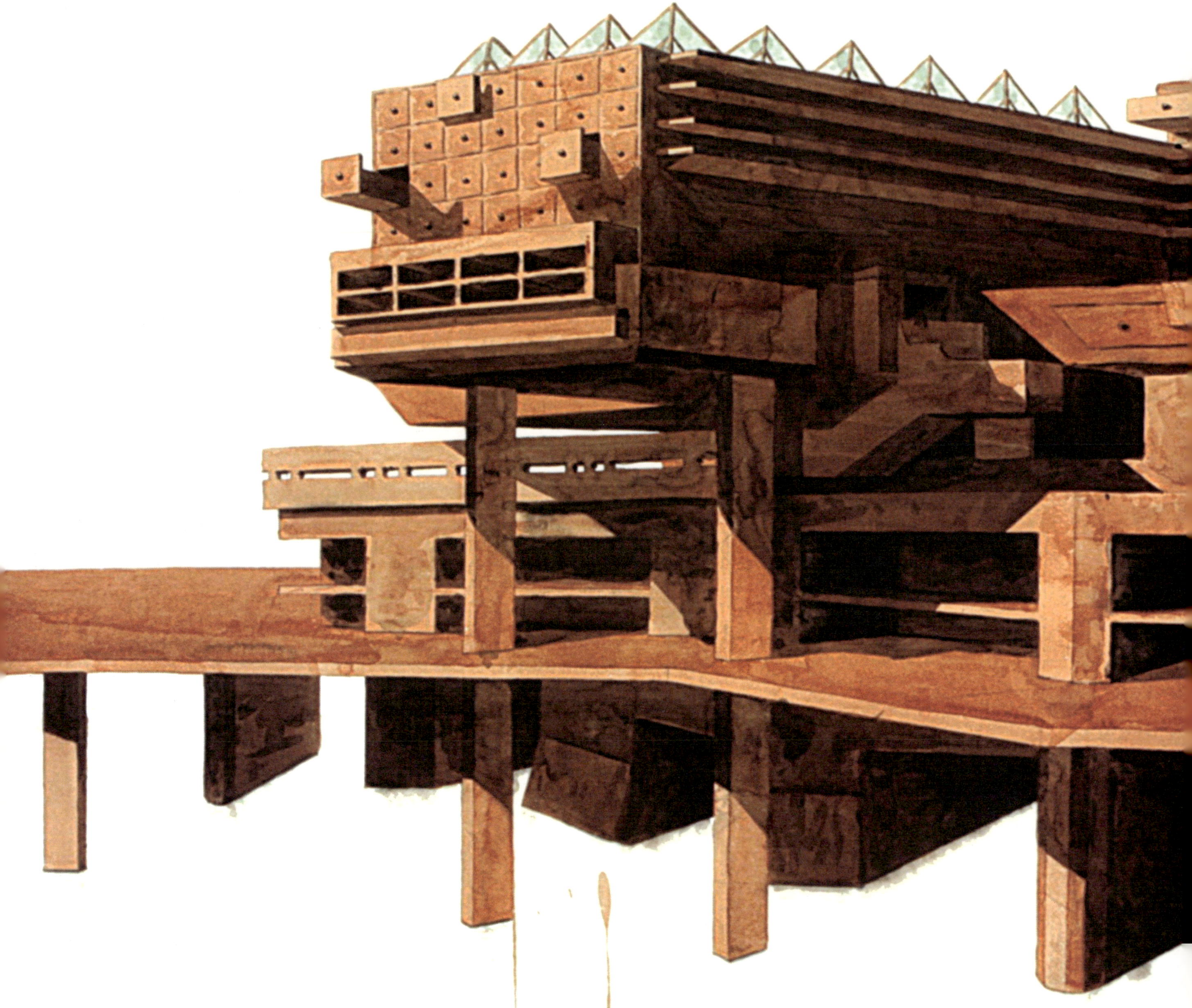

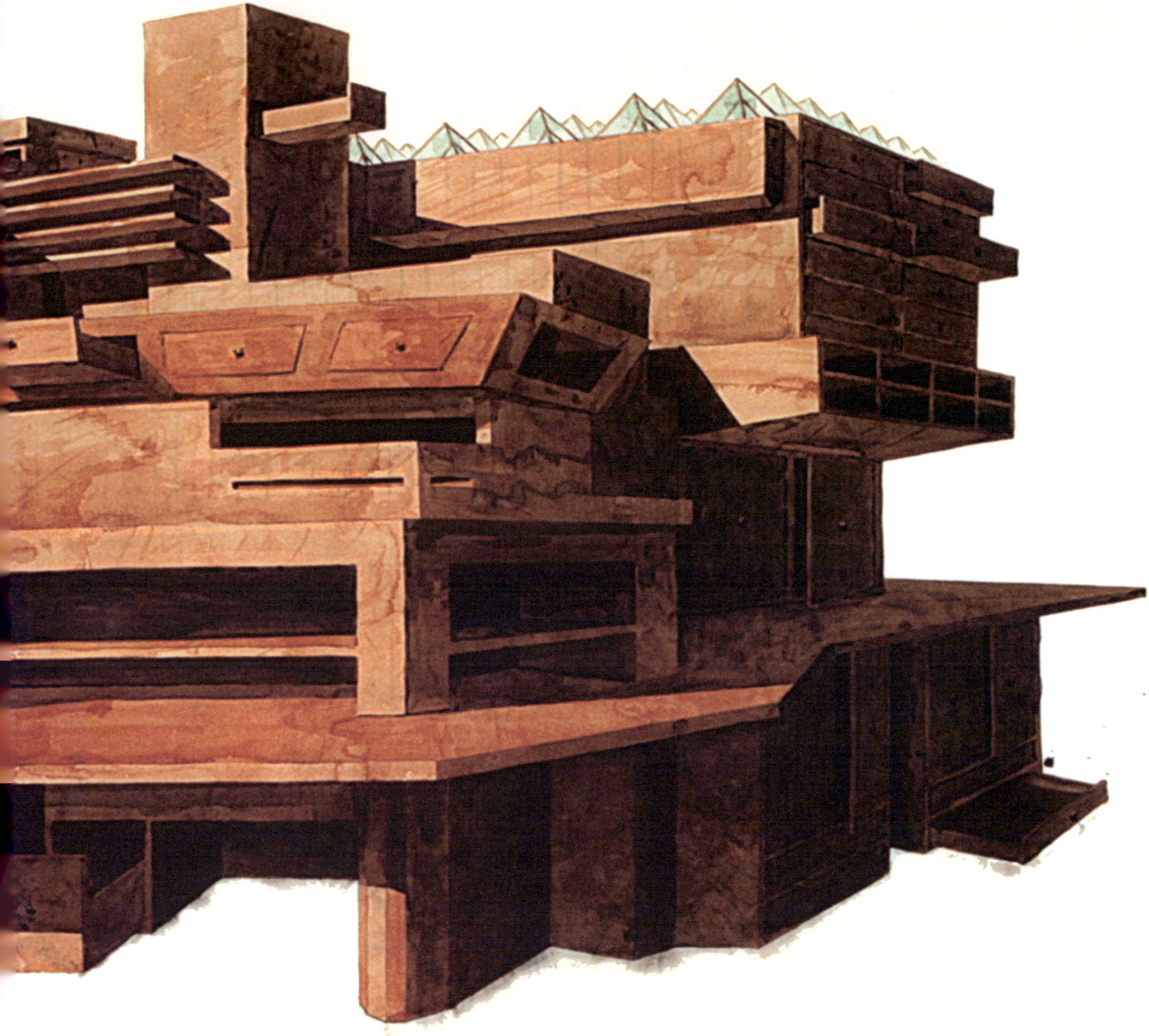

PSYC

BUILD

HO INGS

ARTISTS TAKE ON ARCHITECTURE

ATELIER BOW-WOW
MICHAEL BEUTLER
GELITIN
LOS CARPINTEROS
MIKE NELSON
ERNESTO NETO
TOBIAS PUTRIH
TOMAS SARACENO
DO HO SUH
RACHEL WHITEREAD

PUBLISHED ON THE OCCASION OF THE EXHIBITION *PSYCHO BUILDINGS: ARTISTS TAKE ON ARCHITECTURE*, **THE HAYWARD, LONDON, UK, 28 MAY — 25 AUGUST 2008**

Exhibition curated by Ralph Rugoff
Exhibition organised by Siobhan McCracken
and Richard Parry

Exhibition sponsored by

Bloomberg

With additional support from Outset Contemporary Art Fund and The Henry Moore Foundation

Art Publisher: Caroline Wetherilt
Publishing Co-ordinator: Giselle Osborne
Sales Manager: Deborah Power
Additional editorial assistance by Helen Luckett
Catalogue and typefaces designed by A2/SW/HK
Printed in the UK, with kind thanks to F&G

Psycho Hayward: Atelier Bow-Wow (front cover),
Rachel Whiteread (back cover),
Tobias Putrih (p. 1),
Los Carpinteros (pp. 2-3)

Published by Hayward Publishing,
Southbank Centre, Belvedere Road,
London, SE1 8XX, UK
www.southbankcentre.co.uk

ISBN: 978 1 85332 268 6

Distributed in North America, Central America and South America by D.A.P. / Distributed Art Publishers,
155 Sixth Avenue, 2nd Floor, New York, N.Y. 10013
tel: +212 627 1999
fax: +212 627 9484
www.artbook.com

Distributed outside North and South America
by Cornerhouse Publications
70 Oxford Street, Manchester M1 5NH
tel: +44 (0)161 200 1503
fax: +44 (0)161 200 1504
www.cornerhouse.org/books

CONTENTS

8 SPONSOR'S FOREWORD

11 PREFACE

12 ACKNOWLEDGEMENTS

ESSAYS

17 PSYCHO BUILDINGS
RALPH RUGOFF

29 SPECIES OF SPACES: ART, ARCHITECTURE AND ENVIRONMENT
BRIAN DILLON

39 ART'S USE OF ARCHITECTURE: PLACE, SITE AND SETTING
JANE RENDELL

ARTISTS

50 ATELIER BOW-WOW
DAVID GREENE

62 MICHAEL BEUTLER
FRANCIS MCKEE

74 GELITIN
MIDORI MATSUI

86 LOS CARPINTEROS
TUMELO MOSAKA

98 MIKE NELSON
BRIAN DILLON

110 ERNESTO NETO
PAULO HERKENHOFF

122 TOBIAS PUTRIH
FRANCESCO MANACORDA

134 TOMAS SARACENO
TOM MORTON

146 DO HO SUH
MIWON KWON

158 RACHEL WHITEREAD
IAIN SINCLAIR

170 PSYCHO BUILDINGS: AN ILLUSTRATED HISTORY

177 RELATED EXHIBITIONS

177 BIOGRAPHIES AND SELECTED EXHIBITIONS

180 LIST OF WORKS

180 PICTURE CREDITS

184 NOTES ON THE AUTHORS

ARTS COUNCIL ENGLAND

SOUTHBANK CENTRE HAYWARD PUBLISHING

SPONSOR'S FOREWORD

Gelitin
Psycho Hayward, **2008**

Bloomberg is delighted to sponsor *Psycho Buildings: Artists Take on Architecture* **at The Hayward, a major architectural initiative that invites exciting artists from around the world to radically transform one of London's most iconic public galleries. Combining cutting edge architectural design with innovative artistic vision,** *Psycho Buildings* **creates a series of ten dynamic experimental spaces to engage, provoke and inspire the public both within the gallery and on the public sculpture terraces outside.**

As a global financial communications company, Bloomberg is deeply committed to education and creativity, and to expanding access to art, science and the humanities. Bloomberg has a long history of supporting Southbank Centre and we are particularly proud to be working in partnership with The Hayward on a project that promotes new talent while bringing artists and audiences together in diverse new ways.

Bloomberg

www.bloomberg.com

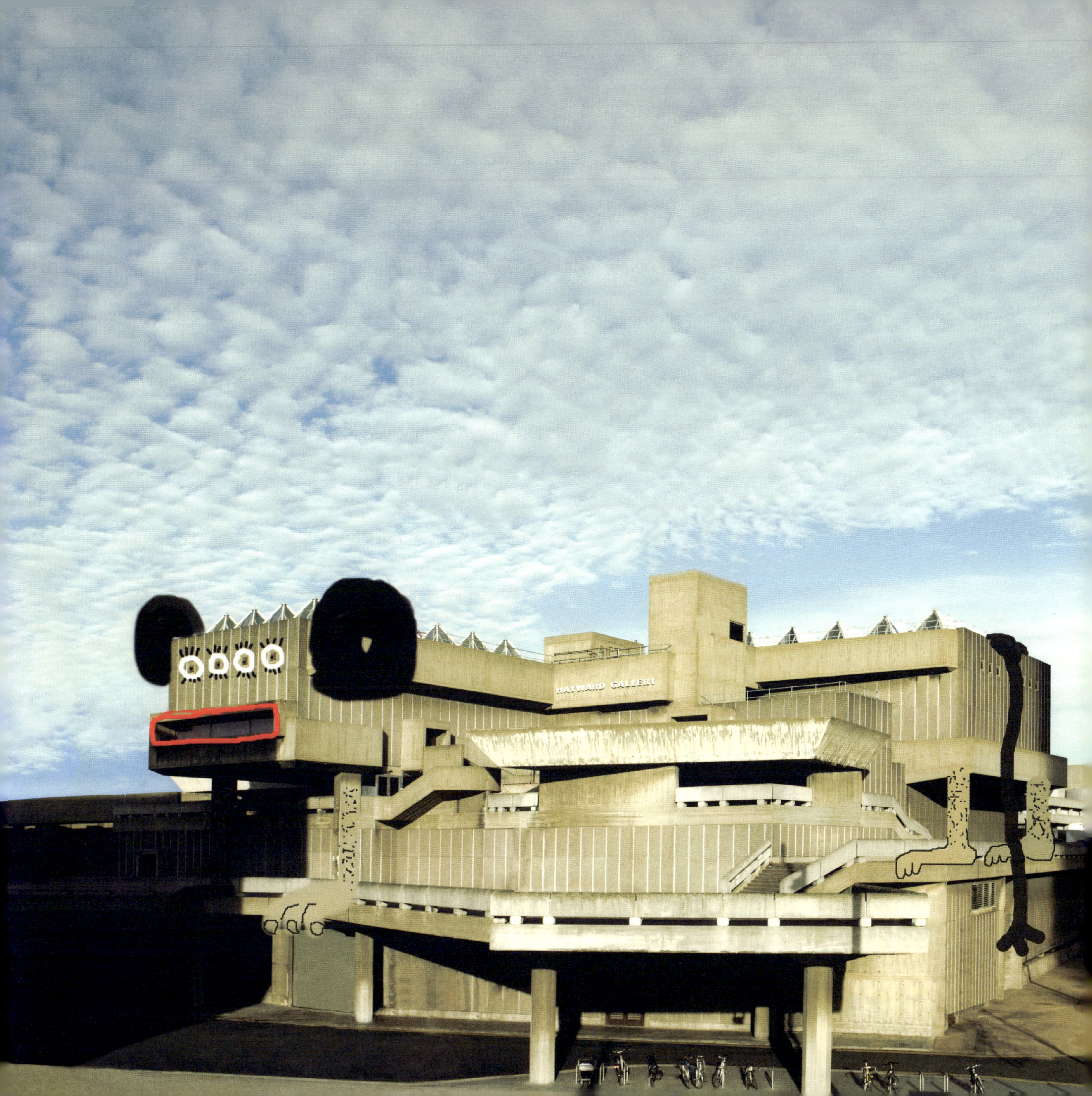
HAYWARD GALLERY

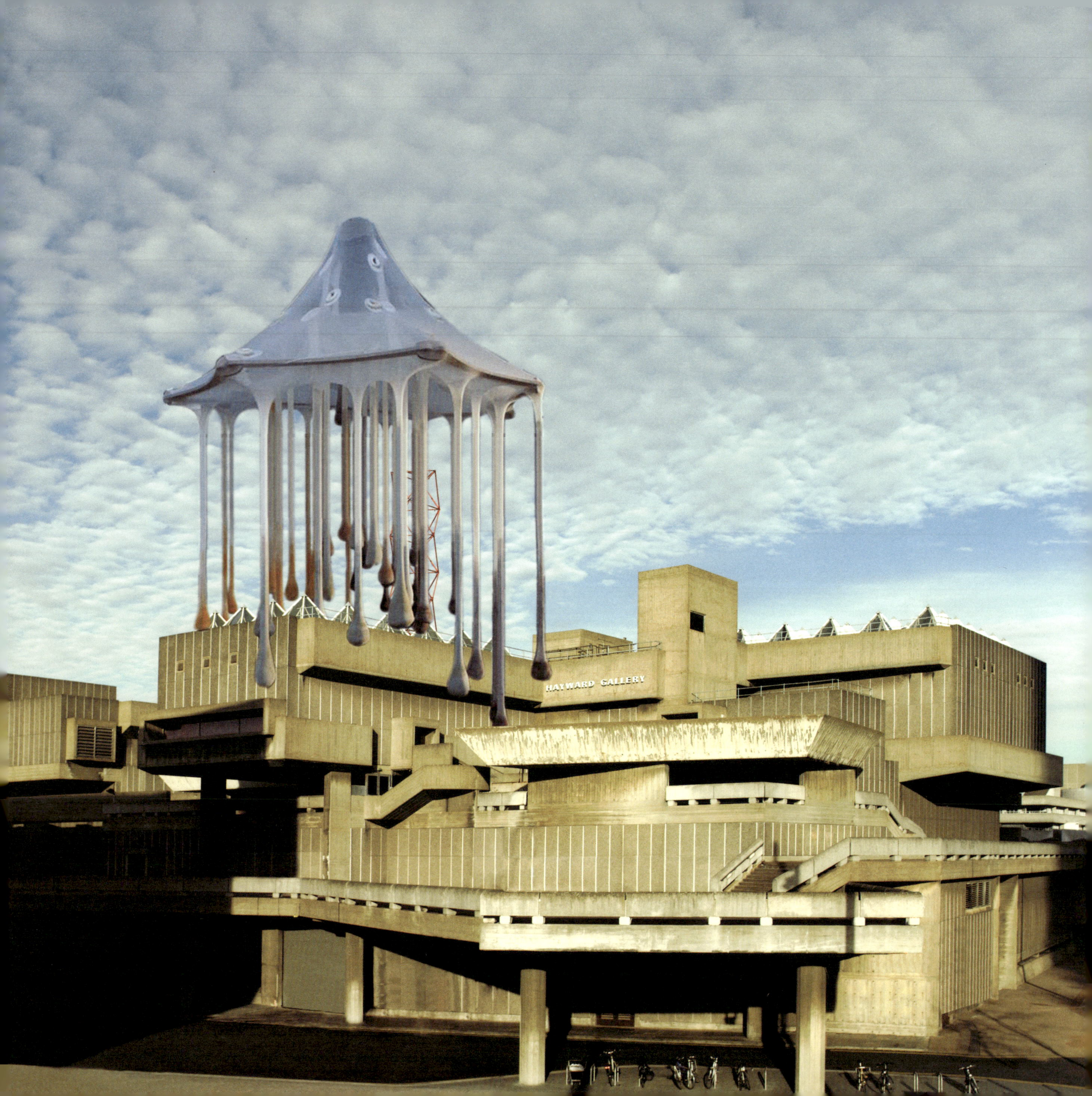
HAYWARD GALLERY

Ernesto Neto
Psycho Hayward, **2008**

PREFACE

Our relationship to space is undergoing a profound metamorphosis. The last piece of *terra incognita* was gobbled up over a century ago, and we are increasingly aware that we live on a finite planet. Uncertainties fuelled by blurring boundaries between suburb and city and public and private domains, as well as anxiety about immigration, all reflect our changing sense of space. And as we spend more and more time logged into the impalpable realms of electronic communications — from the internet to the cash machine, from Google Earth to video game consoles — our tendency to conceive of space in purely visual terms has taken precedence over responses of both thought and action deriving from the use of our other senses.

The contributors to the exhibition *Psycho Buildings: Artists Take on Architecture* aim to reactivate the complexities of our relationship to space, and to prompt us to re-examine our notions about the relationship between the individual and his or her surroundings. Often working against the grain of established architectural practices, they create habitat-like sculptures and architecturally-inflected installations that invite us to consider how built spaces function as social, psychological and perceptual environments. At the same time, their immersive sculptures highlight the crucial role of physical experience in our aesthetic encounters, emphasising what must be experienced rather than merely seen, and actively engaging each visitor as an adventurous participant in the work.

Psycho Buildings marks the 40th anniversary of The Hayward, one of world's most architecturally unique exhibition venues. Designed in the early 1960s by a team of young architects working for the London County Council, The Hayward's baroque brutalism has never conformed to anyone's expectations or model of what an exhibition space should be. Rigorously unconventional, it was conceived as part of an interconnected complex of buildings that make up Southbank Centre, and with its various walkways and sculpture terraces it embodies a democratic posture of access to the public. The building's cast concrete volumes convey a strong sense of spatial physicality while its open-ended interior plan encourages visitors to negotiate their own pathways through an exhibition. In short, The Hayward itself combines many of the elements explored by the artists in this exhibition.

As with any endeavor that involves constructing new spaces, *Psycho Buildings* has been a complex undertaking that has required both ingenuity and dedication on the part of many people. First of all, I would like to thank all of the artists for creating works that inspire and provoke us, and that ultimately lead us to reimagine our relationships to the spaces in which we live. Their studios and galleries have been an essential point of liaison and help during the preparation of this exhibition, and have earned our deep gratitude.

This exhibition could not have been realised without the leading support provided by Bloomberg, and we are immensely grateful for their generosity and boldness in sponsoring such an experimental project. Both Outset Contemporary Art Fund and The Henry Moore Foundation provided crucial support that helped enable artists to create newly commissioned works, and our profound thanks go to both. Our deep appreciation also goes to the following organisations for their indispensable support of this exhibition: Cecil Balmond and Arup; Austrian Cultural Forum London; Benchworks; Goethe-Institut London; The Great Britain Sasakawa Foundation; Korean Cultural Centre UK; ZENDOME GmbH; and Rieck Logistik GmbH & Co.KG.

This book features the work of 11 contributing authors, all of whom have earned our respect and gratitude for their insightful texts. Designers A2/SW/HK have matched their contribution by bringing a sense of intelligence and adventure to the design of this book, the production of which has been expertly managed by Caroline Wetherilt and the Hayward Publishing team.

The exhibition itself has benefited from the ceaseless activity, keen organisational skills and unwavering courage of Assistant Curator Siobhan McCracken, who was ably and enthusiastically joined in the latter stages of its preparation by Assistant Curator Richard Parry. Deputy Director Laura Stevenson brought her considerable skills to many aspects of managing this complex enterprise while Ruth Pelopida, Ed Smith and The Hayward installation team rose to its considerable logistical challenges with a willing spirit and an unalloyed professionalism.

Finally, my thanks go to Chief Executive Michael Lynch AM, Artistic Director Jude Kelly OBE, Southbank Centre's Board of Trustees and the entire organisation for its constant support of this adventure, which has changed and evolved over the past six months as its agenda was continually pushed forward by the creativity of the participating artists.

Ralph Rugoff
Director, The Hayward

ACKNOWLEDGEMENTS

For their significant contributions to this exhibition, we wish to thank:

Cecil Balmond and Triston Simmonds of Arup
Austrian Cultural Forum London
Benchworks
Create One
Goethe-Institut London
The Great Britain Sasakawa Foundation
Korean Cultural Centre UK
Rieck Logistik GmbH & Co.KG
David Derby and Mark Tyler of Price & Myers
ZENDOME GmbH (Carsten Fulland, Michael Schneider and Gordian Overschmidt)

In addition, a number of individuals and firms provided key advice at various stages of planning, and we are grateful for their assistance:

Dennis Ahern, Tectoniks Limited, Professor Denis Weaire, Andreas Weist

The galleries and studios of the participating artists helped in many ways with this exhibition. In particular, we wish to acknowledge the assistance of the following people:

Ticiana Correa, Galeria Fortes Vilaça; Lars Friedrich, Galerie Christian Nagel; Mark Francis, Kay Pallister and Cristina Colomar of Gagosian Gallery; Mariska Nietzman, Lehmann Maupin Gallery; Robin Klasnik, Matt's Gallery; Josie Browne, Stuart Krimko, George Wong of Max Protetch Gallery; Boshko Boskovic, Sean Kelly Gallery, New York; Tanya Bonakdar Gallery

And the following studio assistants:

Gunther Bernhard, Jeonggoo Cho, Tatiana Dager, Christophe Harrington, Jung Kyu Im, Tobias Ingels, Insook Jeon, (Betty) Bo Ra Kim, Bo Ram Kim, Christophe Meier, Marcelo Moletta, Mirai Morita, Simon Morville, Verónica Sedano Alvarez, Eoin Taylor, Emek Ulusay, Ben Washington, Hazel Willis, Sang Hee You

Hayward / Southbank Centre Staff

Many staff at The Hayward and Southbank Centre have contributed to the exhibition and its related programmes in numerous ways. We wish to thank them all for their work, with special thanks going to:

Jenni Carbins, Jeremy Clapham, Alison Cole, Becca Connock, Steve Cook, Froniga Creissen, Sarah Davies, Helen Faulkner, Mark King, Catherine Mallyon, Mike McCart, Britannia Morton, Rafal Niemojewski, Ruth Pelopida, Rebecca Preston, Sarah Sawkins, Julia Sawyer, Toby Skeggs, Ed Smith, Luisa Summers, Laura Try, Terry Vickery, George Walker, Hilton Wells, Imogen Winter, Cathy Woolley, Tony Woolley

For their outstanding work on the installation, we also wish to thank:

John Coles, Jure Mezek, David Wood

Tomas Saraceno
Psycho Hayward, **2008**

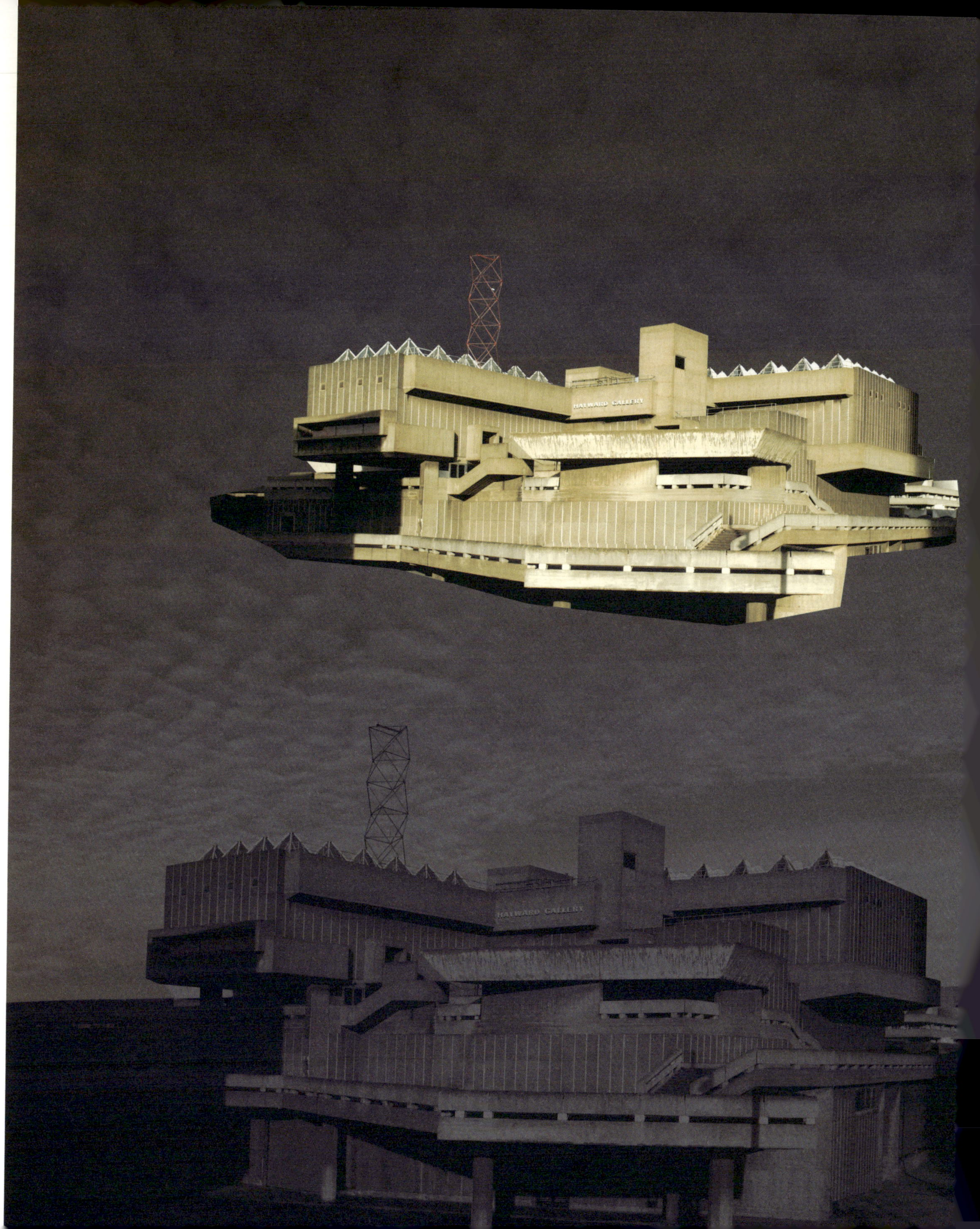

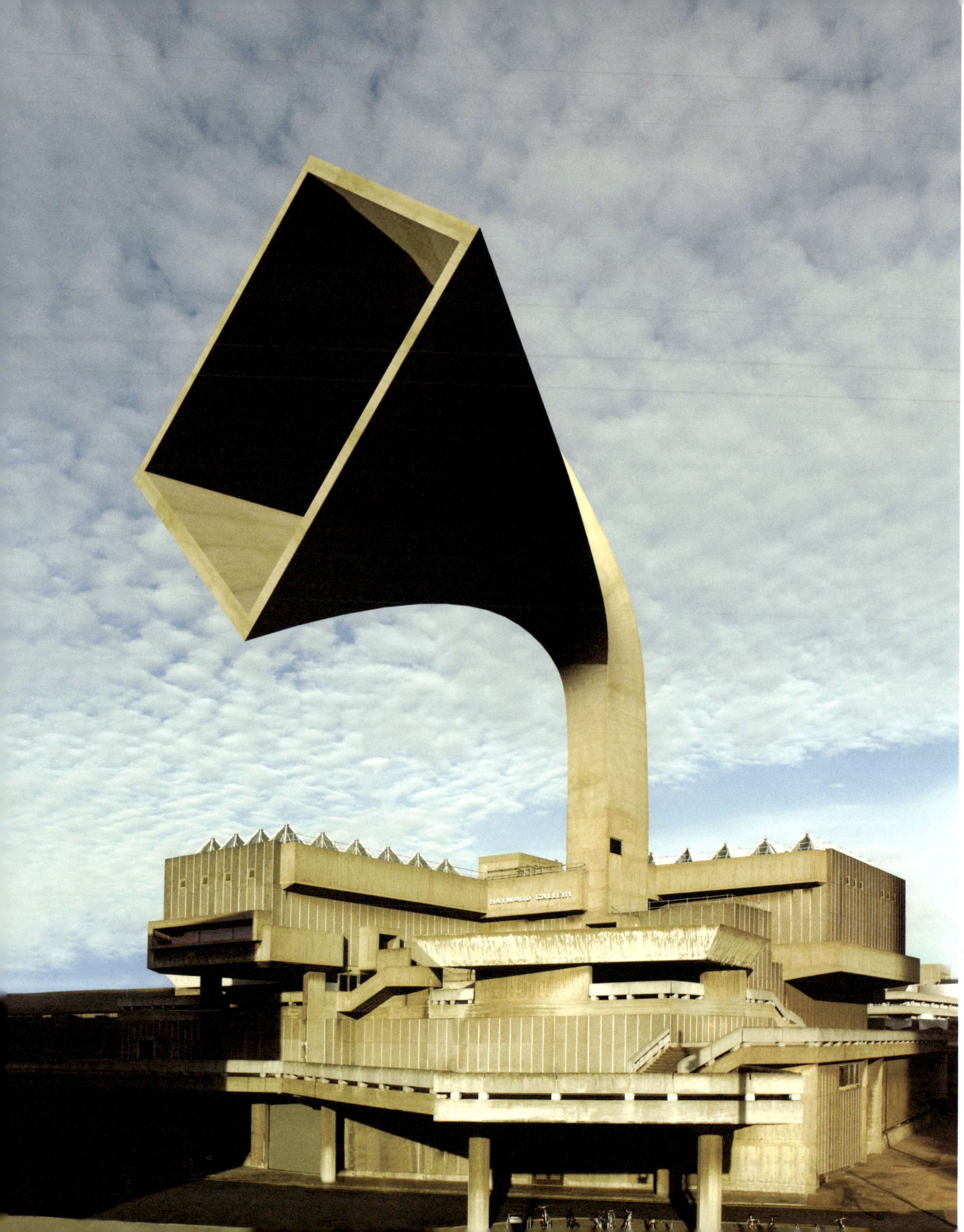

Atelier Bow-Wow
Psycho Hayward, **2008**

ESSAYS

Martin Kippenberger
Images from *Psychobuildings*,
1988

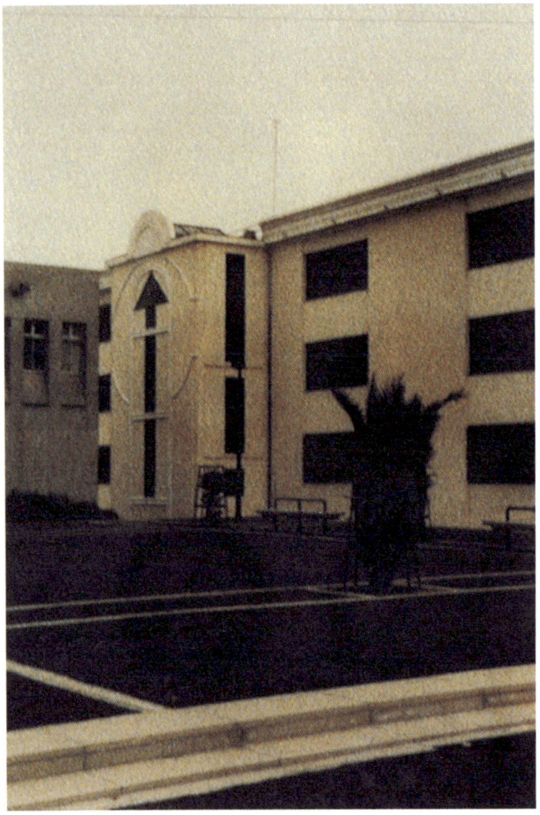

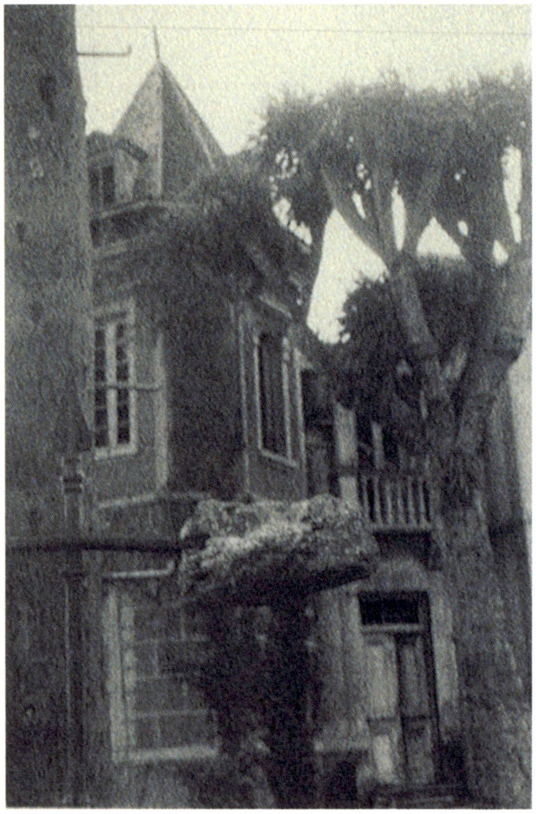

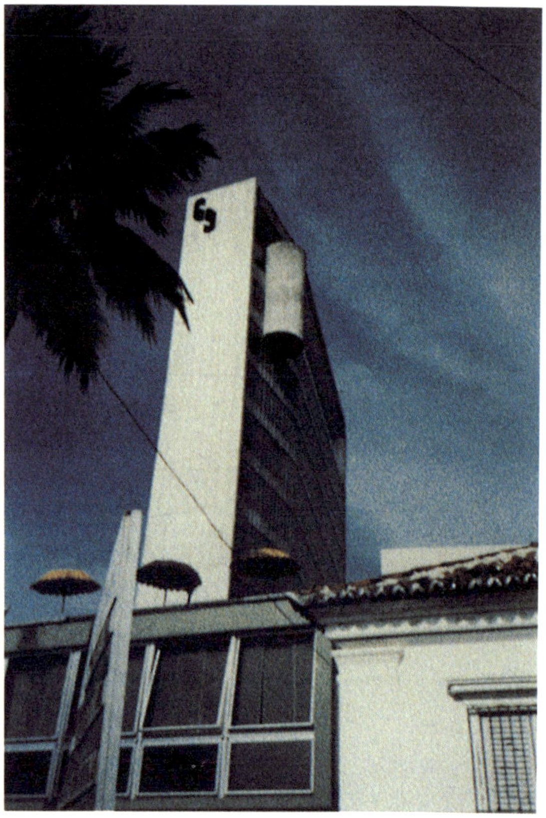

PSYCHO BUILDINGS

RALPH RUGOFF

In 1988, the German artist Martin Kippenberger published a small book of black-and-white photographs entitled *Psychobuildings*. Designed to resemble a publication from a well-known leftist publisher, it featured pictures of architectural structures, some in intermediary states of construction or demolition, that in one way or another conjured eccentric and idiosyncratic spaces, unpredictable alternatives to the homogenised logic of the urban grid. They could be loosely considered *psychotic* — the psychiatric term for a mental state involving a rupture with reality — inasmuch as they constituted breaks in the overly regulated fabric of the modern cityscape. Yet Kippenberger, a master of irony, seemed to hint at something else with this publication: namely, the questionable psychological state of the society that had created not only these kernels of irrational architecture but, more importantly, the straitjacket of metropolitan space that surrounded them. Indeed, rather than pathologise the anomalies that he photographed, the artist seemed to regard them (with affection as well as humour) as antidotes to the seamless sameness of the contemporary built environment. Incongruous bumps on the rectilinear surfaces of the city, they possess the salutary power to disrupt our habitual impulse to comprehend and consume the spaces around us with a single glance.

A psychobuilding, then, is not a symptom of a disorder but a welcome deviation from the rationalisation and abstraction of space that, historically, was one of the great projects of modernist architecture and urban planning. Adapted for the purposes of the exhibition *Psycho Buildings: Artists Take on Architecture*, Kippenberger's phrase seems an apt term for artworks that explore and embody what could be called the architectural unconscious. The artists in *Psycho Buildings* aim to reanimate the ways that we inhabit our surroundings — not only in phenomenological terms, but also by heightening our awareness of the complex social and cultural architecture of our spatial relations. Their work engages us in the political, corporeal and psychological dimensions of built spaces, as well as their formal and material aspects. At the same time, these artists aim to poke holes in our conventional packaging of space in order to reveal its multifarious character and dimensions, its continuity and, at times, its fragmentation.

On one level, their work belongs to an artistic trajectory that spans the past 100 years. Describing the evolution of modern sculpture, the minimalist artist Carl André famously remarked that it had developed from a concern with sculpture as form, to sculpture as structure and finally to sculpture as place. This shift in orientation mirrored an earlier rethinking of architecture as comprised of space, rather than of structural elements like walls and columns. Describing this conceptual turn, architectural historian Anthony Vidler has observed that this notion of space 'was adumbrated as a product of, and experienced through, bodily movement and psychological and optical projection. Space was interior, enveloping, enclosing, ritually sanctioned and structured by the body's motion through it. As such, it tended to break down the rigid stylistic categories of architectural history.'[1] In conjunction with Modernism's preferred vocabulary of reductive geometric forms, adopted by architects and abstract artists alike, this novel focus on space opened up a shared territory between the two disciplines, leading Constantin Brancusi, among others, to insist on their overlapping character.[2]

Beginning with the Futurists and Constructivists of the early twentieth century, and increasingly since the 1960s, sculptors have explored this shared territory by creating works that generate spaces rather than simply occupy them. Reimagining and reworking the traditional territory of architecture as well as sculpture, they have produced models for buildings, freestanding sculptural habitats, environmental installations, and (in the case of Minimalism) works that respond to and seek to formally incorporate the architecture in which they are displayed. Over the past two decades, a growing number of contemporary artists have expanded the terms of this engagement with architecture, mirroring a critical re-evaluation of spatial issues — a 'spatial crisis' as it is often called — that has been articulated in a number of fields including geography, cultural theory, philosophy and even economics.

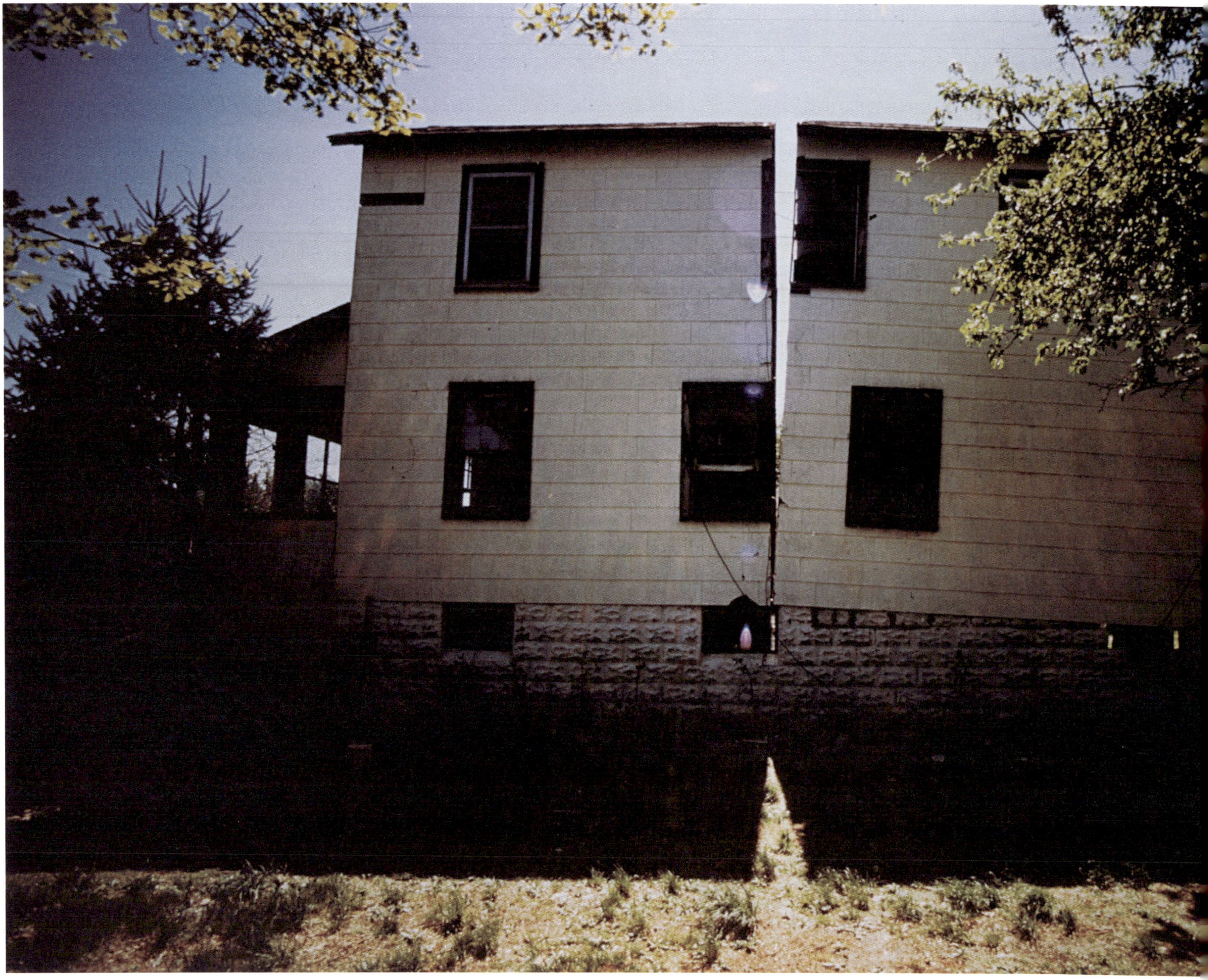

Gordon Matta-Clark
Splitting, **1974**

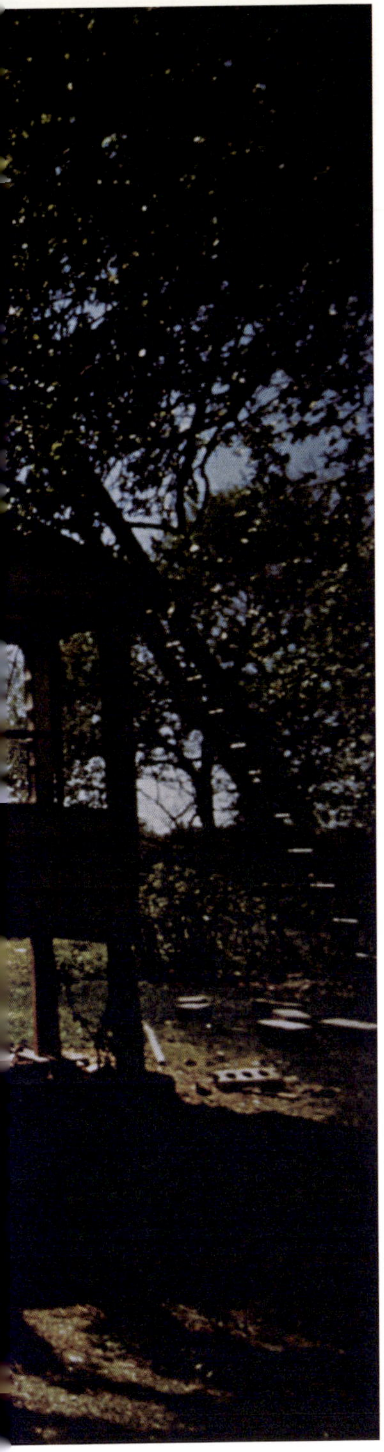

Yet the artists in *Psycho Buildings* are not primarily interested in architecture *per se*, either as a particular discipline or as a formal language to cannibalise. Unlike their numerous contemporaries who critically recycle and revisit the history of modernist architecture or appropriate elements of design in their work, they do not celebrate interdisciplinary practice, a fusing of art and architecture, as a way of (belatedly) questioning the autonomy of either discipline. Diverse and distinct in approach, their work is less engaged with mainstream Modernism than with alternative strains of twentieth-century art and design that explored the multiplicity of our spatial relations. (Key contributors to this history would include Vladimir Tatlin and El Lissitzky, surrealist and 'outsider' architecture, Buckminster Fuller and Frederick Kiesler, and artists from the 1960s and 1970s such as Hélio Oiticica, Gordon Matta-Clark, Robert Smithson, Vito Acconci and Dan Graham.) Likewise, their own architectonic structures, installations and interventions implicate us in spaces that simultaneously assume multiple characters and that are insistently complex rather than consistent. Here, we find architecture not in its functional guise but as a site of desire, memory and doubt, home to personal contingencies and collective histories, the clashing of cultures and coalescing of subjectivities. Refusing to address us as mere spectators, these works implicate us in the spaces they generate, engaging us in ways that are at once visceral and conceptual, and that call attention to what must be experienced rather than merely seen.

This emphasis on the role of the body in spatial perception has paralleled the growing role of media culture in shaping our understanding of space — a circumstance explicitly addressed by several artists in the exhibition. Thanks to our habit of watching life unfold on television, computer and mobile phone screens, and orienting ourselves with virtual tools like Google Earth and GPS satellite navigation, our perception of space has taken on an ever more disembodied quality. For many of us, the world is now mainly intelligible as an endless picture; like the inhabitants of the simulated world portrayed in the 1999 film *The Matrix*, what we experience is no longer space itself but its image.

Los Carpinteros' *Show Room* (2008) plays on this uncanny relationship to space by presenting what appears to be a three-dimensional reconstruction of a photographic image depicting an exploding room. It is a domestic environment furnished, tellingly, with products from Ikea, the global purveyor of ready-made life styles. Fragments from a cinderblock wall and shattered household furnishings hang suspended in the air, while a gaping hole in the wall indicates the point of impact of the blast responsible for this domestic ground zero. The gallery visitor walks through this eerie scene as if somehow entering and navigating a two-dimensional representation, a forensic image from which we may reconstruct the specific nature of the forces unleashed by the detonation. Given the evidence at hand — especially the generic and unlived-in character of the remaining Ikea furnishings — the target of that force seems to be the mass-produced domesticity that is the corollary of a globalised economy. The aggressive social homogenisation carried out by global capital has been answered here by a violent subversion, a shattering of the containerised character of contemporary 'personal' space.

As an image of architectural vulnerability, *Show Room* inevitably calls to mind pictures of the destruction of the World Trade Center — an event experienced around the world through its depictions in the media. Yet for all its evocation of a mortal disaster, Los Carpinteros' installation conspicuously lacks any traces of human inhabitants; the space it presents is devoid of history, a frozen temporal vacuum. Our photographically-conditioned perception limits our experience not only of space, but also of time. 'With the advent of modernity time has vanished from social space,' historian Henri Lefebvre observes. 'Economic space subordinates time to itself; political space expels it as threatening and dangerous (to power) ... Our time, then, this most essential part of lived experience ... is no longer visible to us ... It is concealed in space, hidden under a pile of debris to be disposed of as soon as possible.'[13]

Suggesting a similar imbrication of photographic and architectural space, Do Ho Suh's *Staircase — V* (2003/04/08) presents a life-sized sculpture of a staircase, fashioned from diaphanous red fabric, that ascends from the gallery floor to a ceiling entirely covered with the same material. The domestic scale of the stairway looks out of place in the capacious institutional setting of a public gallery, and combined with its gauzy etherealness, it imbues the work with a haunting dream-like incongruity. A stairway is by nature a transitional passageway, an in-between space, and Suh's work — which is illuminated from above and seems to glow with an internal light — draws out this character in conjuring an experience of architecture that seems to exist in an uncertain dimension poised somewhere between solidity and the projections of memory and cinema. The artist's *Fallen Star 1/5* (2008) makes a much more explicit reference to filmic space in recasting an iconic scene from *The Wizard of Oz*: rendered in startlingly meticulous detail, this sculpture features a 1/5 scale model of Suh's childhood home in Korea (a traditional Hanok-style dwelling) crashing into a similarly scaled model of the New England apartment building where he lived as an art student. The contrast between the two structures — a permeable, semi-transparent cottage and an opaque container of red brick — reveals the role of architecture as an incubator of specific sets of cultural values and spatial relations. However, the apparent violence of their collision — which has apparently split both buildings in half, exposing their interiors — suggests a splintering of identity that is linked not only to cultural discontinuities, but also to the sense of perennial dislocation that characterises our experience of space as a kind of halfway house between the physical and the photographic.

In *Fallen Star 1/5*, as in Los Carpinteros' *Show Room*, the spectre of architectural destruction is commingled with a ghostly unreality. Mike Nelson's *To the Memory of H.P. Lovecraft* (1999, 2008), explores similar terrain but links architectural violence to the traces of an absent body. Transforming the once-pristine gallery into a ravaged site where the walls have been shredded and savaged, with the resulting detritus littering the floor, Nelson's installation presents the entire space of the gallery as a kind of abandoned film set, leaving visitors to reconstruct a narrative or script to account for the state of the space that they are left to explore. The violent clawing of the walls, as well as the inclusion of cage-like barriers around the gallery's various access points, conjures the image of some brutal agent — a wild beast, perhaps — who, for the moment at least, has disappeared from the scene.

Even as it transfigures the physical confines of the gallery architecture into a fictional milieu, Nelson's work simultaneously draws attention to our experience of the space in which art is displayed. Its disturbing evocation of bodily absence calls to mind Brian O'Doherty's account of the contemporary art gallery as a place where 'the presence of that odd piece of furniture, your own body, seems superfluous, an intrusion.' Describing the 'white cube' as an emblematic space of twentieth-century Modernism, O'Doherty adds that its religiously stripped down and abstracted environment 'offers the thought that while eyes and minds are welcome, space-occupying bodies are not.'[4] *To the Memory of H.P. Lovecraft* links this idealised space of vision to the suppression of corporeal experience on which it is predicated — and, as is so often the case in horror fiction, the repressed body returns with a monstrous vengeance. At the same time, Nelson's installation brings us back to a more dimensional and embodied spatial perception: as we inspect the cuts in the walls that reveal the concrete shell of the building behind them, and as we gingerly step over the broken pieces of plasterboard on the floor, we become more aware of both our own bodily presence and our relation to the encasing architectural framework.

As a spatial container that facilitates a disembodied mode of perception, the white cube finds a counterpart in the darkened environs of the modern cinema theatre, yet another example of twentieth-century architecture designed to obliterate our awareness not only of our own body but also of the physical space we inhabit and the world outside. 'The physical confinement of the dark box-like [cinema] indirectly conditions the mind,' noted artist Robert Smithson in a 1966 essay, arguing that the cinema also shuts down temporal perception. 'Time is compressed or stopped inside the movie house ... to spend time in a movie house is to make a "hole" in one's life.'[5] Tobias Putrih's *Venetian, Atmospheric* (2007), a sculpture in the form of a functioning cinema with 30-odd seats, seeks to redress this situation by creating an environment that departs from the insularity of a conventional theatre. Underscoring its temporary (time-based) existence, *Venetian, Atmospheric* is buttressed by scaffolding, as though it were a construction in progress. Inside the structure, visitors encounter a cave-like interior with walls composed of organically shaped slats; calling to mind the interior of a body, its design serves to heighten, rather than diminish, our bodily consciousness. A wrap-around curtain can be adjusted so that the angled slats afford views of the outside world, allowing light inside and a sense of the passing of time. Replacing the model of a black box where viewers lose any sense of their own bodies as well as the other bodies around them, Putrih's permeable sculptural environment restores a dimension of communality to the film-watching experience.

Los Carpinteros
Cold Study of Disaster,
2005

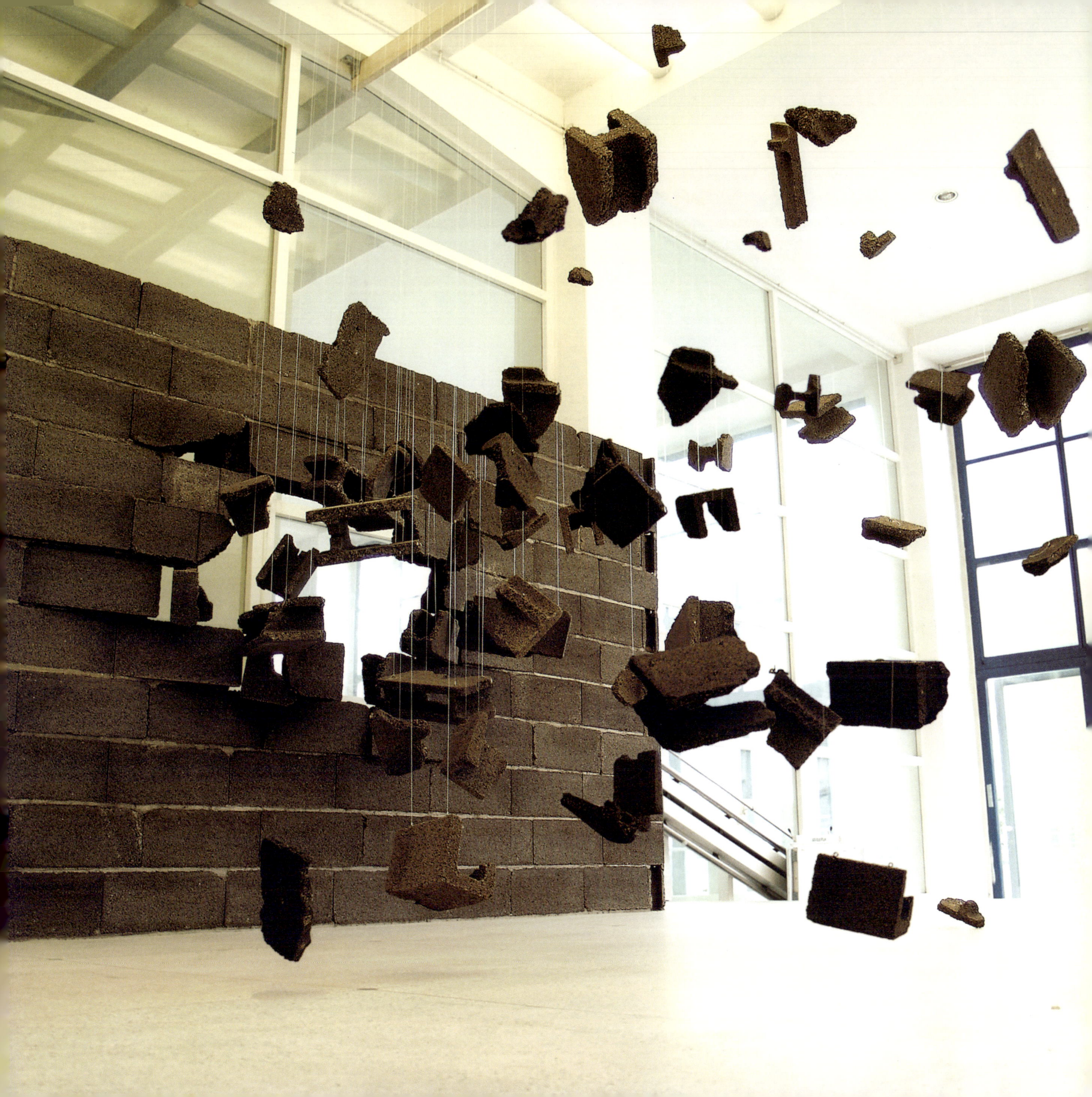

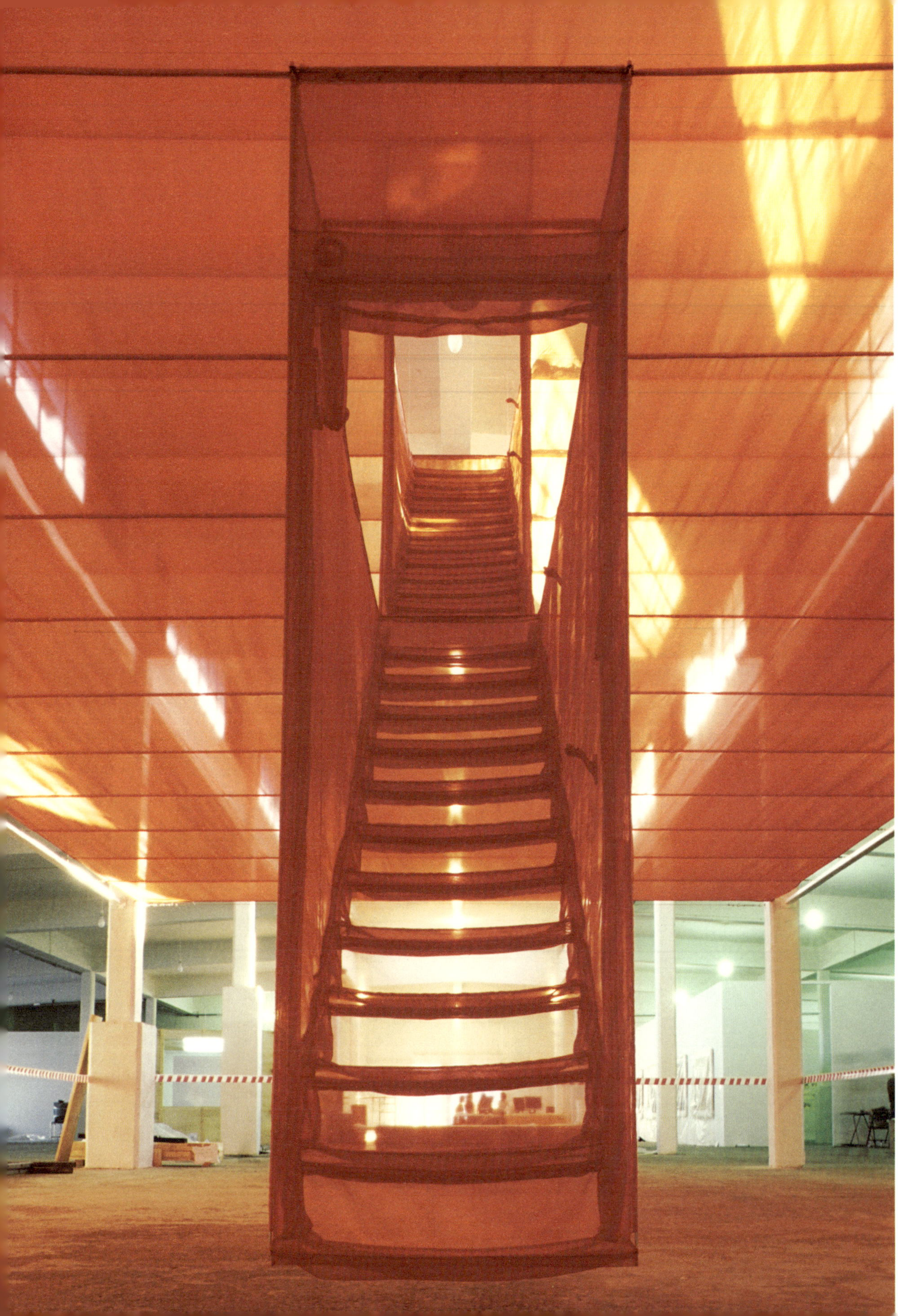

Do Ho Suh
Staircase, **2003**

Venetian, Atmospheric **reminds us that architecture functions not only as a structural container, but also as an optical device that shapes the way we perceive our environs. Sited on The Hayward's northern sculpture terrace, Tomas Saraceno's** *Observatory, Air-Port-City* **(2008), a freestanding dome with a transparent membrane, similarly serves as both shelter and perceptual instrument. On entering the structure's lower level, visitors find themselves inside a clear, air-pressurised 'pillow' with a mirrored floor that reflects the sky overhead; five metres above, the top of the pillow provides an upper floor that visitors access by an external stairway. Stepping out onto a transparent skin, they appear (when seen from below) to be floating in a gravity-free chamber. Thus even as** *Observatory, Air-Port-City***'s low-weight, ephemeral structure looks back to a Utopian tradition of experimental air-supported buildings pioneered by Buckminster Fuller, Saraceno's work simultaneously updates our vision of 'futuristic' architecture as a space for expanding processes of perception.**

The role of built structures in shaping vision is also addressed by Atelier Bow-Wow, a collaborative team composed of Momoyo Kaijima and Yoshiharu Tsukamoto whose practice spans the fields of art and architecture. With *Life Tunnel* **(2008), they have created a crystalline construction with a hybrid identity: it is at once a room, a passageway, a conduit for light, and a kind of walk-in periscope. Featuring reflective walls in its interior, this low-ceilinged, faceted structure leads from one of The Hayward's ground floor galleries into an open well at the rear of the building where it then divides in two, with one section leading visitors up a set of stairs into an adjacent gallery. The other section (accessible only by sight) snakes vertically up the open well, paralleling a free-standing cast concrete staircase, and terminates in one of The Hayward's upper gallery spaces, from which it draws light down to the cave-like spaces below.**

At once a work of temporary architecture, an environmental sculpture and an optical machine, *Life Tunnel* **focuses attention on the perceptual and sensorial role of our bodies (especially as we must alter our posture to navigate its narrow confines). Simultaneously connecting the visitor to different spaces in The Hayward, it highlights the perspectivism of the building as it views, and is viewed by, the visitor moving through it.** *Life Tunnel***'s twisting, multi-directional construction also plays against our customary relationship to the 'transparency' of conventional architecture and a type of space that theorists like Lefebvre and psychoanalyst Jacques Lacan have described as soliciting and entrapping the viewer's desire. Offering the illusion of complete accessibility, architectural space of this kind 'presents desire with a "transparency" which encourages it to surge forth in an attempt to lay claim to an apparently clear field,' Lefebvre observes. 'Of course, this foray comes to naught, for desire encounters no object, nothing desirable, and no work results from its action.'[6] By contrast, Atelier Bow-Wow's structure diverts our desire for an immediately consumable space and reflects it back upon itself, prompting us to explore more playful responses to the impulses that impel us to habitually regard our surroundings in this manner.**

Ernesto Neto's installation, *Life fog frog...Fog frog* **(2008), similarly invites us into interior structures that reveal and perceptually link us to surrounding space.** *Life fog frog...Fog frog* **positions a pair of vaulted domes, made of wooden supports and stretched Lycra and featuring soft foam flooring, in a gallery whose height is bisected by a ceiling also fashioned from Lycra. At once enveloping and yielding, Neto's pliant structures generate a tactile, sensuous space that reminds us that we apprehend our environs by touch as well as by sight. Evoking the interior architecture of the body, they conjoin our sense of the building around us to an awareness of our own corporeal space. At the same time, the work's interlinking, transparent membranes enfold us in a contradictory inside/outside topology. As Bernard Schutze has commented (writing of another work by the artist),[6] 'the viewer in a sense becomes the outside that is contained within the inside of an immersive and organ-like space that "devours" the viewing subject. The viewer's body is thus folded within the skin of the sculptural object and finds itself in the "inside of the outside".'[7]**

Establishing a more fluid relationship between figure and ground than is allowed for by conventional built structures, Neto's installation exposes the continuity and alloverness of space. In doing so, it unpacks those familiar binary oppositions — inside/outside, open/closed, transparent/opaque — that underpin our customary formulations of architectural environments. Here, space appears to be simultaneous, and like that of the body, seems to have neither end nor beginning. Neto's haptic architectonics instead convey a feeling that space is a continuous organism, a field of sensations and tactile interactions in which we are inextricably immersed and through which we are connected to those around us. It reconstitutes in the gallery a temporary version of what historian Giuliana Bruno calls 'the transitorial space of intersubjectivity' — the space of urban culture in which the boundaries of the individual do not end where the body or walls end, but intimately extend into the collective environment of the city.[8]

Architectural structures are not usually in the business of questioning how we relate to them, let alone doubting the nature of their existence, yet Michael Beutler's constructions typically seem to embody an active uncertainty. Departing from the principles of permanence and stability that we tend to associate with architecture, Beutler's Hayward installation suggests a site of process and production. Fabricated from standardised construction materials that are assembled using improvised building techniques simple enough to be self-evident, Beutler's construction engages us in considering the index or the traces of its own making. Rather than a finished product, it embodies a playful process of transformation that imbues the surrounding gallery with a sense of buoyancy and contingency. In presenting space not as a ready-made entity but as an ongoing production, the work draws attention to the temporal aspect of spatial experience. In contrast to the modernist ideal of an artwork that exists in an eternal present, Beutler's sculpture refers us to the time of its making; it evinces a worldliness that places us not only in space but also in relation to a particular (though still unfolding) moment.

In the work of Gelitin, architecture is likewise treated as an arena of action, but one in which the visitor is usually invited to directly participate. A collaborative group of four members (Wolfgang Gantner, Ali Janka, Florian Reither and Tobias Urban), Gelitin explore the social aspects of built spaces, including their collective construction and consumption, and their potential for creating situations of pleasurable encounter, assembly and play. Like the *New Babylon* imagined by Constant Nieuwenhuys, a hypothetical city where the architecture could be continually modified according to the desires of its inhabitants, Gelitin's anarchic structures, fashioned from scavenged wood and furniture and, on occasion, living bodies, function primarily as platforms for libidinally-charged proceedings.[9] For *normally, proceeding and unrestricted with without title* (2008), they have filled The Hayward's western sculpture terrace with water, and have installed a floating dock along with several homemade boats. Visitors are free to row the boats across the flooded terrace, which projects out from the building approximately 40 feet above street level. Engineering sensations of vertigo, dislocation and uncertainty, the work is at once a space of communal recreation and reflection (in a literal as well as figurative sense, as the water's mirror-like surface reflects the sky, the building and the bodies of visitors).

Gelitin's work dramatically alters the exterior of The Hayward, adding an incongruous element (evoking both architectural folly and flood) to the blunt assertiveness of the concrete building. Like much of the work discussed above, it temporarily disengages the gallery's architectural rhetoric and the behavioural prescriptions that it communicates. Encouraging visitors to improvise new uses and meanings for the site, it repurposes a purpose-built structure in a way that incorporates a ludic dimension into our perception of space.

Ernesto Neto
Leviathan Thot, **2006**

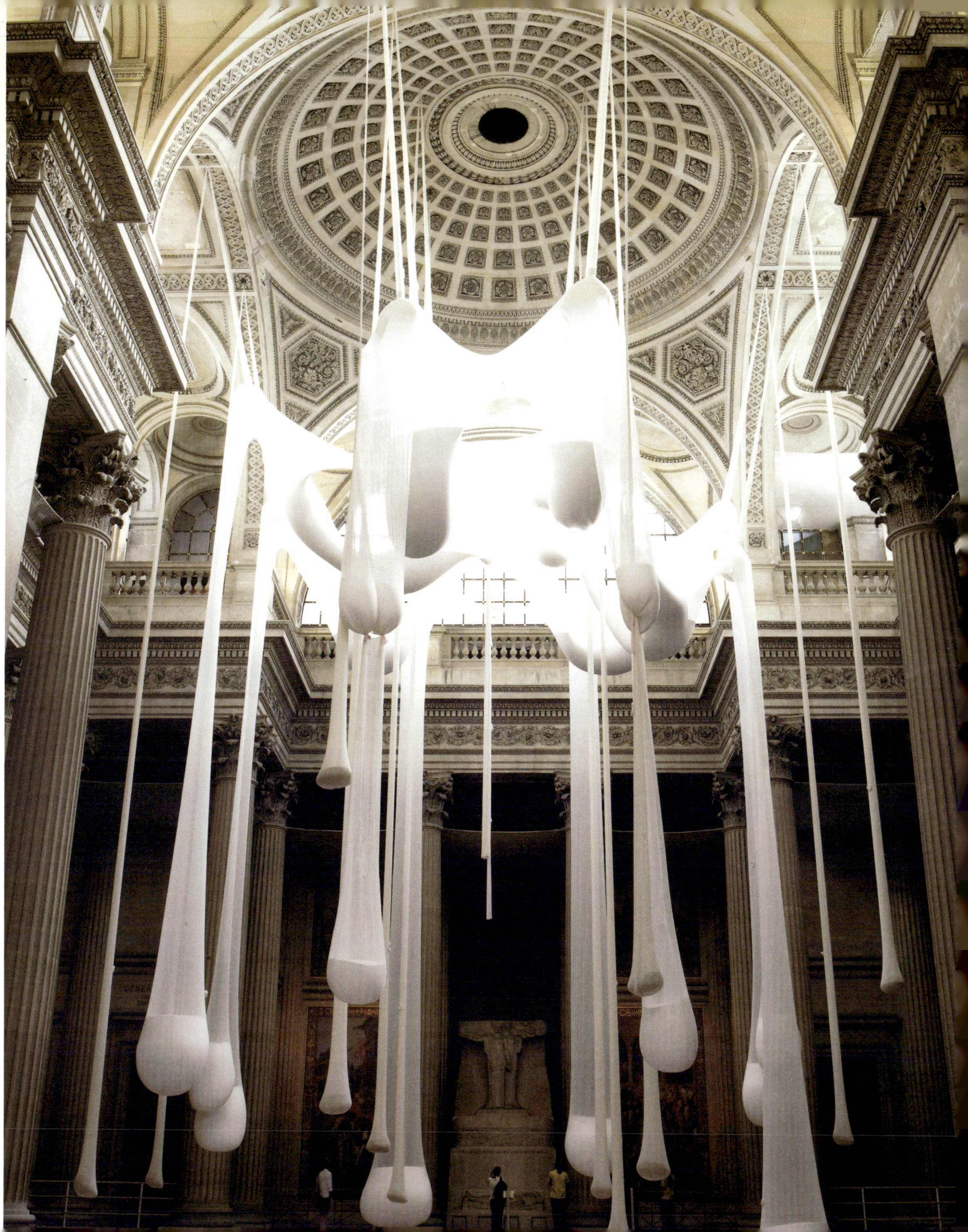

Tobias Putrih
Venetian, Atmospheric, **2007**
(detail)

Rachel Whiteread's *Place* **(2008), engages the field of play in iconic terms by assembling over 200 second-hand dollhouses in an installation that the visitor moves through as if ambulating across a miniature hillside town. The dollhouse, of course, is a space of childhood play that is usually associated with young girls, but** *Place* **appears decidedly gender-neutral. Dolls and their accompanying paraphernalia are conspicuously absent, and the dollhouses themselves remain eerily empty. Placed in a darkened gallery, they are lit from inside, but rather than conjuring signs of life, their illuminated, vacant interiors only intensify the aura of absence emanating from these abandoned play structures. Taken together — and despite the different architectural styles of the individual dollhouses, Whiteread's dimly lit installation stresses their collective identity — they suggest a ghostly monument to a dream of village life. Indeed, their sheer number and densely packed positioning conveys the possibility of endless reproducibility, evoking an anxiety over the loss of clear spatial boundaries and, in particular, the blurred distinction between city and suburb engendered by urban sprawl.**

Whiteread purchased most of the dollhouses from sellers on eBay, and yet the unoccupied containers that she presents seem to have been stripped of their previous histories of play and fantasy; instead these inert boxes (which sit on their own empty shipping crates) put into play thoughts of the architectural relationship between house and sepulchre, the space of the living and the space of the dead. As if recalling historian Lewis Mumford's assertion that 'the city of the dead is the forerunner, almost the core, of every living city,' *Place* **affirms that our collective space is inflected by our relationship to our shared mortality.[10] In this light, Whiteread's installation also conjures a chilling sense of vulnerability: as we look down upon her miniature village our omniscient perspective may call to mind the aerial viewpoint of a spy plane or bomber, and so leads us to reflect on the precariousness of contemporary urban space that results from an almost century-long military practice of bombing inhabited cities.**

In its commingling of elements of fantasy, collectivity, play and death, *Place* **underscores the varied dimensions of our relationship with the built environment. This hybrid relationship with space informs the work of all of the artists in** *Psycho Buildings*. **Rather than box in our processes of spatial perception, their projects engage us in a kind of conceptual ecology where the diverse relationships we maintain with our surroundings co-exist and overlap. Undressing our conventional notions of boundaries and limits, of inside and outside, they expose the possibility of change inherent in space. In doing so, they also call attention to our freedom to re-define the uses we make of our surroundings. That freedom inevitably calls into play our role as members of a collective. Engaging us as participants in shared spaces, the artists in** *Psycho Buildings* **offer us a tonic reminder of the communal character of our involvement with our surroundings — including that of public art galleries.**

Our experience of art, of course, does not begin and end within the walls of a gallery. It extends instead to the ways in which, after encountering these works, we again confront and respond to the spaces in which we live. In inviting us to reimagine the parameters of our spatial experience, then, these artists ultimately prompt us to more clearly grasp the architecture of our everyday behaviour and thought. At the same time, their work does us the great service of intimating how we might escape some of its more confining dimensions and in the process rediscover more active ways of placing ourselves in the world.

1 Anthony Vidler, 'A Dark Space,' in *Rachel Whiteread's House*, Phaidon Press, London, 1995, p. 64.

2 In two oft-quoted statements, Brancusi remarked that, 'True architecture is sculpture,' while also categorising architecture as 'inhabited sculpture'.

3 Henri Lefebvre, *The Production of Space*, Donald Nicholson-Smith (trans.), Blackwell Publishing, Oxford, 1991, pp. 95–96.

4 Brian O'Doherty, *Inside the White Cube: The Ideology of the Gallery Space*, Lapis Press, Los Angeles, 1986, p. 15.

5 Robert Smithson, 'Entropy and the New Monuments', 1966, in *The Writings of Robert Smithson*, Nancy Holt (ed.), New York University Press, New York, 1979, p. 15.

6 Lefebvre, *op. cit.*, p. 97.

7 Bernard Schutze, 'The Skin of Sculpture,' in *Espace*, 75, Spring 2006, p. 26.

8 Giuliana Bruno, '*Site-seeing: Architecture and the Moving Image*', in *Wide Angle*, vol. 19, no. 4, October 1997, pp. 8–24.

9 At a Gelitin exhibition in Munich in 2001, visitors were asked to strip, lubricate themselves with baby oil and squirm down a narrow chute made from other human bodies; in an earlier work using living bodies as architecture, the group created a human elevator with the help of a group of body-builders.

10 Lewis Mumford, *The City in History: Its Origins, Its Transformations, and Its Prospects*, Harcourt, Brace & World, Inc., New York, 1961, p. 7.

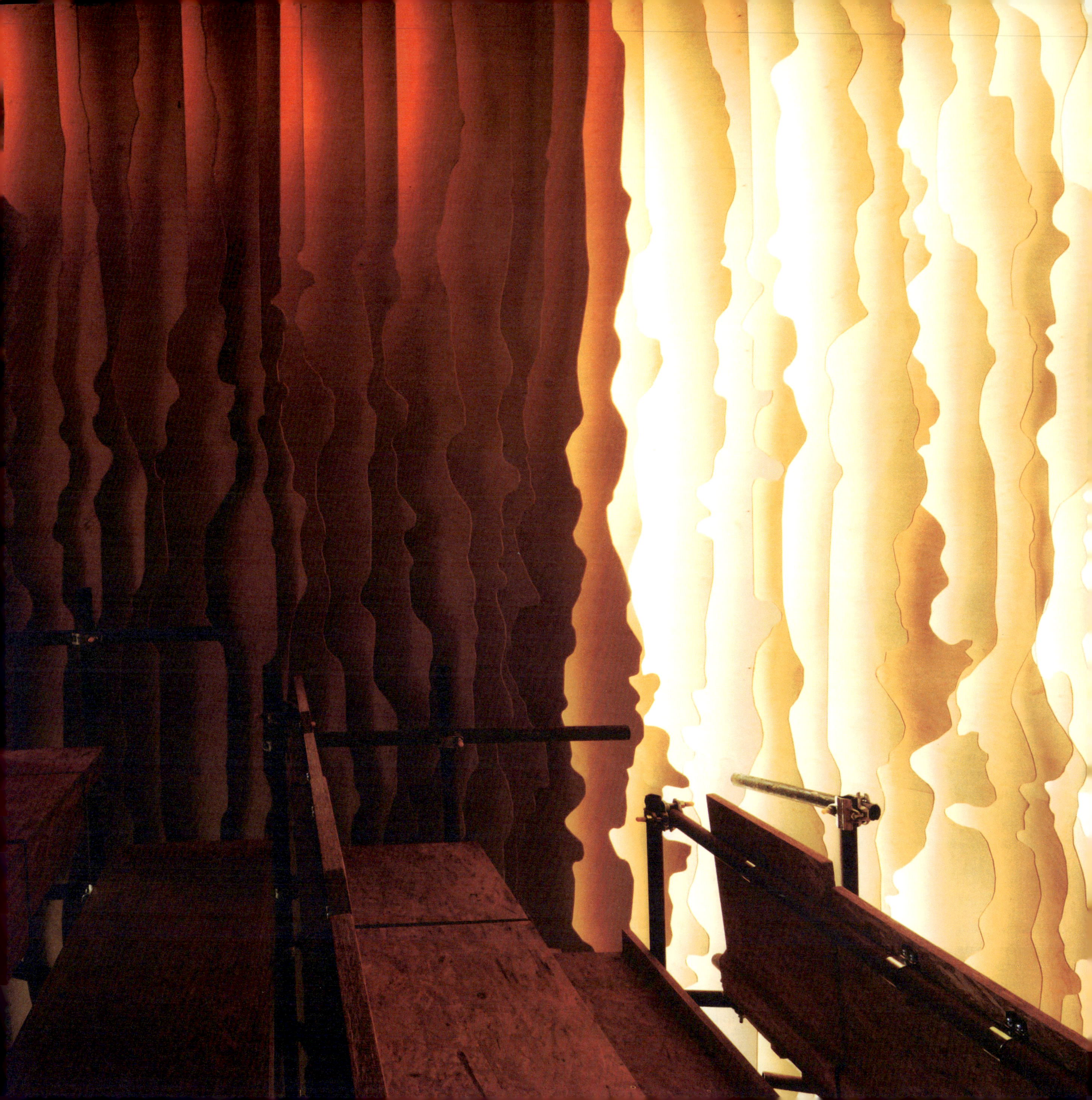

Joseph Paxton
Crystal Palace, **1851**

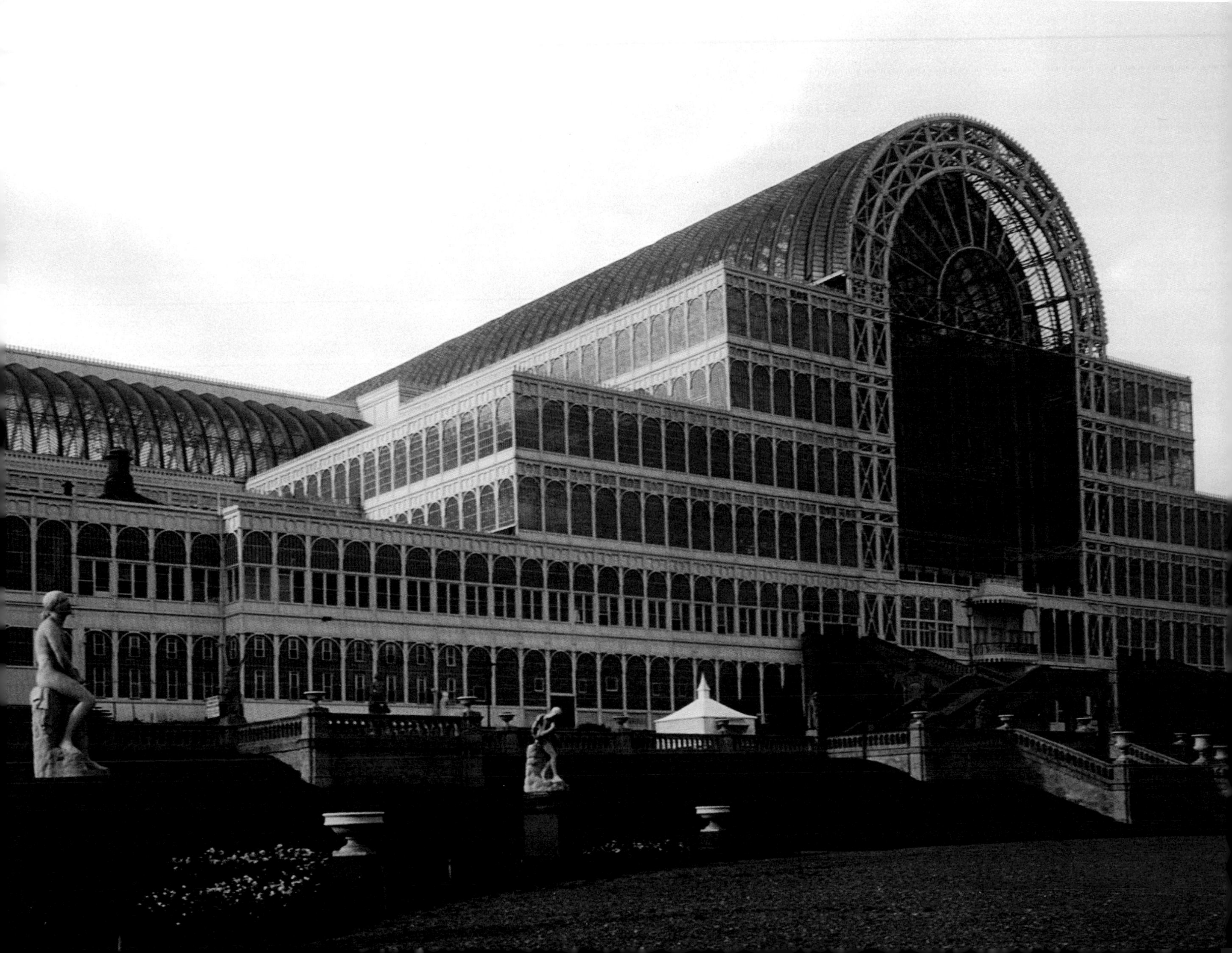

SPECIES OF SPACES: ART, ARCHITECTURE AND ENVIRONMENT

BRIAN DILLON

What kind of spaces do contemporary artists enclose or open up? The artists in *Psycho Buildings* respond in disparate ways to the contemporary practices and the vexed aesthetic and political history of modern architecture. In particular, they seem to address certain ambitions, or even fantasies, that were at the heart of the modernist project of the early twentieth century. In the amorphous, globular environments of Ernesto Neto, for example, or the mobile, airy and Utopian spaces created by Tomas Saraceno, the idea of architecture as both enveloping and liberating lives on, now somewhat fragile and estranged. The obverse modernist urge to blow apart distinctions between inside and outside is literalised in the detonation of space and material in the work of Los Carpinteros, or made psychologically disorienting in Mike Nelson's uncanny labyrinths. We can perhaps identify a handful of exemplary spaces where the artists of the two centuries meet.

Vitrine

In the prehistory of the relation of art to architecture in the twentieth century, a founding image must surely be the Victorian glass house. Many artists and architects of the new century shared a paradoxical dream — a vision of seclusion and transparency — that they had inherited from the designers of the great glass enclosures of the nineteenth century: chief among them, Joseph Paxton and his Crystal Palace, built for the 1851 Great Exhibition in London. The structure was a world in miniature, an independent ecosystem such as had been already confined in zoos and greenhouses. Indeed, our modern notion of a natural environment owes a good deal to the artificially isolated flora and fauna of that time — one thinks, for example, of the 120-year-old Australasian ferns still flourishing beneath the domes of the Kibble Palace glass house at the Botanic Gardens in Glasgow. But the Crystal Palace was also an image of literal enlightenment and societal transparency: commercial transactions, scientific discoveries and technological innovations were exposed (as Karl Marx put it) as 'crystals of [a] social substance, common to them all'.[1] The glass house invited rational scrutiny of economic conditions, while safely sealing the new consumer off from their consequences.

It was also, of course, an aesthetic object: visitors to the Exhibition, and to the many exhibitions that flourished in the coming decades, spoke of the magical glow that such buildings gave off. Paxton's glass edifice, according to the catalogue of 1851, was 'perhaps the only building in the world where the *atmosphere* is perceptible'. In other words, the building seduced or enchanted the spectator: it was as much an image of a society blinded by commodification as it was a picture of perfect social transparency. It was exactly this ambiguity that attracted artists to the new architecture in the coming century. In 1926, for example, stirred by a visit to the gleaming set of Fritz Lang's film *Metropolis*, the Russian filmmaker Sergei Eisenstein conceived of a film wholly devoted to exploring a huge glass building. Though deals were struck with both Paramount and United Artists, and a Pittsburgh glass factory supplied with details of the elaborate sets required, *The Glass House* was never made. Eisenstein's 'comedy of the eye' — initially imagined as almost abstract, a film entirely about things and surfaces — would have exposed both the radical potential of living behind glass and its illusionary qualities, thus putting to the test Walter Benjamin's assertion that 'to live in a glass house is a revolutionary virtue'.[2]

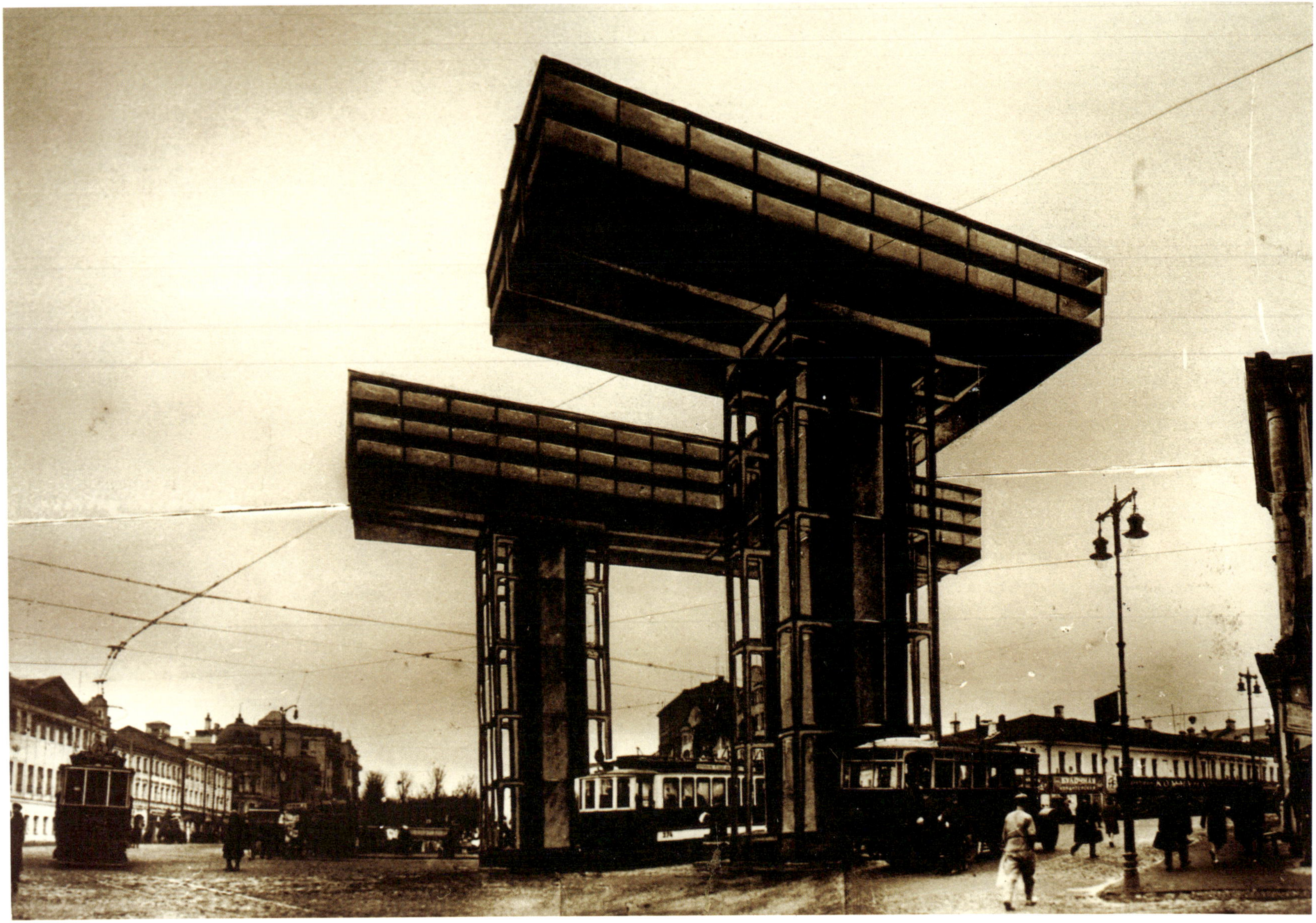

El Lissitzky
Photomontage of the Wolkenbugel (Cloud-Iron), **1925**

Constantin Brancusi
The Endless Column, c.1938

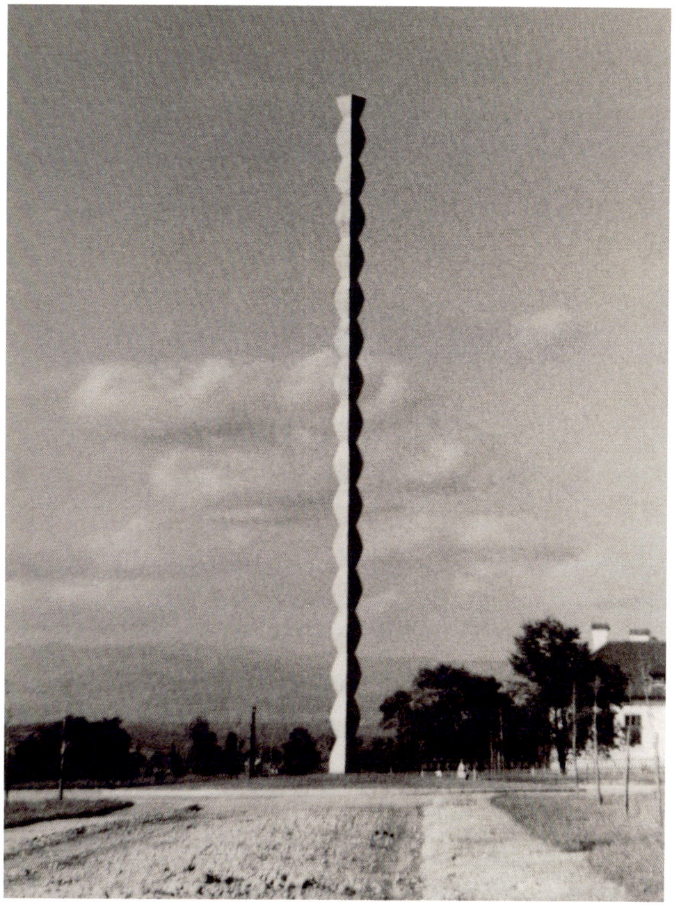

Tower

The notion that architecture could embody by its transparency the actual conditions of a liberated society — an idea canvassed by modernist architects such as Mies van der Rohe but tested to its limits by artists — was nowhere more explicitly put to work than in the early years of the Soviet Union. Eisenstein's suspicion of the glass house as expression of that transparency was prompted by certain constructivist experiments: projected buildings that seemed to promise a society of total control and surveillance as much as liberating visibility. El Lissitzky's unrealised 1925 architectural design, *Cloud-Iron*, in part a counter to the pure verticality of the American skyscraper, imagined vitreous strata that appeared to hover high above the earth, air-locked from historical reality like Jonathan Swift's floating island in *Gulliver's Travels*. Such Utopian towers did not necessarily depend on glass construction: proposing instead an architecture of ideal communication, Konstantin Melnikov's *Building for the Leningradskaya Pravda*, designed in 1924, was to have bristled with slogans and radio masts, elevated reminders of the transformation of society going on, as it were, on the ground.

The most resonant of such projects, and the one that alerts us to the extreme ambiguity of the architectural tower as a symbol of radical artistic and political desires, was Vladimir Tatlin's *Monument to the Third International*, first envisioned in 1919 and only ever realised as a model. In one sense, it is a building filled with the future: the twin spirals of Tatlin's 400-metre-tall tower express the revolutionary impulse as a simple upward striving, while its enclosed and revolving glass volumes (a cube, tetrahedron, cylinder and hemisphere) had practical as well as elemental significance: they were designed to house the legislature, the executive and the propaganda ministry of the Comintern. In another sense, however, the unbuilt tower is already a sort of ruin: an unrealisable monument to the recent past of the Revolution, a relic that the cultural critic Svetlana Boym has called 'a forgotten cosmic station built for the launch that never took place.'[3] A monumental tower (when it is not merely a Babel-like folly) is meant to be a kind of focal point or axis for the space and society that surround it — one thinks here too of Constantin Brancusi's *Endless Column* (c.1938), erected in memory of the Romanian dead of the First World War — but Tatlin's tower seems to point at the same time to the demolition of such ambitions.

Yves Klein
Drawing for *Air Architecture* project, c.1959

Bubble

According to the German philosopher Peter Sloterdijk, whose three-volume work *Spheres* explores the links between politics, atmosphere and environment in the twentieth century, it is possible to map the progress of modern art and architecture according to various ways of enclosing and channelling air. Modernity, argues Sloterdijk, is a kind of *air-conditioning*: an insight that brings together the heated palm houses and exhibition halls of the nineteenth century, the airships and gas attacks of the First World War and the Nazis' even more lethal deployment of gas a generation later. The atmosphere itself constitutes the stakes and the means of modern industry and military might. It is also a charged medium for modern art: Sloterdijk's vivid instance is the appearance of Salvador Dalí at the International Surrealist Exhibition in London in 1936, addressing his audience at the New Burlington Galleries from within a sealed metal diver's helmet (in which, Dalí later wrote, he nearly asphyxiated). We might also recall the glass ampule of Marcel Duchamp's *Air de Paris* (1919) and his broader interest in bodily and mechanical conduits for gas, fluid and energy.

Perhaps the most ambitious artistic conjunction of pneumatics and architecture, however, is that first imagined by Yves Klein in 1959, while the artist was at work on a series of murals for the Gelsenkirchen Theatre near Düsseldorf. Klein, whose interest in empty space was already evident from his vacant exhibition *Le vide* in Paris the previous year, conceived a series of fire-and-water fountains for the plaza in front of the theatre, and went so far as to patent his invention, noting its 'decorative purpose'. Before long, the scheme had grown in Klein's mind to encompass a new way of enclosing space, an 'air architecture' whose materials were the insubstantial elements themselves: air, fire and water. Architecture, he wrote, 'is space, and thus it is everything'; contemporary buildings remained hampered by the one feature that even Mies van der Rohe's glass structures had not succeeded in removing: that is, the roof. Klein's elemental architecture would finally obliterate the distinction between inside and outside, liberating the individual beneath a pure blue sky.

The drawings that Klein completed appear to constitute the *ne plus ultra* of the dream of a transparent architecture. They are also its *reductio ad absurdum*. Vast precincts stretch to the horizon, apparently open to the elements but in fact protected above by implausibly violent jets of warm air and walled by fountains of fire and water. All practical amenities have been buried underground, glassed over and accessed by discreet stairways. The inhabitants, cushioned on beds of pure air, live naked and liberated: 'the concept of secrecy, still common in our world, has disappeared in this city which is flooded with light and completely open to the outside community and is perfect, free, individualistic, impersonal.'[4] This vision has affinities with the work of the Dutch artist Constant Nieuwenhuys, a contemporary of Klein's whose *New Babylon* was a projected cityscape made of standardised components but endlessly adaptable and liberated from the territorial constraints of traditional dwelling. Constant pictured its ideal inhabitant as a nomad whose potential for creativity and play had at last been released from traditional buildings and ways of being. Architecture, pursued to the furthest extreme by artists, had finally evanesced, become immaterial. This disappearance inevitably conjures, once again, the prospect of ruin: Klein's ideal, elemental space starts to look like the result of entropic disarray or even terminal decline.

Dome

Klein's air architecture encloses a nagging paradox: on one level, he longs for the complete dissolution of built space; on another, he imagines a world pneumatically sealed off: his airy plazas may as well be glassed in. In this, he resembles the visionary architect and inventor Buckminster Fuller, whose perfection of the concept and construction of the geodesic dome is his most famous contribution to the atmospherics of the twentieth century. Buckminster Fuller's interest in dome-like, hermetic structures had begun in 1927 with his *Dymaxion House*: a cylindrical aluminium living space, complete with Buckminster Fuller's own modular fittings and topped by a rotating ventilator. This vision of a self-enclosed and technologically sophisticated dwelling was later expanded, in the geodesic domes, to englobe factories, military installations, and even (this last only in Buckminster Fuller's imagination) whole cities or districts, such as a vast tract of Manhattan. In his *Cloud Nine* project, Buckminster Fuller went further and proposed complete spheres, one mile in diameter, that would float above the earth, each housing several thousand inhabitants in eco-friendly independence of the earth below. As with Klein, the dream is one of liberation through atmospheric autonomy.

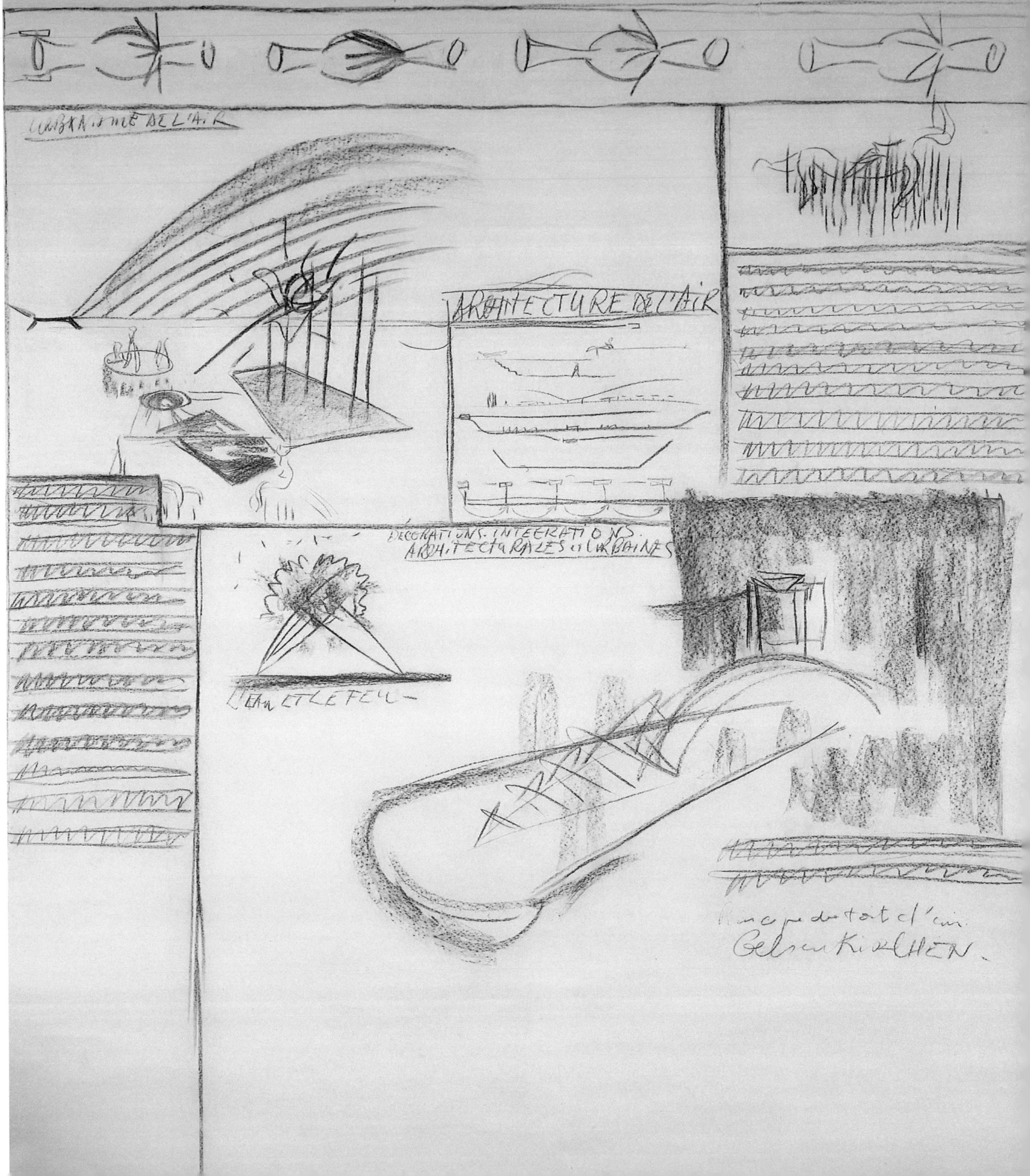
URBANISME DE L'AIR
ARCHITECTURE DE L'AIR
DÉCORATIONS. INTÉGRATIONS.
ARCHITECTURALES et URBAINES
L'EAU ET LE FEU
Gelsenkirchen.

Buckminster Fuller
Proposal for an airborne habitat:
Cloud Nine, **1958**

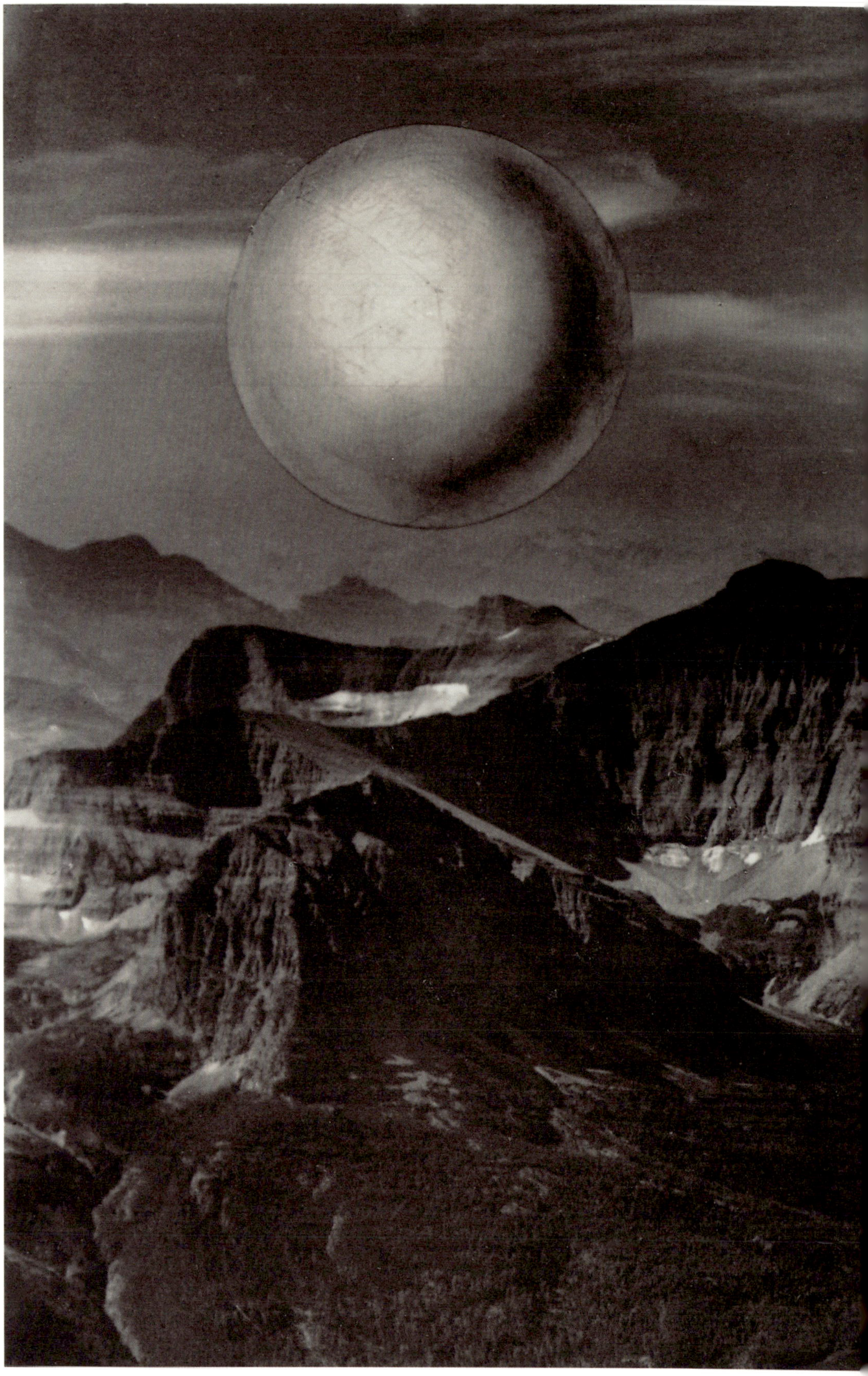

In the late 1960s, Robert Smithson asserted that Buckminster Fuller had in part anticipated the sculpture and installation art of the era — he shared, for example, the ambition to create a total, immersive environment and a new way of inhabiting space. The difference, however, was that Buckminster Fuller had 'a notion of entropy as a kind of devil that he must fight against and recycle':[5] he remained committed to a securely sealed, discrete, ordered architectural space, resisting the Kleinian disintegration of forms. In time, as in the 1972 film *Silent Running* — a parable of future ecological disaster — the sovereign dome would come to seem an image of dashed Utopian hopes. So much so that Sloterdijk has recently proposed, satirically, a 'pneumatic parliament': a dome that could be airdropped and inflated at short notice (thus ensuring swift and efficient democratisation) in any of the world's so-called 'failed states'.

Grotto

The architectural appropriations and imaginings of the art of first half of the twentieth century were for the most part concerned with communal living or creation: they were visions of architecture as politics, whether serene or anarchistic. There were, of course, notable exceptions: Duchamp's atmospherics are condensed and gnomic; Klein's very public architecture (which does away with the notion of privacy *tout court*) is at the same time a personal, even megalomaniac, project. But the artist of this period who most obsessively modelled and remodelled the concept of a private architecture — and in the process pushed at the limits of art as an immersive architectural experience — was perhaps Kurt Schwitters. Beginning around 1919, at his house in Hannover, with the construction of a tower of disparate materials that he named the *Column of Erotic Misery*, Schwitters expanded his post-Cubist collage of wood, cardboard, iron and discarded furniture until it colonised several rooms. 'As the sculpture grows bigger and bigger', he wrote, 'valleys, hollows, caves appear, and these lead a life of their own within the overall structure. The juxtaposed surfaces give rise to forms twisting in every direction, spiralling upward ... Shapes are curiously bent or otherwise twisted until their complete dissolution is achieved.'[6]

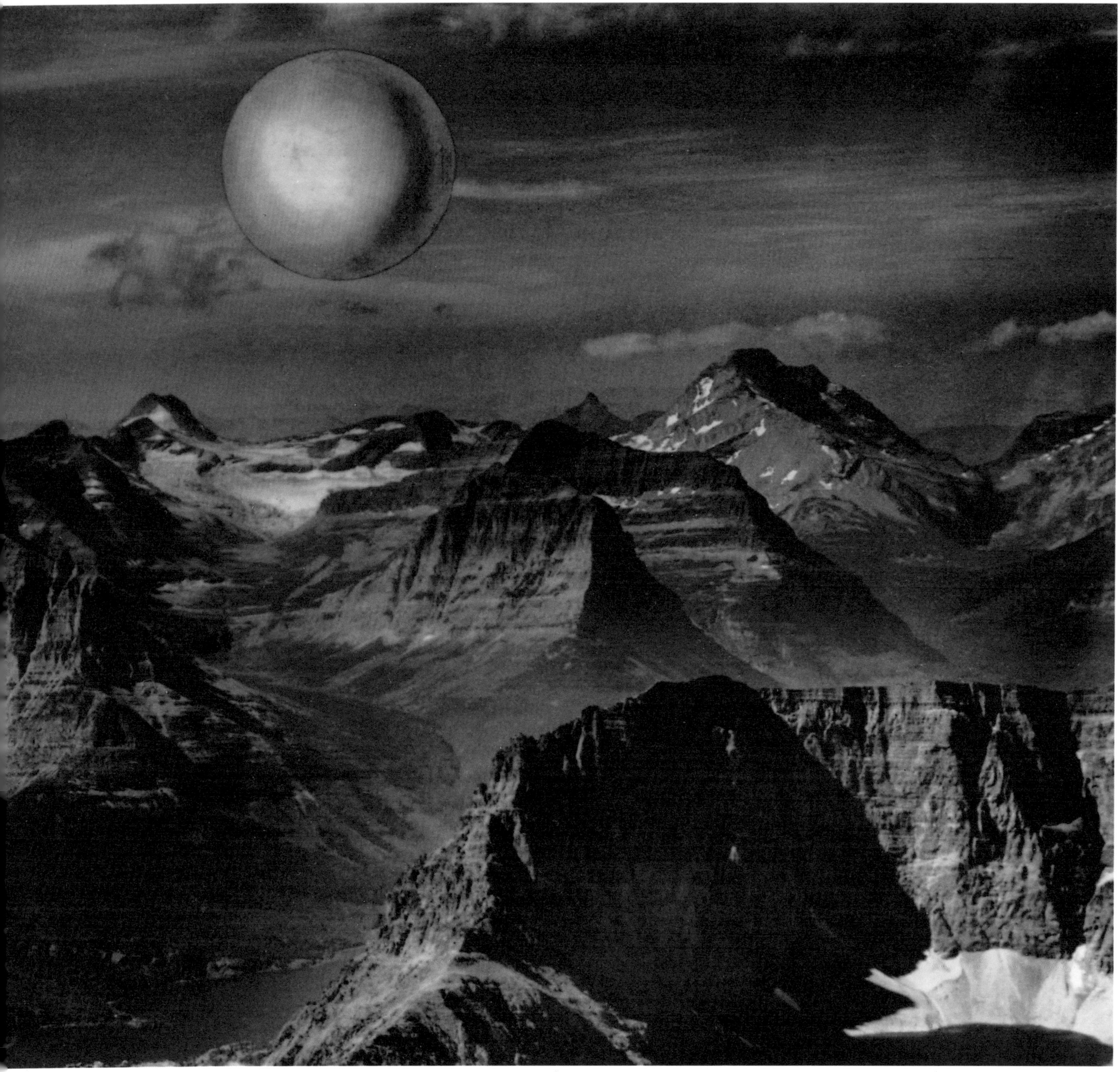

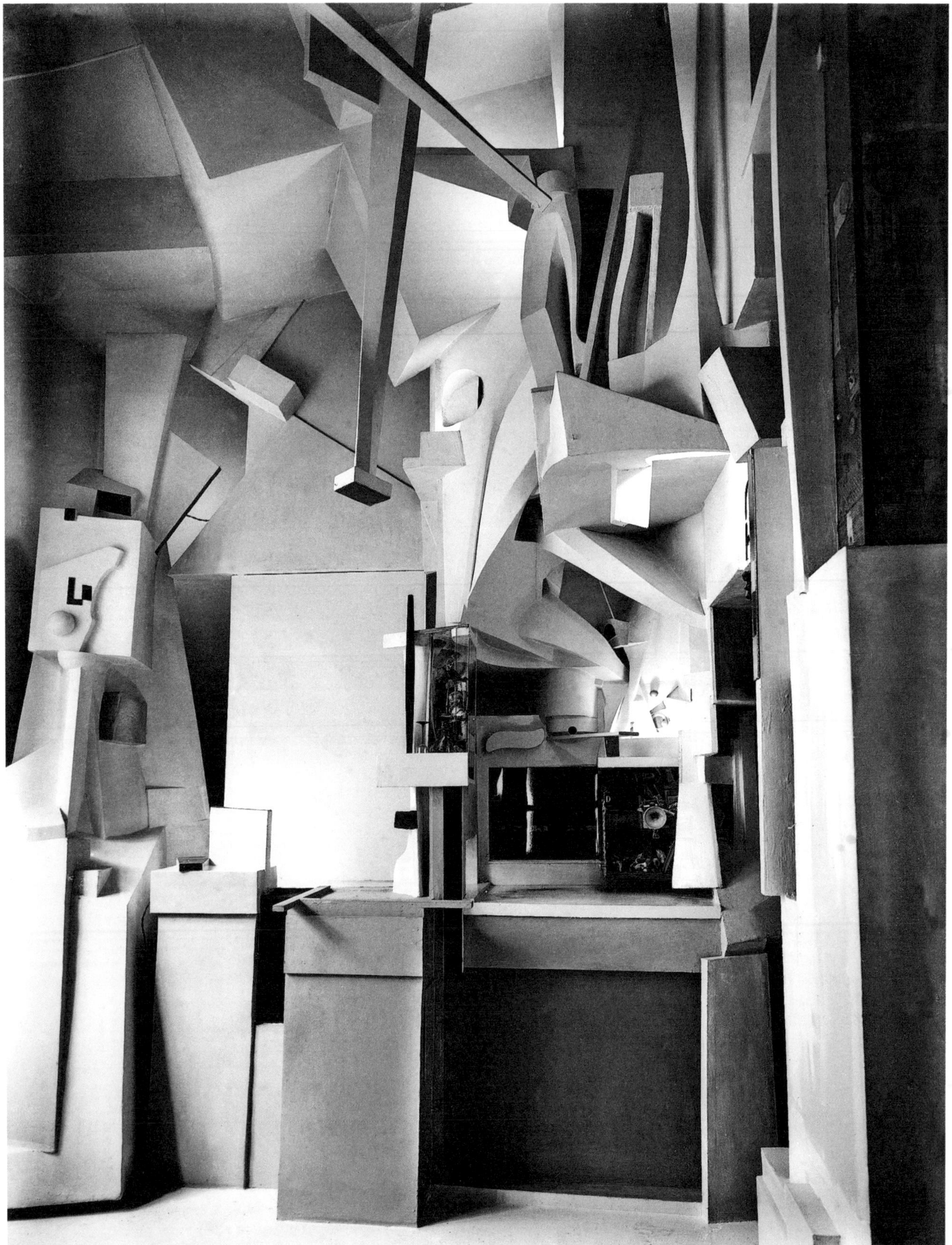

Kurt Schwitters
Merzbau, **c.1932**
(detail)

The *Merzbau*, as Schwitters titled this Constructivist-Gothic labyrinth, was both a fantastic grotto and an archive of the artist's own work: fragments of sculpture, collage and writing, as well as found objects, were progressively plastered over and enclosed in the building's chaotic, almost vegetal substance. It was 'an abstract sculpture into which people can go':[7] a total work of art and a self-enclosing environment or installation. But this most hermetic of artist's architectures led also to a kind of opening up of space, a dissolving of the walls of the 'gallery', and a composition, as Schwitters put it, without boundaries. The original *Merzbau* was destroyed by Allied bombing in 1943; a second version, built in exile in Norway, was also consumed by fire. In its final iteration — the *Merzbarn*, built in the Lake District in the UK in 1947 — the work is little more than a decayed hut and a single wall on which the artist worked in the months before his death. In a prospective hint at the fractured edifice of Smithson's *Partially Buried Woodshed* (1970), the dream of a self-enveloped art that would be inseparable from architecture starts to dissolve into the landscape and history that surround it.

The five discrete architectural types described here do not exhaust the responses of artists to architecture in the first half of the twentieth century. Nor do they exactly map onto the ideas, environments and habitats explored by the artists who succeeded them, or to the work of the contemporary artists in *Psycho Buildings*. Rather, these illustrative spaces are best understood as slightly dilapidated architectural neighbours to the works in the exhibition. They embody both the ambition toward a complete and autonomous environment that exercises some of the artists (albeit today in a more sceptical register than their precursors) and the explosion or dispersal of architectural space that is an abiding concern of others. An air-conditioned corridor, with digressive off-shoots towards alternate histories, runs between one era and the other.

1 Karl Marx, *Capital*, David McLellan (ed.), Oxford University Press, Oxford, 1999, p. 15.

2 'Surrealism', in *Reflections*, Edmund Jephcott (trans.), Harcourt Brace Jovanovich, New York, 1978, p. 180.

3 Svetlana Boym, *The Future of Nostalgia*, Basic Books, New York, 2001, p. 133.

4 Yves Klein, 'Project of an Air Architecture: Collaboration Ruhnau-Klein', in *Zero*, 113, 1973, quoted in Sidra Stich, Yves Klein, Cantz, Stuttgart, 1994, p. 126.

5 Robert Smithson, 'Entropy Made Visible', in Jack Flam (ed.), *Robert Smithson: The Collected Writings*, University of California Press, Berkeley/Los Angeles, 1996, p. 203.

6 Kurt Schwitters, 'CoEM', in *Transition*, no. 24, 1930, p. 92.

7 Kurt Schwitters, letter to Alfred Barr, 23 November 1936, quoted in John Elderfield, *Kurt Schwitters*, Thames and Hudson, London, 1985, p. 156.

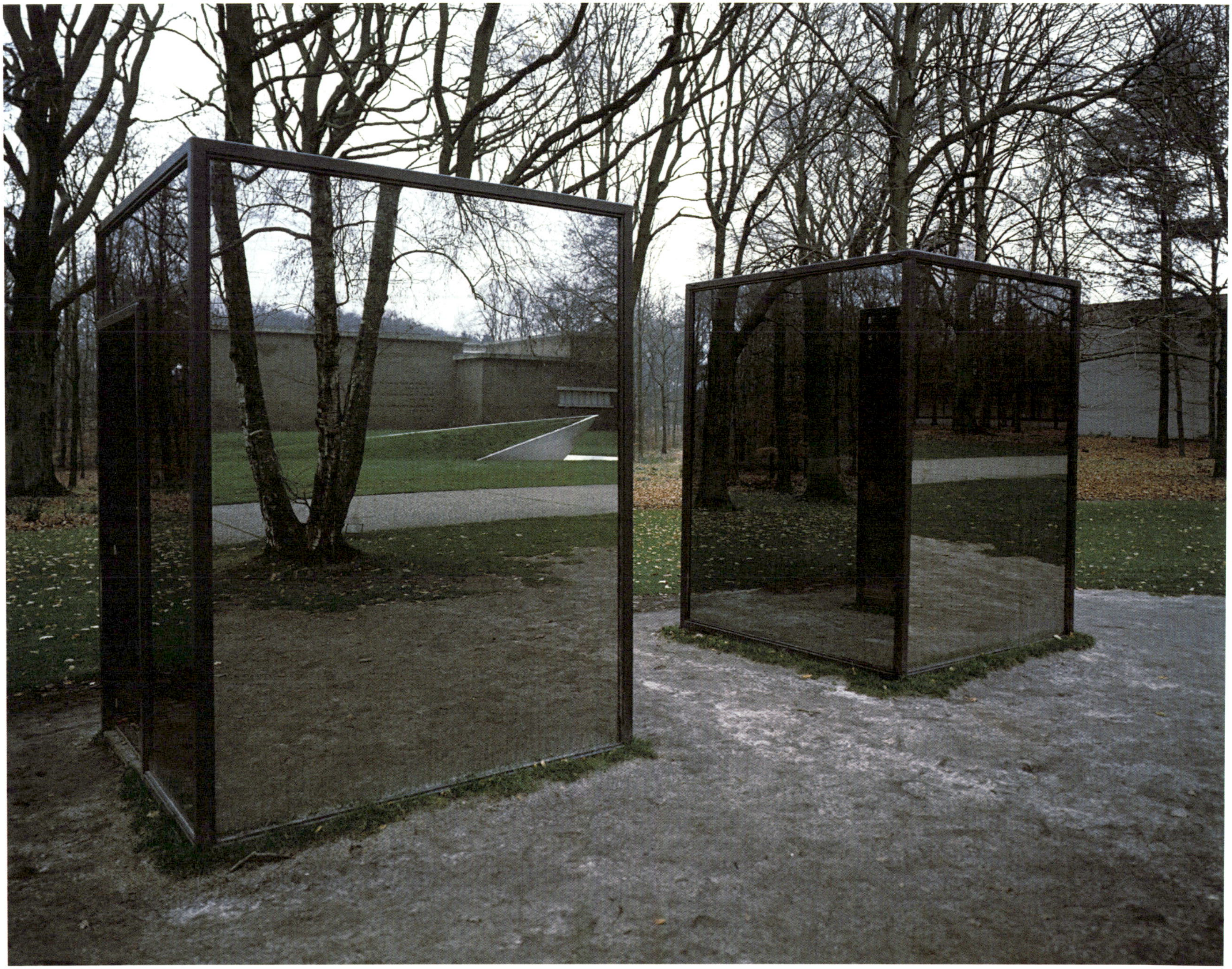

Dan Graham
Two Adjacent Pavilions, **1978–81**

ART'S USE OF ARCHITECTURE: PLACE, SITE AND SETTING

JANE RENDELL

Art and architecture are frequently differentiated in terms of their relationship to 'function' or 'use'. Unlike architecture, art may not be useful in pragmatic terms, for example in responding directly to social needs, providing shelter or somewhere in which to perform open-heart surgery, but we could say that art provides a place for other kinds of function – self-reflection, critical thinking and social change. If we consider this expanded version of the term function in relation to architecture, we realise that architecture is seldom given the opportunity to consider the construction of critical concepts and spatial relations as its most important purpose. Architecture's potential is most often realised in contemporary art, especially in current works that, in reworking architectural forms within the gallery setting, decontextualise architecture. In this way, they allow a new way of responding to architecture, one that draws attention to those qualities that are often overlooked.

There are many possible ways of framing an exhibition such as *Psycho Buildings*, which comprises architectural works by a diverse range of international artists practicing today. This essay looks backwards to the 1960s in order to draw attention to a number of architectural themes that emerge in the art of that period. These include architecture's role in producing place, critiquing site and imagining settings.[1] These interests figured as key aspects of the art of the 1960s, but also continue to preoccupy contemporary artists engaged in architectural investigations, albeit in ways that are being continually revised, reworked and rethought.

Sculpture as Place

In February 1966, in his essay 'Notes on Sculpture, Parts 1 and 2', artist Robert Morris argued that, unlike pictorial work, sculpture was not illusionist but had a 'literal nature', and that clearer distinctions needed to be made between sculpture's 'tactile nature' and the 'optical sensibilities involved in painting'.[2] In June of the same year, art critic David Antin wrote that sculpture was 'a specific space in which the observer is thrust, namely it is a place.'[3] Again, in October the same year, critic David Bourdon quoted artist Carl André's account of the development of modern sculpture from form, through structure, to place, and noted André's statement on *Cuts*, his show in March 1967 at the Dwan Gallery in Los Angeles, 'I now use the material as the cut in space.'[4] For artist Dennis Oppenheim, 1967 was *the year* when the 'notion of sculpture as place was manifest'.[5] In the same issue of *Artforum* in Part 2 of his 'Notes on Sculpture', Morris, following sculptor Tony Smith, took up the question of scale and located minimalist work at a human scale between the private object and public monument, as one term in an expanded situation.[6]

The architectural installations of Brazilian artist Hélio Oiticica from this period combine an interest in the formal qualities of architectural structures – open and closed, formal and informal – with different kinds of sensual experience. Oiticica's early works, such as *Bolides Caixas* (1963–), are tiny environments, boxes made of painted plywood, too small to be inhabited. Considered in relation to the inhabitable scale of the open mazes of hanging coloured panels comprising *Núcleos* (1960–66), the saturated hues of the closed cabins of the *Penetrables* (1961–) and the *Parangolés* (1964–71), incorporating various fabrics – capes, flags, banners and tents – designed to be worn while dancing, it is possible to think of his early work as a model for his later structures. The political relevance of the cultural sensuality of Oiticica's fabrications is perhaps most clear in *Tropicália* (1967), where a setting composed of a closed wooden labyrinthine structure with various fabrics, plants, parrots and sand, installed at the Museu de Arte Moderna in Rio de Janeiro, had to be 'penetrated' in order to be experienced.[7]

Robert Smithson
Partially Buried Woodshed,
1970

Over a similar time period, Dan Graham was also critiquing architecture's forms and value systems from the suburban — in photo-essays like his 1967 *Homes for America* — to the corporate, in the construction of his pavilion projects.[8] Graham's first outdoor pavilion work, *Two Adjacent Pavilions*, was first shown at *Documenta 7*, Kassel, Germany, in 1982. The twin pavilions had identical walls of two-way mirror glass, but there was a transparent glass ceiling in one and a dark ceiling in the other, resulting in the construction of two quite different experiences. Since two-way mirror glass can appear transparent or reflective depending on light levels, when the sun was shining, the viewers under the transparent ceiling were able to see themselves reflected in the mirrored walls and at the same time be seen by viewers outside, while those under the dark ceiling looked at the outside world rather than their own reflections, and could hardly be viewed from the outside.

Graham explored the potential of the pavilion form and two-way mirror glass in numerous other site-specific projects. In *Rooftop Urban Park Project*, a small urban park constructed on the roof of the Dia building in Chelsea, New York, in the 1980s, the pavilion consisted of a glass rectangle surrounding a cylindrical form also constructed of glass. Due to different lighting conditions, at times the viewer could look through the pavilion and see the grids of the façades of the downtown steel and glass skyscrapers on the skyline. At other times, they were confronted by their own reflection, looking back. Like many other works by Graham, *Two-Way Mirror Cylinder Inside Cube* (1981–91) combines the cube and cylinder. The cube references the grid of the city and modernist architecture, while the cylinder refers to the water towers perched on the surrounding roofs, while also relating the surface of the body to the horizon line.[9] The work questions the limits of the gallery — architecturally and institutionally — but also follows Graham's provocation of the viewer's critical as well as his/her physical engagement.

In art critic Hal Foster's reading of Minimalism, the sculpture is 'off the pedestal' in relation to the viewer, 'repositioned among objects and redefined in terms of place'.[10] He argues that in order to create a direct physical relationship with the viewer, Minimalism replaced the idealist Cartesian 'I think' and the abstract expressionist 'I express' with 'I perceive'.[11] Refusing the distinction between the perceptual experience offered by Minimalism and the intellectual challenge posed by Conceptualism, in demanding that the viewer operate not just perceptually, but also conceptually, artists like Oiticica and Graham set the scene for the development of what has come to be described as Post-Minimalism. Their sculptures investigate the relation between viewer and work, not only through the literal physical experience of the here and now, but also by exploring processes that are abstract and ideological as well as visibly and tangibly present.

Architecture as the Site of Institutional Critique

Robert Smithson described the shift in his own artistic practice at this time from an interest in specific objects to a more relational way of 'seeing' the world, where the works 'became a preoccupation with place'.[12] Exploring architecture through his interest in entropy, his *Partially Buried Woodshed* (1970) was intended to demonstrate this principle of disintegration through the dumping of earth on top of an empty shed until it collapsed. Smithson also documented entropy in existing architecture in works such as *A Tour of the Monuments of Passaic, New Jersey* (1967) and *Hotel Palenque* (1969).[13] The former, a photo-essay, describes the material qualities of entropy in enormous industrial structures that at the time of their construction were already deteriorating. The latter, originally a lecture to architecture students, now a slide installation and sound recording, outlines Smithson's concept of a 'ruin in reverse', through his visit to a Mexican hotel which was decaying while also being renovated, enacting 'places of little organisation and no direction', as Smithson described the space between site and non-site.[14] Smithson's consideration of the dialectical relation between the site of the work and the non-site of the documentation of the work in the gallery presents the spatial aspect of his art as key to understanding his critique of art and architecture.[15]

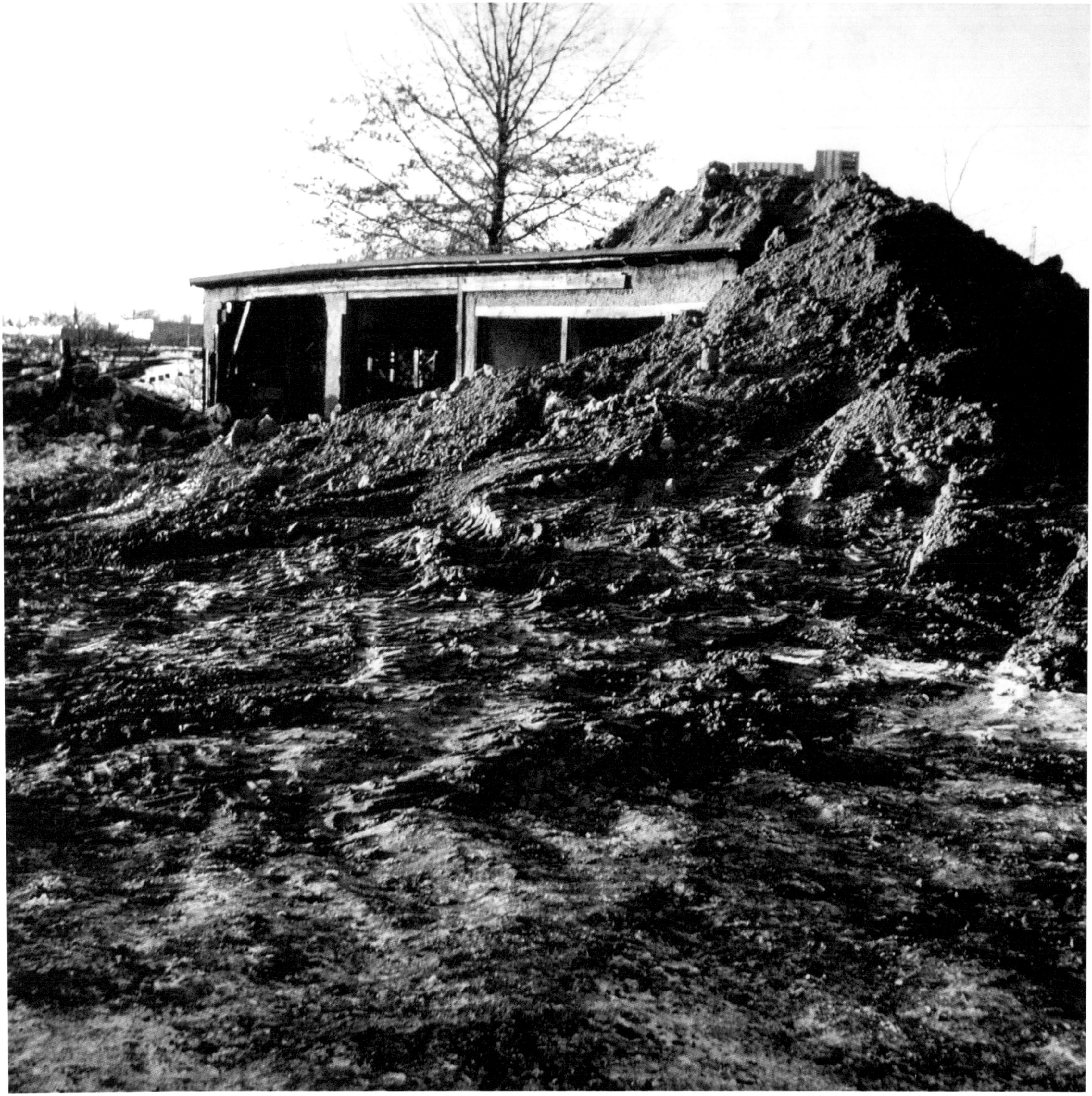

Gordon Matta-Clark
Window Blowout, **1976**

In the early 1970s, Michael Asher's work utilised the principle of material subtraction to focus critical attention on the institutional role of architecture from an experiential perspective. For his untitled work at the Claire Copley Gallery, Los Angeles, in 1974, he removed the partition between the office and exhibition space, revealing the usually hidden operations that allow the gallery to function economically to the viewer, but also exposing the viewer to the curator, thus making both subjects conscious of their activities as producers and consumers of art.[16] For his 1976 installation at the Clocktower Gallery of the Institute for Art and Urban Resources in New York, Asher removed all the windows and doors connecting the gallery to the external environment. This opened the interior to fluctuations in temperature, direct light and moisture, thus using perceptual change to promote critical reflection on the limits of art and the viewing experience.

These types of disruptions have been extended into contexts other than galleries. Built structures, which tend to represent the value systems of dominant cultures, have provided opportunities for critical art practitioners to make visible structures of oppression. Gordon Matta-Clark's anarchitecture is perhaps the clearest expression of insertions into architecture, which operate through negation — performative acts of destruction or building cuts — which in turn create new temporary architectures. For example, in *Splitting* (1974) Matta-Clark sawed two parallel slices through a wood-frame house in Englewood, New Jersey, removing the material between the two cuts, and in *Day's End* (1975) he removed part of the floor and roof of a derelict pier in Manhattan. In *Conical Intersect* (1975), for the *Biennale de Paris*, Matta-Clark cut a large cone-shaped hole through two seventeenth-century townhouses, which were to be knocked down to construct the Centre Georges Pompidou. But his most explosive act against architecture and its associated institutions must be his 'participation' in an exhibition alongside well-known architects in 1976 at the Institute of Architecture and Urban Studies in New York: on the afternoon of the exhibition's private view he shot out all the Institute's windows with a BB gun as a means of linking the abstraction of modernist architecture with its production of disastrous urban housing projects, the facades of which typically featured shattered windows.

Matta-Clark's work focuses attention on the ambivalence of the attraction between art and architecture, where the fascination is not without repulsion. Architecture's curiosity about art is in no small way connected with the perception of art as a potentially subversive activity, whose relative freedom from economic pressures and social demands can make it appear superfluous; while the appeal of architecture's so-called purposefulness for art, its cultural and functional role, reveals its more sinister side in the potentially despotic aspect of the control and power considered integral to the identity of the architect.

The Setting

Art critic Claire Bishop has argued that installation art is best understood in terms of its treatment of the viewing subject — perceptually, politically and psychologically.[18] For this reason, it might be that *Psycho Buildings*' predecessors lie in the use of the gallery as a performance space that dissolves the boundaries between subject and object. In his essay 'The Work of Art in the Age of Mechanical Reproduction' (1936), Walter Benjamin differentiated between concentration as the optical mode of viewing a painting, in which the work absorbs the viewer, and distraction as the tactile experience of architecture, in which the viewer absorbs the work.[19] The insertion of structures, objects, sounds and texts into the gallery context has produced complex architectural scenes, which both absorb and are absorbed by the viewer. They invite a viewer to move through the work, drawing out meanings over time. And, through varying modes of interaction, they involve activities that draw on personal memories, cultural references and imagined scenarios.

Kurt Schwitters' *Merzbau*[20] and the phenomenon of the 'total installation' described by Ilya Kabakov, provide environments that immerse their viewers in alternative worlds through the production of narrative and theatrical settings, which involve the viewer in fictional constructions as well as sensual and visual experience.[21] This might include inviting the viewer to imagine an 'elsewhere', when the gallery is arranged to replicate another place — as is the case with Lucas Samaras' 1964 *Room*, for which the artist transported his bedroom-studio from his parents' home in New Jersey to the Green Gallery on West 57th Street in New York.

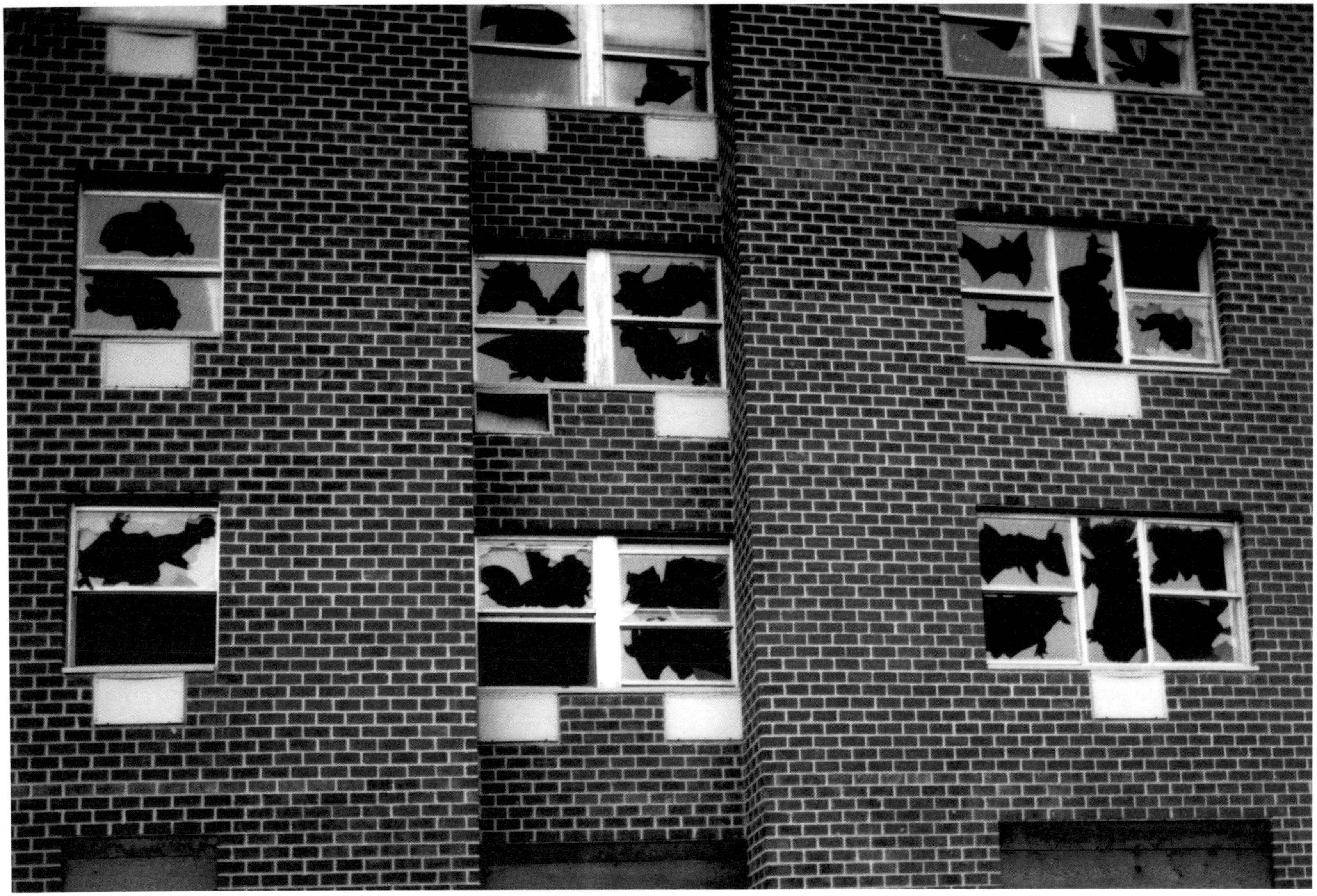

An act of duplication might also involve some invention, as in Paul Thek's carefully choreographed and symbolic 'processions' or 'ensembles' — ritualised architectural spaces — such as *Pyramid/A Work in Progress* (1971–72), which recreated the artist's working environment and included a boat, bathtub, piano and other items.[22] An installation might also be a hybrid fabrication, part fact and part fiction, where fantasy blends with the everyday, and reality departs due to the miniaturised way in which it is repeated; for instance, in the feminist works comprising *Womanhouse* (1972), a project organised by Miriam Shapiro and Judy Chicago in an old Hollywood mansion.[23]

The interest in architecture here can be distinguished from the minimalist and conceptual art of the 1960s and 1970s in terms of the complex forms of occupation that the work requires in order *to function* or to be used. This highlights a specific articulation of, in Umberto Eco's words, the 'open work', where the viewer is invited to imaginatively complete the work. In his important essay, 'The Poetics of the Open Work' (1962), which prefigures the discussion of relational aesthetics by some 30 years, Eco shifts the grounds of viewer experience from contemplation to use.[24] In demanding imaginative as well as perceptual and conceptual modes of use, these works are inhabited both consciously and unconsciously.

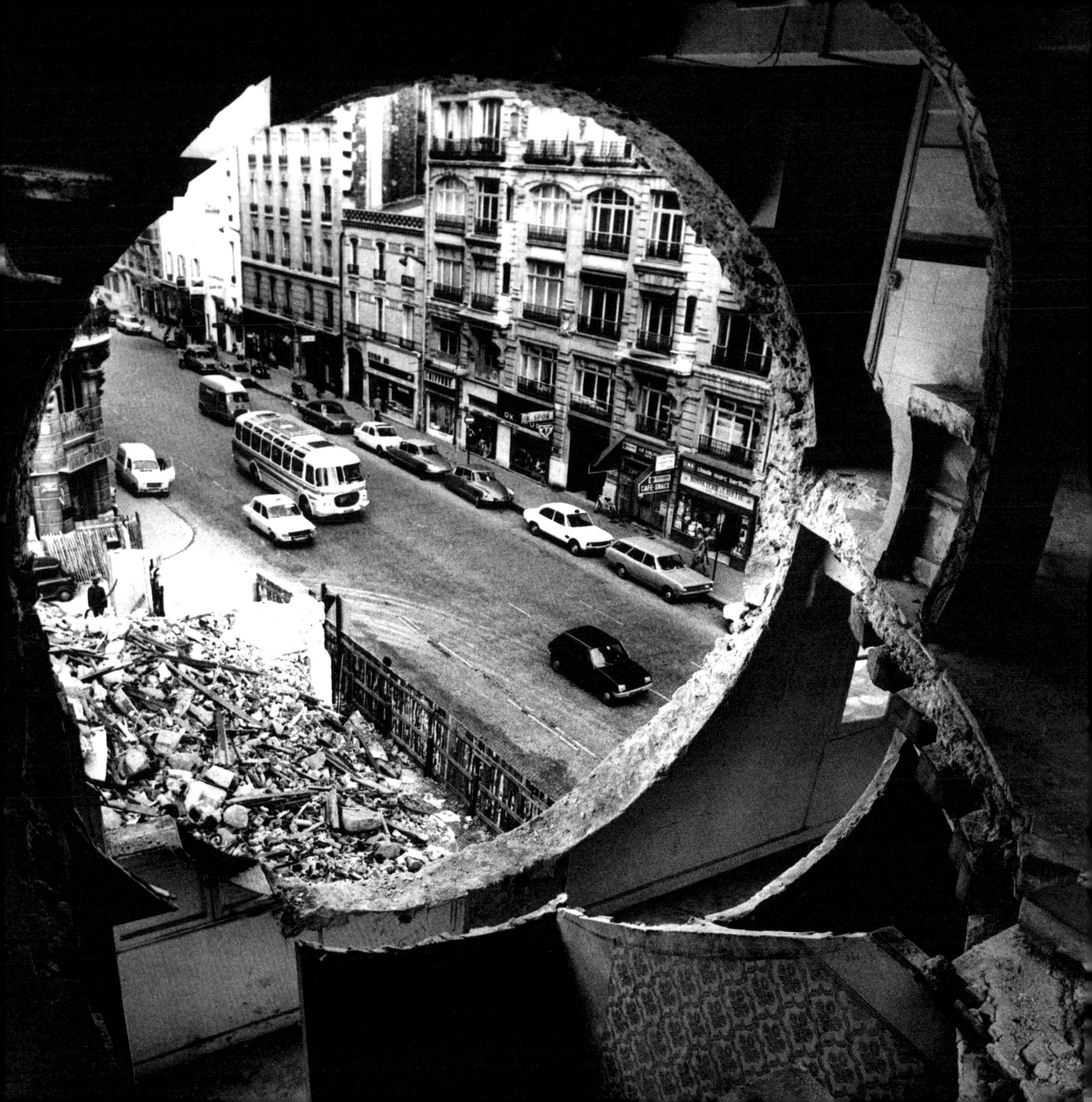
CAFE-SNACK
claude marc bertho

Gordon Matta-Clark
Conical Intersect, **1975**

It may be helpful therefore to consider *Psycho Buildings* in relation to the psychoanalytical notion of 'setting', a term used to describe the main conditions of treatment within which the psychoanalytic encounter occurs. Following Sigmund Freud, these conditions include 'arrangements' about time and money, as well as 'certain ceremonials' governing the physical positions of analysand (lying on a couch and speaking) and analyst (sitting behind the analysand on a chair and listening).[25] Coined by Donald Winnicott, 'as the sum of all the details of management that are more or less accepted by all psychoanalysts',[26] the term has been modified by other analysts. In the work of José Bleger, the setting comprises both the process of psychoanalysis and the non-process or frame, which provides a set of constants, or limits, to the 'behaviours' that occur within it.[27] And, in terms of its spatial configuration, Jean Laplanche considers the setting a double-walled tub.[28] For André Green, it is a casing or casket that holds the 'jewel' of the psychoanalytic process.[29]

Green has drawn attention to the setting not as a static tableau, but as a psychoanalytic apparatus; not as a representation of psychic structure, but as an expression of it. For Green, the position of the consulting room between inside and outside relates to its function as a transitional space between analyst and analysand, as does its typology as a closed space different from both inner and outer worlds, 'The consulting room ... is different from the outside space, and it is different, from what we can imagine, from inner space. It has a specificity of its own.'[30] In Green's work the setting is a 'homologue' for what he calls the third element in analysis, the 'analytic object', which is formed through the analytic association between analyst and analysand.[31] 'The analytic object', Green argues, 'is neither internal (to the analysand or to the analyst), nor external (to either the one or the other), but is situated between the two ... in the intermediate area of potential space, the space of 'overlap' demarcated by the analytic setting.'[32]

In many ways, the closed space of the gallery operates as a setting for an encounter between user and artwork, involving the process of engaging with a work and the non-process or frame in which one is 'invited' to engage with the work. This setting includes then the frame of the physical space of the gallery: the hours of opening, admission fees, provision of refreshments and facilities, the presence of invigilators, and rules of occupation, as well as the process of encountering art. As 'analytic object', the architecture of the artwork provokes a response in the user that is not only physical or conceptual but also psychic. The contemporary artworks in *Psycho Buildings*, in engaging with the psychic dimension of architecture, are best understood with reference to the setting as a spatial term that frames the provocation of transference — the work of psychoanalysis. Through spatial processes of displacement and disorientation, uncanny experiences associated with repetition and play indicate the presence of the unconscious in the unexpected dimensions conjured by these works.

In choosing to highlight the 1960s as the most relevant precedent for this show, what has been suggested? In the art of the 1960s, architecture often featured as the gallery, with its institutional structure, material limitation and cosy relation with commerce, but it also operated as a mediating threshold between private lives and public concerns through which individuals related to the wider environment. Through the late 1970s and into the 1980s, the art world's interest in architecture appeared to diminish; art's criticality pointed in a different direction, towards a sceptical questioning, sometimes an ambivalent celebration, of mass consumption, visual spectacle and the commodification of art. But the return of architecture in the art of the late 1990s and 2000s is not a repetition of the work of the 1960s and 1970s. There is still a fascination with architecture's dark side, with its ability to control and order, but the manifestation of power affects the viewer both consciously and unconsciously. Artists in *Psycho Buildings* explore architecture's psyche, through the production of places, sites and settings, which engender spatial experiences that connect the viewer psychically, as well as perceptually and conceptually, to broader social issues and cultural phenomena.

1 In developing the concept of critical spatial practice in art, I discuss the difference between the terms space, place and site. See Jane Rendell, *Art and Architecture: A Place Between*, I.B. Tauris, London, 2006. In my forthcoming book *Site-Writing: The Architecture of Art Criticism*, I explore criticism itself as a critical spatial practice, where interaction between the critic and the work operates as a form of setting. See also Miwon Kwon, *One Place After Another: Site-Specific Art and Locational Identity*, MIT, Cambridge, Mass., 2002; and the discussion of place in Claire Doherty (ed.), *Thinking of the Outside: New Art and the City of Bristol*, University of the West of England and Bristol Legible City in Association with Arnolfini, 2005, pp. 9–10.

2 Robert Morris, 'Notes on Sculpture 1–3', in Charles Harrison and Paul Wood (eds), *Art in Theory 1900–1990: An Anthology of Changing Ideas*, Blackwell, Oxford, 1992, p. 814. Part 1 was first published in *Artforum*, February 1966, pp. 42–44.

3 See David Antin, 'What is an Environment?', in *Art News*, April, 1966, referenced in Suzaan Boettger, *Earthworks: Art and the Landscape of the Sixties*, University of California Press, Los Angeles, 2002, p. 211.

4 David Bourdon, 'The Razed Sites of Carl André', in Gregory Battcock (ed.), *Minimalism: A Critical Anthology*, University of California Press, Berkeley/Los Angeles, 1995, pp. 103–108. Reprinted from *Artforum*, October 1966, pp. 103–104.

5 Germano Celant, *Dennis Oppenheim*, Charta, Milan, 1997, p. 29.

6 Robert Morris, op. cit., p. 816. Part 2 was first published in *Artforum*, October 1966, pp. 20–23.

7 Claire Bishop argues that the sensorial experience of *Tropicália* has to be understood as 'activated spectatorship' in relation to the oppressive Brazilian regime of the mid 1960s onwards. See Claire Bishop, *Installation Art: A Critical History*, Tate Publishing, London, 2005. Her point can be extended to suggest that the various kinds of spatial experience involved in installation art need to be understood within their specific historical and cultural contexts.

8 See for example, Dan Graham, *Pavilions*, Kunsthalle Bern, 1983; Dan Graham, *Pavilions*, Kunstverein München, 1988; and Martin Köttering and Roland Nachtigäller (eds), *Dan Graham: Two-Way Mirror Pavilions 1989–1996*, Städtische Galerie Nordhorn, 1996.

9 The park includes a pavilion designed by the artist Dan Graham in collaboration with architects Moji Baratloo and Clifton Balch and a video salon with a coffee bar showing work selected by the artist. See leaflet published by Dia Center for the Arts, Dan Graham, 'Rooftop Urban Park Project', long-term installation, consisting of Dan Graham 'Two-Way Mirror Cylinder Inside Cube' (1981–91), and Design Collaboration, Baratloo-Balch Architects, 'Video Salon'.

10 Hal Foster, *The Return of the Real: The Avant-Garde at the End of the Century*, MIT, Cambridge, Mass., 2001, p. 38.

11 Ibid., p. 43.

12 Robert Smithson, 'Interview with Robert Smithson for the Archives of American Art/Smithsonian Institution', (1972), in Jack Flam (ed.), *Robert Smithson: The Collected Writings*, University of California Press, Berkeley/Los Angeles, 1996, p. 296.

13 See Robert Smithson, 'Entropy and New Monuments', (1966), in ibid., pp. 10–23, and Robert Smithson, 'A Tour of the Monuments of Passaic, New Jersey', (1967), in ibid., pp. 68–74.

14 See Robert Smithson quoted in Neville Wakefield, 'Yucatan is Elsewhere: On Robert Smithson's *Hotel Palenque*', in *Parkett*, 43, 1995, p. 133. See http://www.robertsmithson.com/essays/palenque.htm.

15 For specific descriptions of his site/non-site dialectic see Robert Smithson, 'Towards the Development of an Air Terminal Site', (1967), in ibid., p. 291, Robert Smithson, '"Earth" (1969) Symposium at White Museum, Cornell University', in ibid., p. 178, and Robert Smithson, 'The Spiral Jetty', (1972), in ibid., pp. 152–153.

16 See for example Benjamin H. D. Buchloh (ed.), *Michael Asher, Writings 1973–1983 on Works 1969–1979*, Nova Scotia College of Art and Design and Museum of Contemporary Art, Los Angeles, 1984, pp. 76–81.

17 See Kirsi Peltomaki, 'Affect and Spectatorial Agency: Viewing Institutional Critique in the 1970s', in *Art Journal*, Winter 2007.

18 See Claire Bishop, op cit., pp. 6–13.

19 Walter Benjamin, 'The Work of Art in the Age of Mechanical Reproduction', completed in 1936 and translated by Harry Zohn, in Hannah Arendt (ed.), *Illuminations*, Fontana, London, 1992, pp. 231, 233.

20 See for example http://www.merzbau.org/Schwitters.html.

21 Ilya Kabakov, *On the 'Total' Installation*, Cantz Verlag, Bonn, 1995, p. 273.

22 See for example http://www.ptproject.net/introduction.php.

23 See for example http://as-ap.org/sider/resources.cfm.

24 Umberto Eco, 'The Poetics of the Open Work', (1962), in Claire Bishop (ed.), *Participation: Documents of Contemporary Art*, Whitechapel, London, and MIT, Cambridge, Mass, 2006, pp. 20–40.

25 Sigmund Freud, 'On Beginning the Treatment (Further Recommendations on the Technique of Psycho-Analysis I)', (1913), *The Standard Edition of the Complete Psychological Works of Sigmund Freud, Volume XII (1911–1913): The Case of Schreber, Papers on Technique and Other Works*, pp. 121–144, 126, 133.

26 Luciana Nissin Momigliano, 'The Analytic Setting: a Theme with Variations', in *Continuity and Change in Psychoanalysis: Letters from Milan*, Karnca Books, London and New York, 1992, pp. 33–61, 33–34.

27 José Bleger, 'Psycho-Analysis of the Psycho-Analytic Frame', in *International Journal of Psycho-Analysis*, 1967, 48, pp. 511–519, 518.

28 The French term used is 'baquet'. See Jean Laplanche, 'Transference: its Provocation by the Analyst', in *Essays on Otherness*, Routledge, London, 1999, pp. 214–233, 226, note.

29 The French word used is '*écrin*'. See André Green, *Key Ideas for a Contemporary Psychoanalysis: Misrecognition and Recognition of the Unconscious*, Routledge, London, 2005, p. 33, note.

30 'Dialogues with André Green', in Gregorio Kohon (ed.), *The Dead Mother: The Work of André Green*, Routledge, London, published in association with the Institute of Psycho-Analysis, 1999, p. 29.

31 André Green, 'The Analyst, Symbolization and Absence in the Analytic Setting (On Changes in Analytic Practice and Analytic Experience) – In Memory of D. W. Winnicott', in *International Journal of Psycho-Analysis*, 1975, 56, pp. 1–22, 12.

32 André Green, 'Potential Space in Psychoanalysis: The Object in the Setting', in Simon A. Grolnick and Leonard Barkin (eds), *Between Reality and Fantasy: Transitional Objects and Phenomena*, Jason Aronson Inc., New York and London, 1978, pp. 169–189, 180.

Robert Morris
Untitled (Box for Standing),
1961

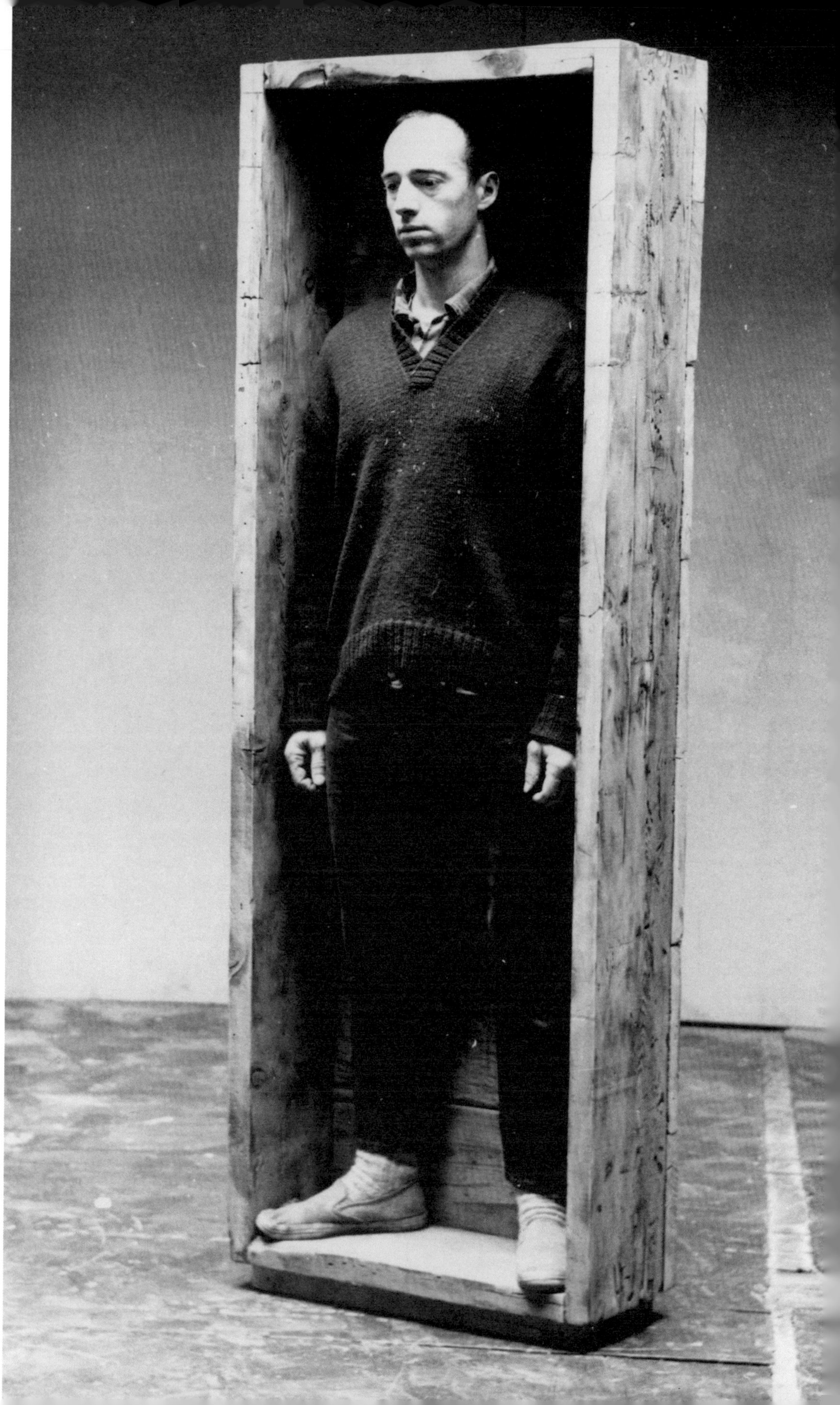

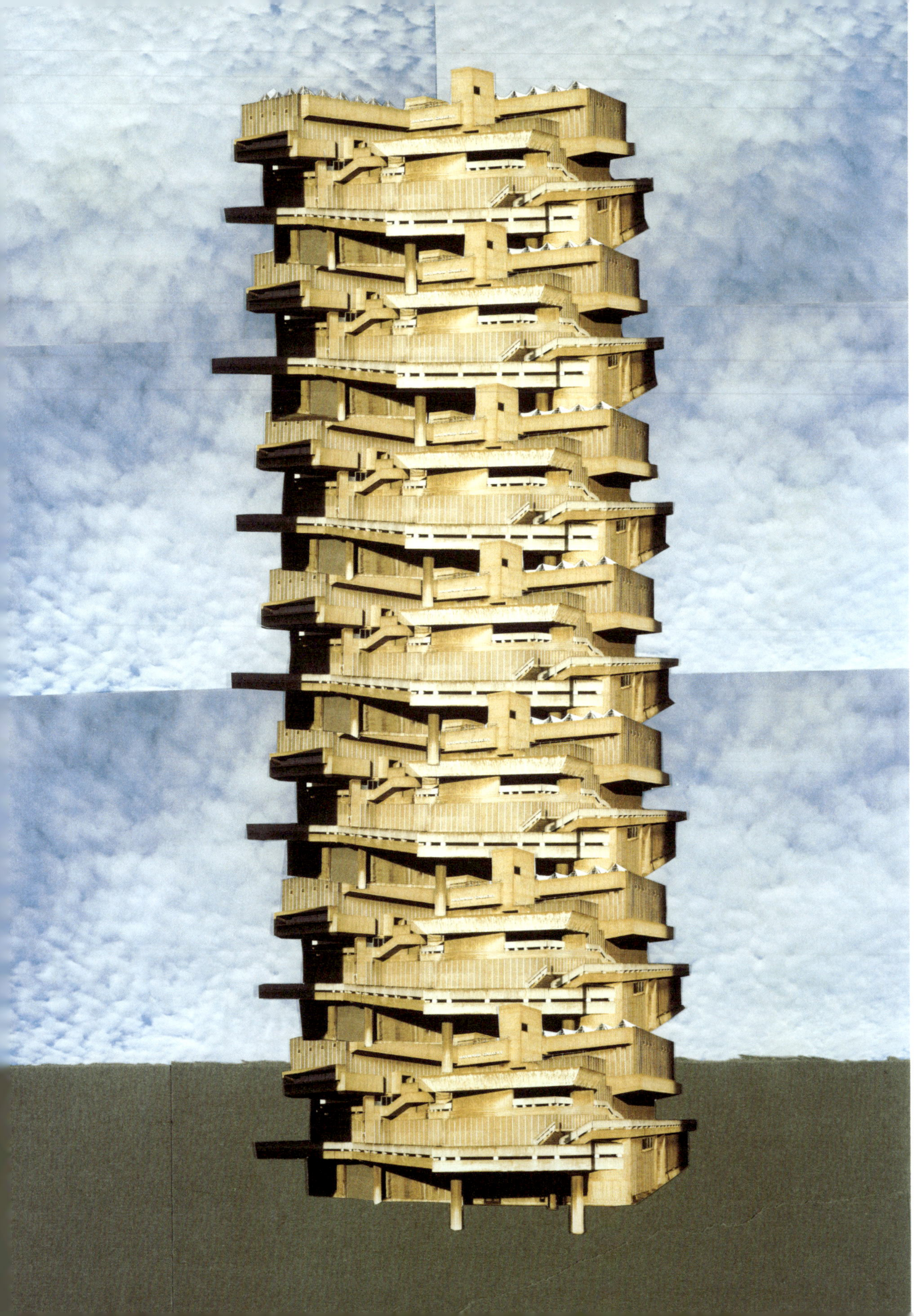

Rachel Whiteread
Psycho Building, **2008**

ARTISTS

Life Tunnel, **2008**

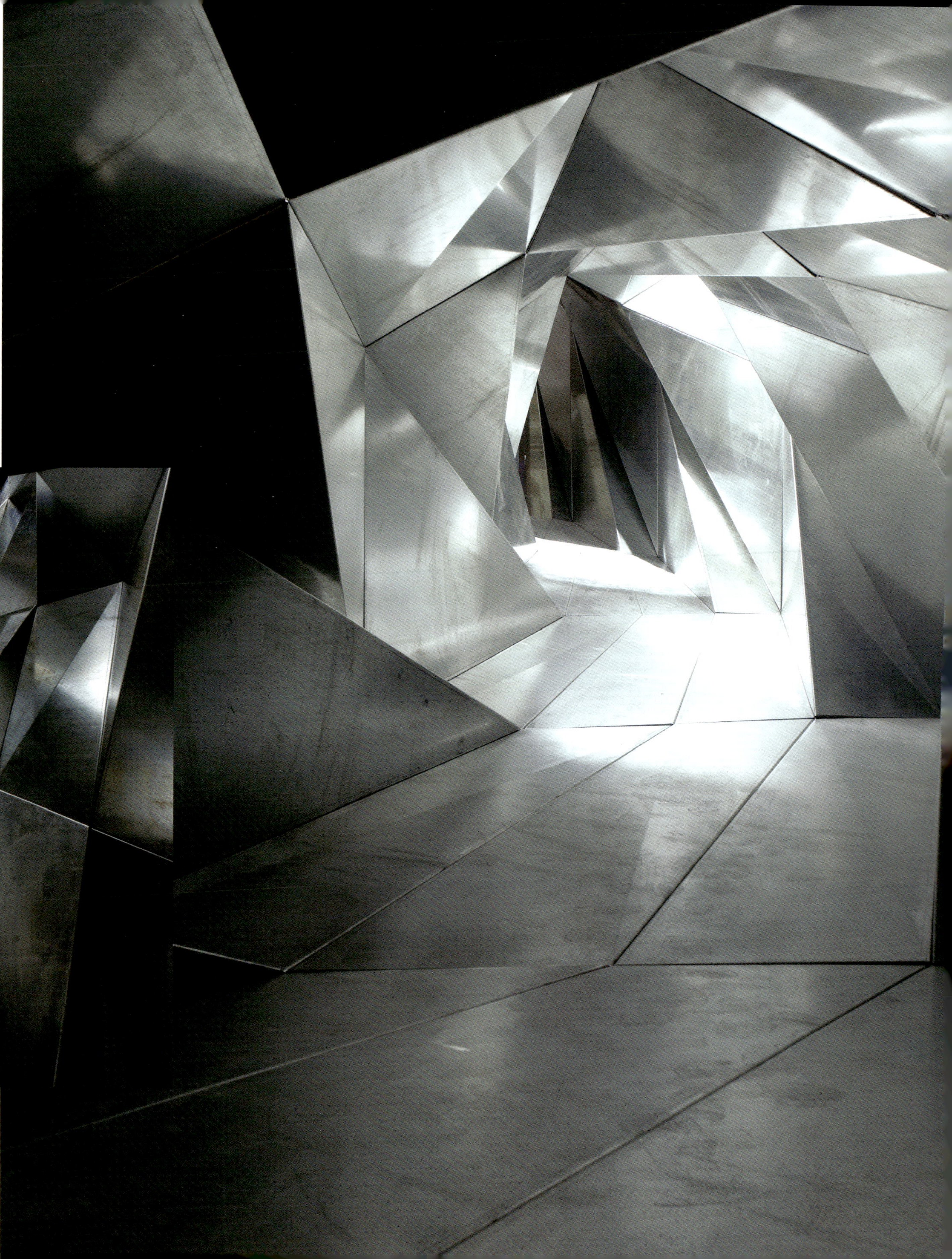

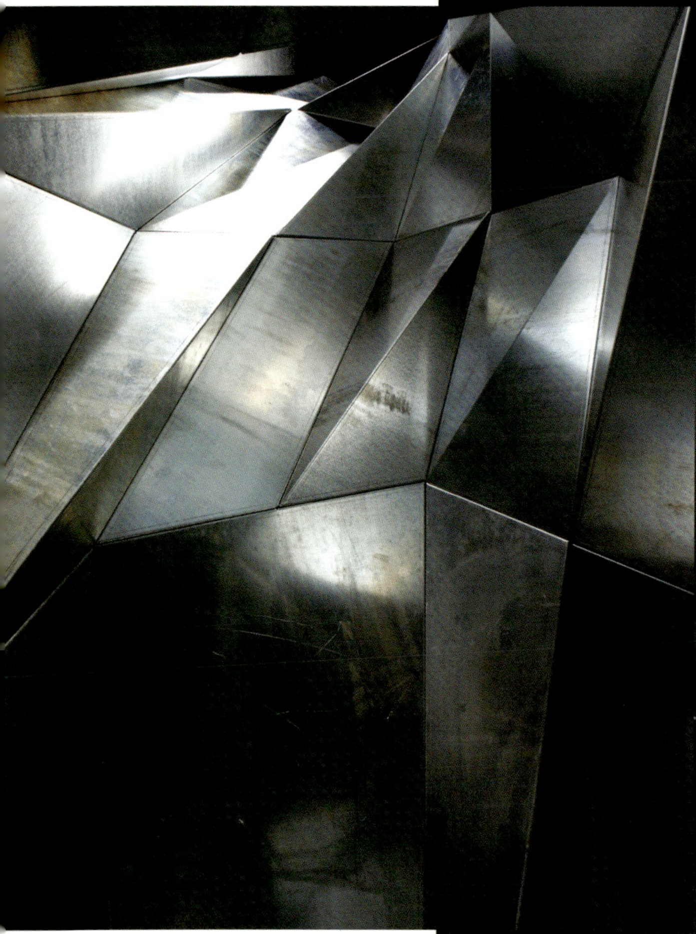

ATELIER BOW-WOW

DAVID GREENE

The Tokyo-based architectural office Atelier Bow-Wow was formed in 1992 by Yoshiharu Tsukamoto and Momoyo Kaijima. The duo work in a wide range of creative disciplines: the name itself says much about the nature of their varied output, which slides effortlessly between art practice, building architecture (which includes, remarkably for such a young practice, an extensive body of domestic architecture: they have designed more than 20 detached houses), constructing events and writing books. Their books, in particular, are a kind of research that informs their built work.

Their name is a hybrid of the French word for 'studio' and the childish English name for a dog or the noise it makes. In Japan, their name is yet another hybrid, Atelier Wan: 'because Japanese dogs bark Wan', explains Kaijima.[1] Bow Wow, Wan Wan, clearly they are anxious to disassociate their work and themselves from the respectable orthodoxies of the architectural profession and brand themselves as a group not imprisoned by the category 'architect'. Many young architects now employ this naming tactic, but Atelier Bow-Wow stand out from the rest because of their allegiance to the pleasures and possibilities of working in what we could call architecture in the expanded field. Their pleasure in words continues into their built work, and many of their houses are carefully named: Black Dog House, Juicy House, House without Depth.

We could say they are Neo-Dadaists. They use wit, humour and puns. They like to surprise, and they use and take delight in what Marcel Duchamp called the ready-made. In their book *Pet Architecture Guidebook* (2001), where they act as urban detectives, small even tiny buildings that frequently inhabit the left-over spaces and gaps in the city fabric are systematically catalogued as readymade architecture, ad-hoc collections of steps, fans, windows, signs, wires, etc. Importantly, they admire the way these impossibly small structures, on sites sometimes only two-metres wide, are always customised by the users.

Following on from the readymades of *Pet Architecture Guidebook*, these young architects claim to produce 'micro public space' in their projects. They say that micro means small but at the same time individual, thus the smallest public space might be seen as a public space for just one person. It is at this point that they begin to make intellectual claims for this 'micro public' realm, referring to the theories of the French Neo-Marxist philosopher Henri Lefebvre, in particular, his book *The Production of Space*. But they also have an appetite for serious play, and in this way, they have more in common with the artist Richard Prince and his serious jokes.

Atelier Bow-Wow like to join up words: for instance, 'Subdivurban' (Sub-divided suburbia?) and 'Commersidence' (a mixture of residential and commercial activity). They are fascinated by mixture, and so they assembled a book called *Made in Tokyo* (2001), which is a kind of guide book of buildings that Rem Koolhaas might call 'cross-programmed' (a word used in Schools of Architecture that means a mixture of functions). This book is a collection of unlikely hybrid Tokyo ready-mades, and it includes a bus terminal, public housing and a golf course on a garage. Mixtures of function can be found in any large city, but through the precision and elegance of Atelier Bow-Wow's documentation in this small book they remind us that architecture is everywhere.

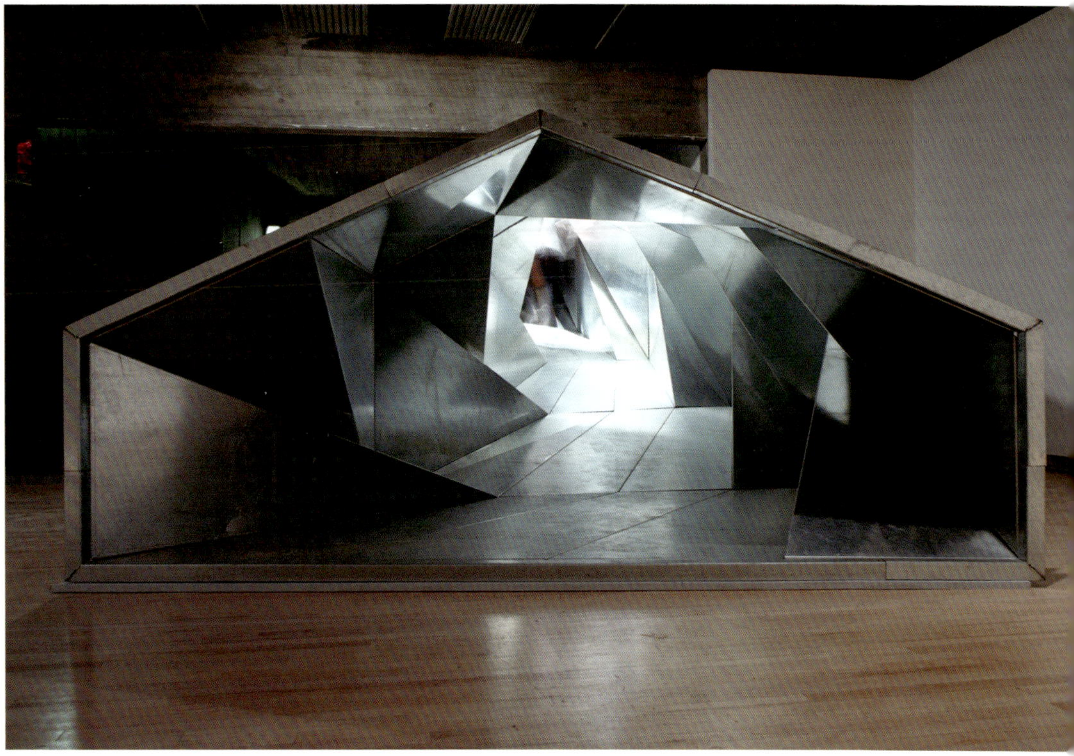

Life Tunnel, 2008

In 1992 and 1994, respectively, Atelier Bow-Wow designed a kiosk for vegetables and a public kitchen, a project that reminds us of their allegiance to the Situationists who argued that the city's events were more important than its buildings. Atelier Bow-Wow like to see the house as an event; they say that they started to think that domestic space could be organised in a personal way so that, for instance, once you took a bath and took off your clothes, you could put them in the laundry right away and, afterwards, on your way out, you could pass the balcony and hang them out to dry. Event equals house. Small things, but important; *Pet Architecture* things, micro space things, hybrid things. Inevitably, this principal has been carried on to larger public 'things', such as their design for the Hanamidori Cultural Centre in Tokyo. At this greater scale, the test will be whether they can still employ the same humour and hybridity, and can overcome the difficulty of changing from being observers of the city's details to being participants in their making. This journey is one familiar to all architects, and indeed to all of us, as it encompasses a reconciliation of ideals with reality.

Atelier Bow-Wow make us remember the powerful slogan 'small is beautiful'. Maybe we should measure their Hayward exhibit *Life Tunnel* in their own terms: 'Every time we are invited to participate in art events in different cities, we create a *micro public space* using the framework of an art exhibition. We go there a few months before the exhibition and observe the behaviour of the city and people. Then we design something based on this observation.'[2]

1 Email from the artists, February 2008.

2 '*Atelier Bow-Wow: Tokyo Anatomy*', www.archinect.com/features, 22 May 2007.

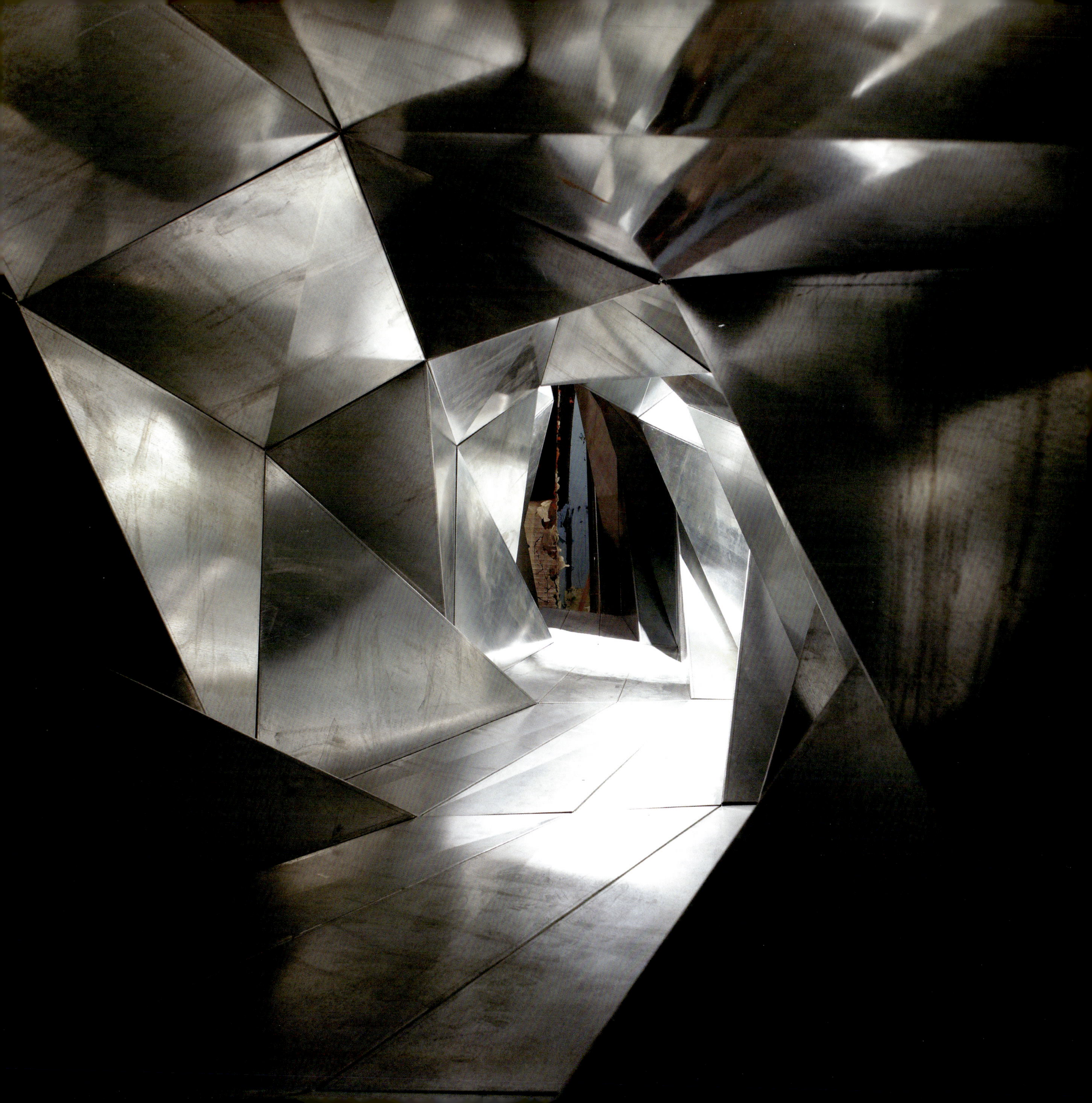

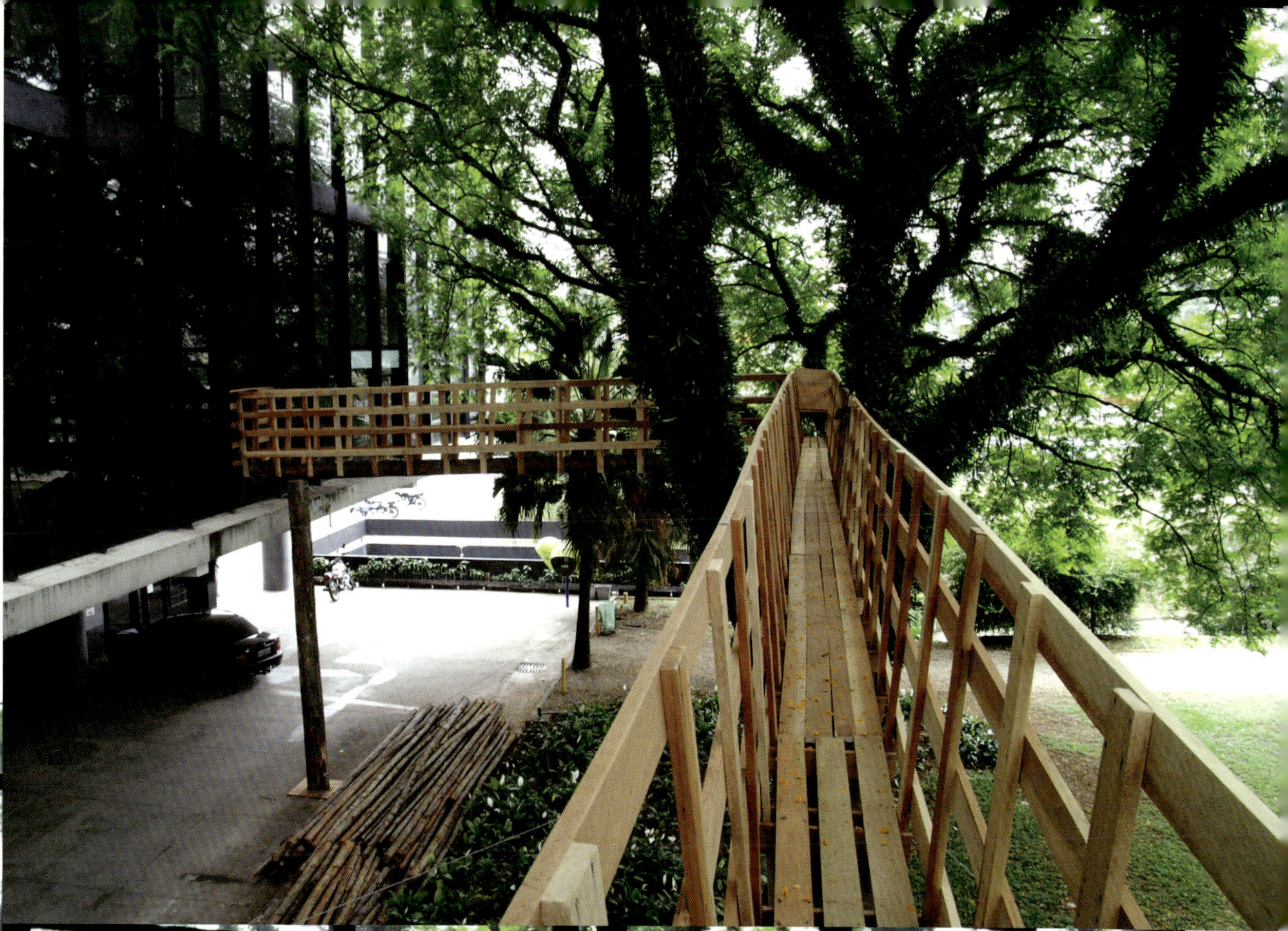

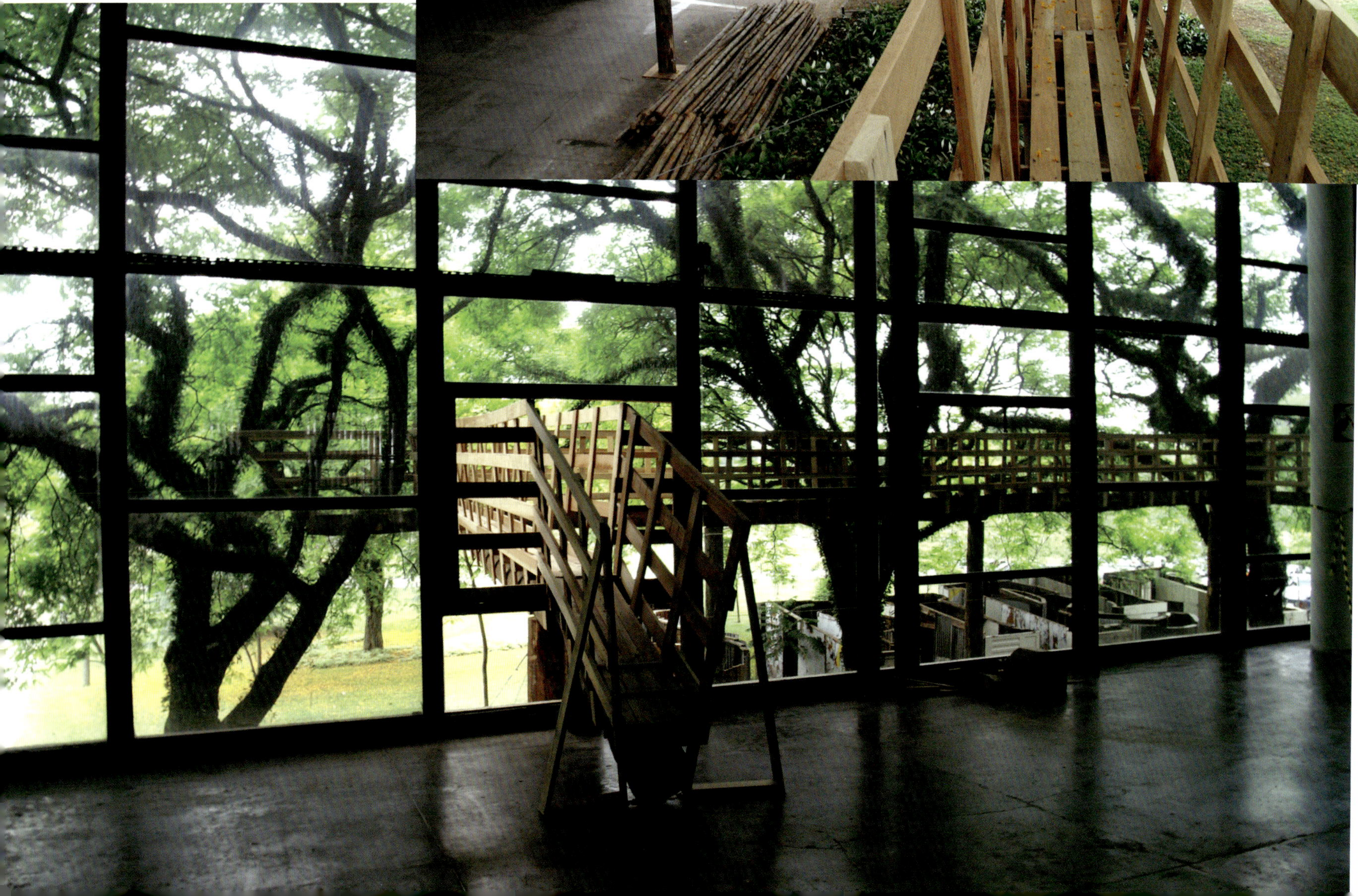

Monkey Way, **2006**

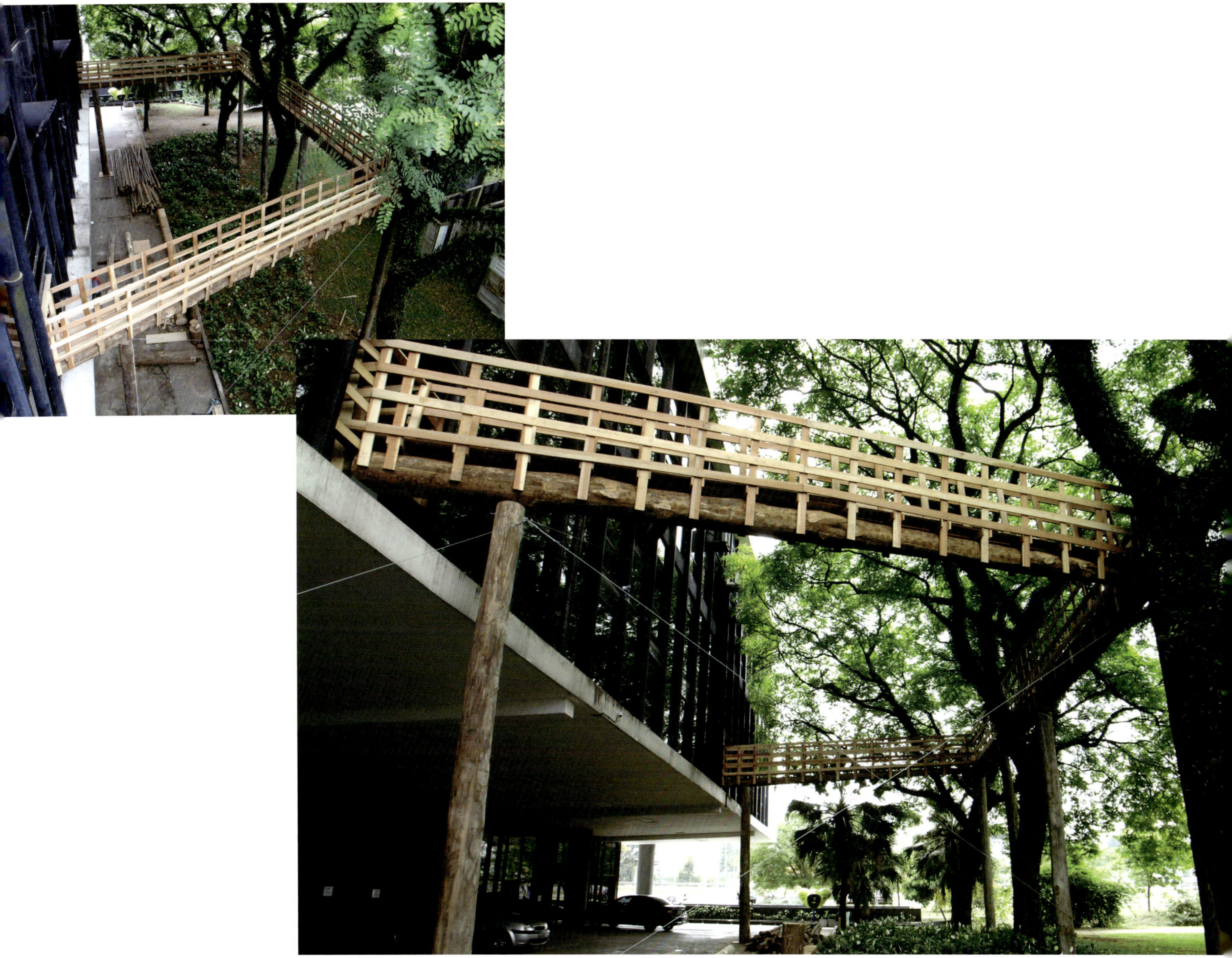

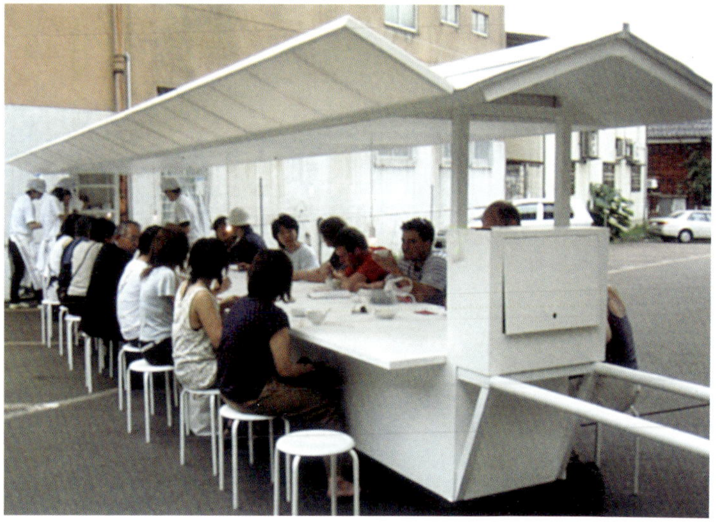

White Limousine Yatai, **2003**

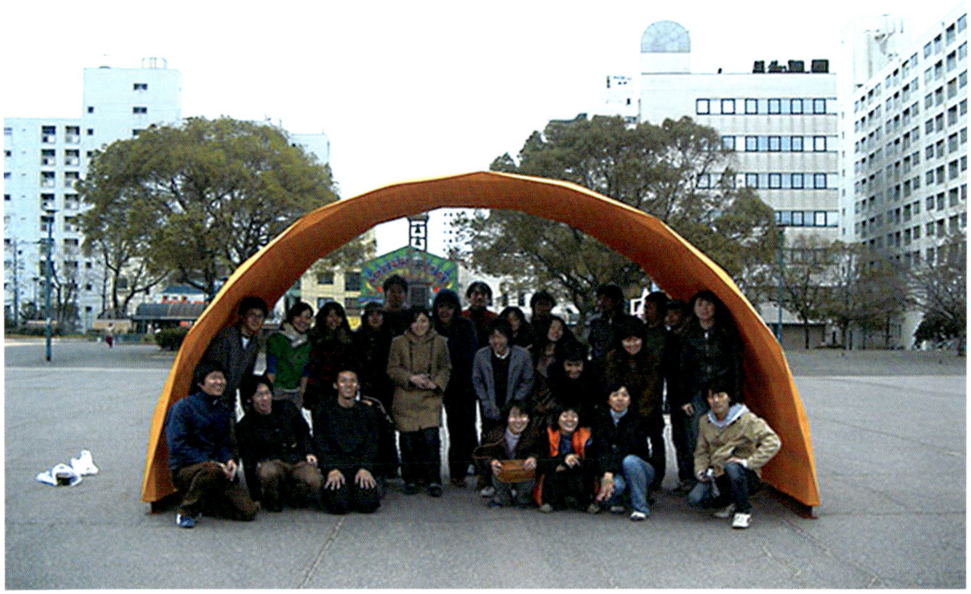

Jumbo Origamic Arch Orange, **2005**

Pet Architecture TAS, **2003**

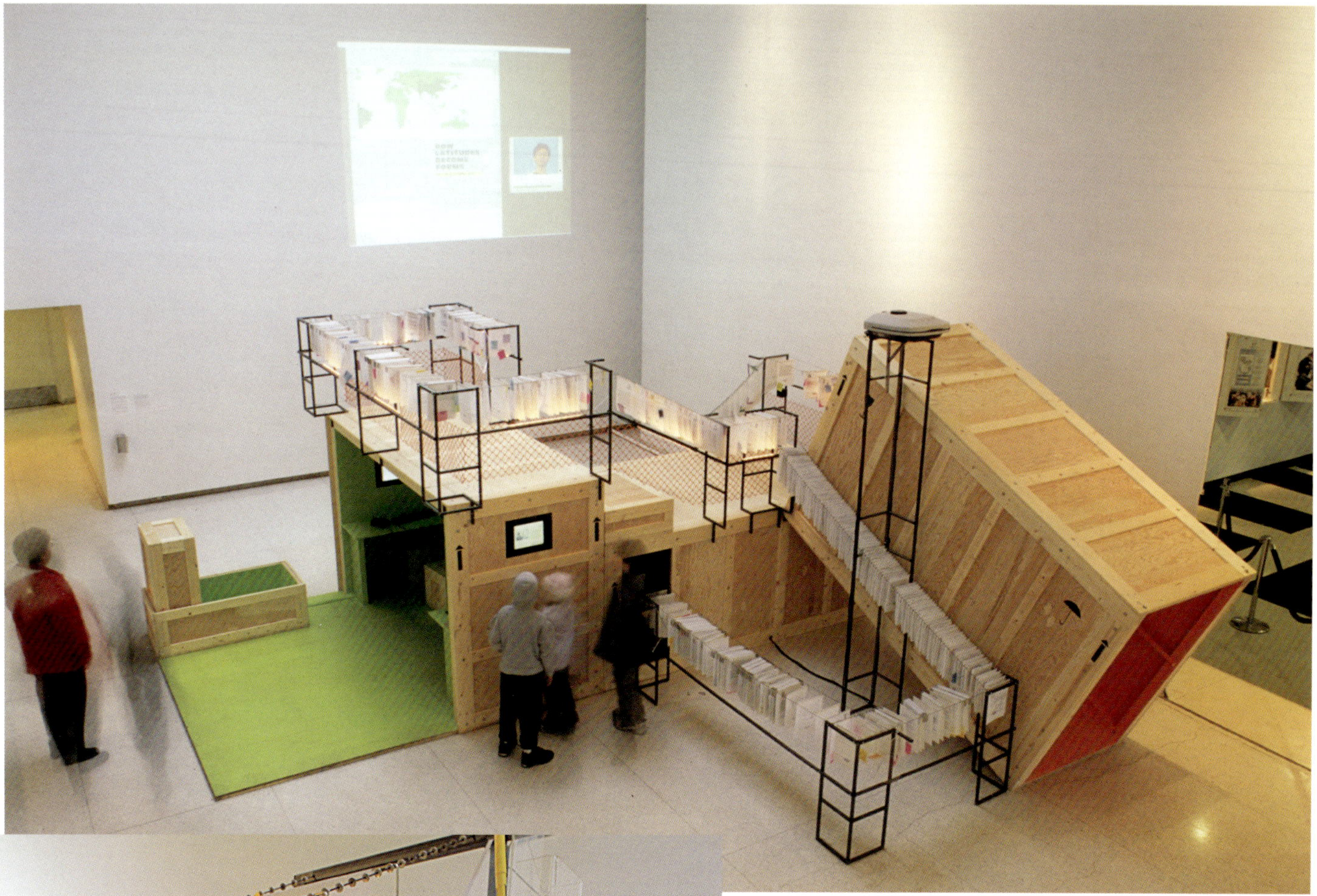

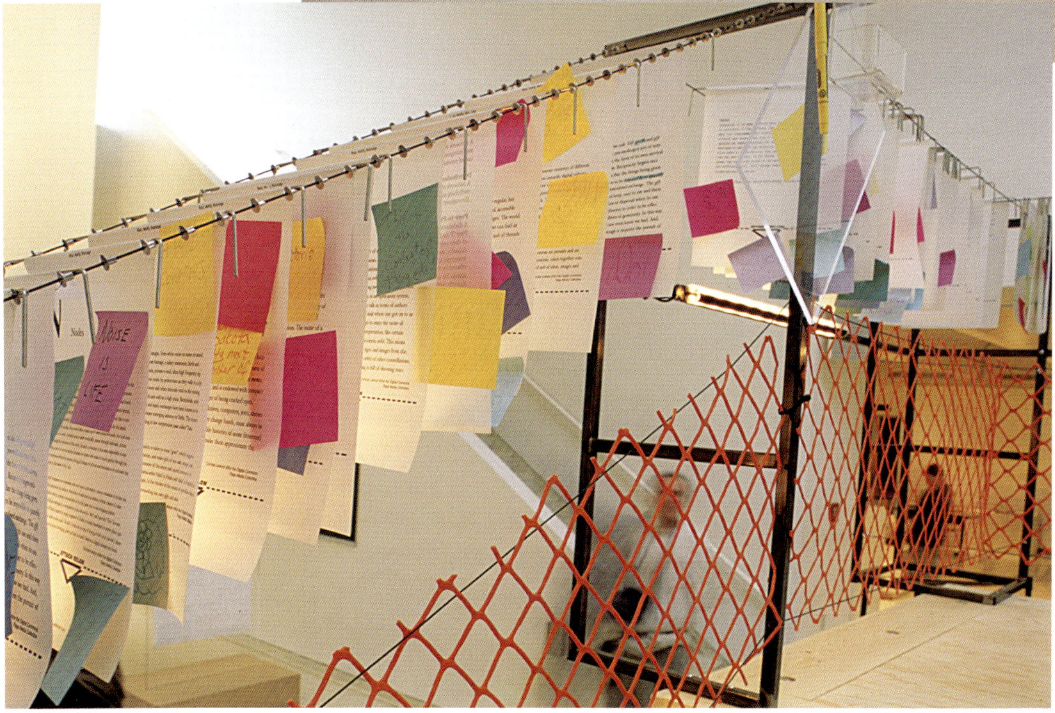

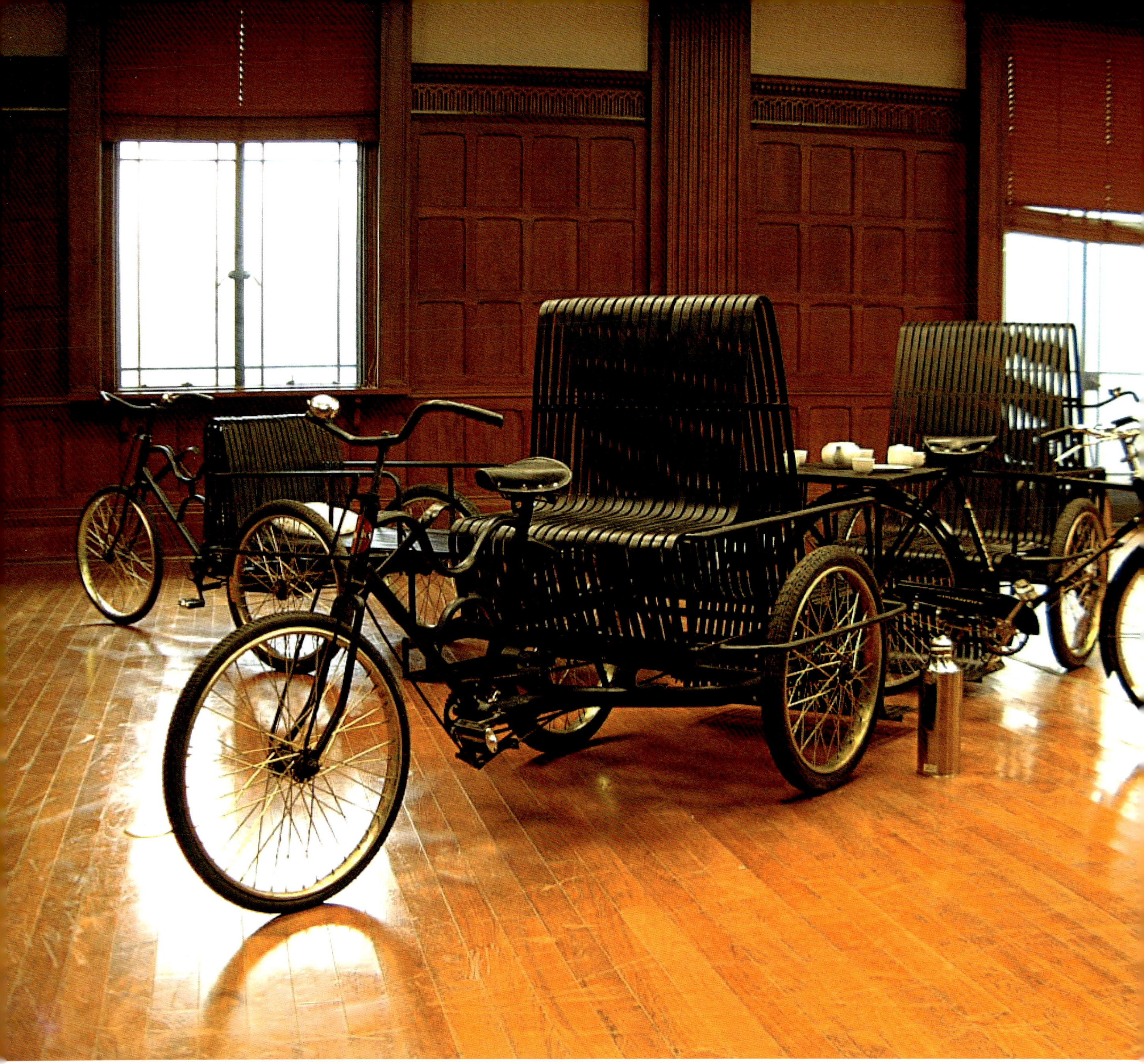

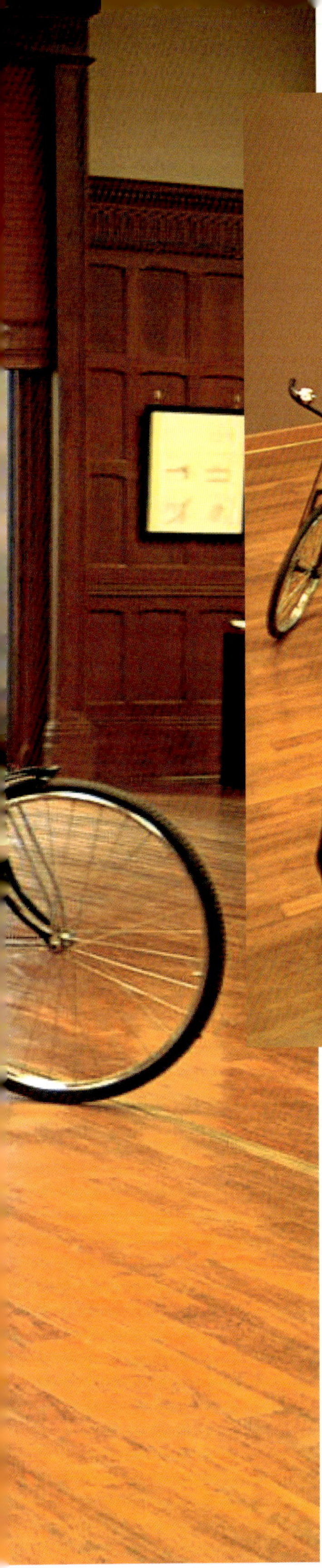

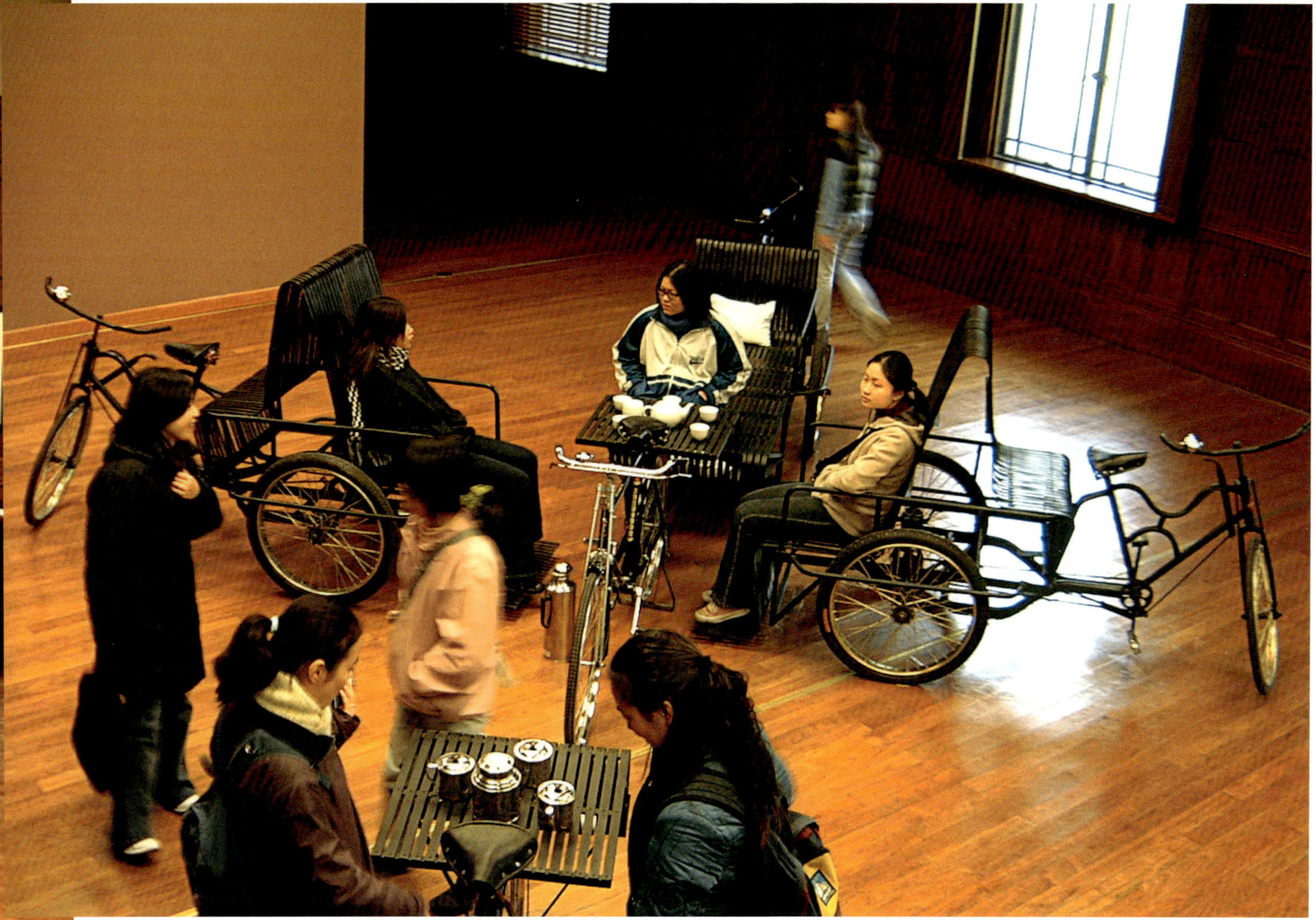

Furnicycle, **2002**

overleaf
Manga Pod, **2002**

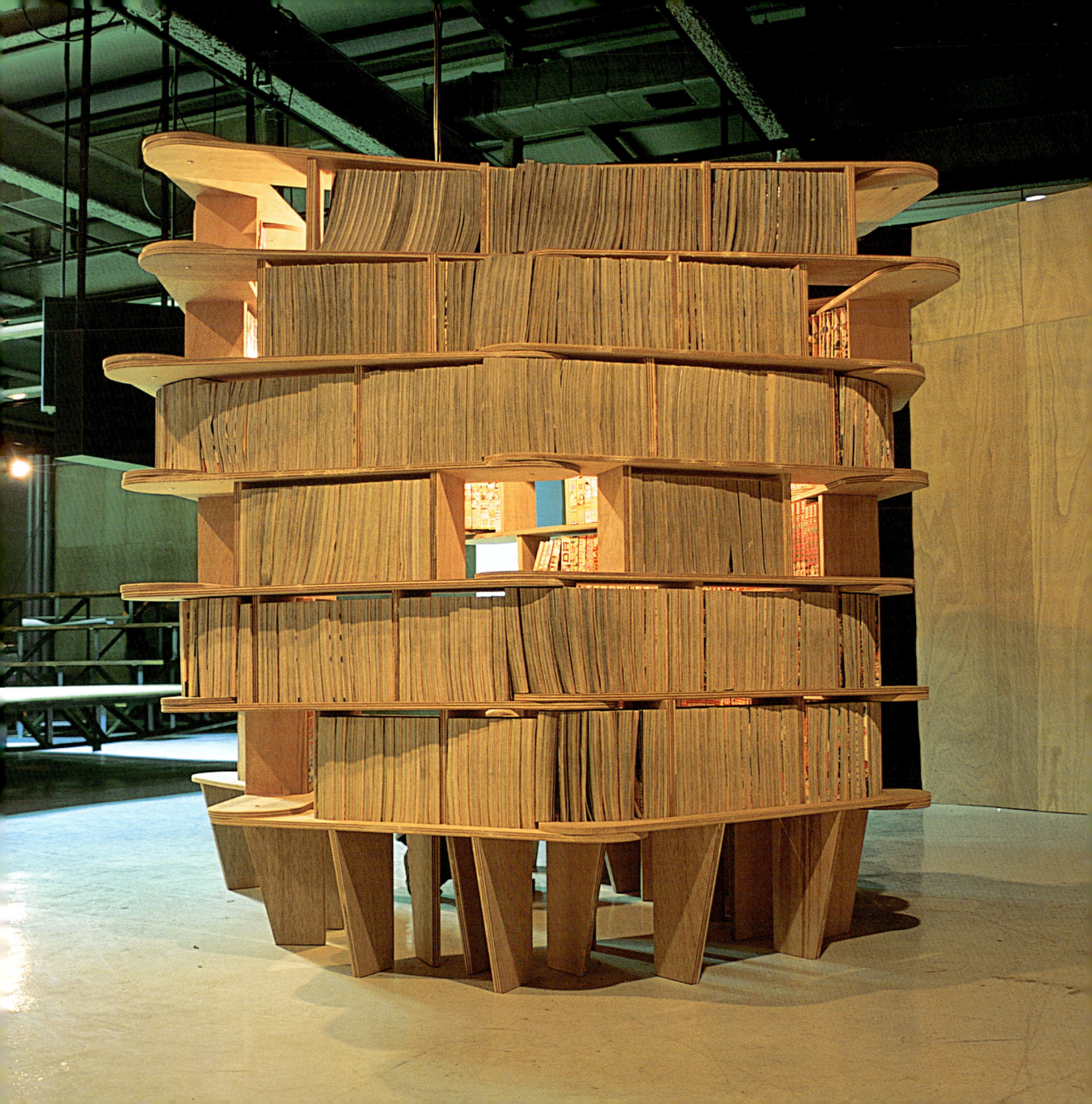

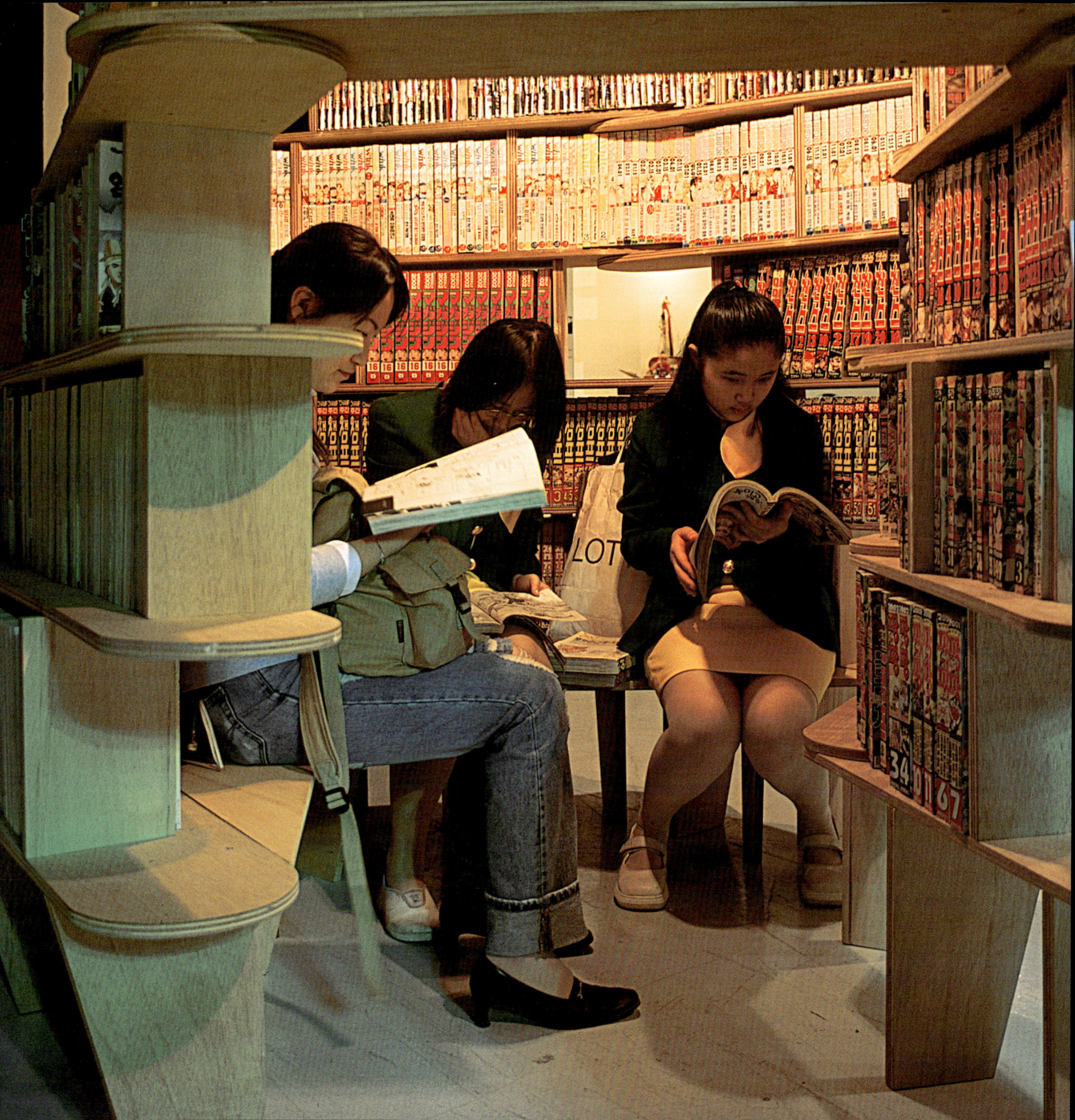
LOT

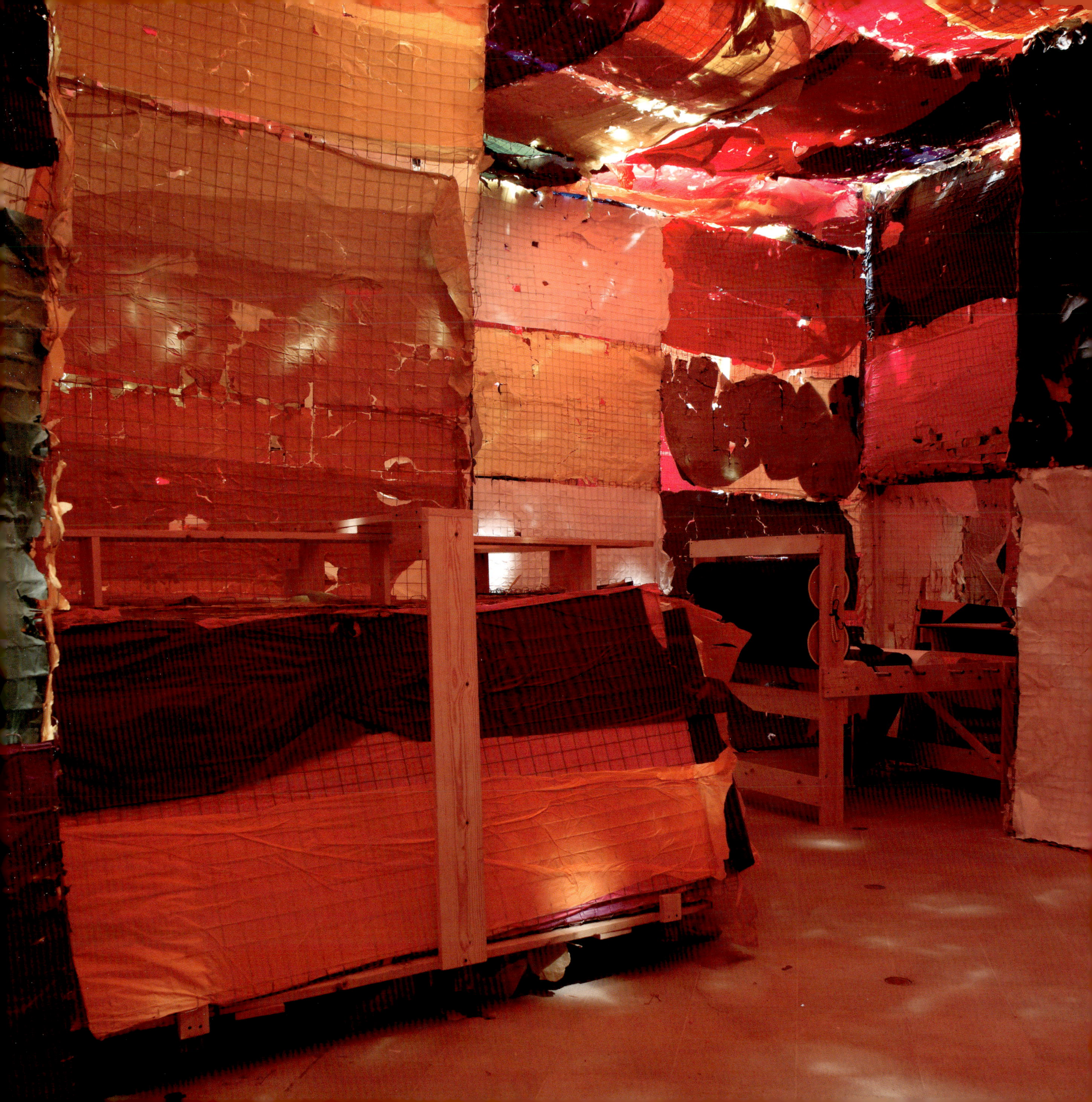

Sandwiches, Dobbels and Burgers, **2008**

MICHAEL BEUTLER

FRANCIS MCKEE

We live in a world increasingly determined by transience, and cities of the twenty-first century are in a continuous state of flux. In the 1970s and 1980s, cranes signalled gentrification as developers moved into abandoned industrial areas, converting them into apartment blocks, leisure facilities or shopping precincts. Now, cranes have become a permanent feature of the landscape as this accelerated process endlessly reshapes every city. At one time, these transformations might have been seen as a stage in modernist development, a moving forward towards a more utopian future, a new stability. Today, though, this process of perpetual mutation is an end in itself. The German sculptor Michael Beutler is highly sensitive to this phenomenon and his work reflects many of the often-contradictory signals that characterise the contemporary built environment. His approach to sculpture and to his artistic practice in general also demonstrates a realignment of the artist within this new, mutable, context.

Beutler is often associated with standardised construction materials. To shape his materials, Beutler first constructs a series of machines, themselves handmade and, in terms of appearance, pitched somewhere between medieval siege machinery and nineteenth-century looms. Each machine has a particular function — corrugating paper, stretching plastic, bending materials or mangling aluminium. They magnify labour, reminding us of the sheer physical effort of work as well as the more celebrated virtues of the 'handmade' object. They are used to manufacture or mould the materials of the artwork, becoming art themselves in the process, pointing back towards the world of craft and forward to the world of mechanisation. Like many of Beutler's objects, they are in a state of becoming rather than being clearly defined. And the shaped materials that emerge from these machines underline this state of transience.

In Frankfurt in 2005, Beutler constructed sculptural pieces across the city that hinted at a variety of urban forms — boxes or makeshift shelters, rough models of tower blocks, classical porticos and modernist columns. The sculptures, in bright yellow, stood out against the drabness of city streets, creating an intense but unreal presence, almost virtual. In 2006, Beutler constructed a maze in the grounds of the Palladian style Villa Manin in Italy, responding constantly to the landscape around the piece. The maze, with its secret doors and small balconies, harked back to the great classical garden labyrinths and glowed in the Italian light. At the same time, the insistent yellow plastic evoked urban building sites, and Beutler built it knowing the rain would rust the links and ties that held it together while the material itself would stain and children would perforate its surface.

In 2007, the artist continued to explore the relationship between his work and archetypal historical buildings. At Portikus in Frankfurt, he used sandwiches of wire mesh wrapped in transparent flower paper to create a vast edifice within the gallery, leaving only a thin passageway between the structure and the gallery walls. The grids and paper were woven together to create surfaces that were coloured and then jumped on, creating battered and perforated panels linked together to form what Beutler entitled, *Portikus Castle*. **The structure dwarfed visitors and pushed them to the margins of the gallery or sucked them into its innards where they found themselves under a colourful dome. Again, the piece fell between a classic building form and a makeshift shelter that bore the bruises of its construction process. It was not an attempt to imitate a castle in these raw materials but rather it was the creation of a structure that leaned toward the definition of a castle, something in the state of becoming rather than something complete and classifiable.**

A playfulness is evident throughout Beutler's art practice, from the machines that mangle and mould his materials to the bright, organic forms of the sculptures he produces. Each piece involves the pleasure of colour and the active participation of the audience as they navigate a landscape or cityscape to engage with the work. They are each close to recognition — a portico, a maze, a tower — but each playfully refuses complete identification. At times, there is a resemblance to children's play areas, and yet the works also invite thought. Their intervention into a particular landscape prompts us to re-examine that environment and its own architectural and aesthetic values. The empathy with which Beutler constructs each piece creates a dialogue with its surroundings that brings us back to the basics of form and function.

In preparing for The Hayward exhibition, just such concerns have been on the artist's mind. The brutalist gallery, with its concrete spaces, already points to the basics of architecture. Beutler, though, looks to games such as the German-made formendomino, which replaces domino dots with archetypal geometric forms such as triangles, squares and circles. The game itself seems to be a children's version of The Style Game, devised by Hermann Finsterlin in 1921. Finsterlin, a German Expressionist architect, used painted wooden blocks in basic geometric shapes to construct models of pyramids, domed temples, pagodas and cathedrals.

The game was typical of the work of a group of elite architects called the Crystal Chain who called for a revolution in architecture. In their correspondence and sketches they pushed each other to create fantastical buildings in organic, utopian cities. The drawings for Finsterlin's own buildings seemed to depict living creatures — breathing, moving structures that would be impossible to tether to any one site. The relationship between his style game and his architectural practice can be summed up in a quote from another member of the Crystal Chain group, Paul Scheerbart, who said, 'In style, play is the goal — In play, the goal is style — The goal reached, play and style are one.'[1] Such an approach seems close to that of Beutler, whose sculptures often seem to blur the interface between the work and its surrounding environment. By making it difficult to separate the piece from its site, a symbiotic relationship between the two is formed, a joint continuous becoming.

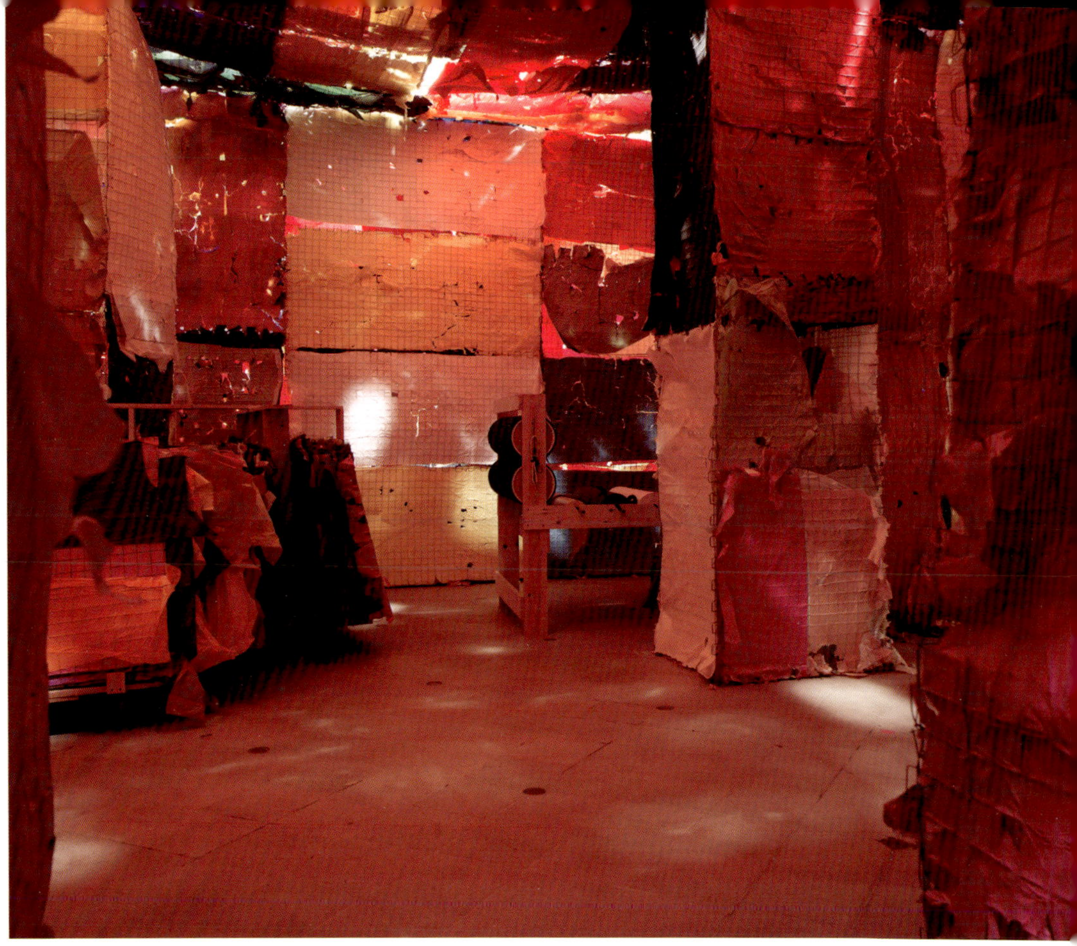

Sandwiches, Dobbels and Burgers, **2008**
overleaf
A-Frame, **2007**

A levelling impulse also seems important in the work of Michael Beutler. In another of his monumental sculptures, for the Lufthansa Aviation Centre in 2006, he devised a vast pagoda built from aluminium. The aspiring tower, reaching to the heavens, is brought back to earth by the humble hut and root-bound by the discipline of gardening. Its hybrid culture, grafting temple and shed, points again to the nomadic, constantly mutating culture we inhabit. Like many of his works, the pagoda teeters on the edge of ruin. The grand structures implied in the pieces all contain the seeds of their own collapse and, in the materials Beutler uses, the ruin of each is foreseen. This architectural genre, the ruin, was deliberately cultivated in the late eighteenth and early nineteenth century. More often in history, though, the ruin emerges in an improvisatory way, surviving or collapsing under the pressures of weather, war, looting and time. A ruin is undergoing a slow transformation, always in a state of becoming. The ruin, then, is a shadow that is always present in Beutler's work.

1 http://findarticles.com/p/articles/mi_m1248/is_n10_v82/ai_15821899/print.

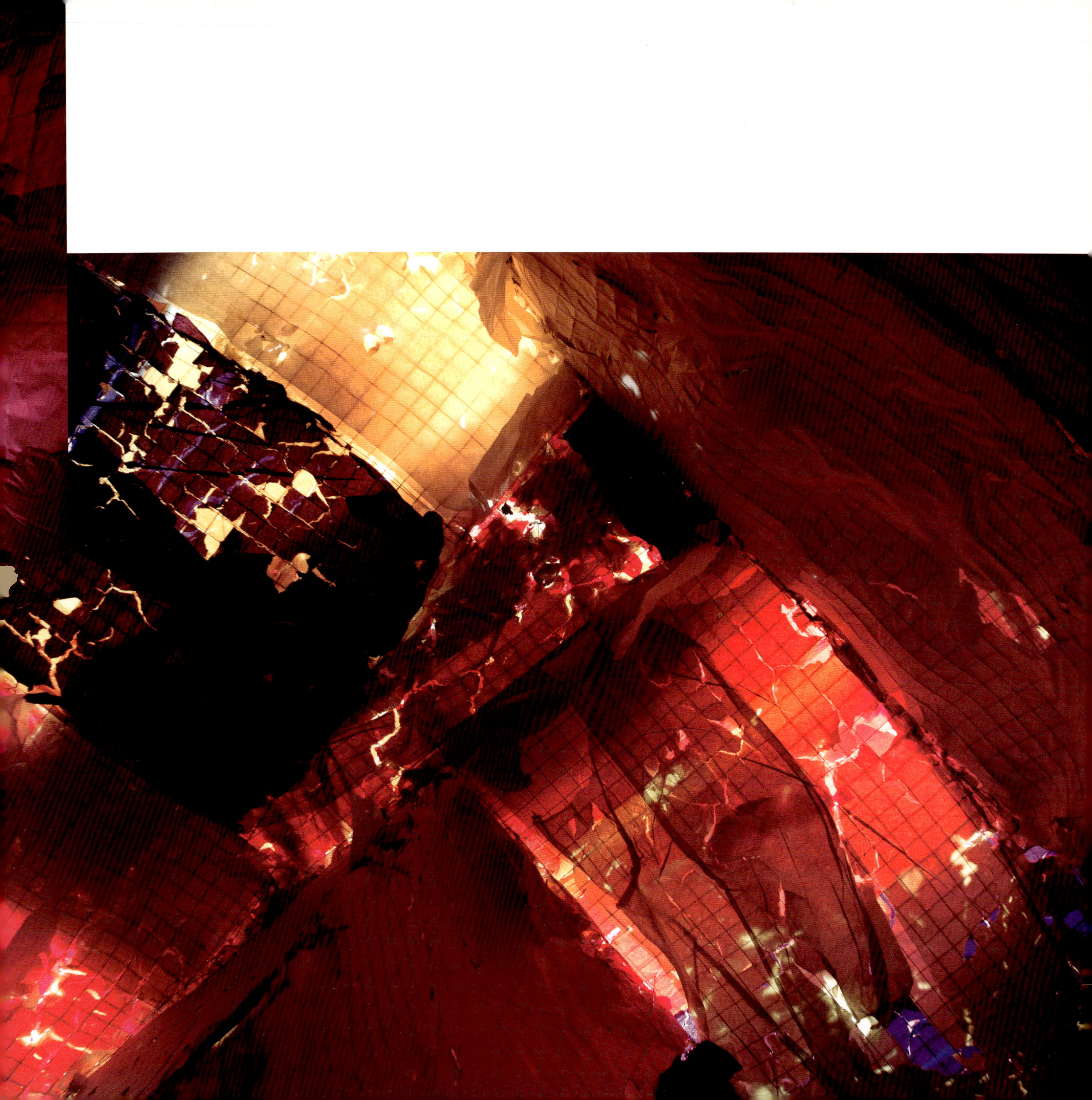

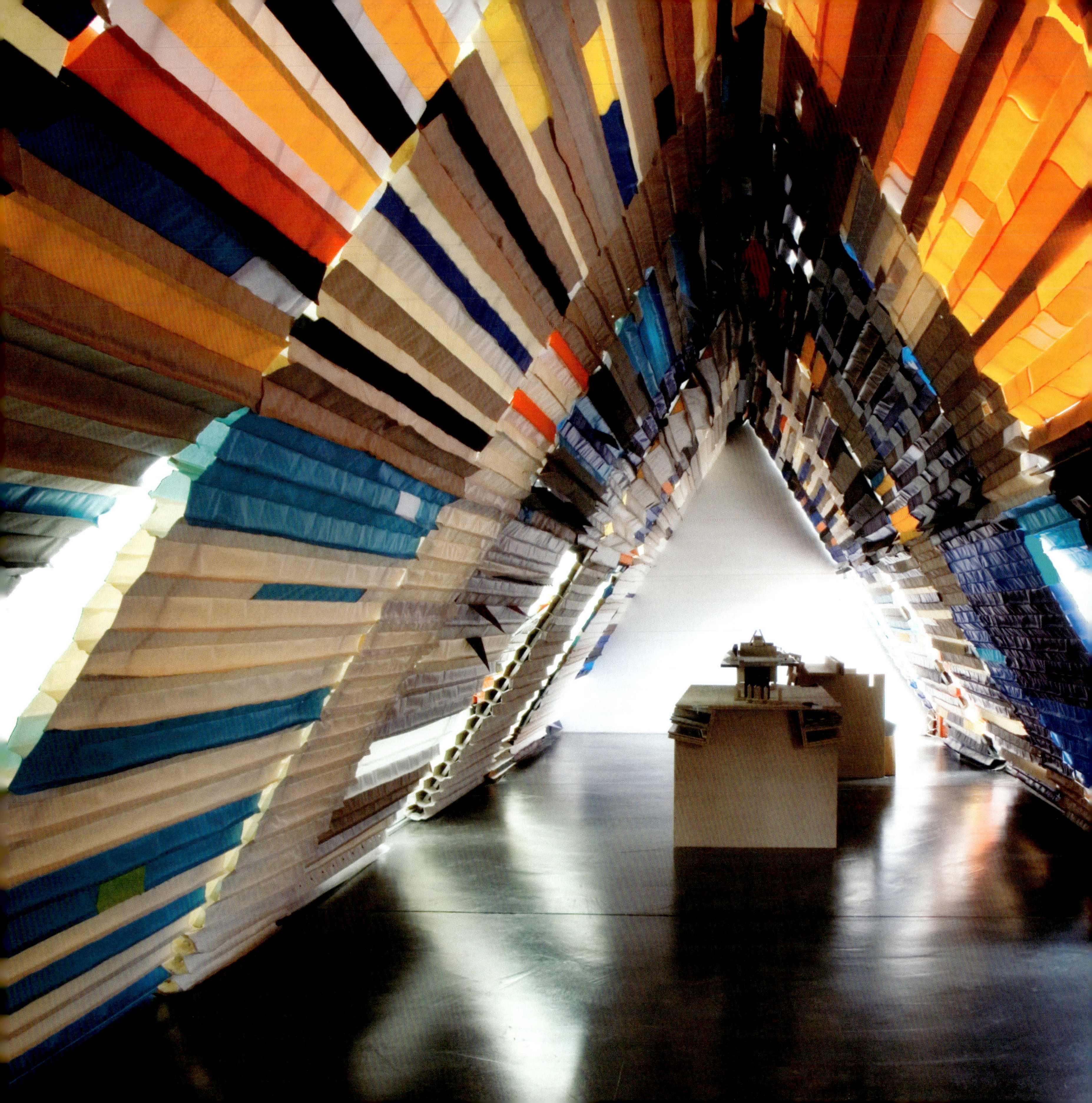

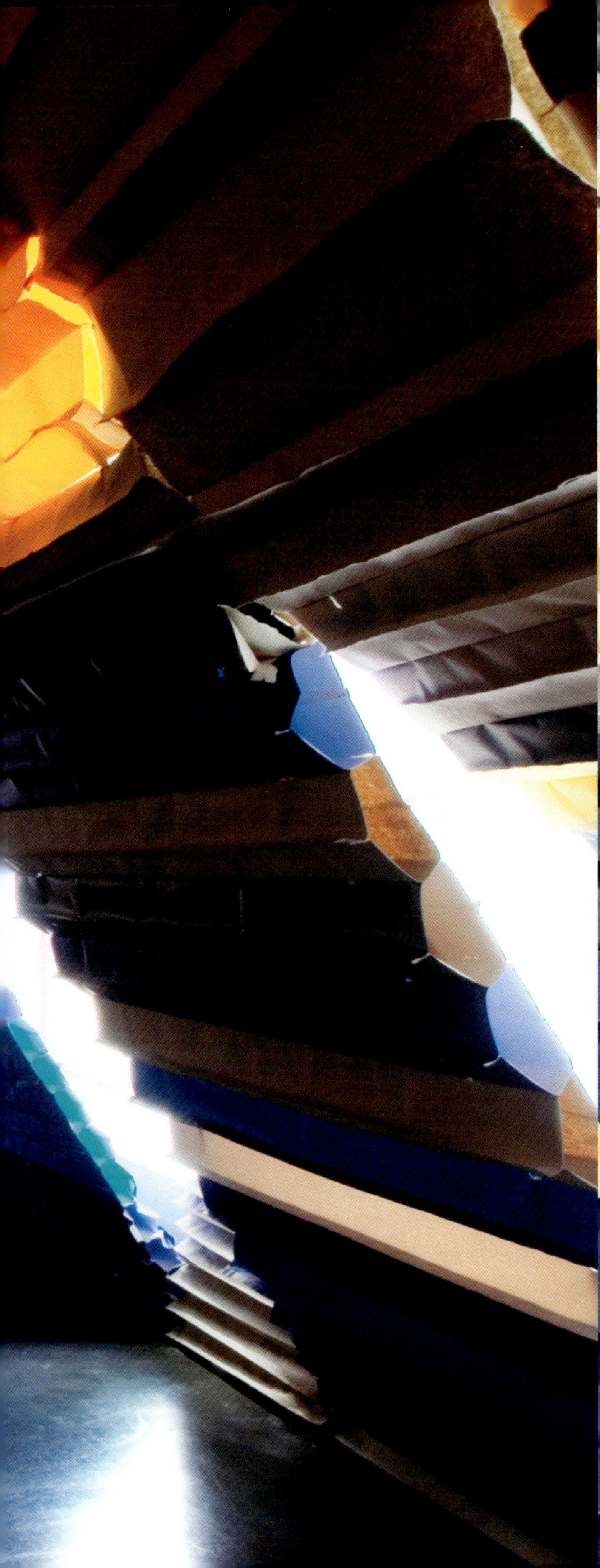
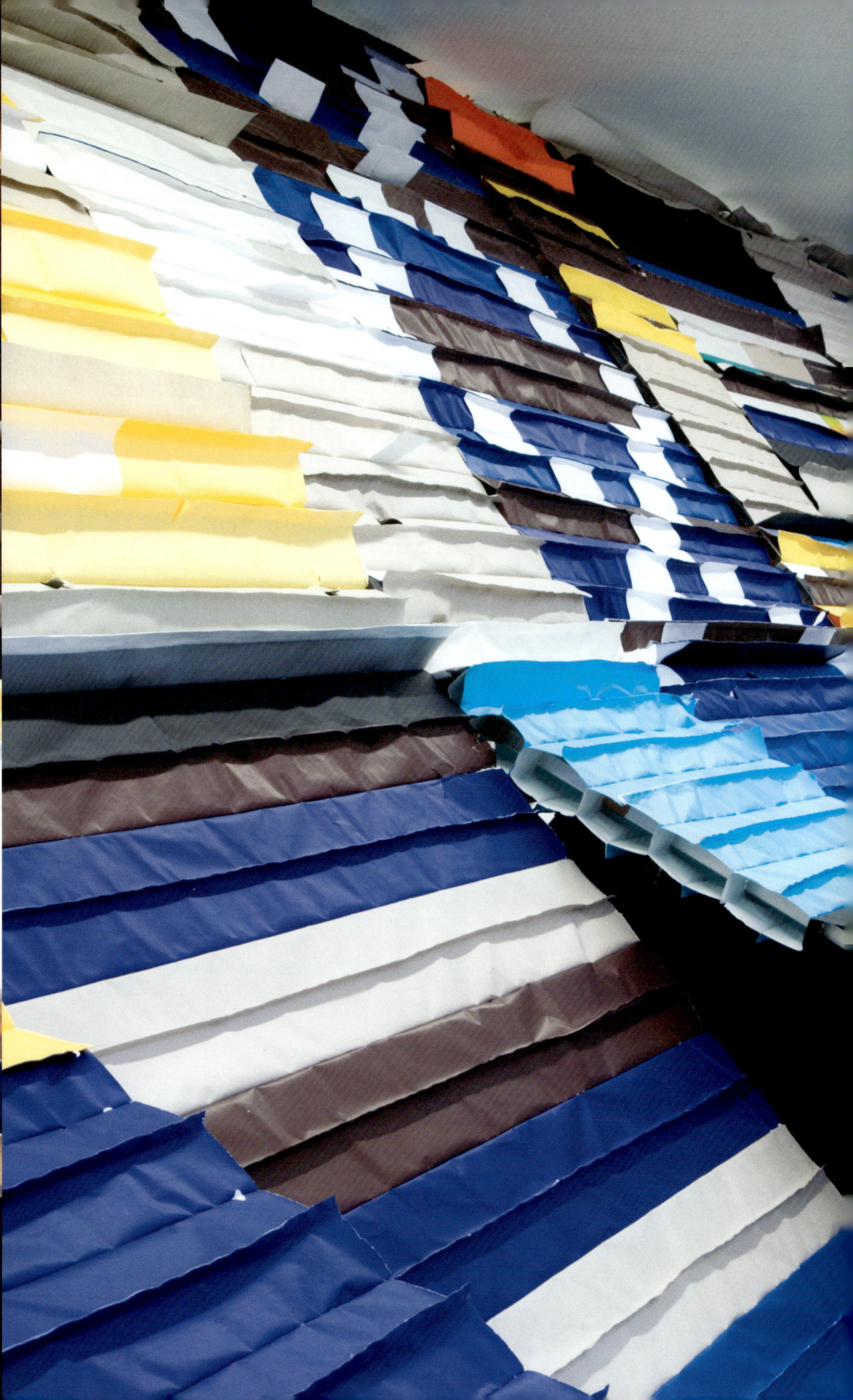

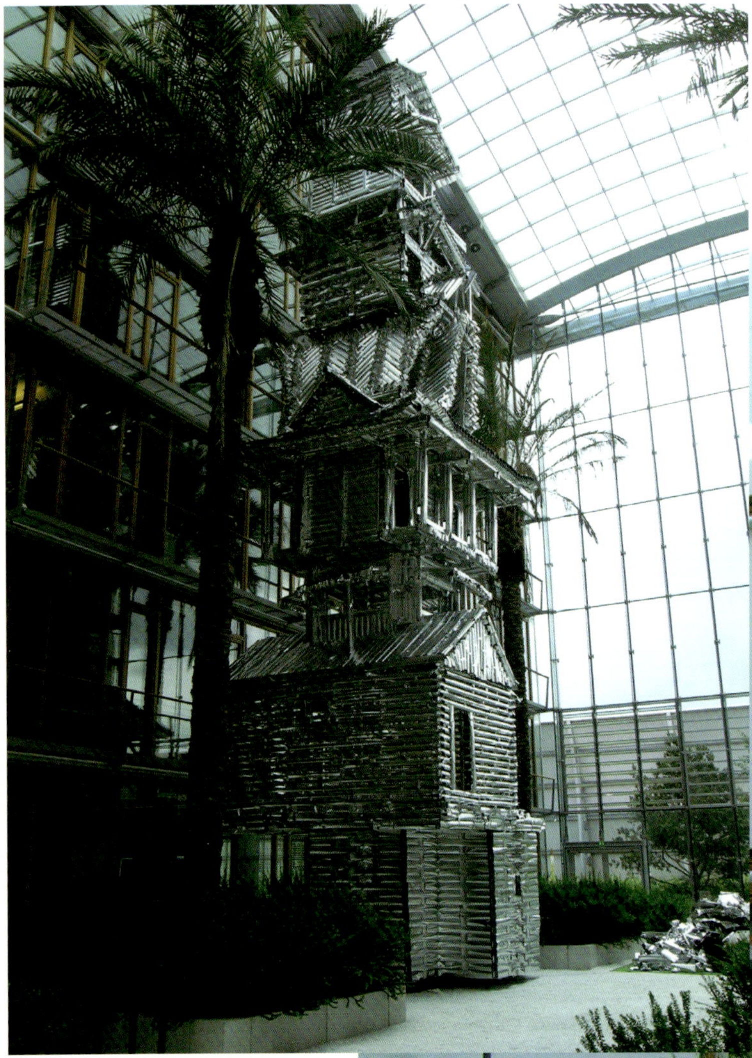

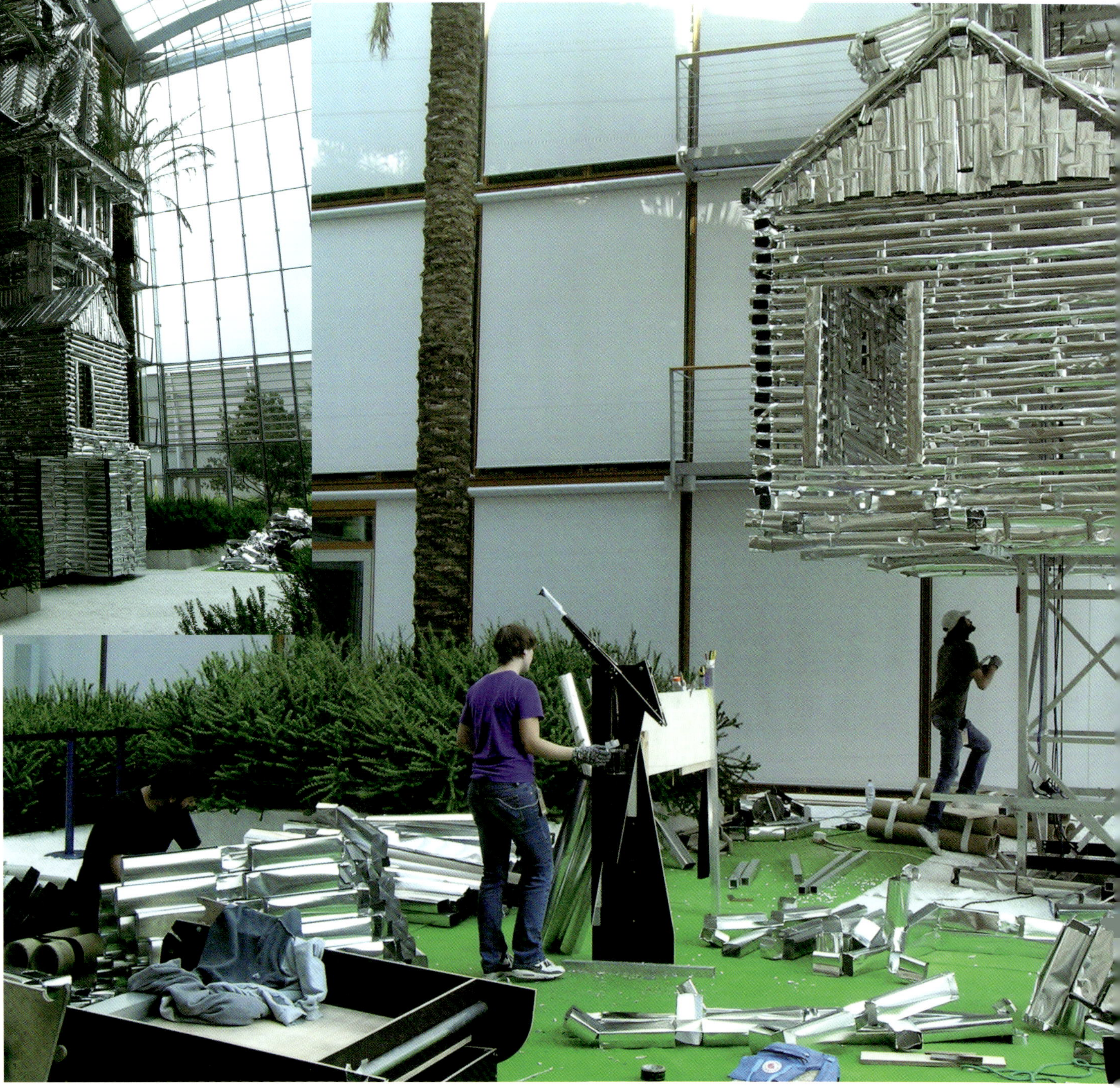

Aluminium Pagode, **2006**

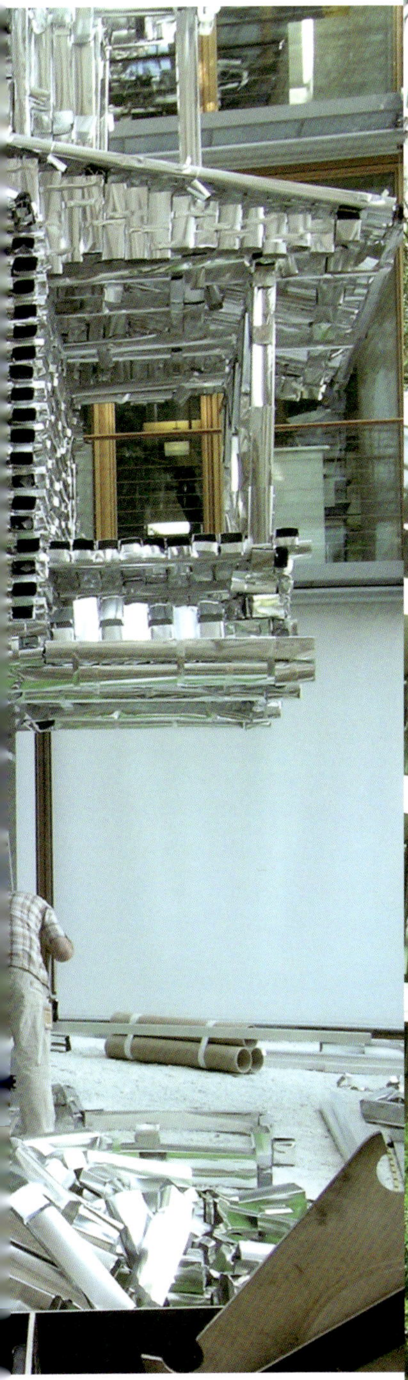

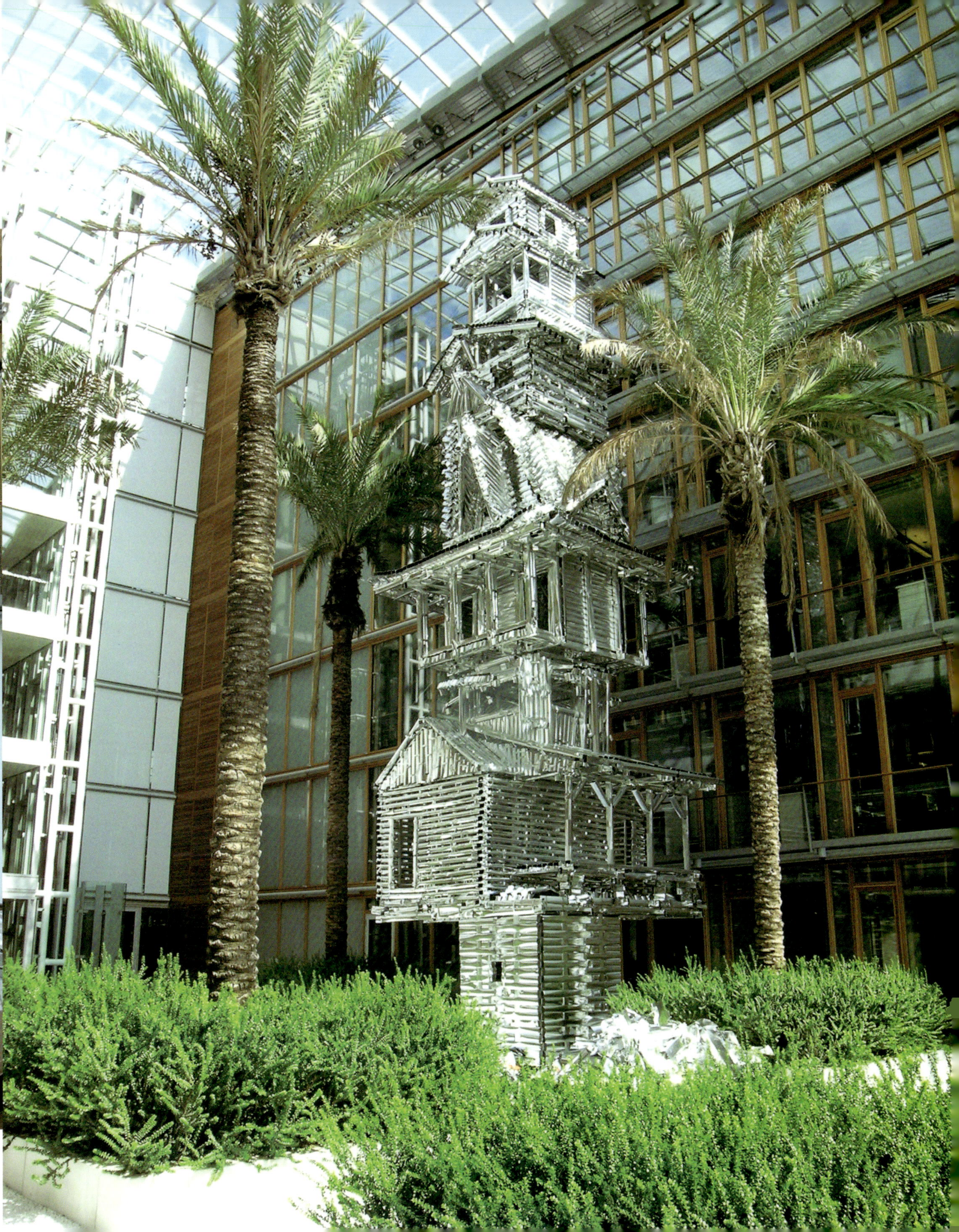

below
Manin City, **2006**
right
Outdoor-yellow 9, **2004**
overleaf
Glashaus, **2002**

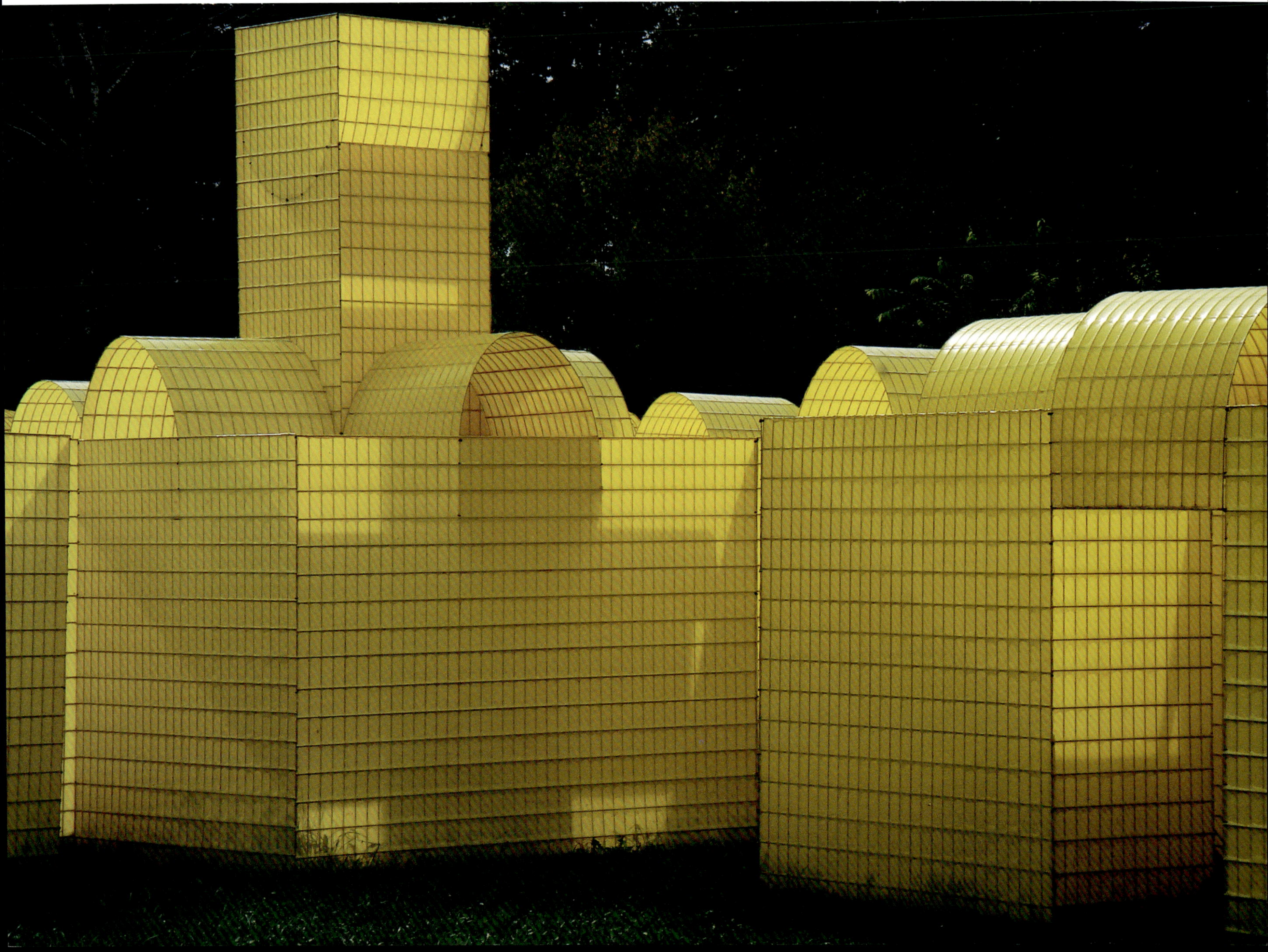

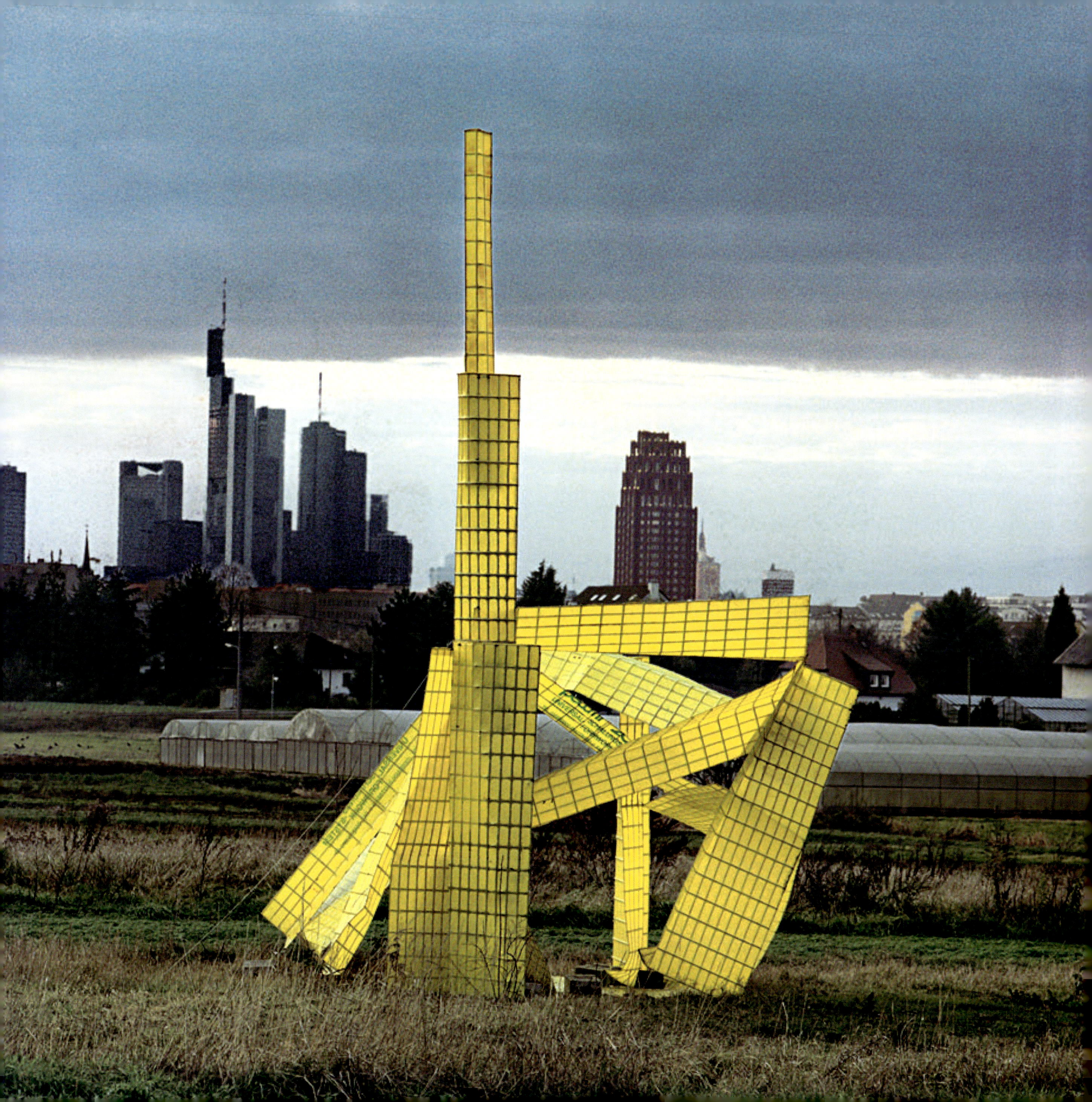

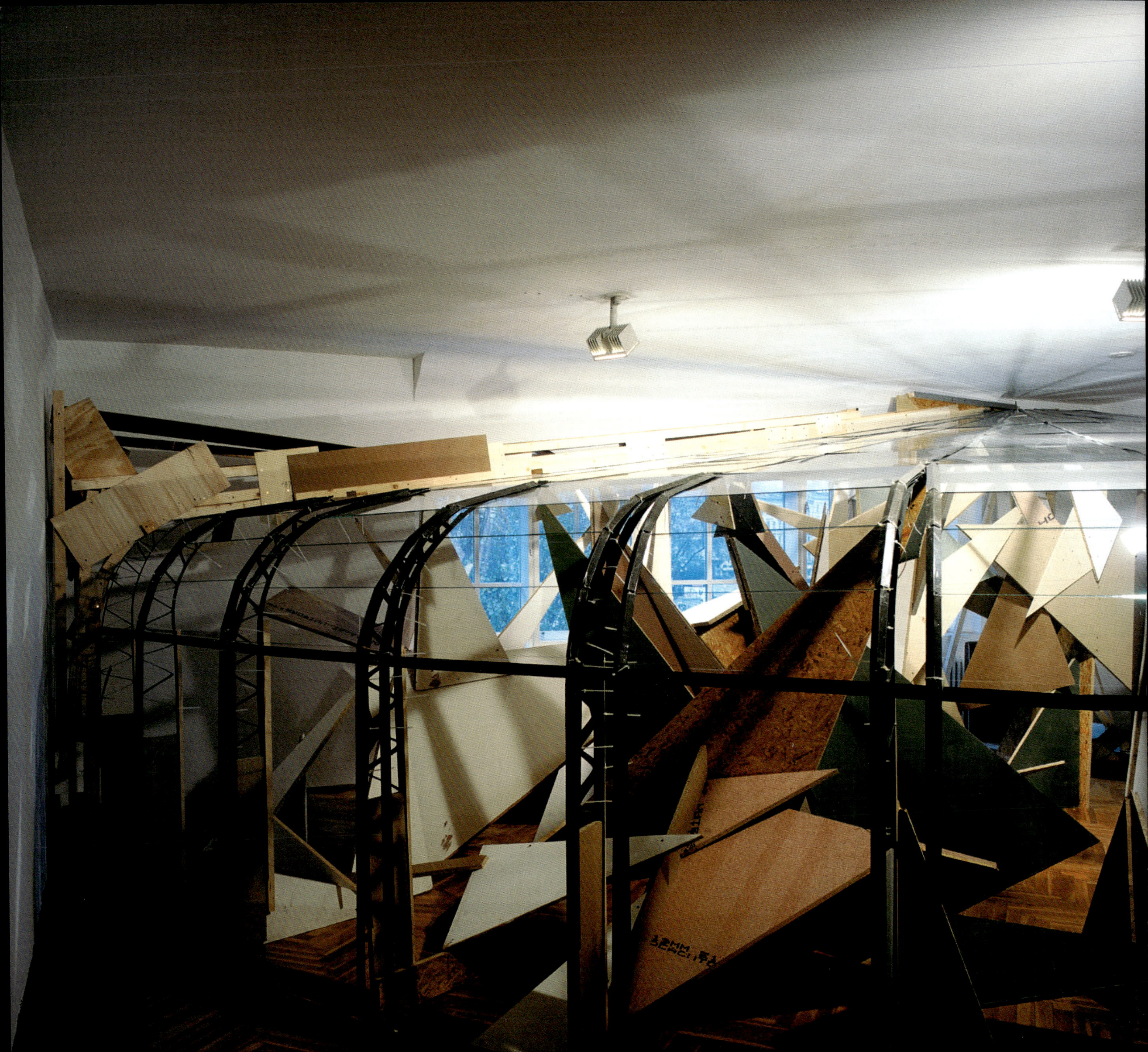

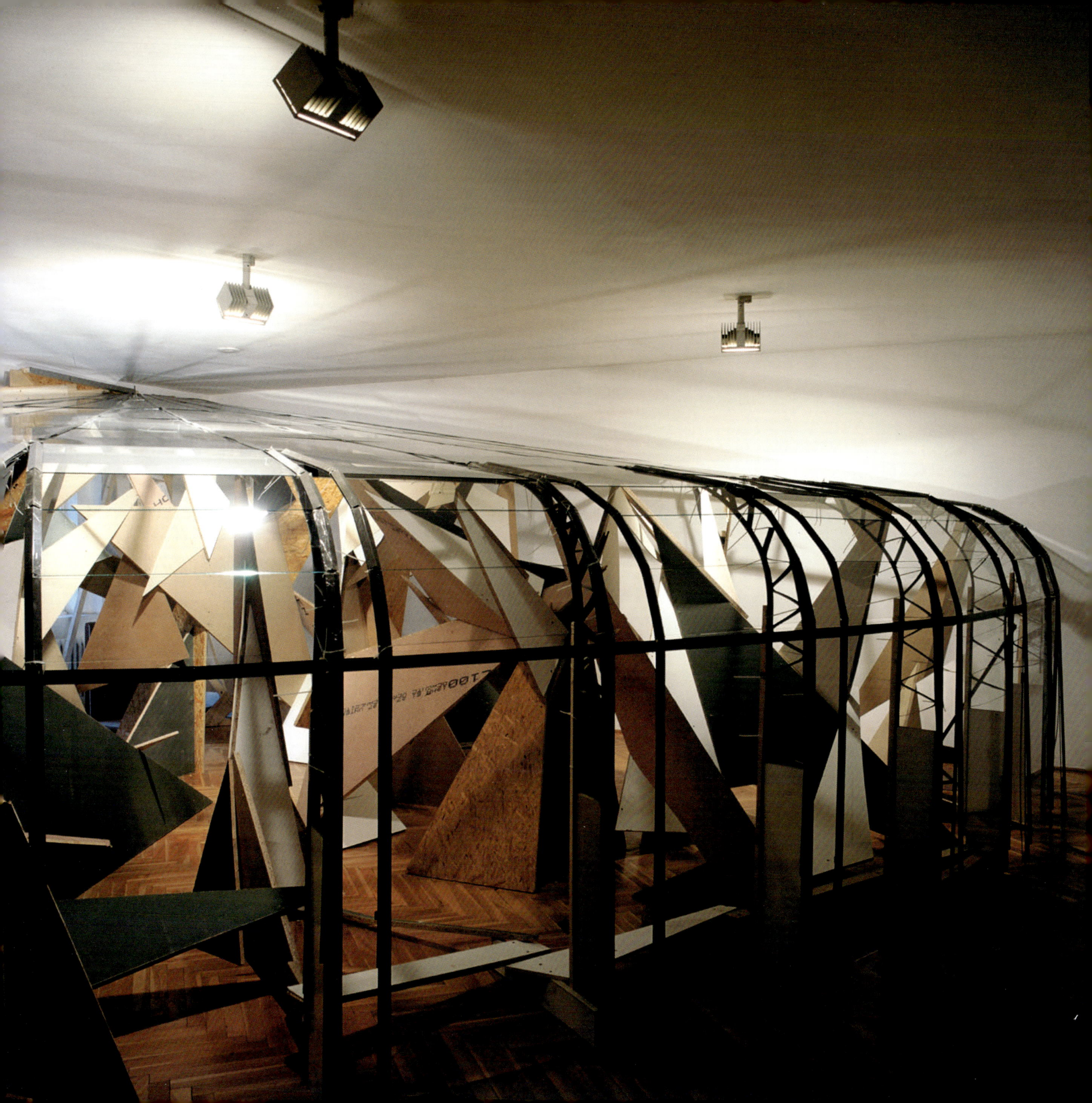

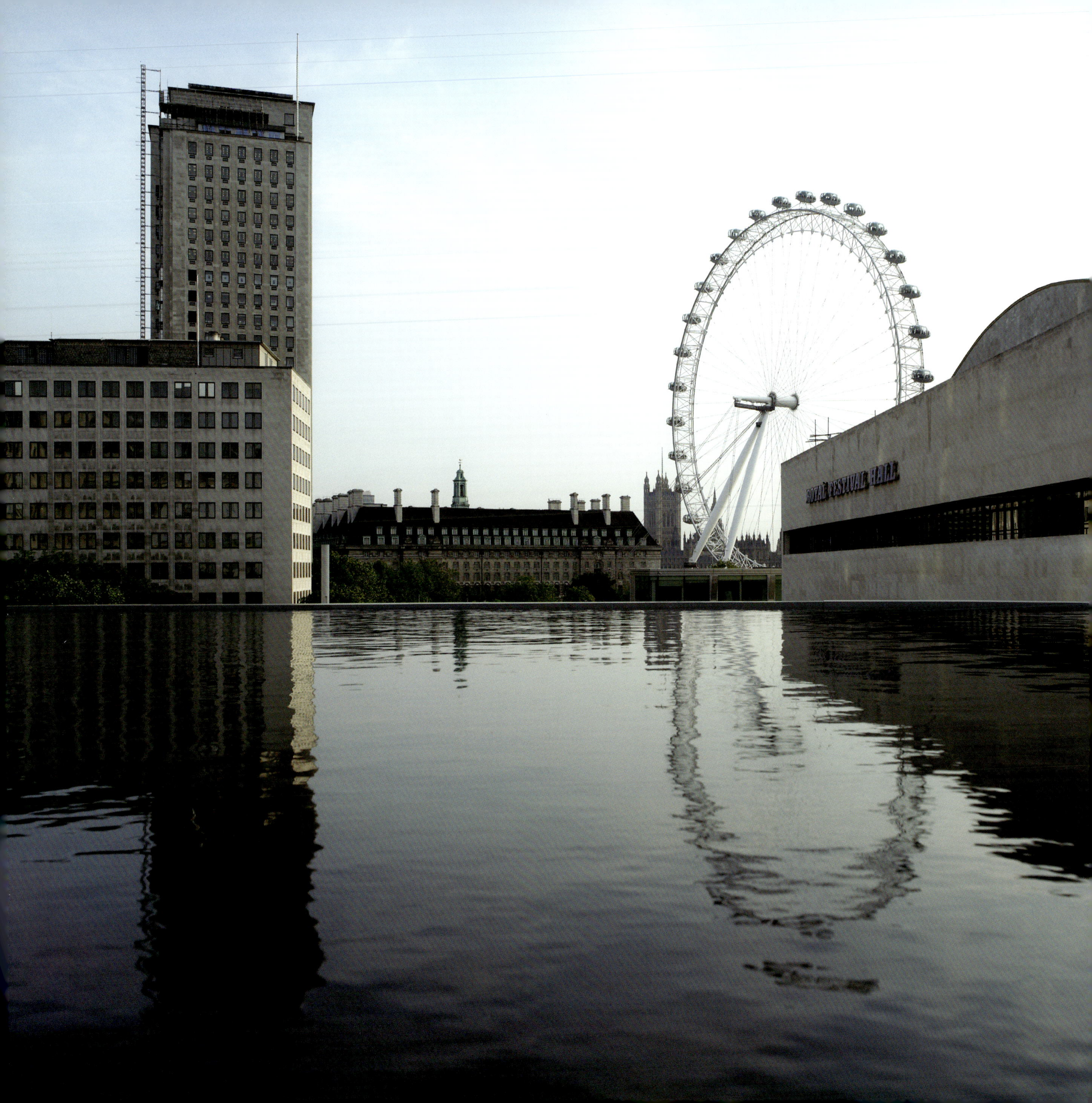
ROYAL FESTIVAL HALL

normally, proceeding and unrestricted with without title, **2008**

GELITIN

MIDORI MATSUI

The Viennese artist unit Gelitin (Wolfgang Gantner, Ali Janka, Florian Reither and Tobias Urban), active since 1993, mix performance, sculpture and architecture to create spaces in which the spectators' senses are physically challenged and perceptions about their body and surroundings are altered. They bring such natural elements as water, mud and fire into the gallery, or exploit existing conditions of the space like height as central resources of their actions. Their introduction of natural elements into the gallery aggressively challenges its original functions, which are dedicated to aesthetic contemplation, creating physical environments that are beyond the spectators' control, and eliciting responses that are beyond rational discretion. Gelitin's emphasis on audience participation, intervention in the authoritative functions of public buildings, creation of communicative situations within galleries, as well as the involvement of immediately affective physical elements as the catalyst of the renewal of perception, strongly link their practices with the experiential tendencies of the 1960s' and 1970s' avant-garde, including Fluxus, International Situationism and Land Art. At the same time, elements of boyish mischief, reminiscent of childhood games, enhance the spectators' sense of fun and freedom, making Gelitin's conceptual work human and empowering.

In their 2005 project *Sweatwat*, **for example, Gelitin converted the Gagosian Gallery in London into a 24-hour open house for a week, flooding the gallery's interior with water. The work invited the participants to take off their shoes or clothes to bathe in the water, liberating them from decorum. Filled with heaps of stacked-up furniture, household appliances and Gelitin's eccentric interactive sculptures, the space evoked childhood memories, such as the children's game of imagining a bedroom as a realm of adventure.**

The playful modification of architecture's original function into a place of perceptual transformation is exemplified by Gelitin's performance project *The B-Thing* **(2000) and by their exhibition** *Chinese Synthese Leberkäse* **(2006). In** *The B-Thing*, **Gelitin created a temporary and illegal balcony that protruded from the window of their room on the 91st floor of World Trade Center in New York, where they then had an artist residence. The act of standing for a few minutes on the balcony made them physically experience the precariousness of their condition, which they had created but could not control. By changing the spectator's position from the inside to the outside, the performance transformed the effect of overlooking the world from a high window from a sense of omnipotence into feelings of vulnerability.**

Gelitin's interventions also turn the austerity of an exhibition space into a playground of association and sensory discoveries. In *Chinese Synthese Leberkäse*, they created a unique installation on each floor of the main building of Kunsthaus Bregenz, which contains three exhibition floors and a ground floor. On each level, Gelitin showed respectively: a public toilet that allowed the spectators to look at their bottoms reflected in a mirror, tableaux loaded with small objects resembling volcanic debris, three temporary movie theatres structured like children's secret headquarters, and a mud volcano and pool. Gathering together elements of excretion, cave exploration and sedimentation from different sources, the installations indicated the continuity of the unformed processes of human body and mind, and the earth's cycle of decomposition and reconstitution, urging the spectators to integrate disparate features into an organic vision of this continuity. Accentuating the building's structural specificity, Gelitin's focus on the formlessness of mud nevertheless subverted the serenity of its minimalist design and its steel-and-glass construction, which gathers light like a lamp.

Gelitin's interest in unformed natural processes as a catalyst for new perception finds a predecessor in the ideas and Land Art projects of Robert Smithson. Smithson emphasised a parallel between unformed natural processes and the randomness of human thought, creating sculptural environments that enabled spectators to discover connections through the experience of boundlessness. His 1970 Land Art project *Spiral Jetty*, a 1,500-foot long spiralling path protruding from the shore into the Great Salt Lake in Utah defied comprehension from a single viewpoint, demanding the spectators to realise its shape by walking to the end of the path. In a similar way, Gelitin's 2005 work *Rabbit*, a 60-metre long and 6-metre high, pink stuffed rabbit installed on an obscure hill in Piemonte, Italy, encouraged the spectators to feel its expansiveness and materiality by climbing or walking on it. Exposed to natural decay, *Rabbit* also recapitulated Smithson's idea of making a decomposing monument, while its association with cartoon characters enhanced the joy of playful interaction.

Gelitin's installation for The Hayward brings together various conceptual points of their former projects: construction of an interactive space, introduction of natural elements, and creative exploitation of existing architectural structures, to bring about new relations between spectators and their surroundings. Flooding The Hayward's west-facing sculpture terrace, Gelitin have created a one-metre deep pond where spectators can row in boats, floating above busy Belvedere Road. The simple device conjures up a vision of a natural retreat in the midst of a London cityscape, involving the spectators as part of the pastoral vision. Boating 40 feet above ground, the participants simultaneously feel exhilaration and dizziness; surrounded by the water that floods the pond's edges, they feel a nearly complete immersion in their surroundings. Although the perception of height and rimlessness is visual, its physical effects enable the spectators to have a tactile understanding of the space.

Gelitin's experiential approach finds a sympathetic voice in contemporary architecture, where the users' actions and surrounding environments become the structural determinant of designs, and 'randomness' is maintained as the inherent principle. And, inheriting the same conceptual shifts from form to experience as practiced by artists in the 1960s and 1970s, but opening them towards more exuberant expressions, Gelitin embrace the ineluctability of physical experience as the source of new knowledge, discovering fresh ways of interacting with familiar or functionally-delimited places.

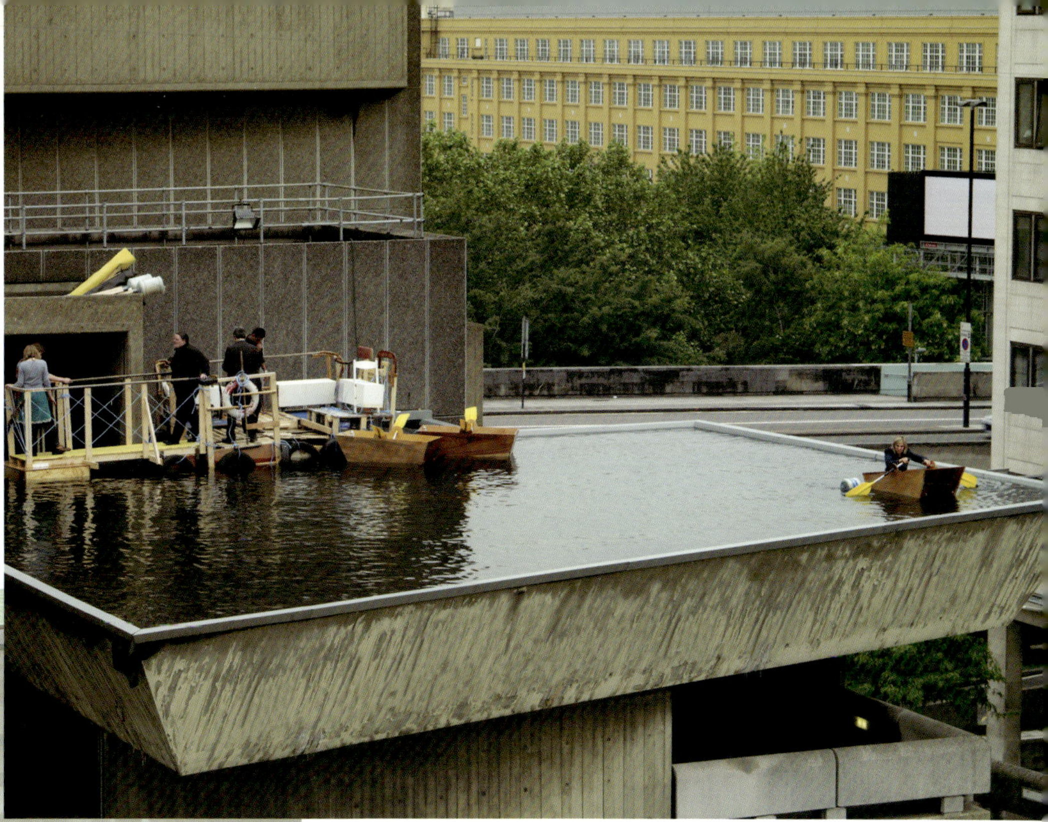

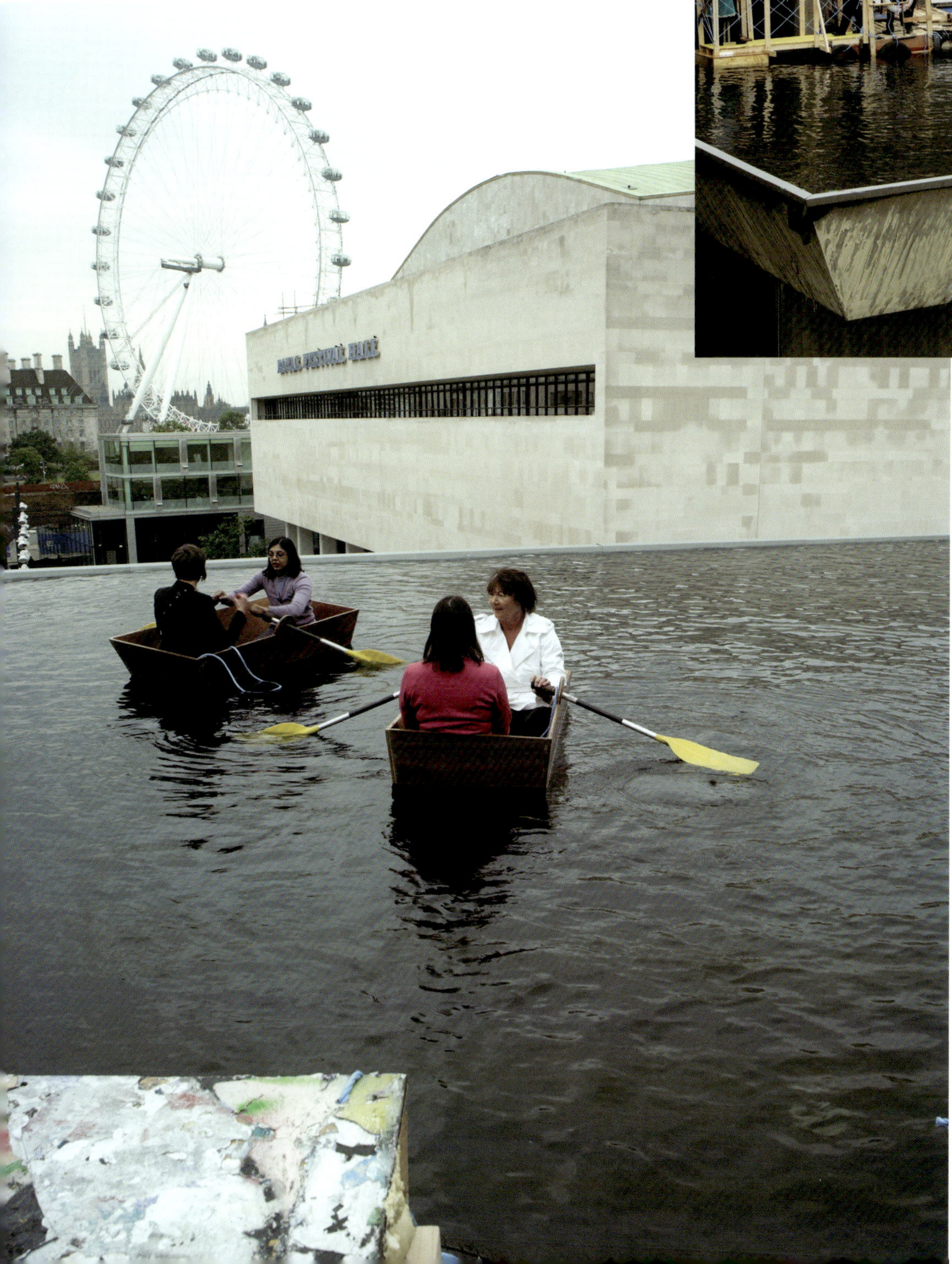

normally, proceeding and unrestricted with without title, **2008**

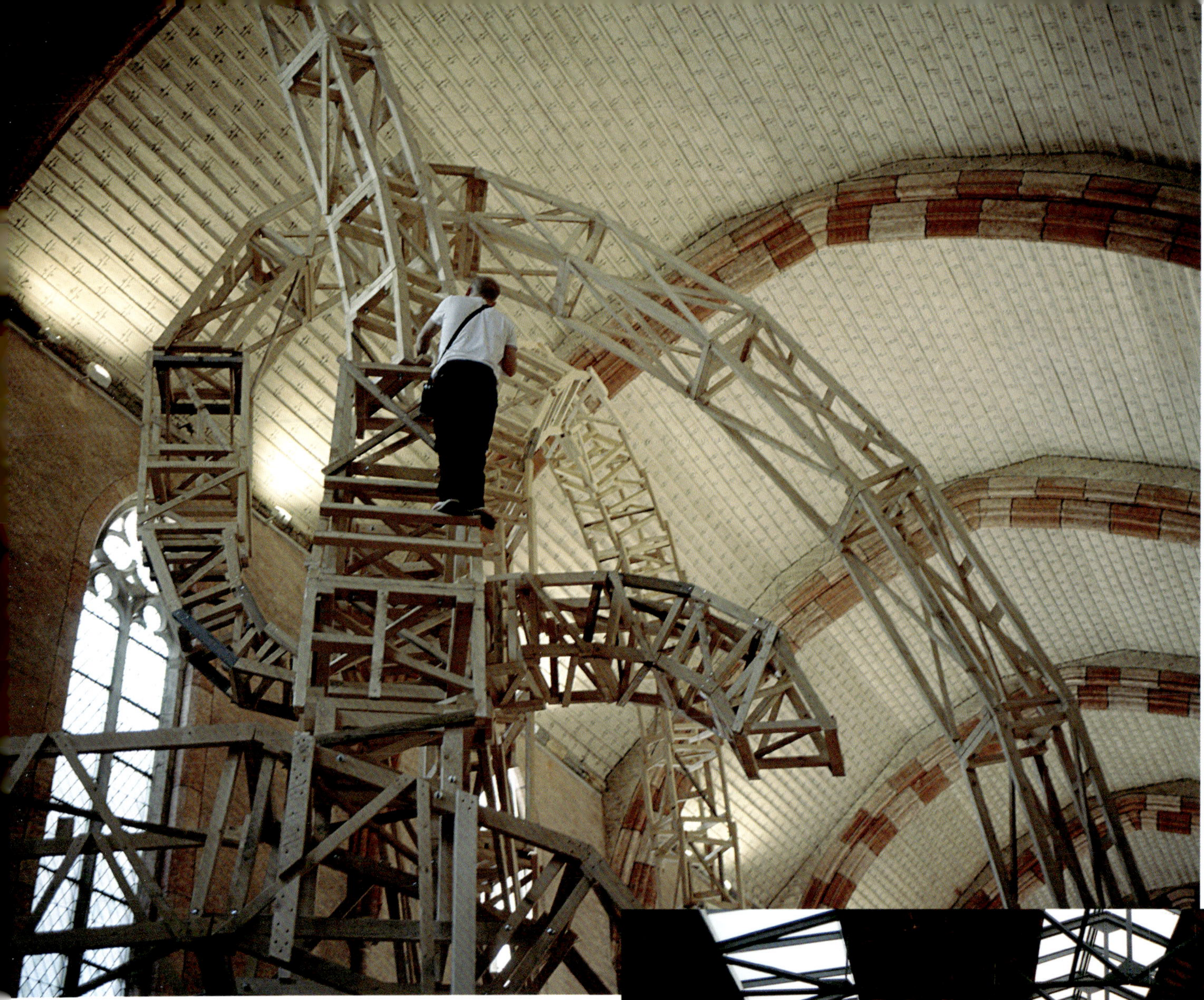

Stellungswechsel 500, **2007**

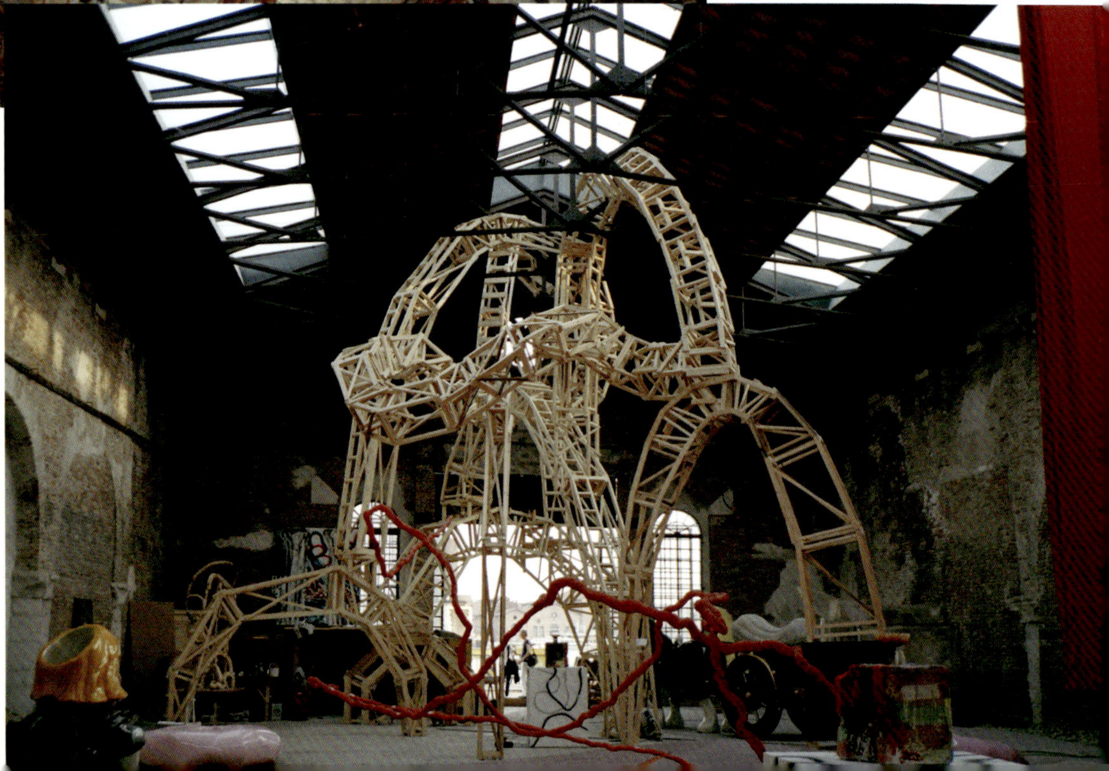

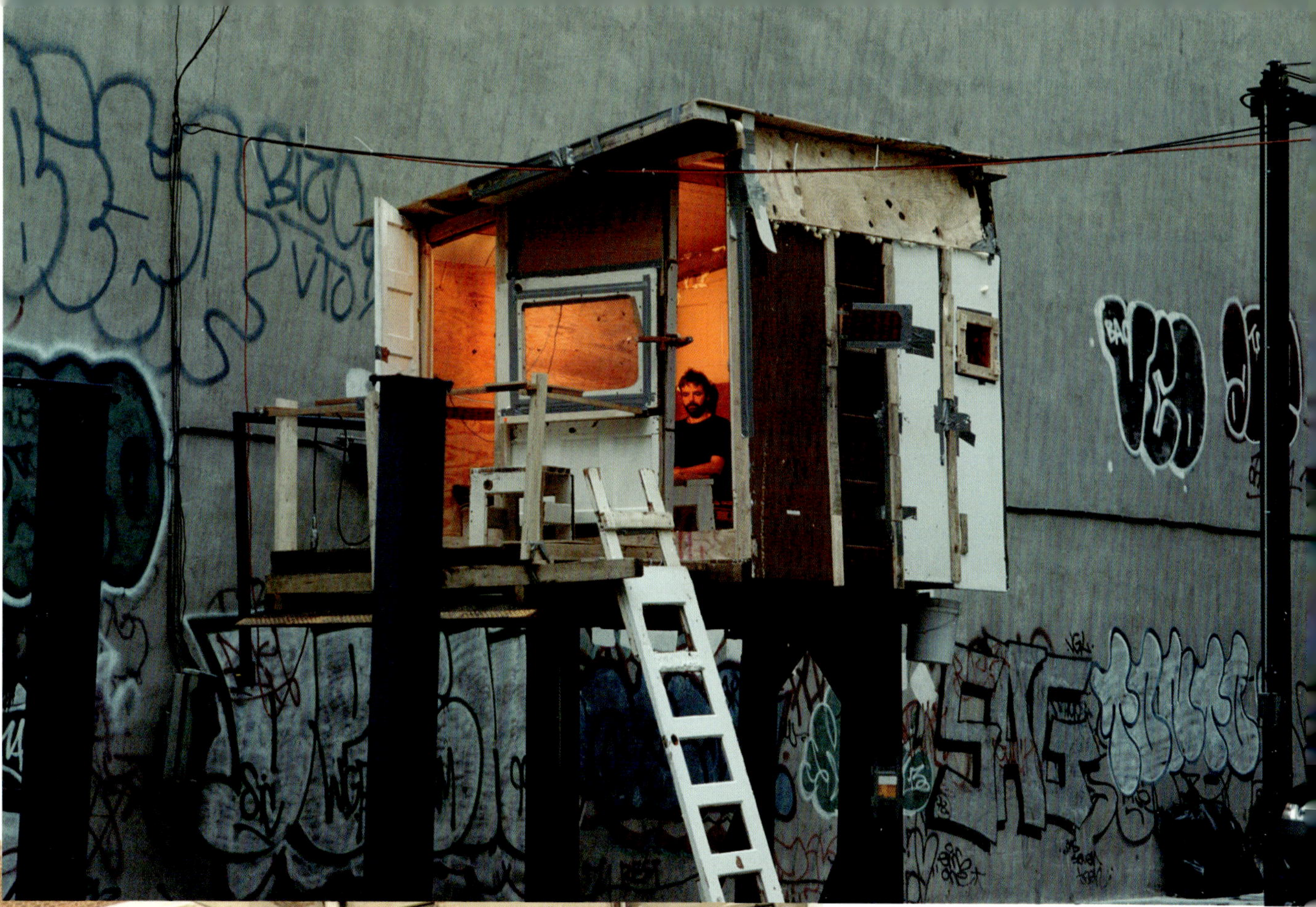

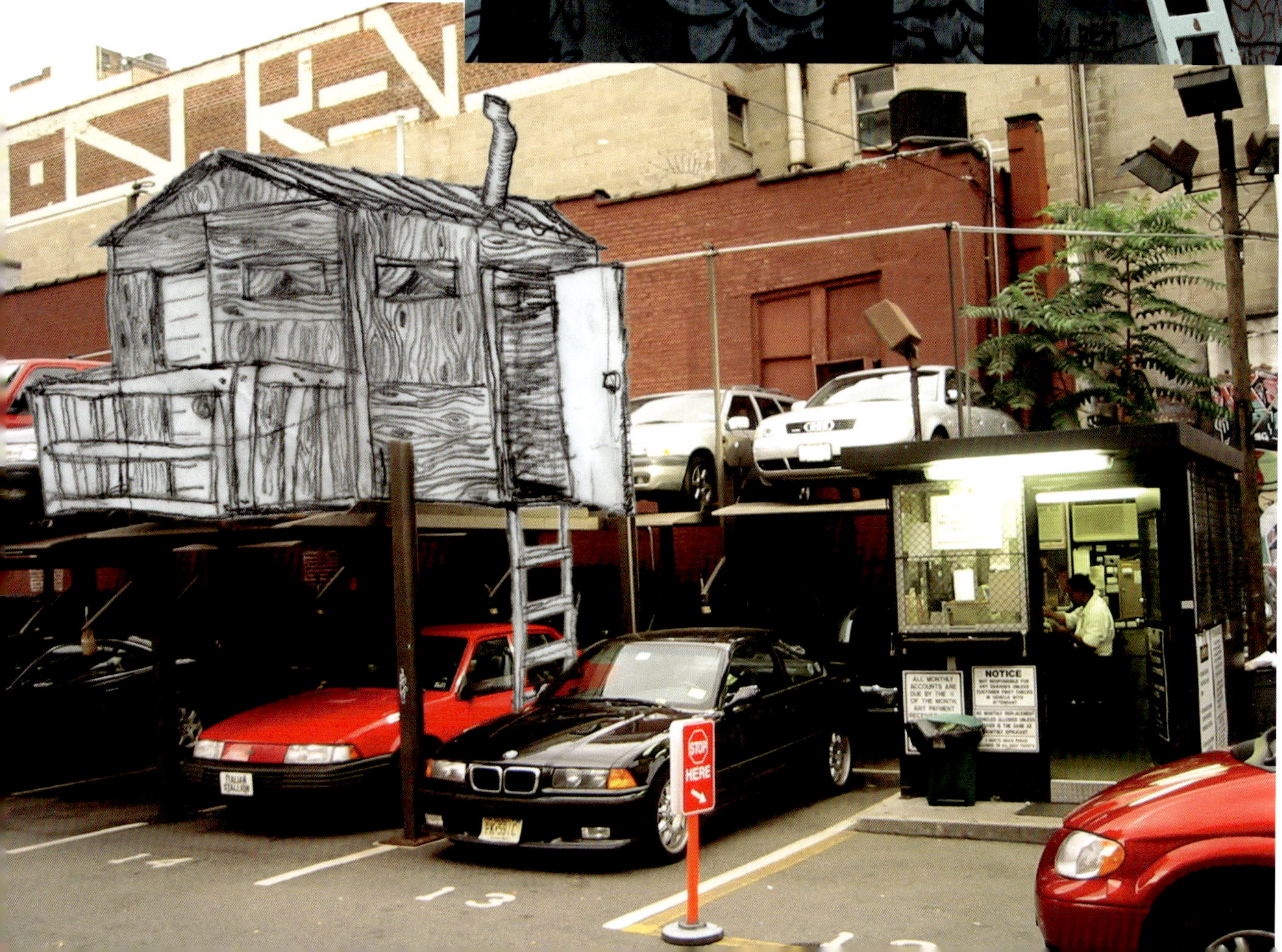

Stephan With PH Please!, **2002**

below
Kinosaal, **2006**
right
Kacksaal, **2006**

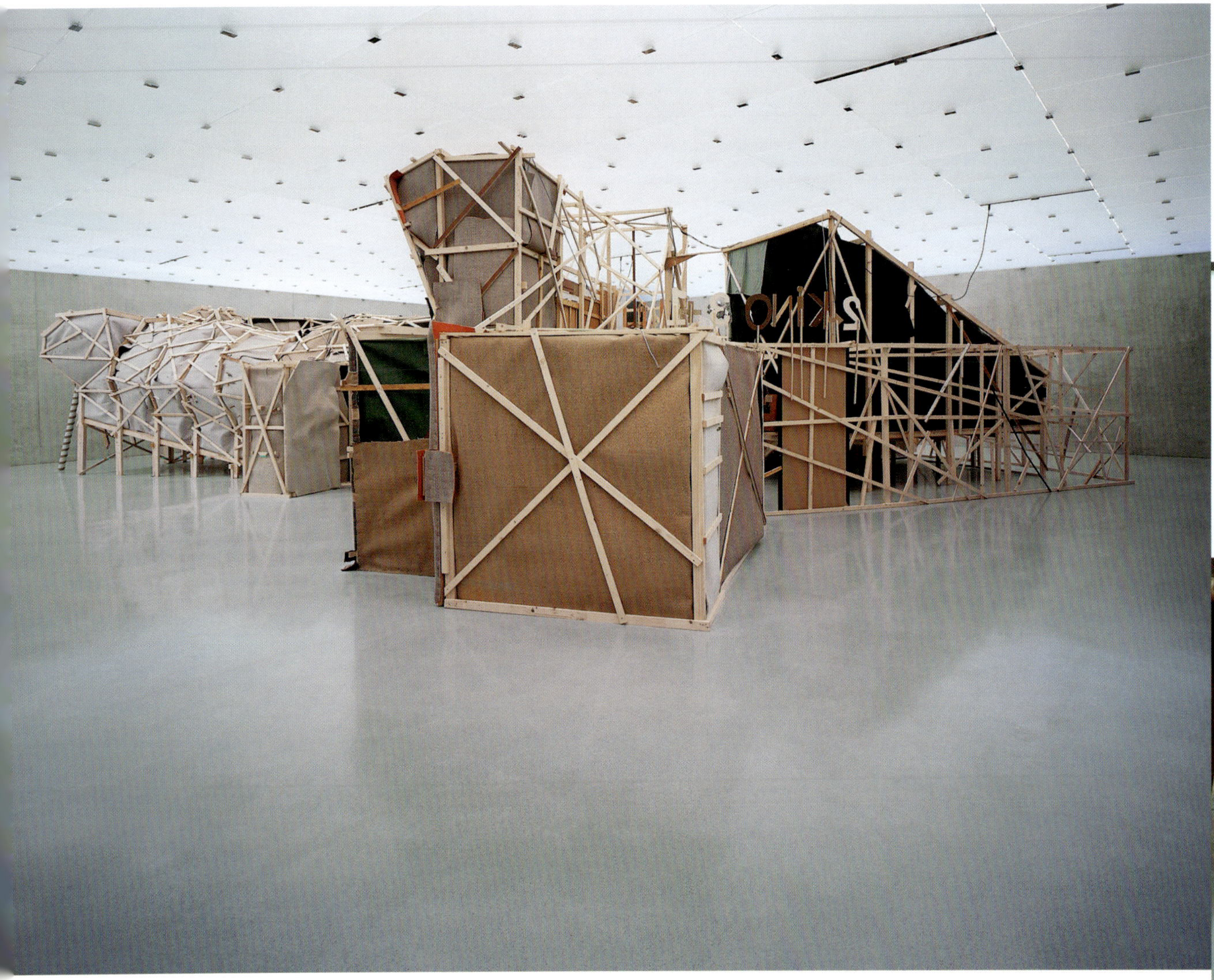

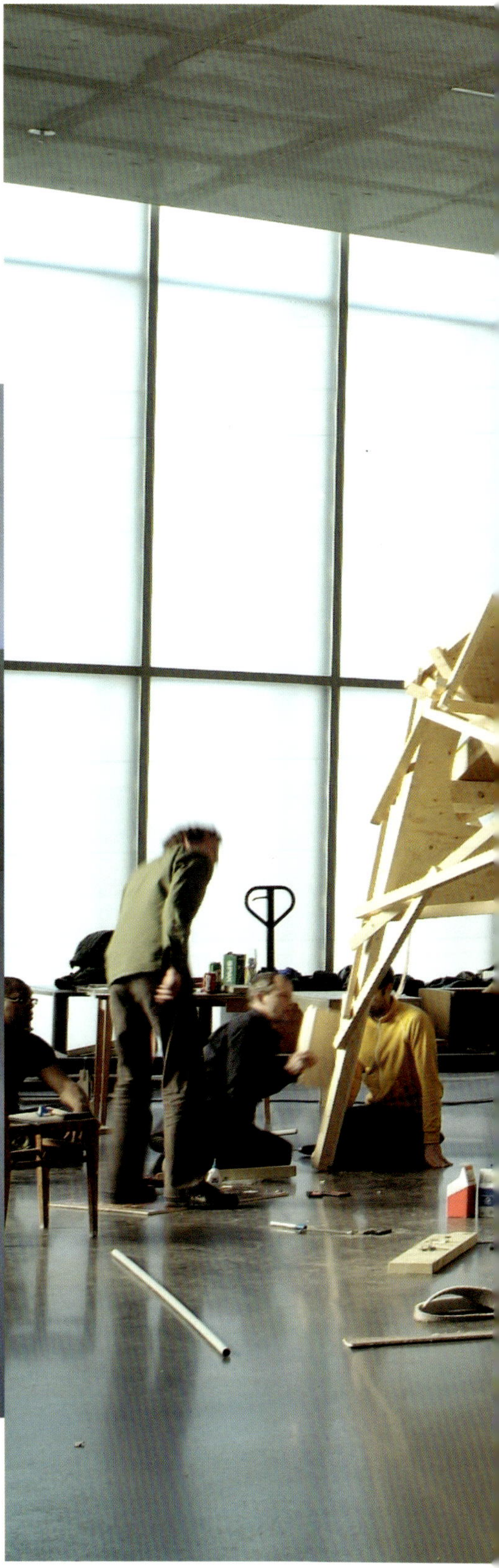

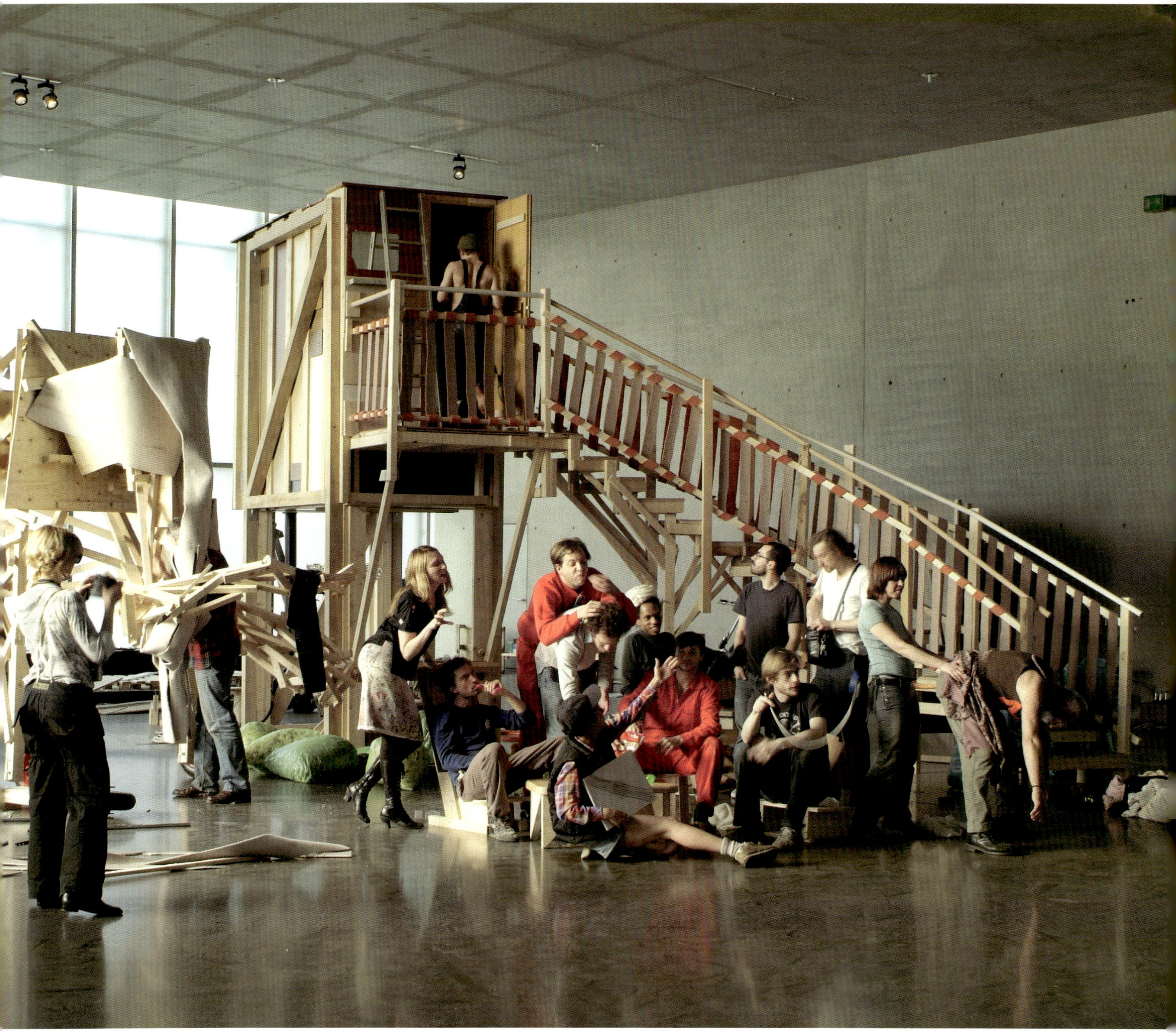

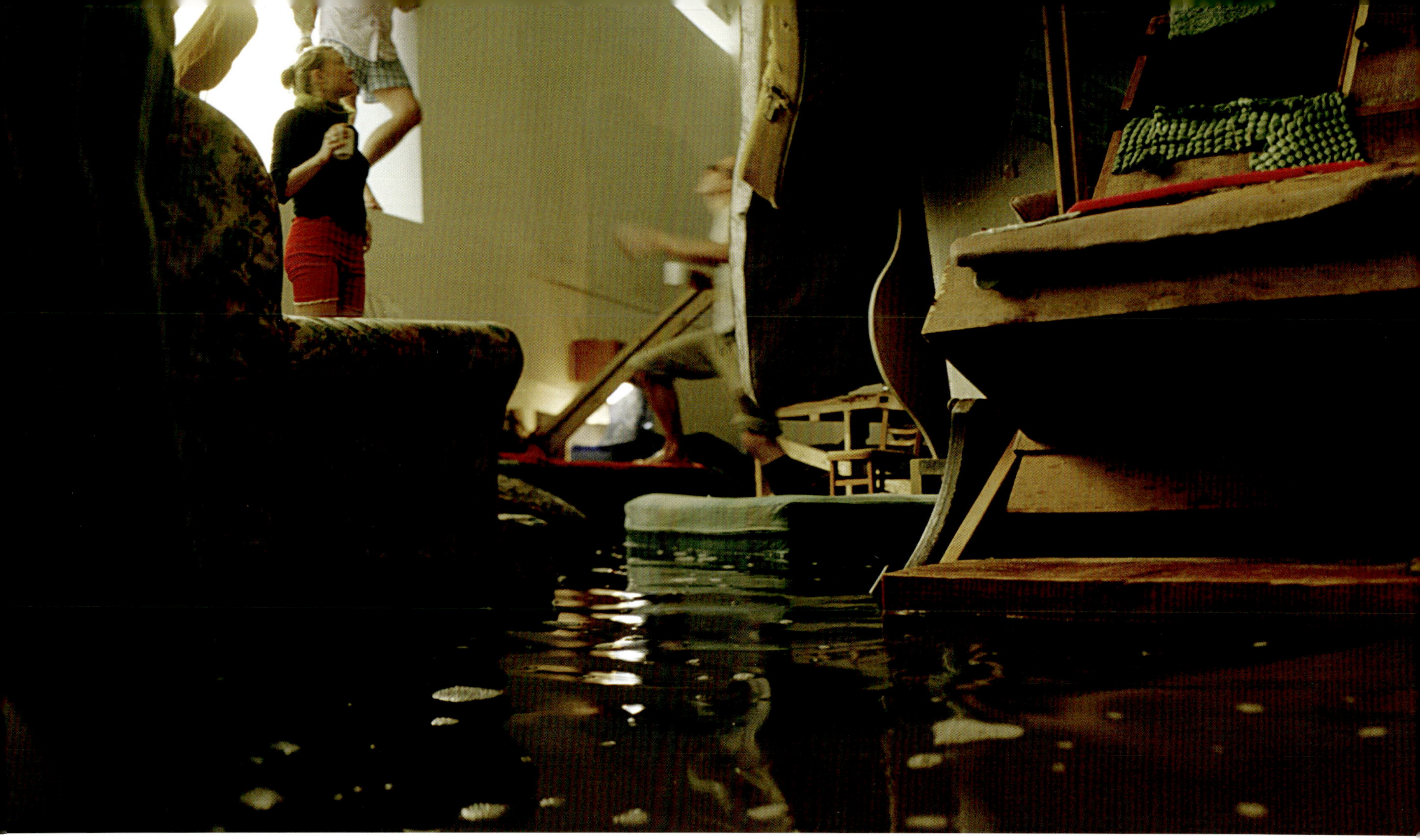

Sweatwat, **2005**

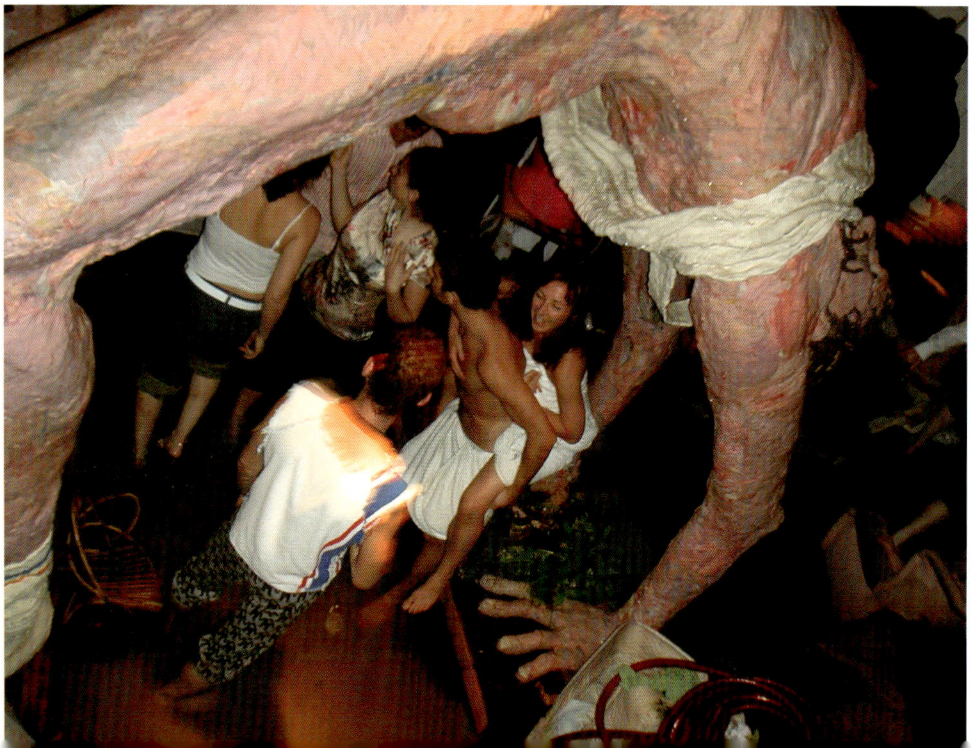

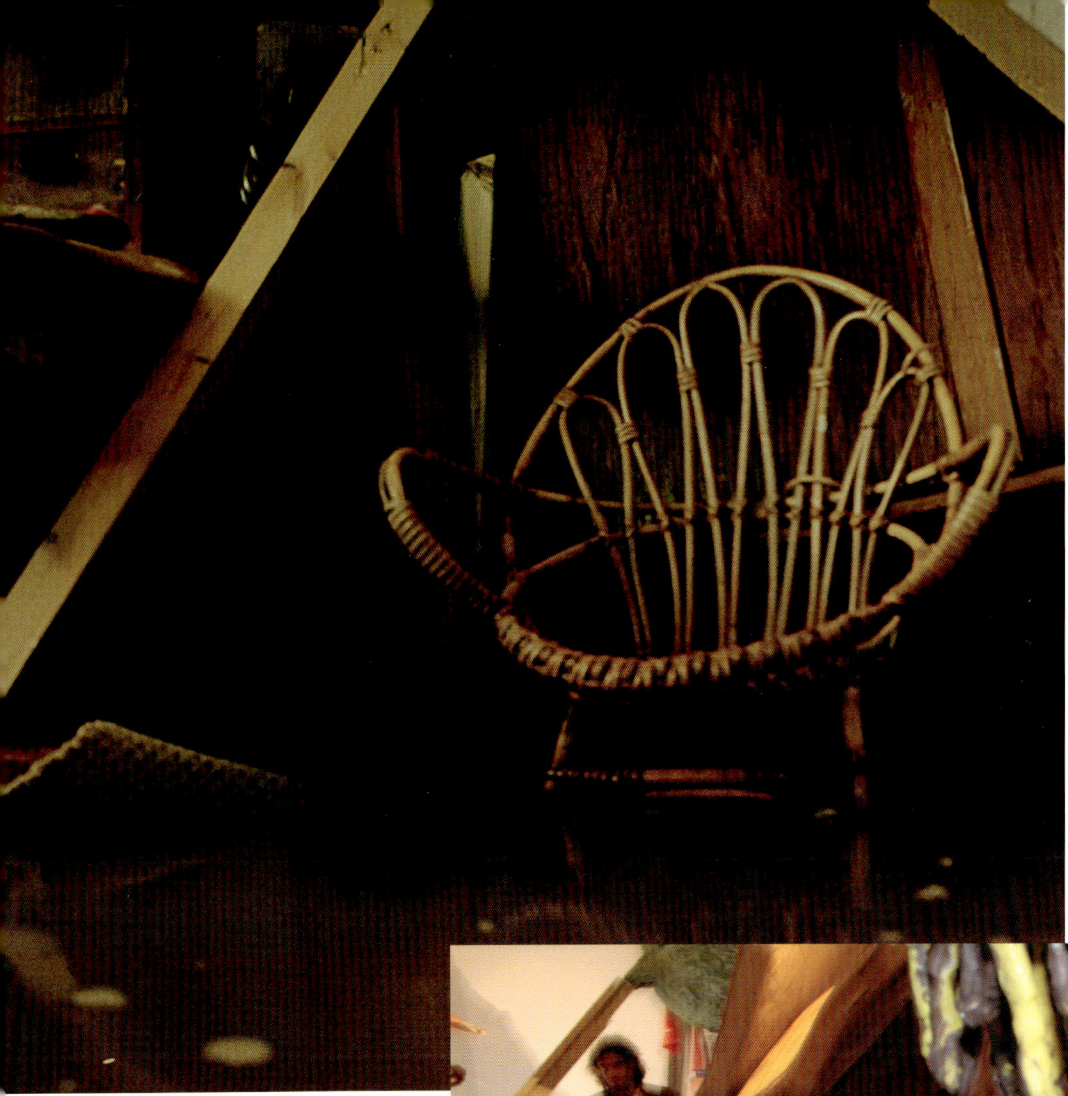

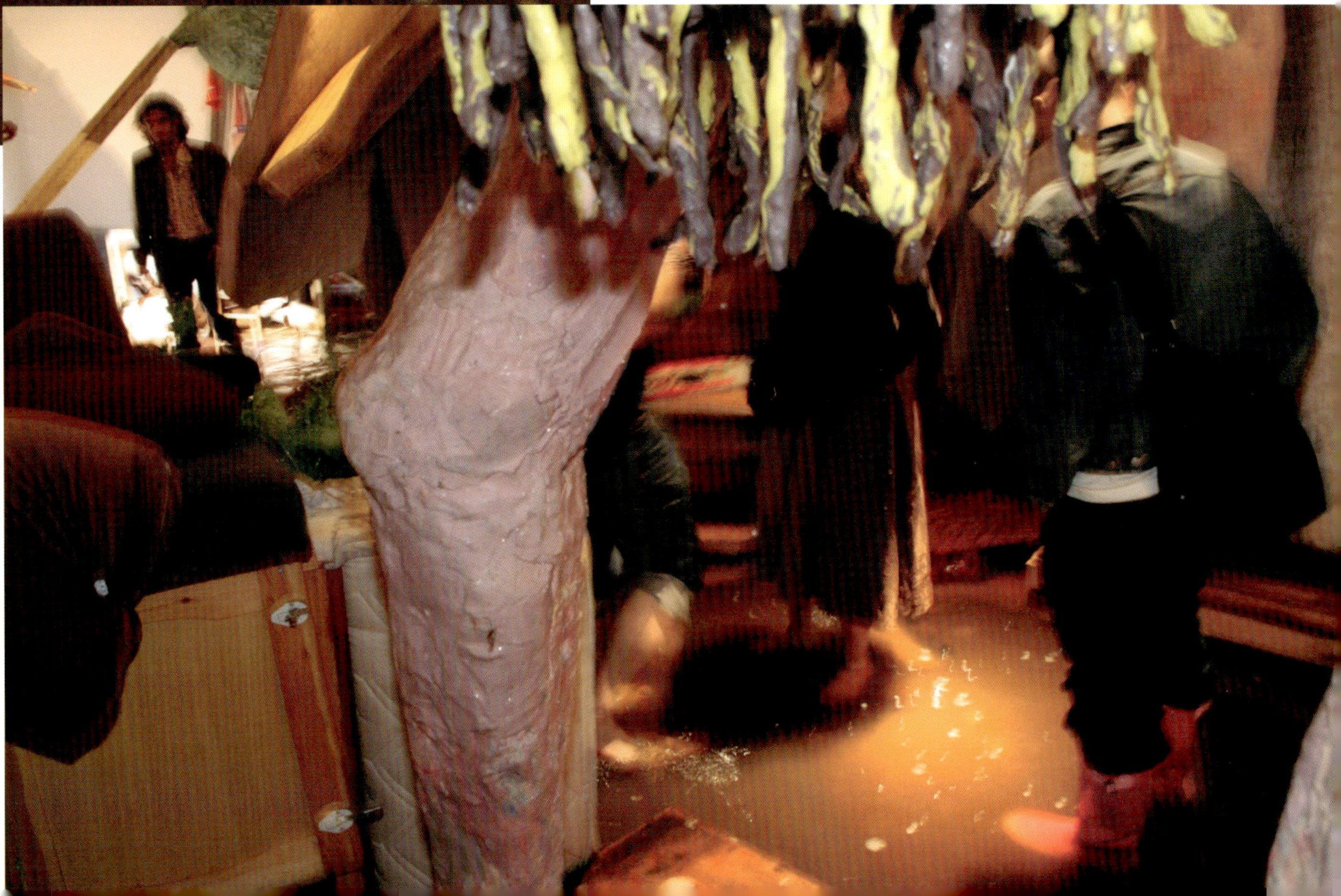

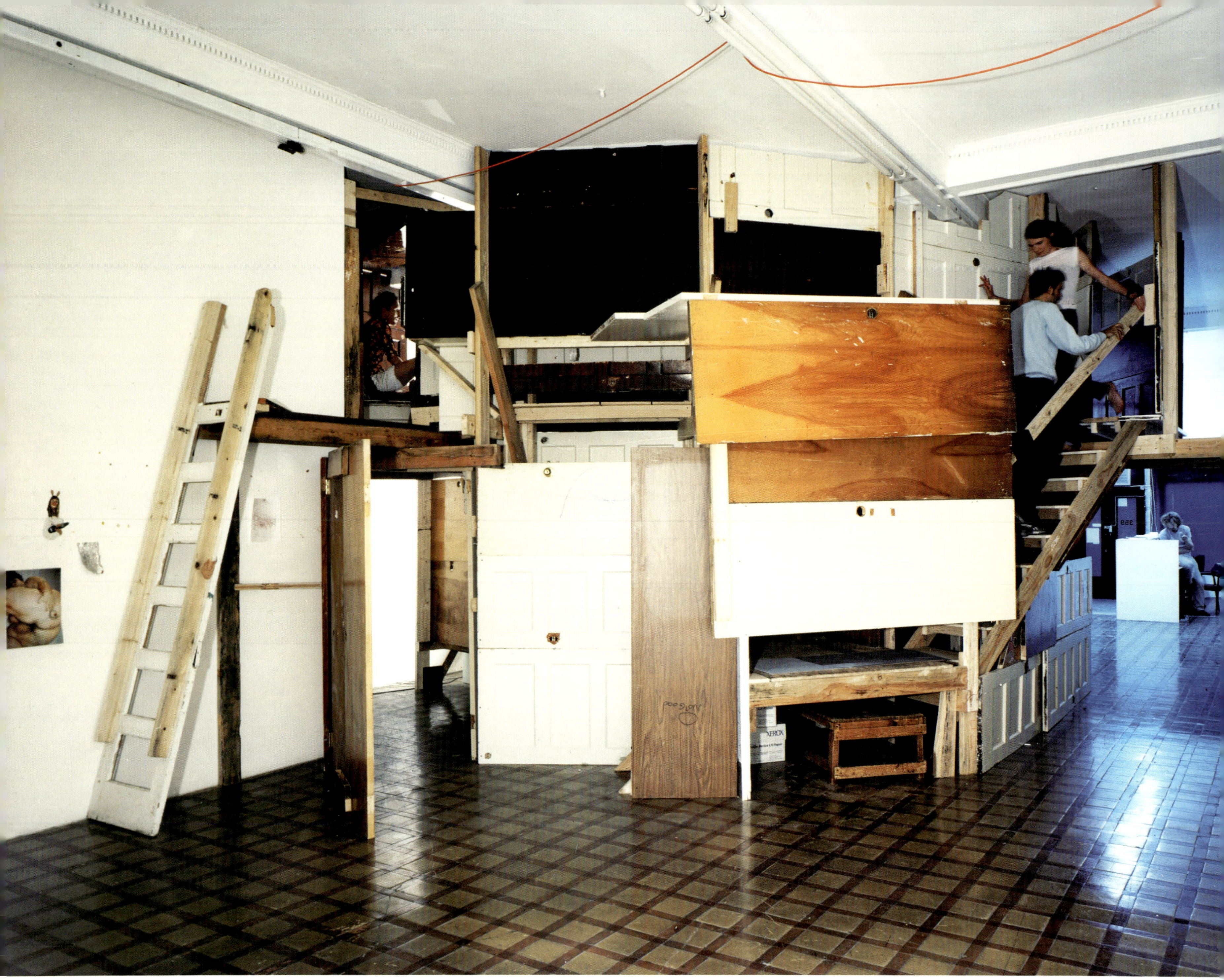

Coliseum, **2001**

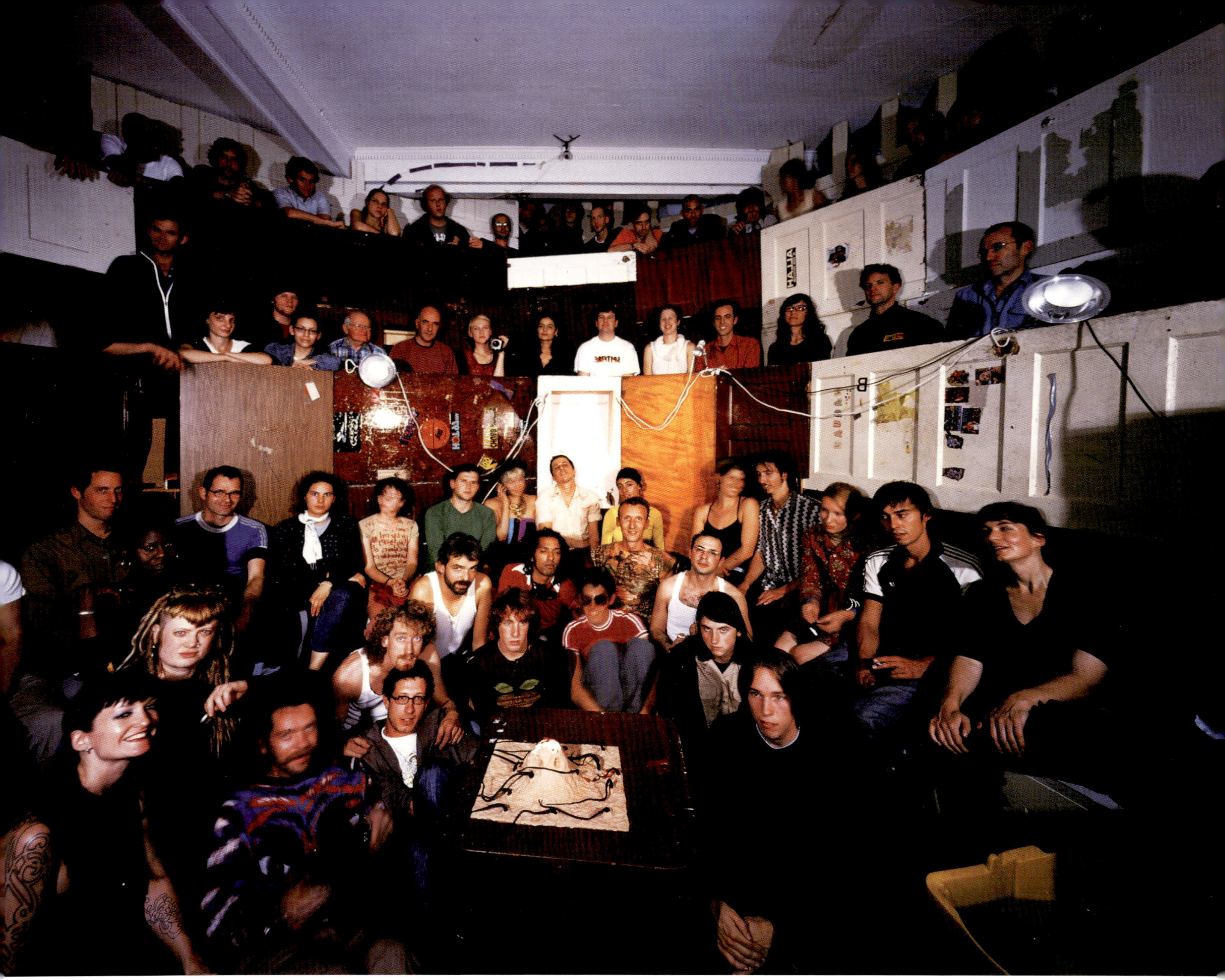

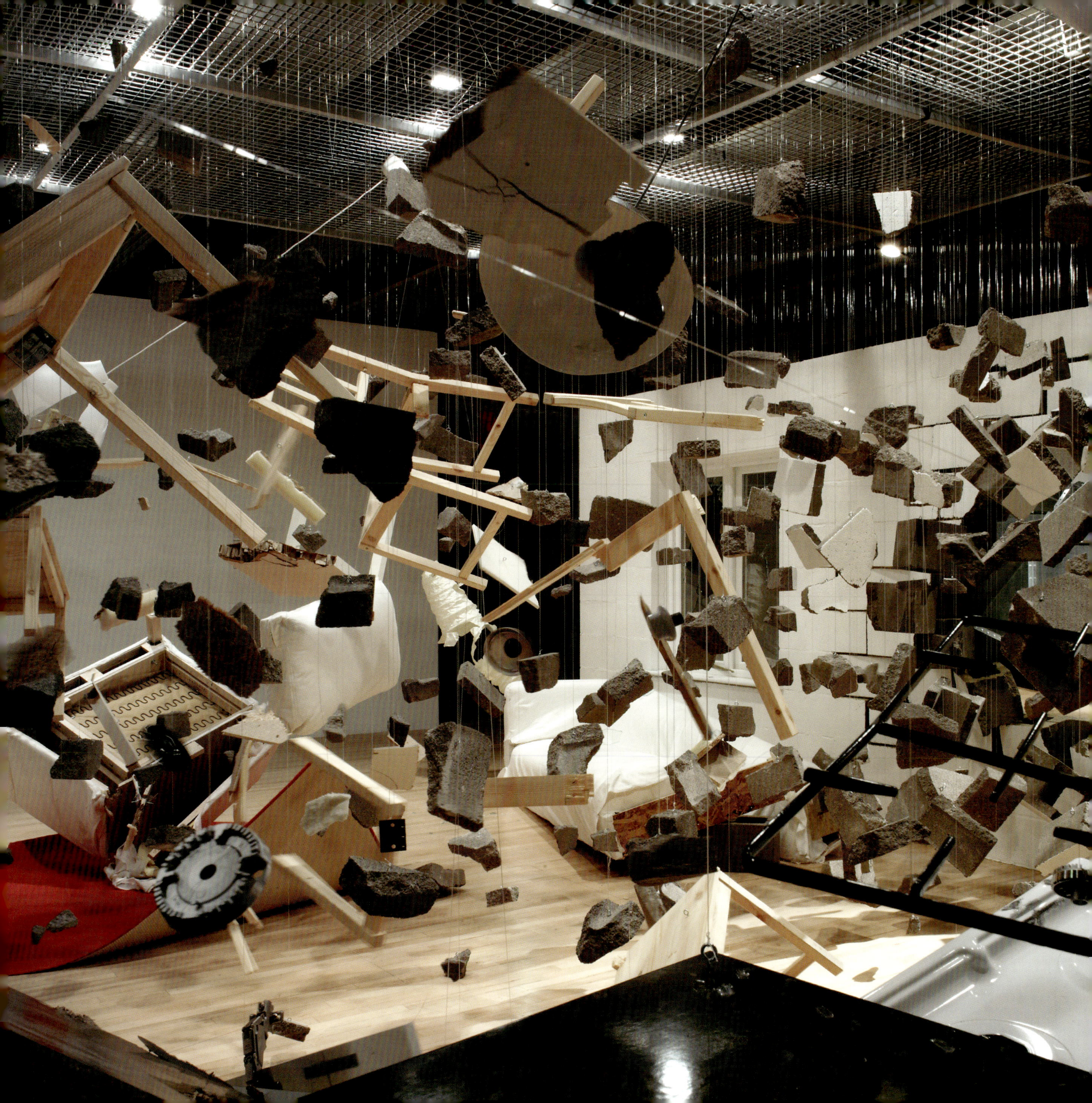

Show Room, **2008**

LOS CARPINTEROS

TUMELO MOSAKA

There are no hard distinctions between what is real and what is unreal, nor between what is true and what is false. A thing is not necessarily either true or false; it can be both true and false.[1]

Los Carpinteros blur the lines between life, art, craft and politics, drawing upon known architectural landmarks and furniture designs. Central to their practice is the inquiry into 'how art is made' and 'for whom'. Their work is inspired by the architecture and urban designs in and around the colonial city of Havana, Cuba. They use recycled and found materials to build sculptural forms that are loaded with political overtones. Since the 1990s, they have emerged as a critical voice in Cuba, making art that is significantly relevant to their context while employing metaphors and dual meanings to evade censorship. Forced by the political conditions in Cuba, the artists find subtle ways to critique the status quo, bringing to attention the poverty and inequality that has been underplayed by the government.

The collective was formed in 1991 by the trio Alexandre Arrechea, Marco Castillo and Dagoberto Rodríguez, and only in 1994 adopted the name 'Los Carpinteros', meaning 'The Carpenters'. Since 2003, they've worked as a duo (Castillo and Rodríguez), denouncing the concept of the individual author as genius and embracing older guild traditions by skilled labourers, whose creativity is evident throughout the architectural landscape of Havana. They embrace certain socialist tendencies such as working collectively towards a common goal to effect social change. The production model that they've adopted entails them conceptualising and designing the work then releasing it to be fabricated by experts, eliminating any record of the makers' signature. Their earlier works are typically made from wood by hand tools often associated with carpenters. And, by applying functional designs to mundane objects, Los Carpinteros explore social contexts without being overtly political. However, art in Cuba remains very much tied to the politics and history of the island's struggle for identity and autonomy from its colonial past and its present relationship with the United States.

Through their work, Los Carpinteros comment on the adverse circumstances and ironies of daily life, especially in Havana where the artists live part-time. Facing the harsh realities of socio-economic conditions and deteriorating infrastructure in the country, they have continued to be resourceful in creating work that addresses more universal human conditions. These works follow a pattern marked by ongoing series such as *Transportable City* **(2000),** *Transportable Columns* **(2001),** *Prison* **(2003) and** *Watch Towers* **(2002), which focus on the physical and psychological experience of entrapment and displacement evident in the region.**

Watch Towers, **for example, suggests surveillance, isolation and the control of physical space. The tall structures are constructed out of industrial metal and transparent green glass, like that of a greenhouse. They resemble lookout posts at prisons and military camps, built for protection and control, which is emphasised by the height of the towers. They are rendered ineffective and fragile because of the transparent glass interior. As such, they no longer serve as law enforcing outposts, and have become vulnerable and iconic symbols of power. Like sentinels, they stand anchored to the ground as pillars of authority.**

Show Room, **2008**

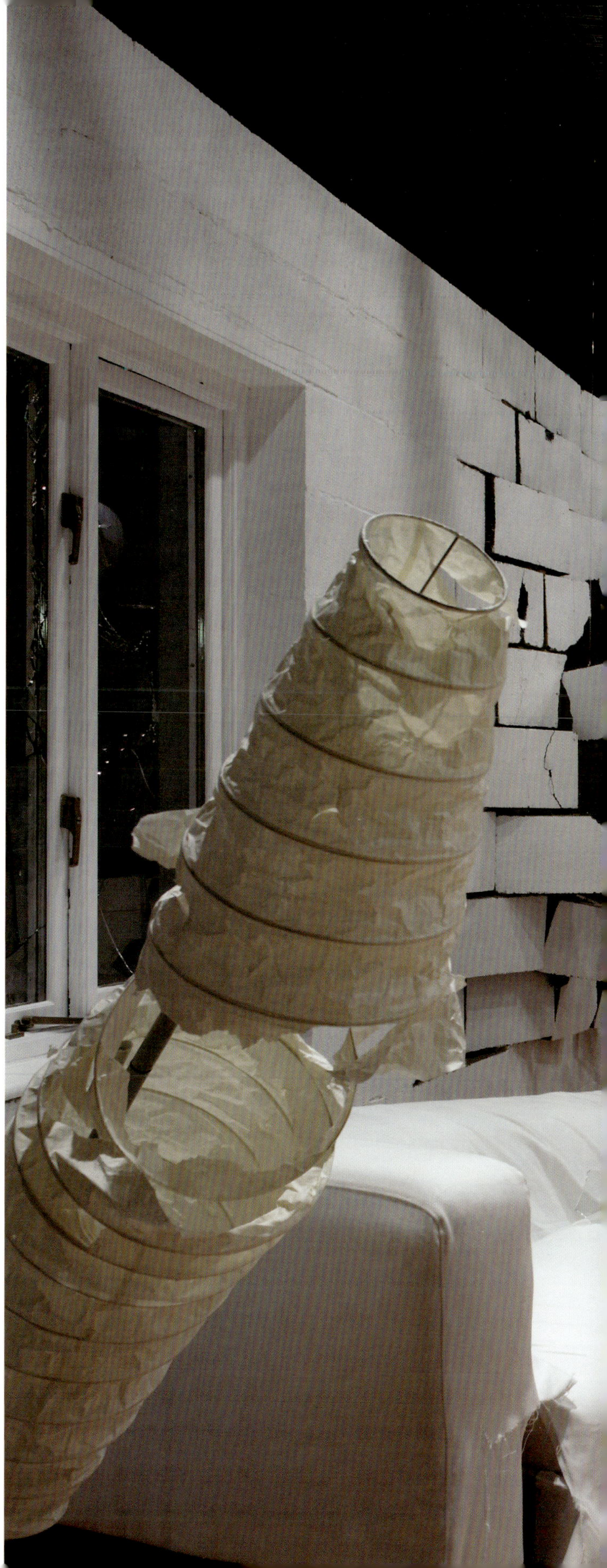

Today, given existing global networks and access to technology, it is without doubt that nationhood is no longer limited to a singular culture or region, but rather has become more complex and diverse as populations are no longer geographically or culturally restricted. *Show Room* (2008) demonstrates the possible collapse and change of man-made borders separating people along the lines of ethnicity and nationality, especially the geographical separation enforced by physical borders. With brick fragments suspended in mid-air, almost suggesting a frozen moment as in a photograph or film still, at first glance the scene looks unreal — like a dream where reality collides with the imaginary. The air of stillness is ominous, as if it's the quiet before the storm.

The solid wall in the work represents officialdom. Its rigid, formal structure and grey colour is reminiscent of the bureaucratic systems associated with governments. At the centre, the wall is blasted open to suggest a forced intrusion. This breach proposes an opening hole upon which new possibilities can be considered. We are left wondering who or what might have caused this destruction and why it is frozen in time. One clue lies in recent history, where such events as the demolition of the Berlin Wall indicated a dramatic change and end to the Cold War.

Recently, developments in Cuba have begun to show some change. Fidel Castro's official resignation has signalled a transformation that is still to be tested. The prevalent mood is that the country can no longer continue along the same path. Los Carpinteros draw our attention to the winds of chance sweeping through the country and charting new directions. They have continued to produce work that not only resonates locally, but also has universal appeal. Working with existing forms stripped of their original meaning, they create metaphors for us to decipher and challenge our understanding of the world. They search for truth, which is sometimes evasive, and yet through their art-making they find meaning in the truths and falsities prevailing in daily life.

1 **Extract from Harold Pinter,** *Art, Truth and Politics*, **2005**

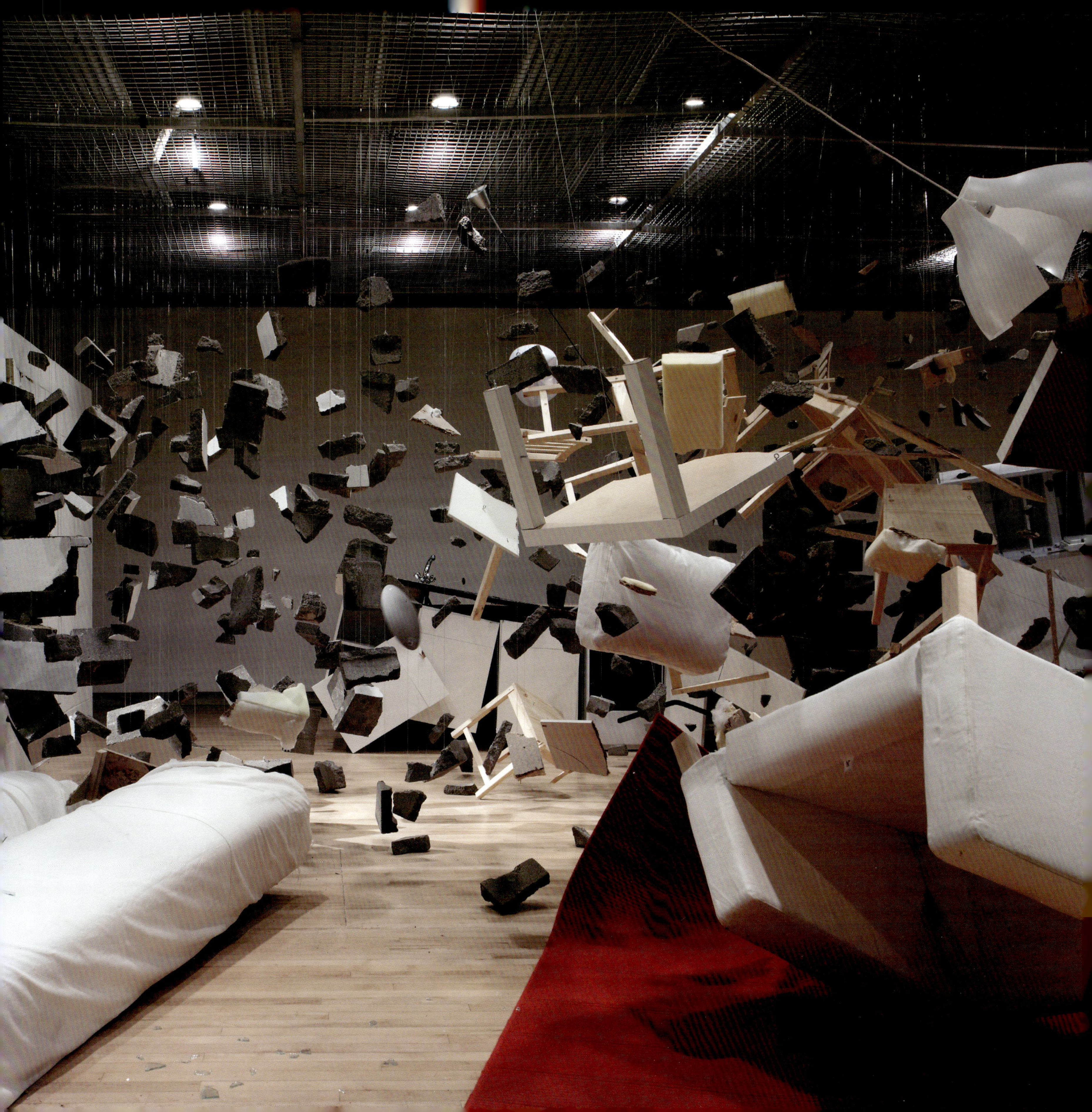

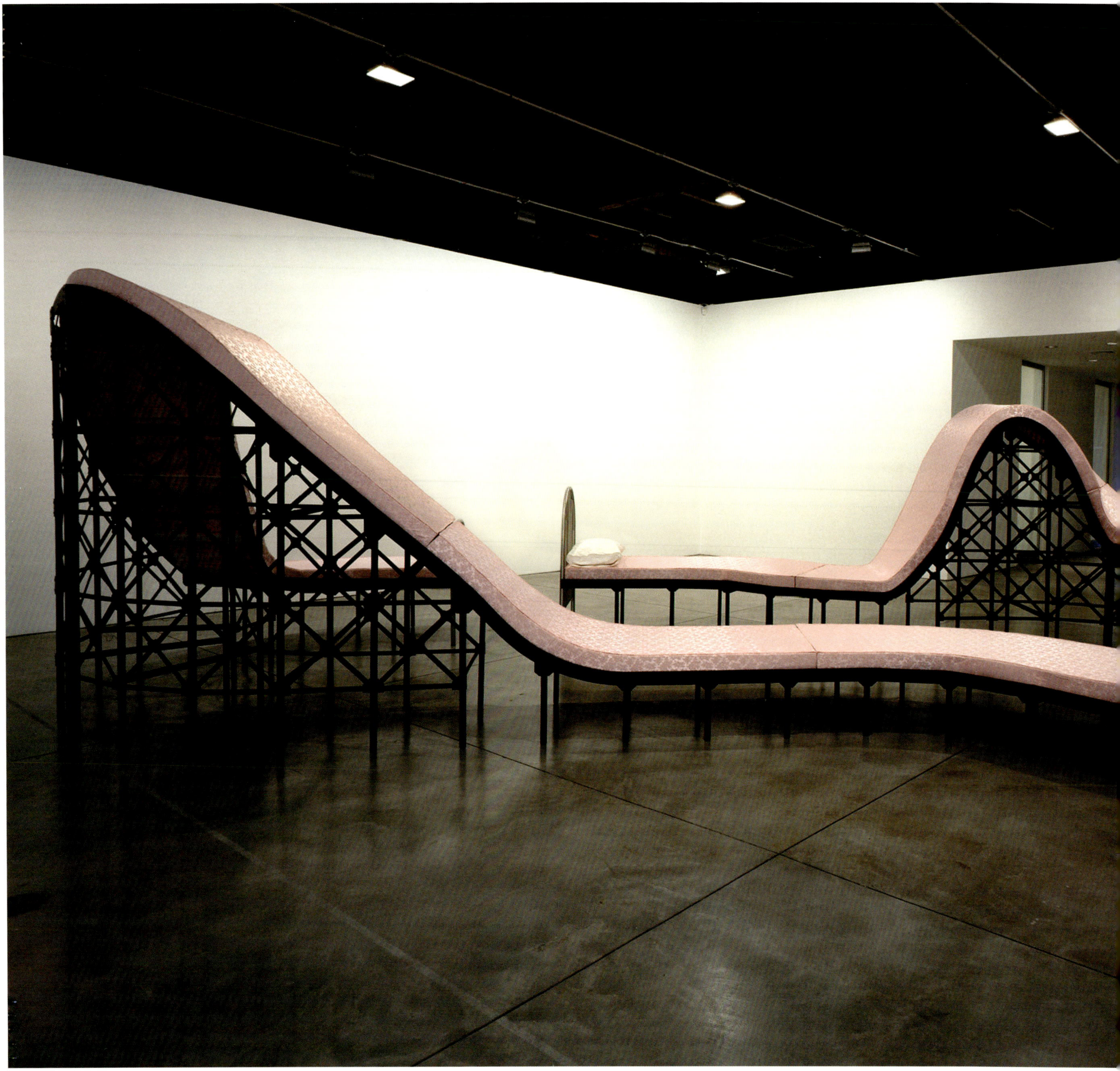

La Montaña Rusa, **2008**

overleaf
Felled Lighthouse, **2006**
Watch Towers, **2002**

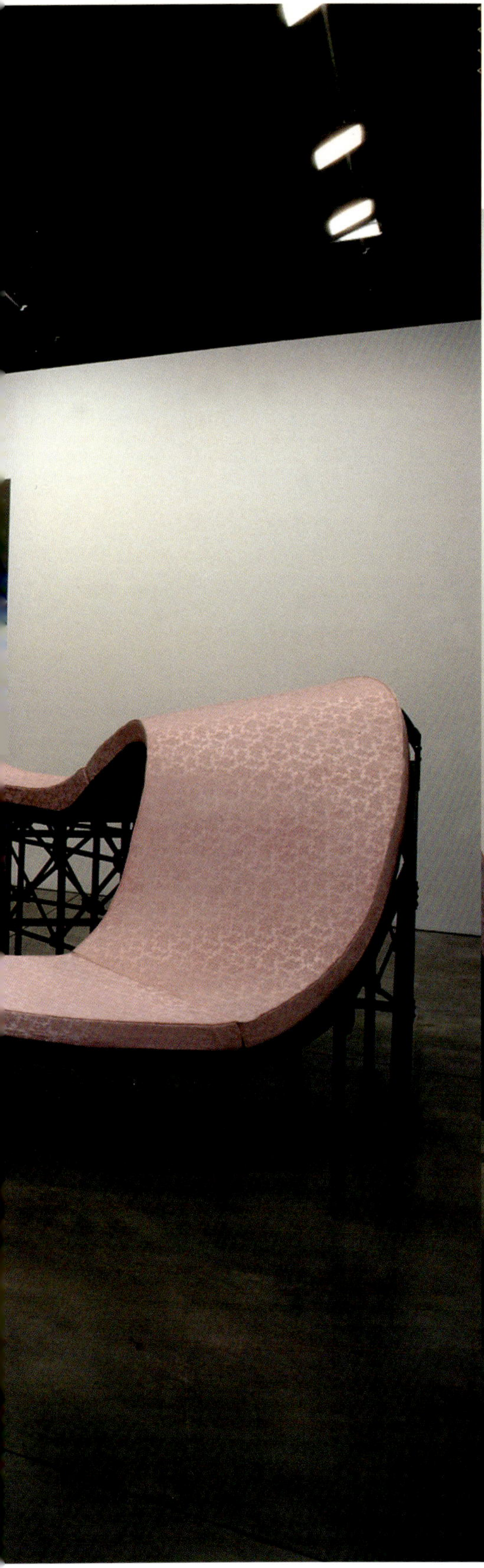

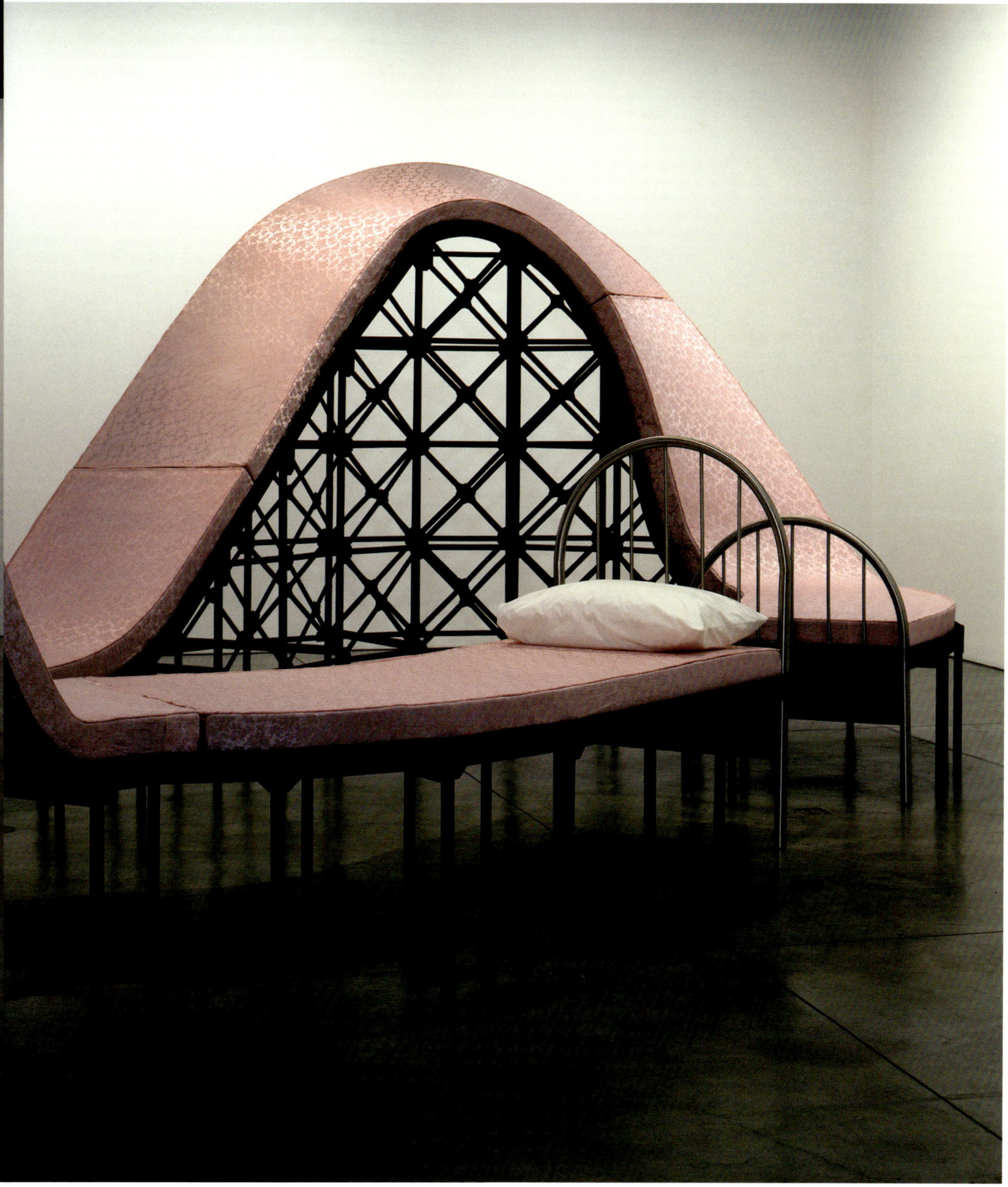

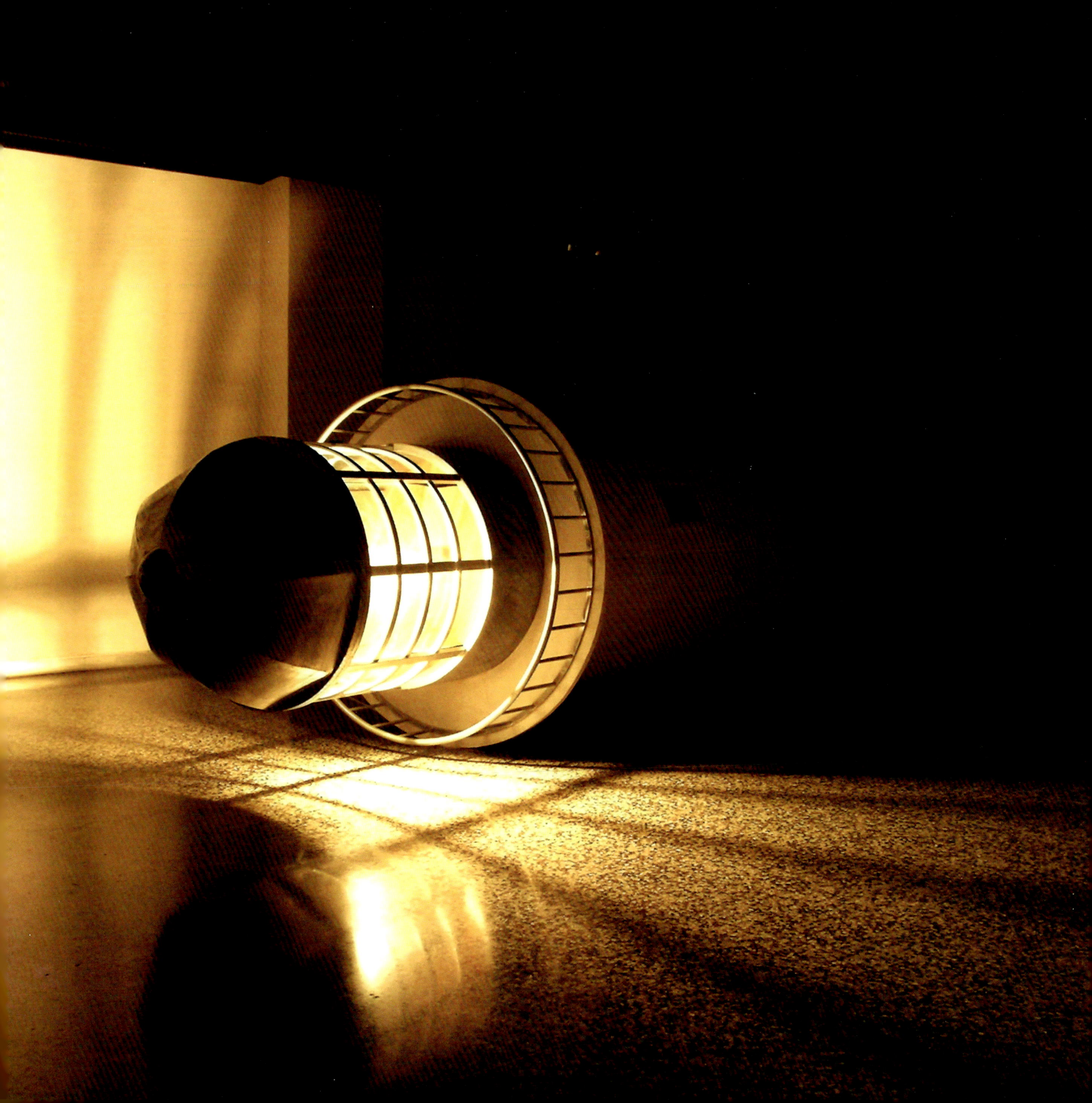

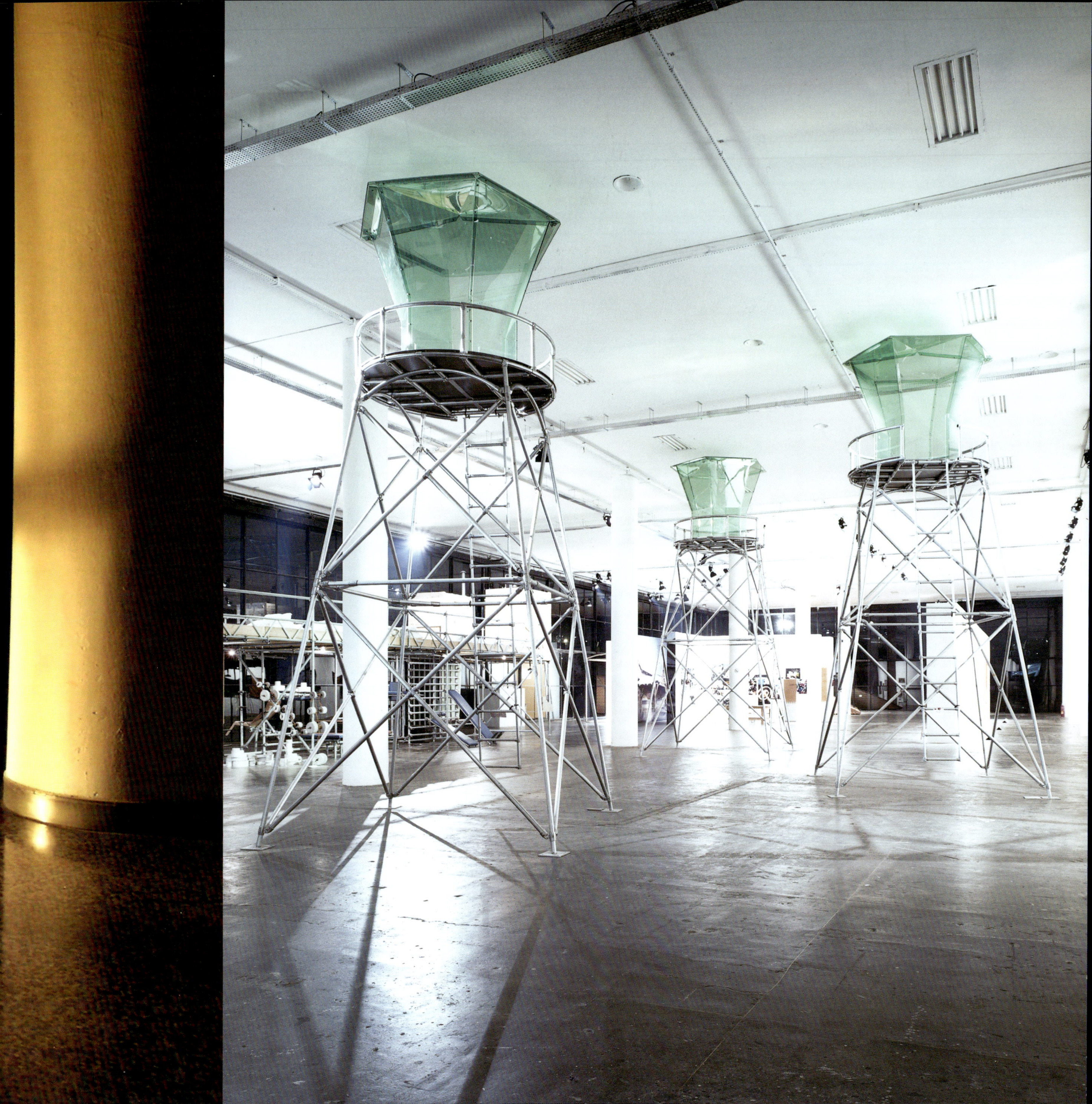

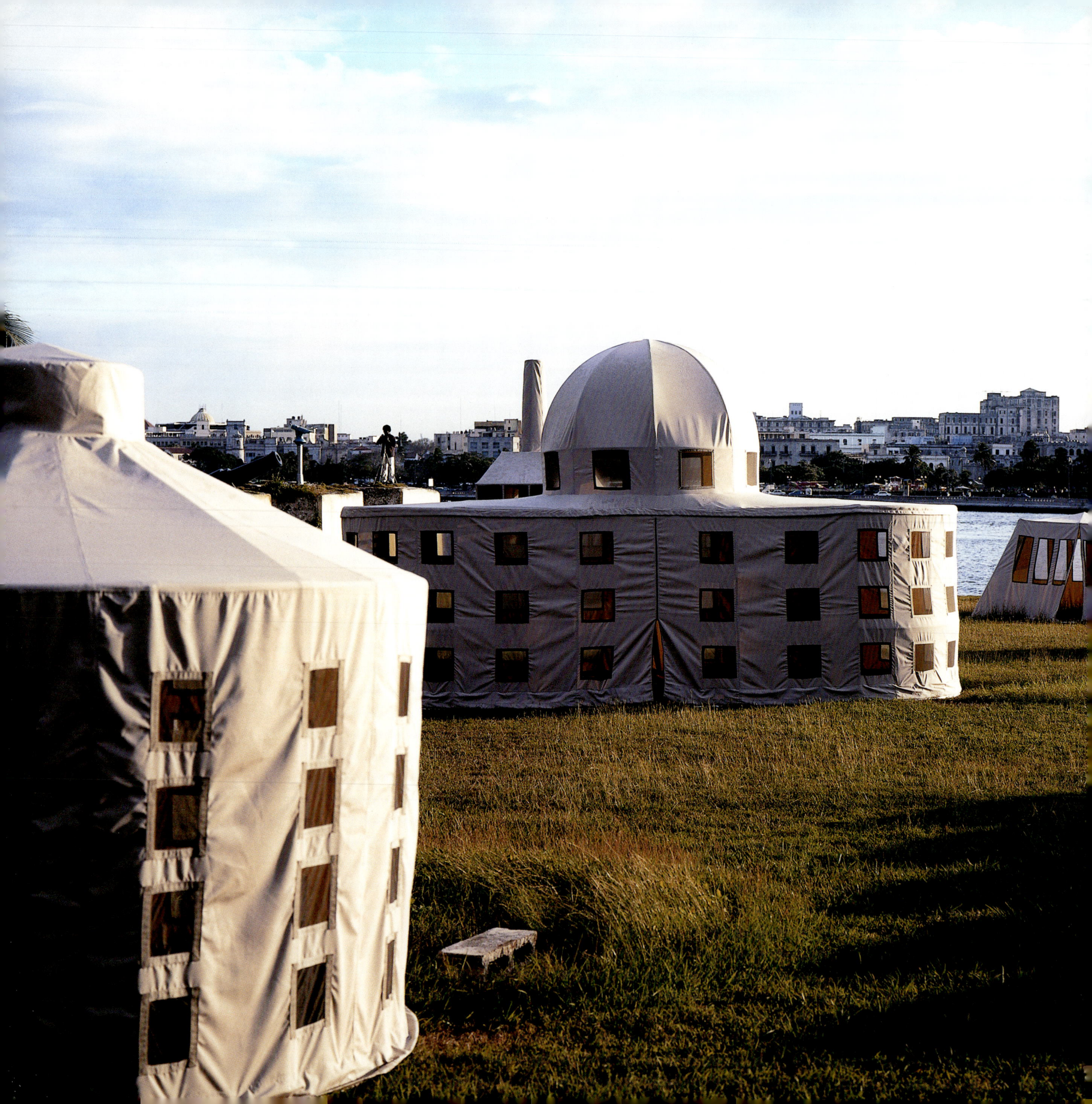

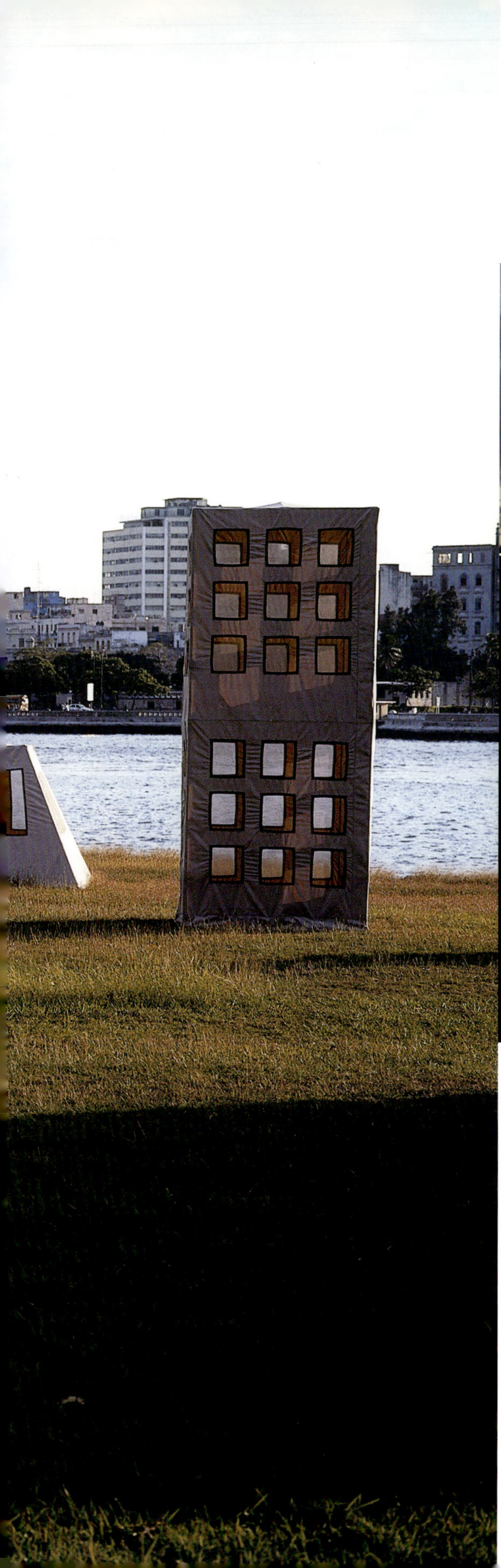

Transportable City, **2000**

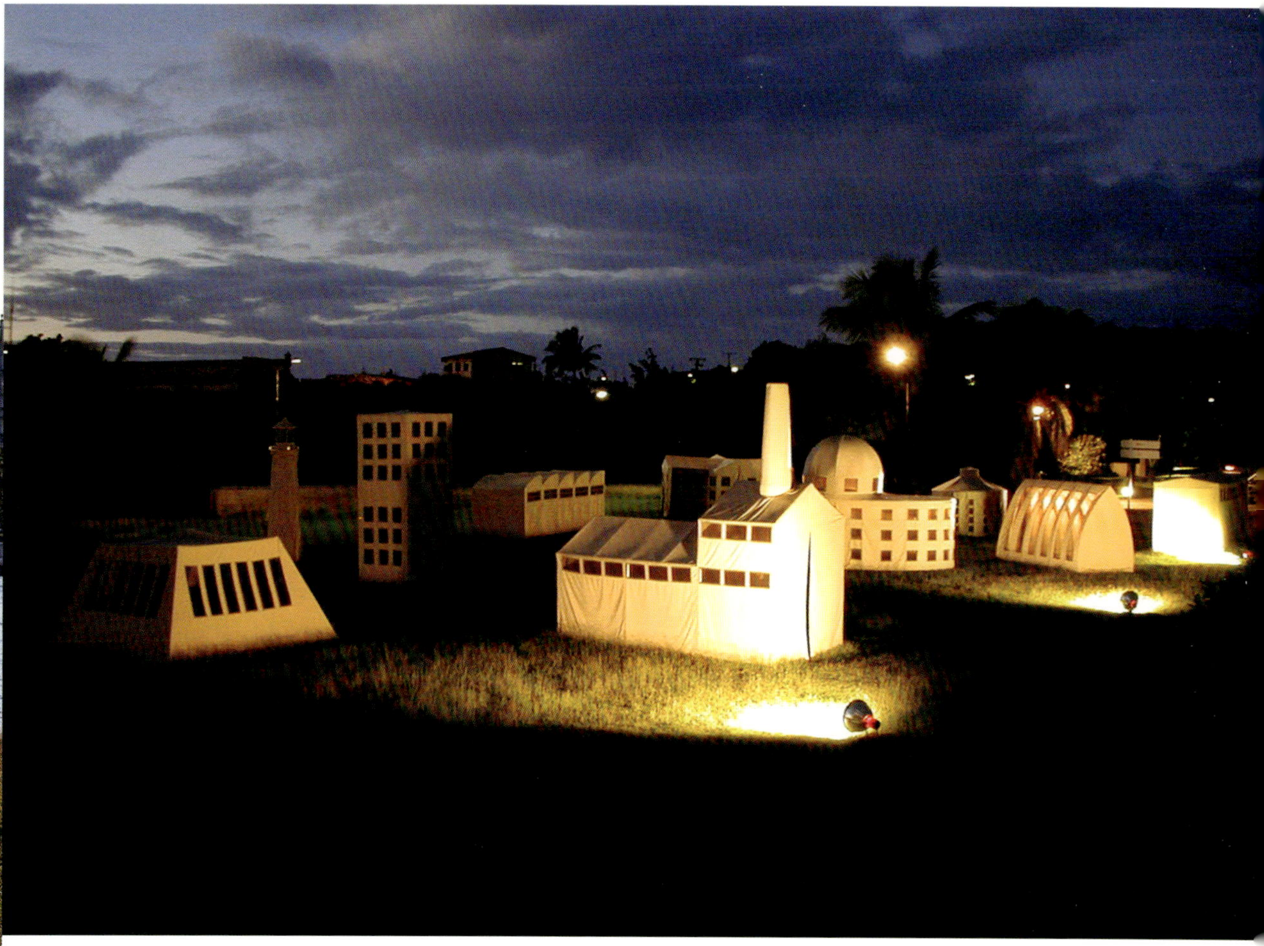

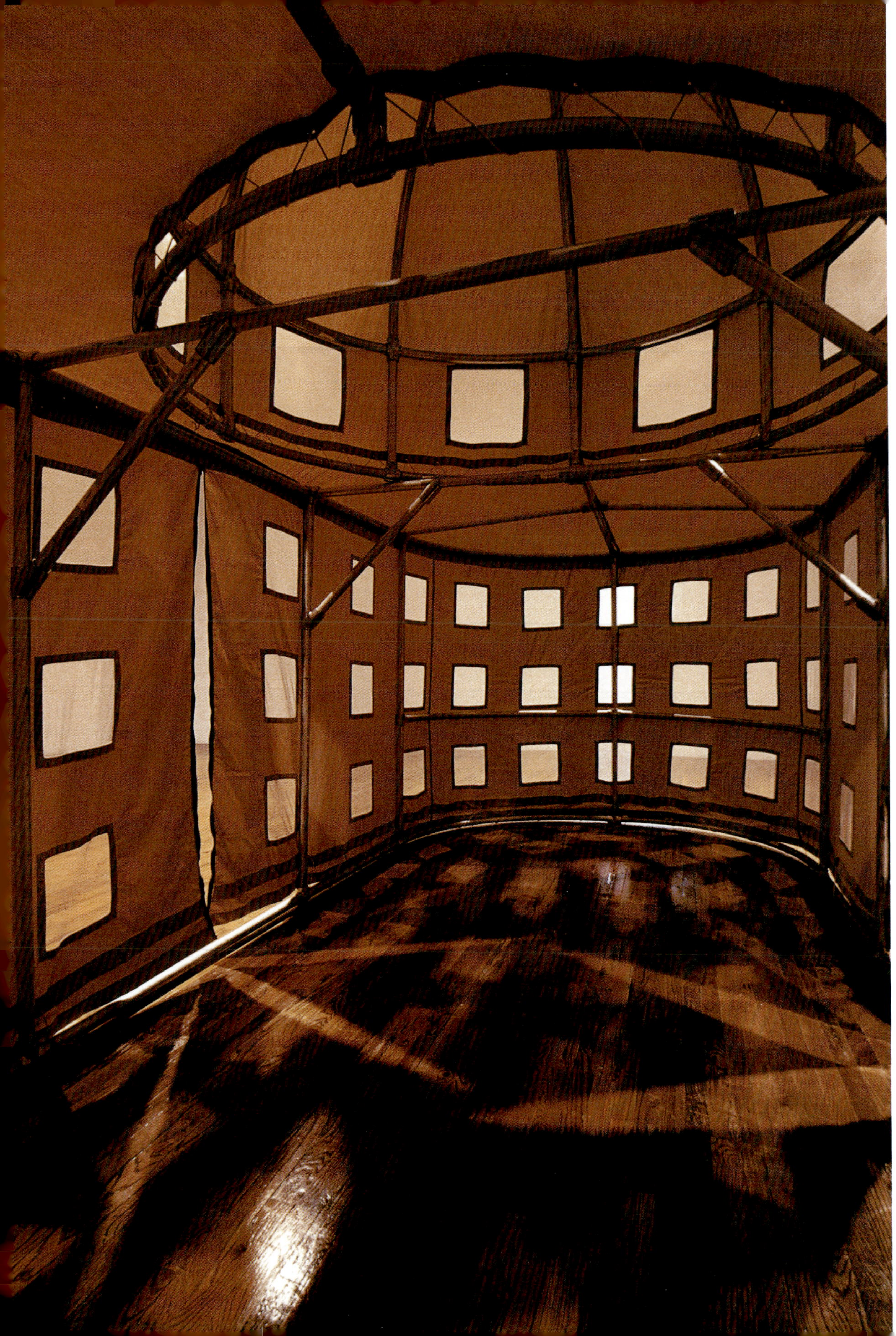

Transportable City, **2000**

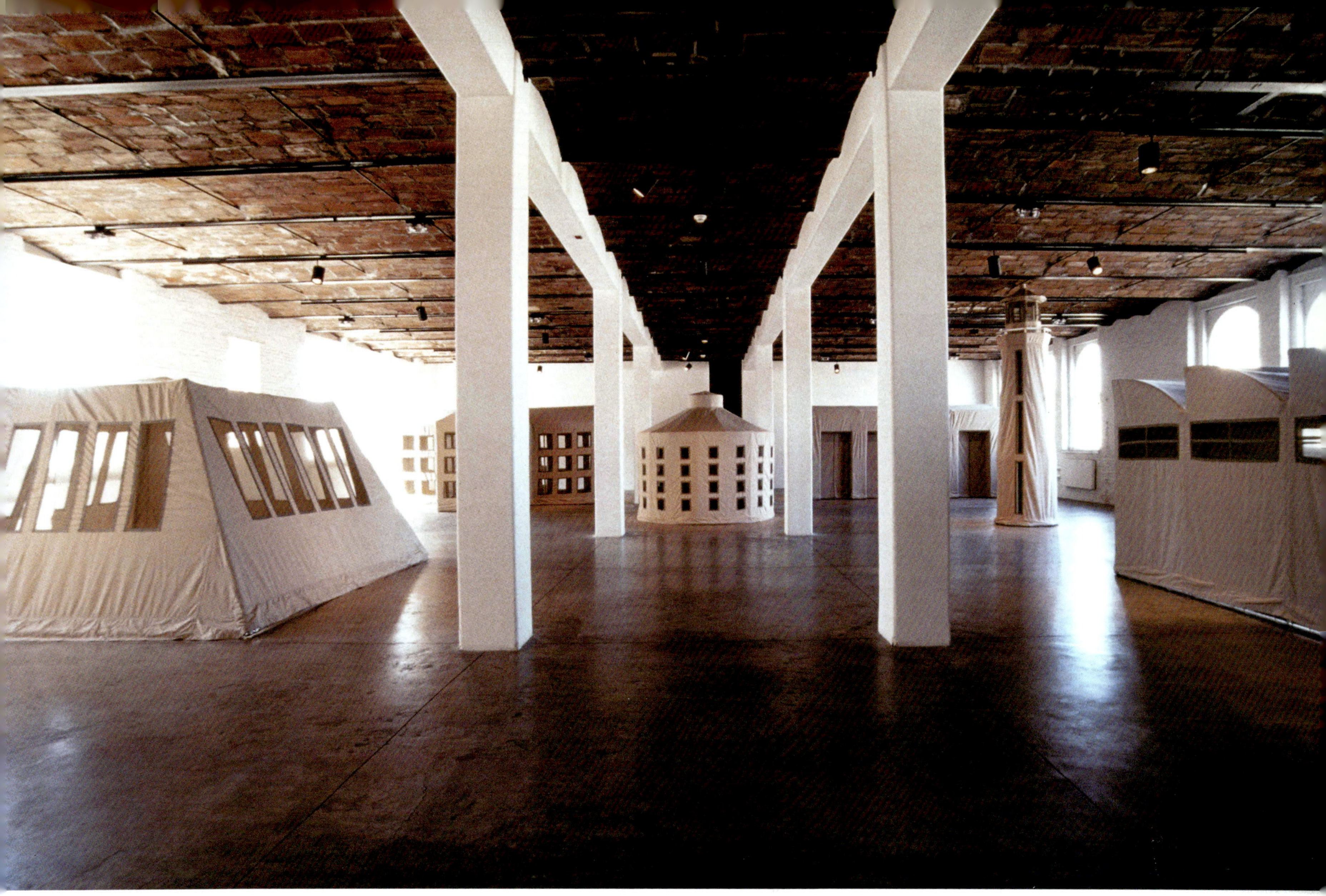

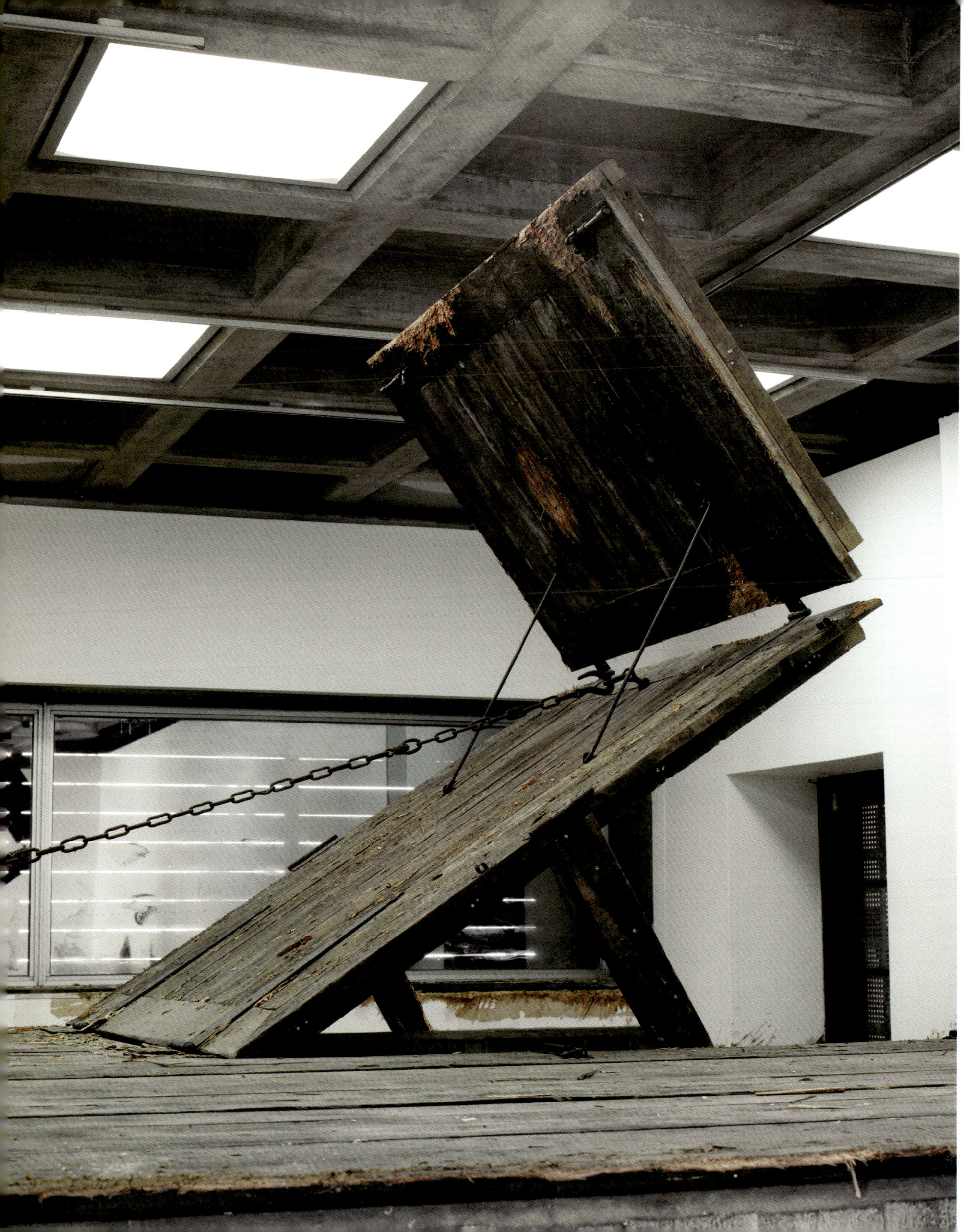

To the Memory of H.P. Lovecraft, **1999, 2008**

MIKE NELSON
BRIAN DILLON

Stepping inside one of Mike Nelson's extremely unsettling installations, one has the sense of travelling in time as well as space: the present recedes as we penetrate his maze-like imagination. The meticulously contrived but dingy labyrinths, the gloomy chambers in which enigmatic objects lie about in careful disarray, the disorienting corridors and crawlspaces: all of them seem to suggest that we have arrived too early or too late upon the scene. Something has transpired here, or is about to happen, and in that uncertainty lies a good deal of the power of Nelson's art. The architectural volumes he constructs or cannibalises resemble, at best, the shoddy back-lot to everyday life — glum dwellings and offices, artists' studios or alchemists' laboratories. At worst, they look like the kind of lair where a serial killer meditates his next abomination, or the scene of the crime itself. If the artist is a sort of architect, his materials are the stuff of nightmares.

Nelson's work is often called 'uncanny', following Sigmund Freud's famous essay on the subject from 1919. Architecture itself, writes Freud, can unnerve us as easily as any violent, ghoulish or apparently supernatural phenomenon: 'one may wander about in a dark strange room, looking for the door or the electric switch, and collide time after time with the same piece of furniture.' Nelson is a connoisseur of such alarmingly recursive interiors: literary and cultural references to them cling to his works like cobwebs. The architectural dreams of Thomas De Quincey, the metaphysical labyrinths of Jorge Luis Borges, the decaying ghost ship of Edgar Allan Poe's *Manuscript Found in a Bottle*: **all of these and many more quotations nestle in the shadows of his architectural fictions. More contemporary citations proliferate too — the weirdly organic décor of the** *Alien* **films, for example, or even the limitless, paradoxical interior of the Tardis in** *Doctor Who*.

Among these reference points, the horror writer H.P. Lovecraft occupies a special place. His particular skill was in imagining horrifically ambiguous beings, things that were scarcely of this world at all, and yet partly human. Nelson's Hayward installation, *To the Memory of H.P. Lovecraft*, **in fact, takes its title from a homage to the writer — a story by Borges,** *There Are More Things* **— that concerns an eerie house, renovated in the most bizarre fashion. Its rooms have been expanded as if to accommodate some marauding creature; the new furniture does not seem to fit the human form. The tale's narrator is appalled but curious, and at length encounters the monstrous inhabitant — but Borges declines to describe it. This is the 'thing' that, according to the conceit of the piece, Nelson has set loose in the gallery, where it has ripped the place to shreds. The thing, we might say, is ambiguity itself.**

To the Memory of H.P. Lovecraft **was first shown at the Collective Gallery in Edinburgh in 1999. (It was in Edinburgh, it's worth recalling, that Robert Louis Stevenson first conceived** *The Strange Case of Dr. Jekyll and Mr. Hyde*, **with its locked laboratory and windowless dissecting room where the monster Hyde hangs out.) A heavy steel reinforced door was hung at the gallery entrance, as though every effort had been made to contain the animal (or alien) energy within. Up to a certain height — the level that the imaginary creature could reach — the artificial walls were scored and lacerated: as if, said Nelson, the beast had tried to eat its way out of the gallery. The installation has not been reconstructed since: what we have at The Hayward is thus a kind of horror-movie sequel: the return of the barely repressed, instinctual, untamed and inhuman thing.**

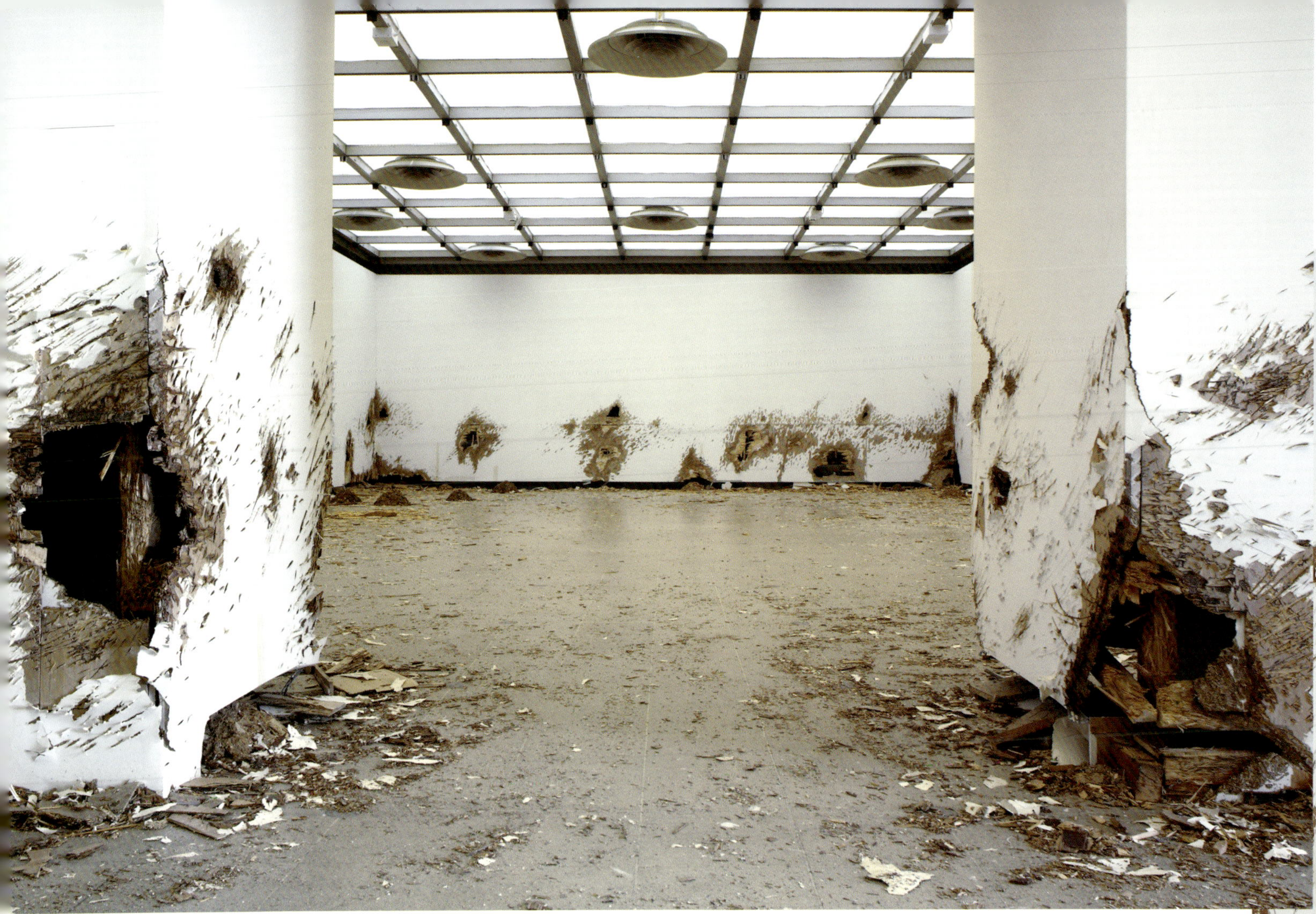

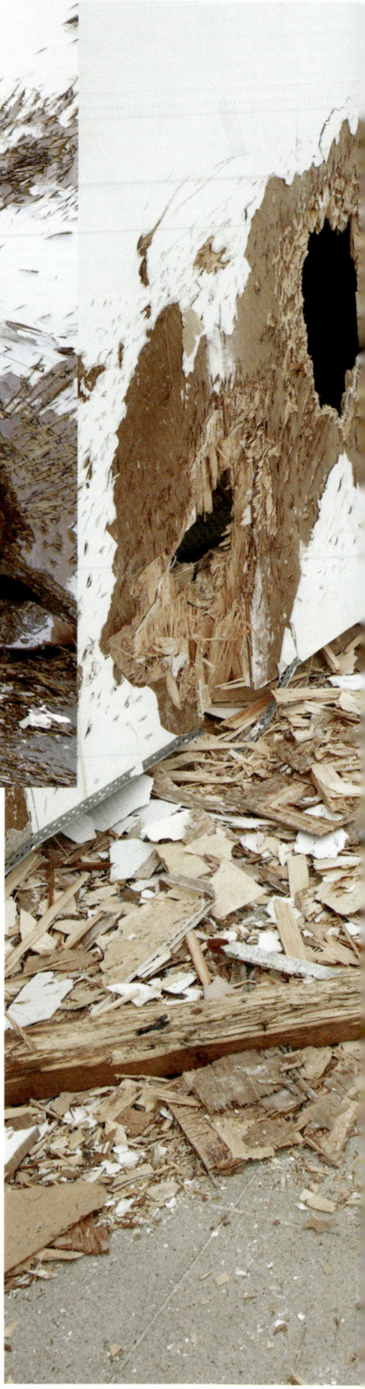

Of course, there is really no such beast, and Nelson is too interesting an artist to simply play, in a strictly Gothic style, on the idea of caged unconscious urges. *To the Memory of H.P. Lovecraft* is also a somewhat sly comment on the claims made in recent decades for the ability of installation art to disrupt the white cube of the gallery space. What the critic Brian O'Doherty has called 'the suave extensions of the space, the pristine clarity': these have been comprehensively eroded by artists as diverse as Robert Smithson, Gordon Matta-Clark, Ilya Kabakov and, latterly, Nelson himself with his weird intersticial spaces insinuated into the traditional precincts of the gallery or museum. The assault on the space and substance of the institution seems all the more dramatic when its object is the implacable concrete Modernism of The Hayward. By imagining the provocateur as a literal monster, however, Nelson emphasises the melodramatic, hysterical, almost cartoon-like urge to artistic revolt.

This is not to say that Nelson's take on the matter of art and architecture is just so much art-historical in-jokery, or that the elaborate veils of reference and recollection in his works are evidence of an air-locked aestheticism. Far from it; *To the Memory of H.P. Lovecraft* actually bears today a considerable political weight. In its first incarnation, the work predated the expansion of global terror and the wars in Afghanistan and Iraq: catastrophes that have time and again over the last decade reminded us of the intimacy of architecture as a practice with policies of concealed horror. It is impossible to enter the labyrinths that Nelson makes now and not think of Abu Ghraib, Guantanamo, kidnapper's cells and the dimly-lit carceral archipelago constructed out of sight by the CIA — places that the light of reason always reaches too late. Nelson's art asks us to consider the unseen interiors of history as much as the architecture of our own psyches — he invites us to emulate the narrator of Borges' tale: 'curiosity overcame my fear, and I did not shut my eyes'.

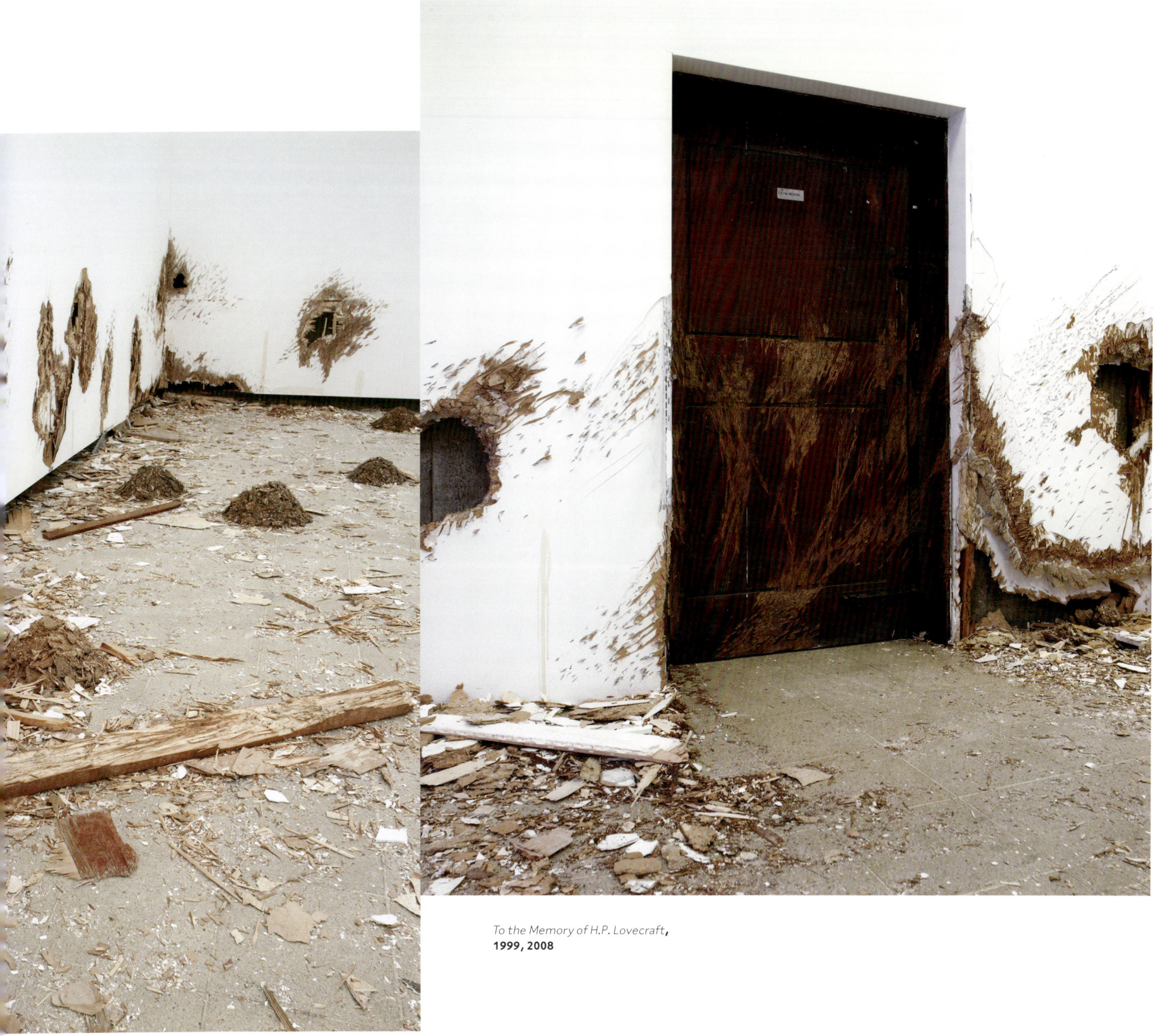

To the Memory of H.P. Lovecraft,
1999, 2008

Triple Bluff Canyon, **2004**

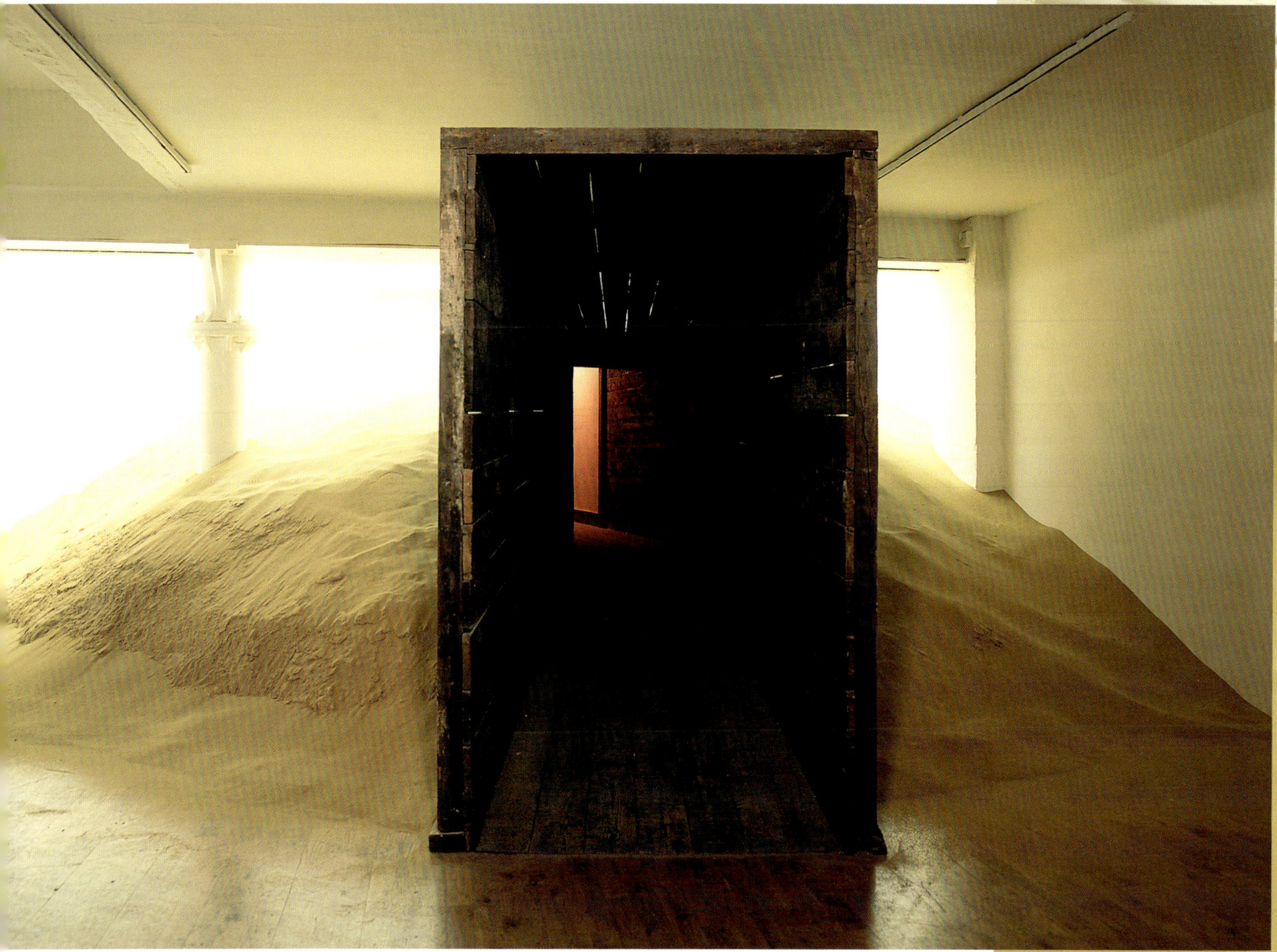

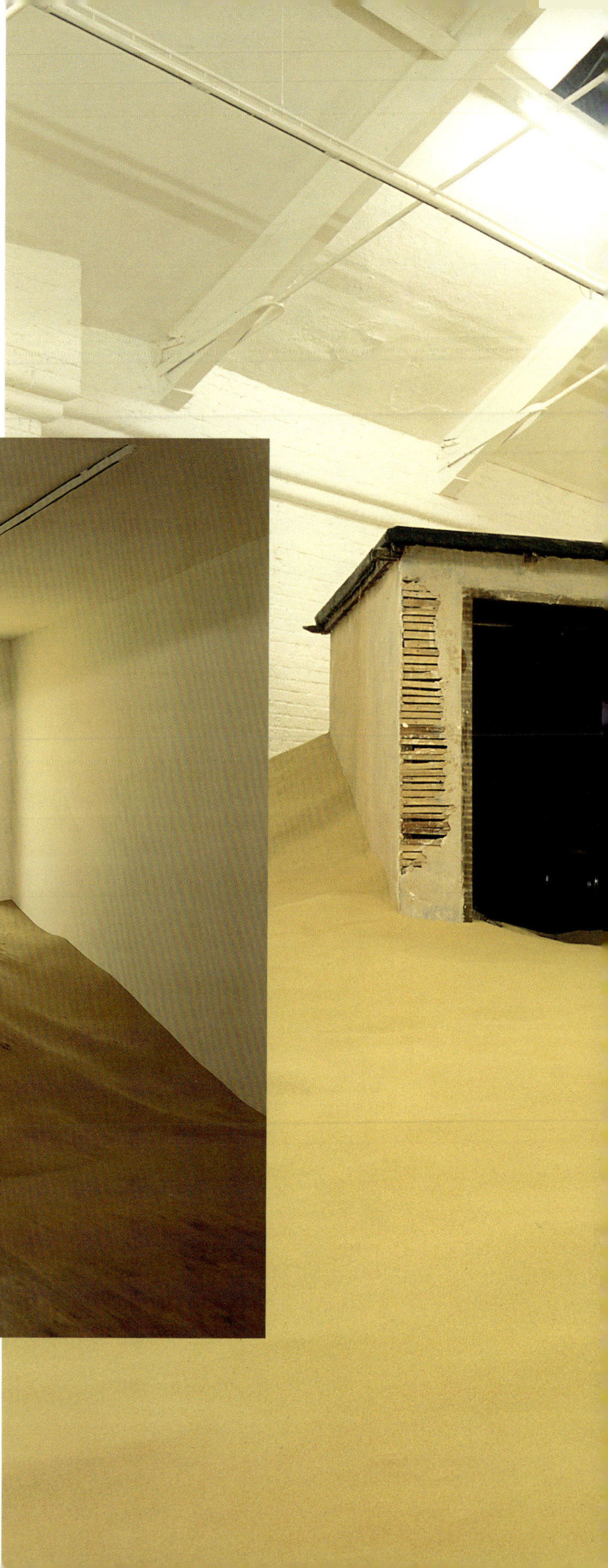

overleaf
Magazin: Büyük Valide Han, **2003**

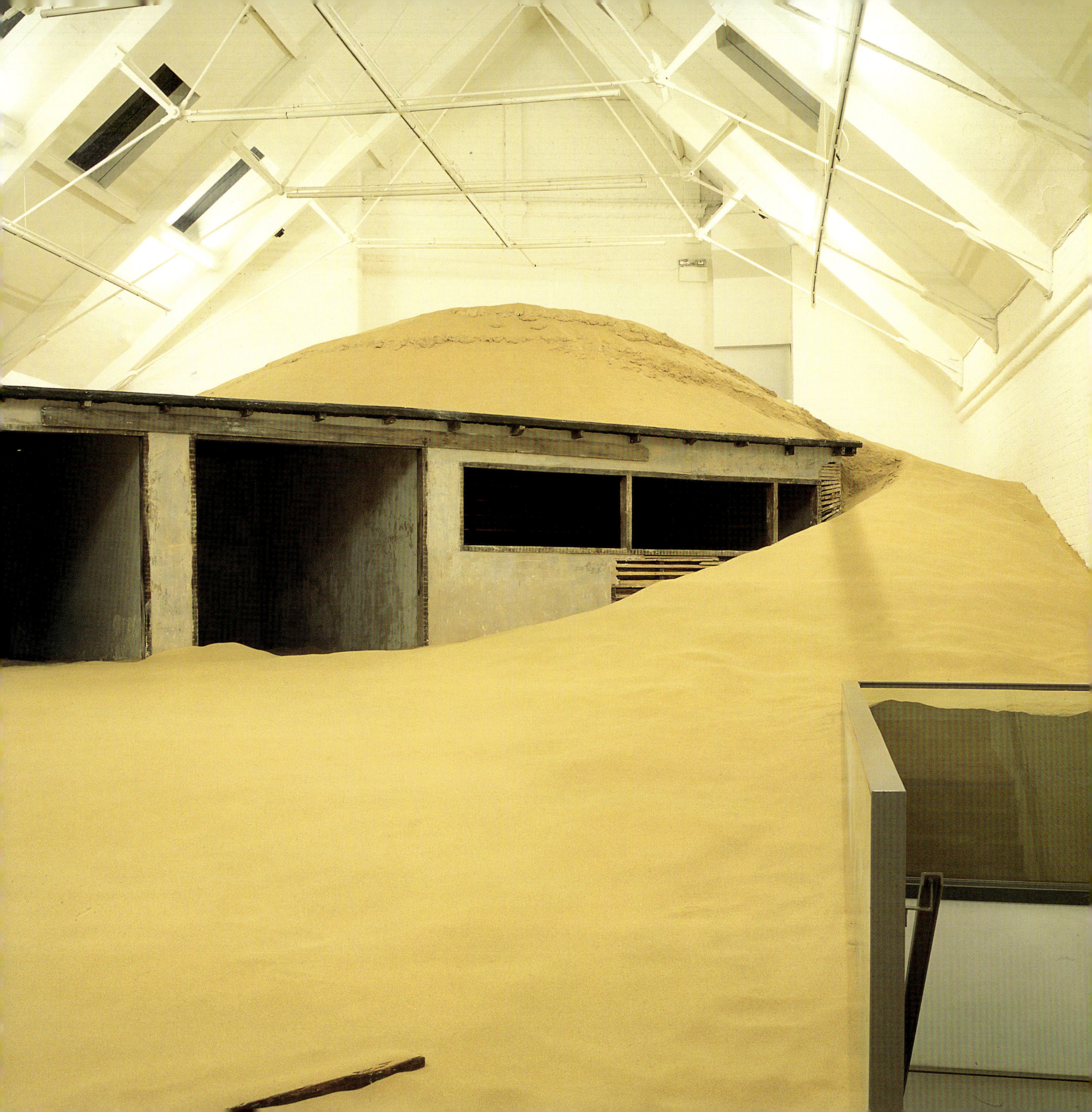

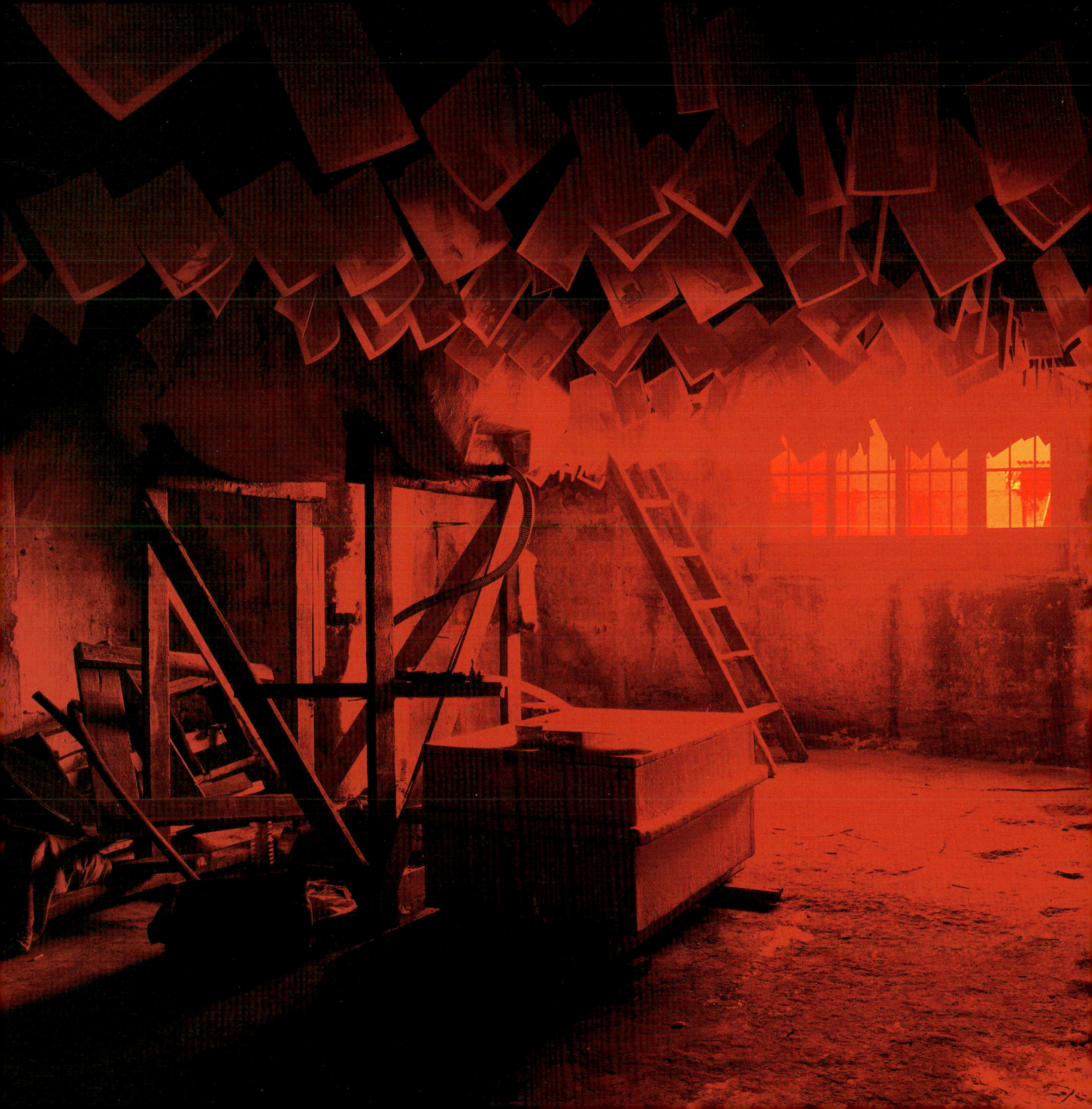

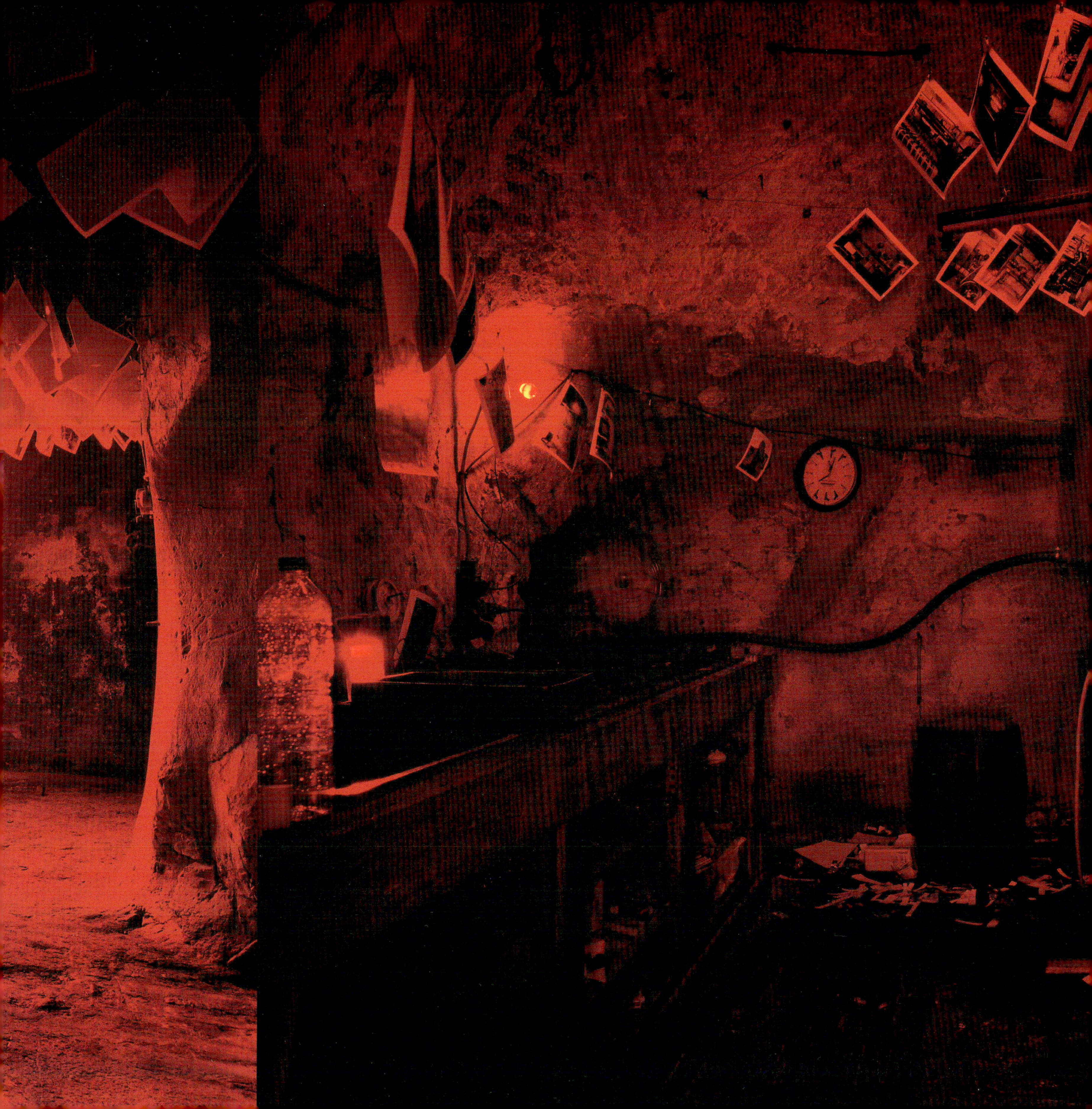

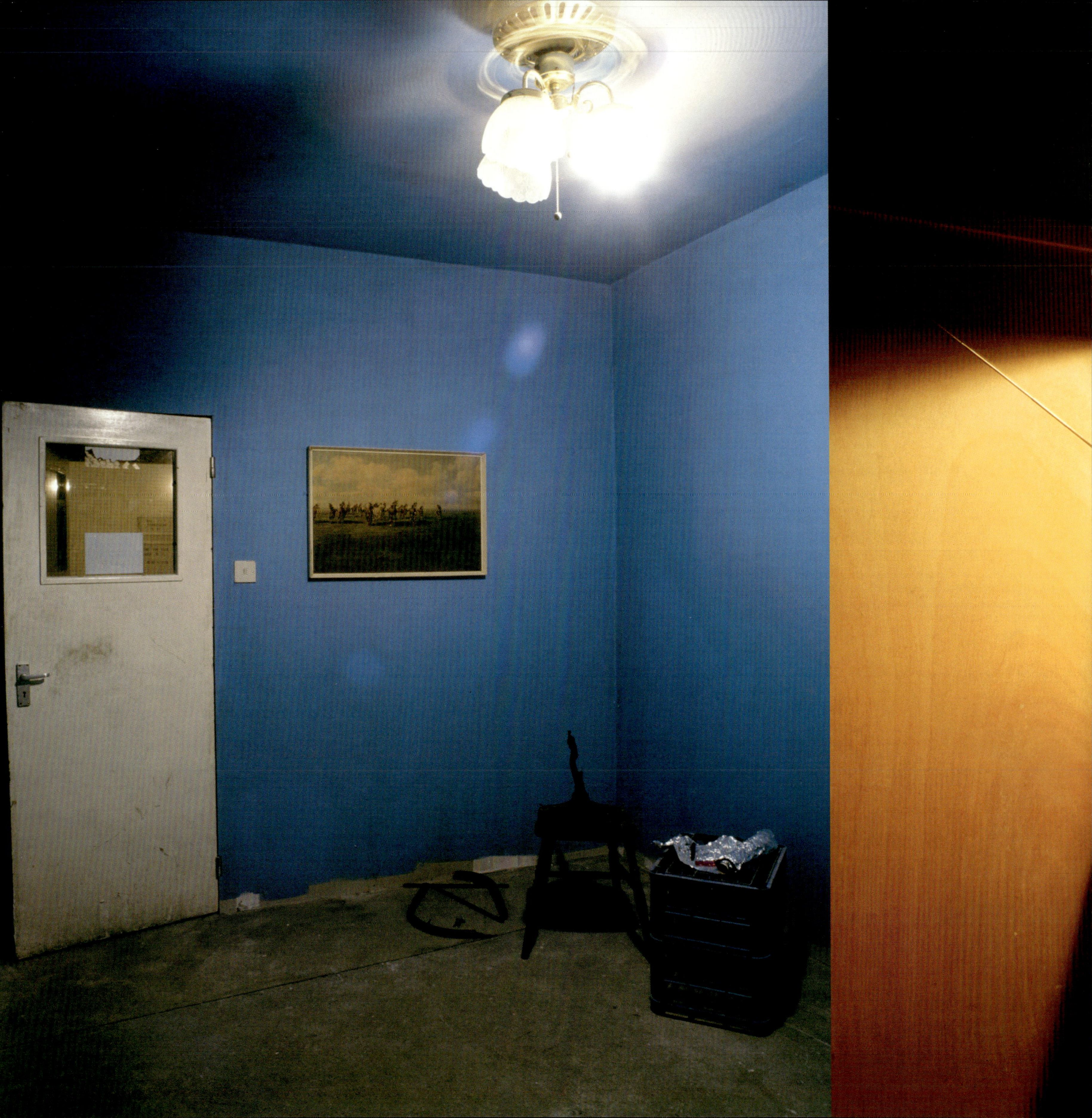

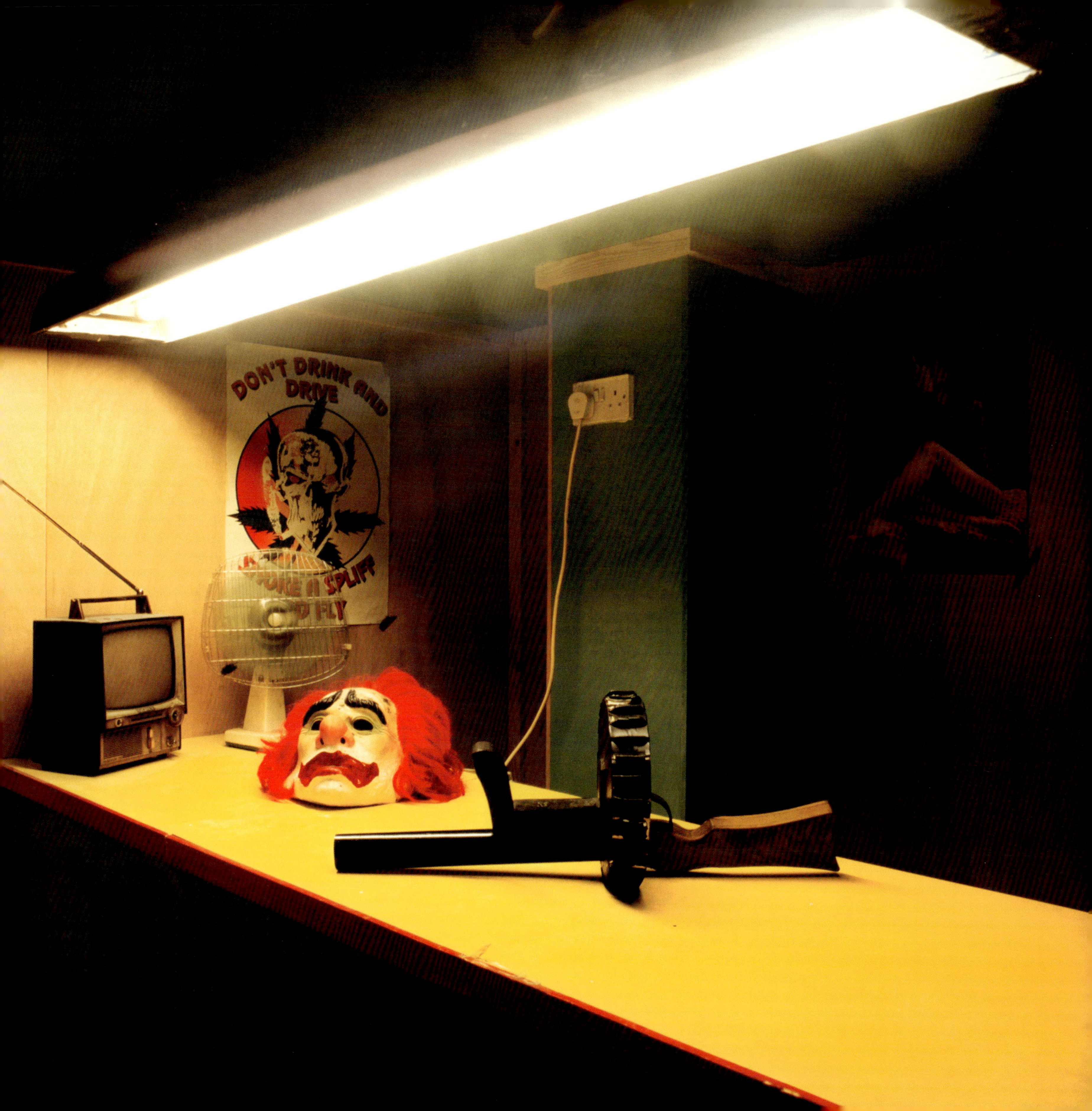
DON'T DRINK AND
DRIVE

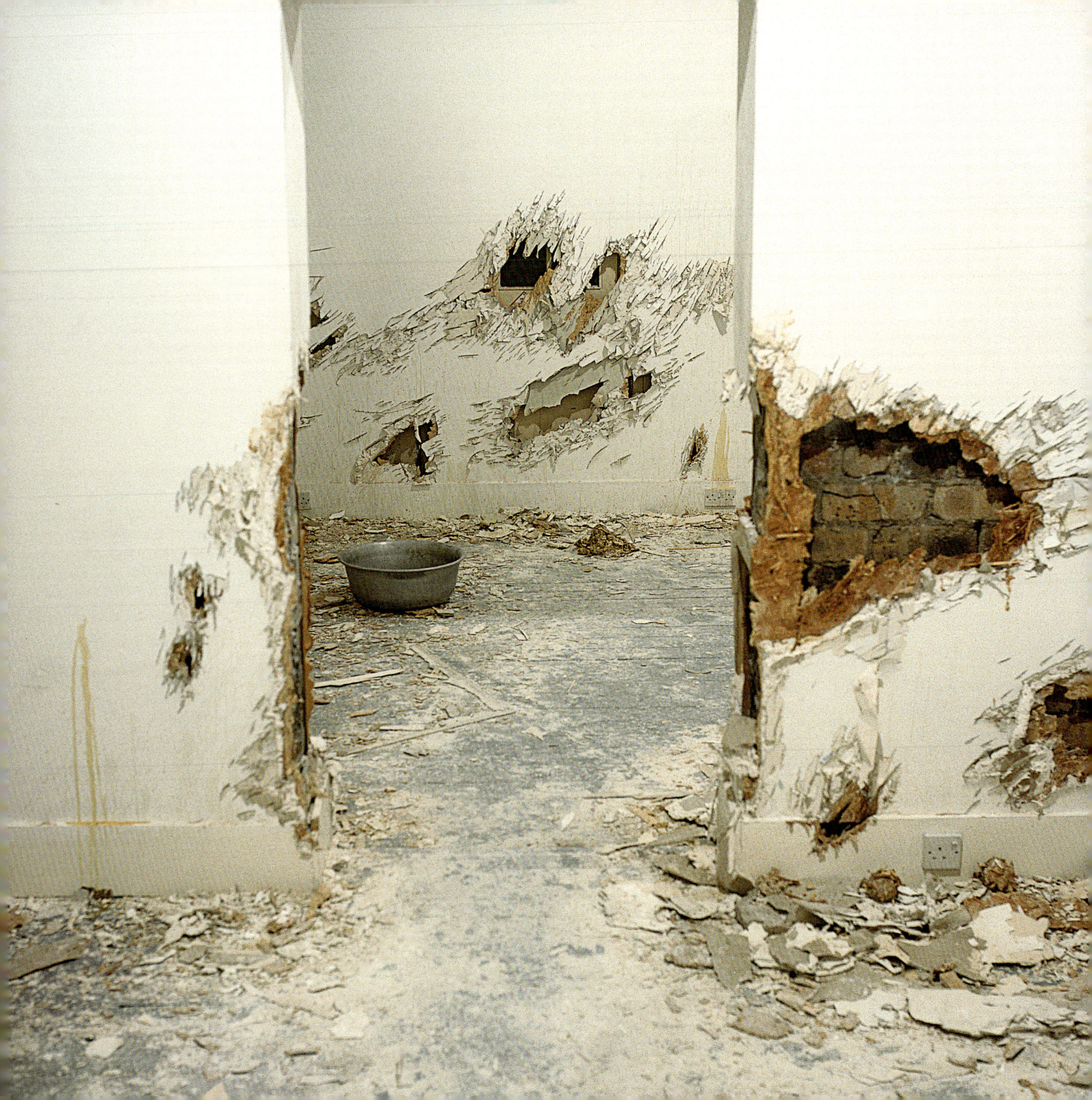

previous spread
The Coral Reef, **2000**
left
To the Memory of H.P. Lovecraft, **1999**
right
Barker Ranch, **1996**

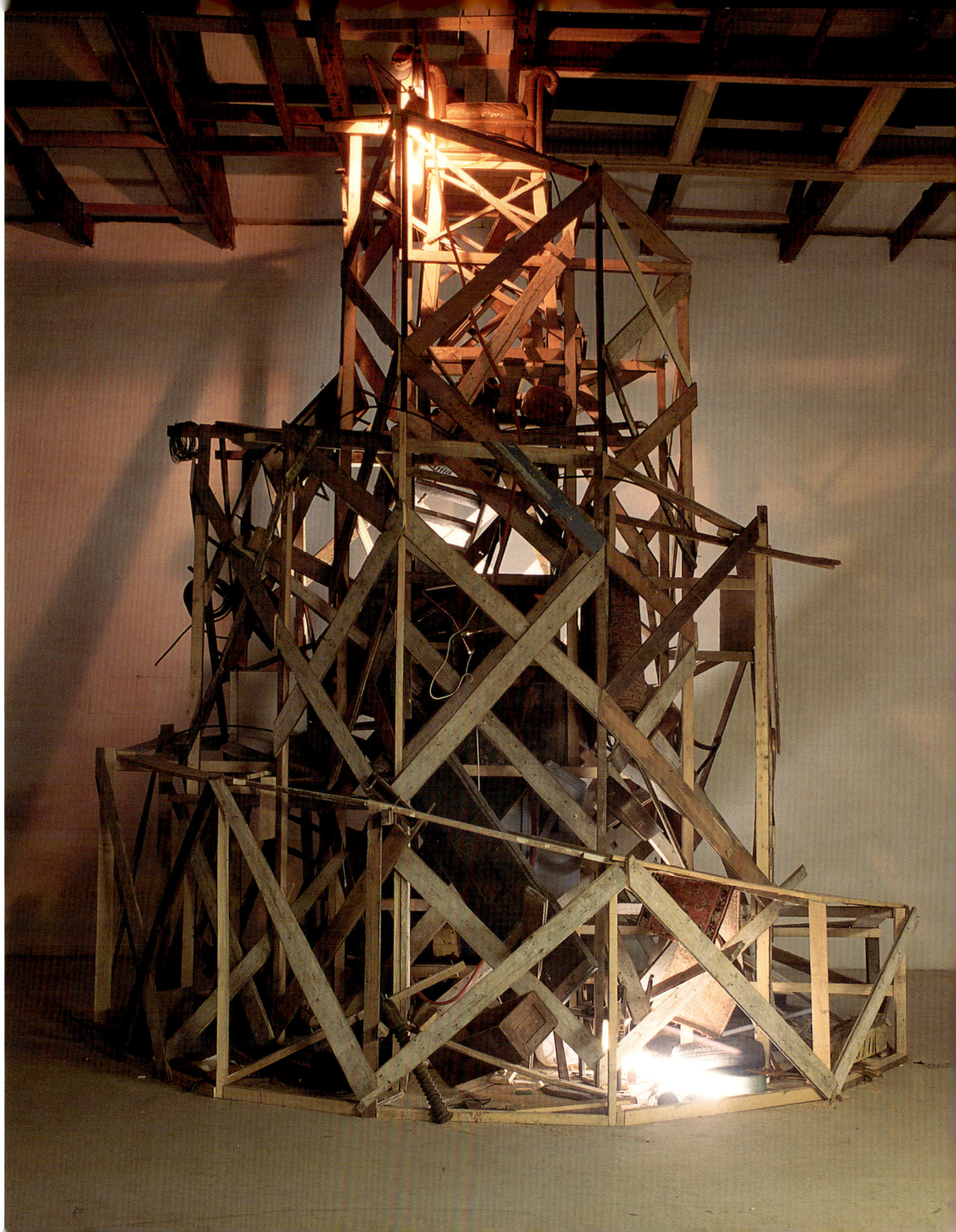

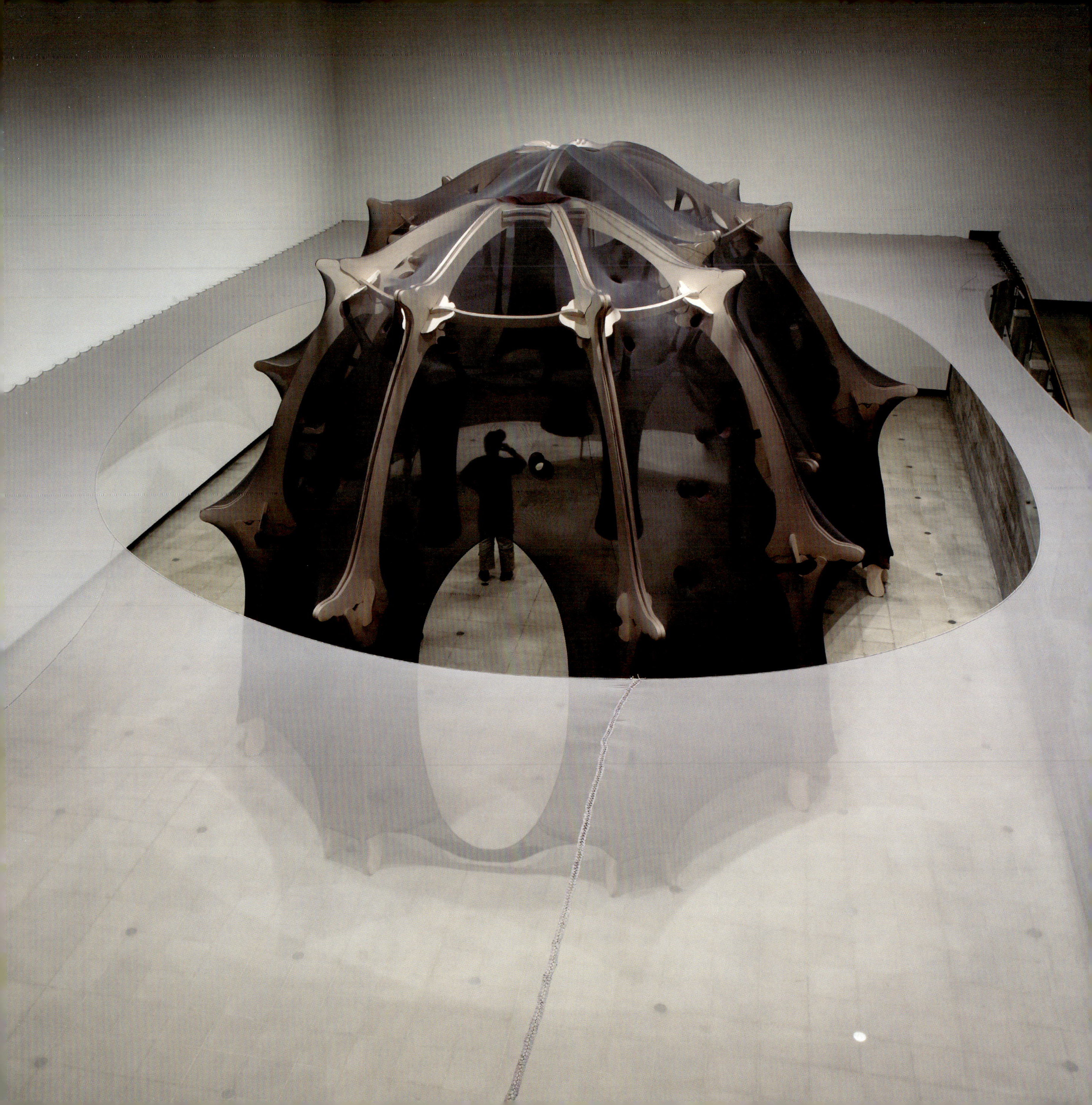

Life fog frog...Fog frog, **2008**

ERNESTO NETO

PAULO HERKENHOFF

Brazilian artist Ernesto Neto's architecture is based on the anatomical essential. 'It is a mammal architecture, only skin and bones, with no stuffing', says the artist about his new work, *Life fog frog...Fog frog*, for The Hayward's *Psycho Buildings* exhibition.[1] *Life fog frog... Fog frog* creates a spatial and sensory labyrinth for viewers to explore, and a transparent screen captures the actions of the public within. A low ceiling of transparent Lyric fabric divides the gallery into two layers, and the pressure of the transparent fabric on the wooden structure completes the corporeal architecture of a two-room Being — head and trunk (and 'subjective and implied limbs', as the artist says). Allowing us to simultaneously glimpse both internal and external structures, Neto's installation links biology and architecture with spaces that solicit social interaction.

The engineering of Neto's work is based on the conversion of physical laws into diagrams of movements — porosity, elasticity, fluid mechanics or gravity — and his materials rely on the potential of the viewer's imagination. In Neto's 1987 sculpture *Barra/bola (Bar/ball)*, a small rubber ball was pressured against a wall by an iron bar resting on the floor. Tension is attraction — there was a kind of harmony between the two surfaces. The sculpture was made by the bar's touch on the ball. To separate the objects — the bar and ball — would have meant no sculpture, a return to the ordinary. The poetic momentum in *Bar/ball* was the delicate touch between the mass of the objects and the velocity of the act that articulated them. Connection was the sculpture's ignition.

In Neto's corporeal architecture one can trace a link to neoclassical architectural utopias of the eighteenth century. According to French architect Claude Ledoux, if form evoked function, a whorehouse would have the shape of a phallus. Following the neoclassical ideal of order, Ledoux projected the *Ideal City* of Chaux in the form of a sphere. Likewise, architect Etienne-Louis Boullée proposed an enormous sphere for the *Cenotaph for Newton* (1784). Minuscule spheres formed the blood of Neto's *Leviathan Thot*, which was assembled in the Panthéon in Paris in 2006.

It is useful to distinguish the architecture of Neto's new work *Life fog frog... Fog frog* from the architectural work of the artist and sculptor Louise Bourgeois and the *Arte Povera* movement. In Bourgeois' work, the artist addresses themes of protection against abandonment, control or overcoming childhood traumas. Through her sculpture, she attempts to defend herself against repression, fear, solitude and existential complaints. In contrast to Bourgeois, however, Ernesto Neto does not operate with sublimation nor does he attribute an external symbolic value to the unique experience of each work. His spaces are based on collective sheltering, and the visitors to his works are able to share in a delicate game of desire.

The igloos of *Arte Povera* artist Mario Merz, begun in 1968, on the other hand, reiterate principles such as constructive paradigms, relations between nature and culture, the image of the nomad artist and the material as an anthropological index. But Neto doesn't corroborate the grammar of *Arte Povera*. If Merz's igloos reiterate transcendentalism, the sensuality of Neto's spaces is based on science, body politics and the immanent experience of sensorial pleasures.

In the ambit of forms, Neto places himself closer to the visionary architecture of Frederick Kiesler and his biomorphic shapes of buildings and furniture. Nevertheless, it is not biomorphism that constitutes the core of Neto's eroticism, but a participative sensorial perception. For Bourgeois, geometry is stability in the world, for Neto it's a path of the turbulences of the libido: the sculpture is an assemblage of energy. Its most productive relation with a constructive tradition is found in installations subsequent to Neoconcretism.

Neto's work should also be viewed in the context of twentieth-century Brazilian art and culture, which displayed a balance between experimental avant-garde and historical references. In 1928, Brazilian poet Oswald de Andrade published his *Manifesto Antropófago* (Cannibal Manifesto), which asserts that cultural emancipation can be achieved through an autonomous poetical language that absorbs other cultures within a Brazilian identity. 'Only anthropophagy unites us. [...] The only things that interest me are those that are not mine', wrote Andrade. The Brazilian post-war movement of Neoconcretism (1959–61), established by Hélio Oiticica, Amilcar de Castro, Lygia Clark, Lygia Pape and Franz Weissmann, reasserted the subjective in the field of concrete art. Influenced by the ideas of French philosopher Maurice Merleau-Ponty, Neoconcretism replaced mechanical geometry by the phenomenology of perception, and artists such as Clark and Oiticica worked with all of the senses — for instance, the olfactory qualities of spices and scents — to heighten the visual experience. Ernesto Neto continues in this tradition, often using spices to enhance the visitor's perception.

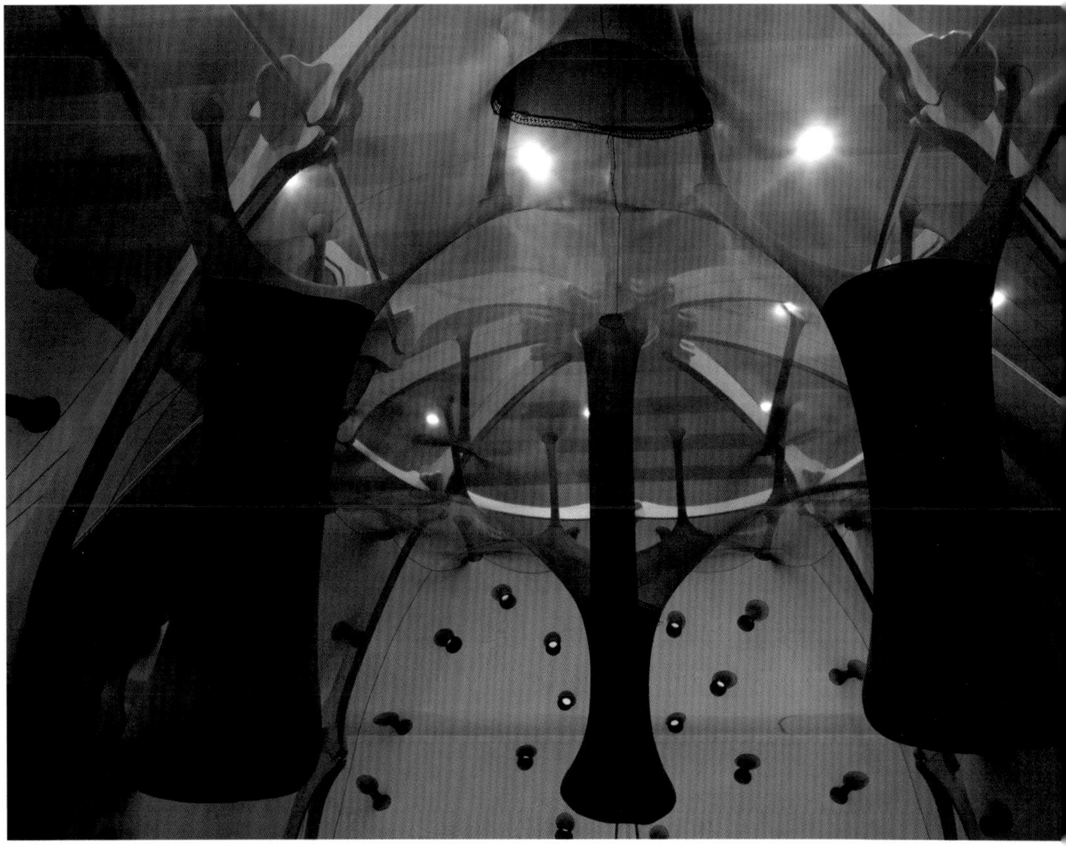

Neto's objects affirm desire and his architecture establishes pluri-relational experiences, like those between spheres and socks. His 'wheel of pleasures',[2] includes sensual games with shadows, soft volumes, wooden structural modules, colour, scents, rumours and relations with music, shelter, words, hymens, transparency and tension of fabrics as excited skins — all senses are elated. More than sex appeal, his work constitutes diagrams of sexual drive confronting seduction. Neto erotises the architectural experience. In his art, he says, 'there is something of a feminine practice', nevertheless, 'through a masculine hand, I believe in masculine-feminine continuity.'[3]

Translated by Renato Rezende

1 Conversation with the artist, 2 August 2008.
2 This is a reference to a homonymous work by Lygia Pape.
3 Email from the artist, 26 June 2006.

Life fog frog...Fog frog, **2008**

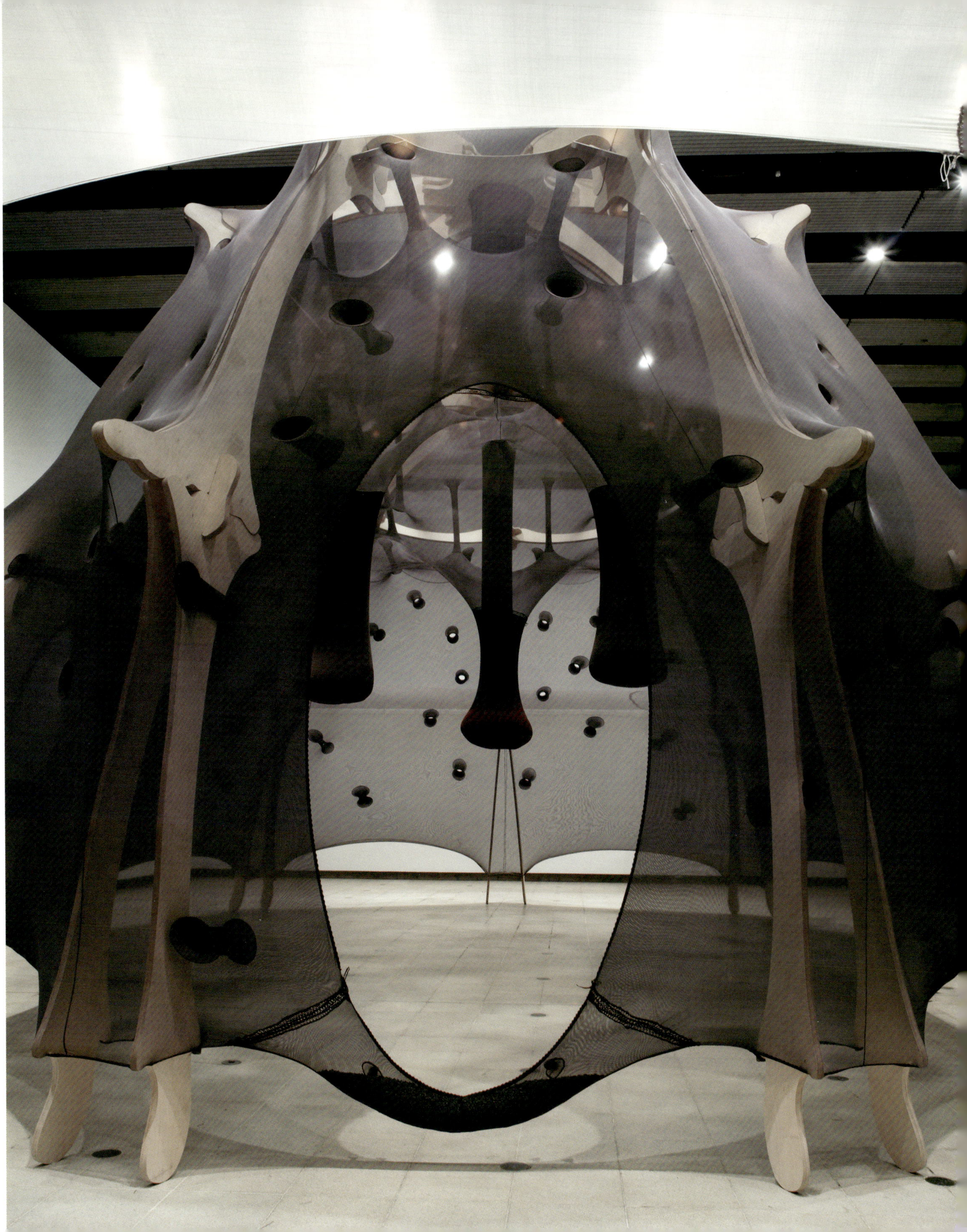

previous spread
The Creature, **2006**

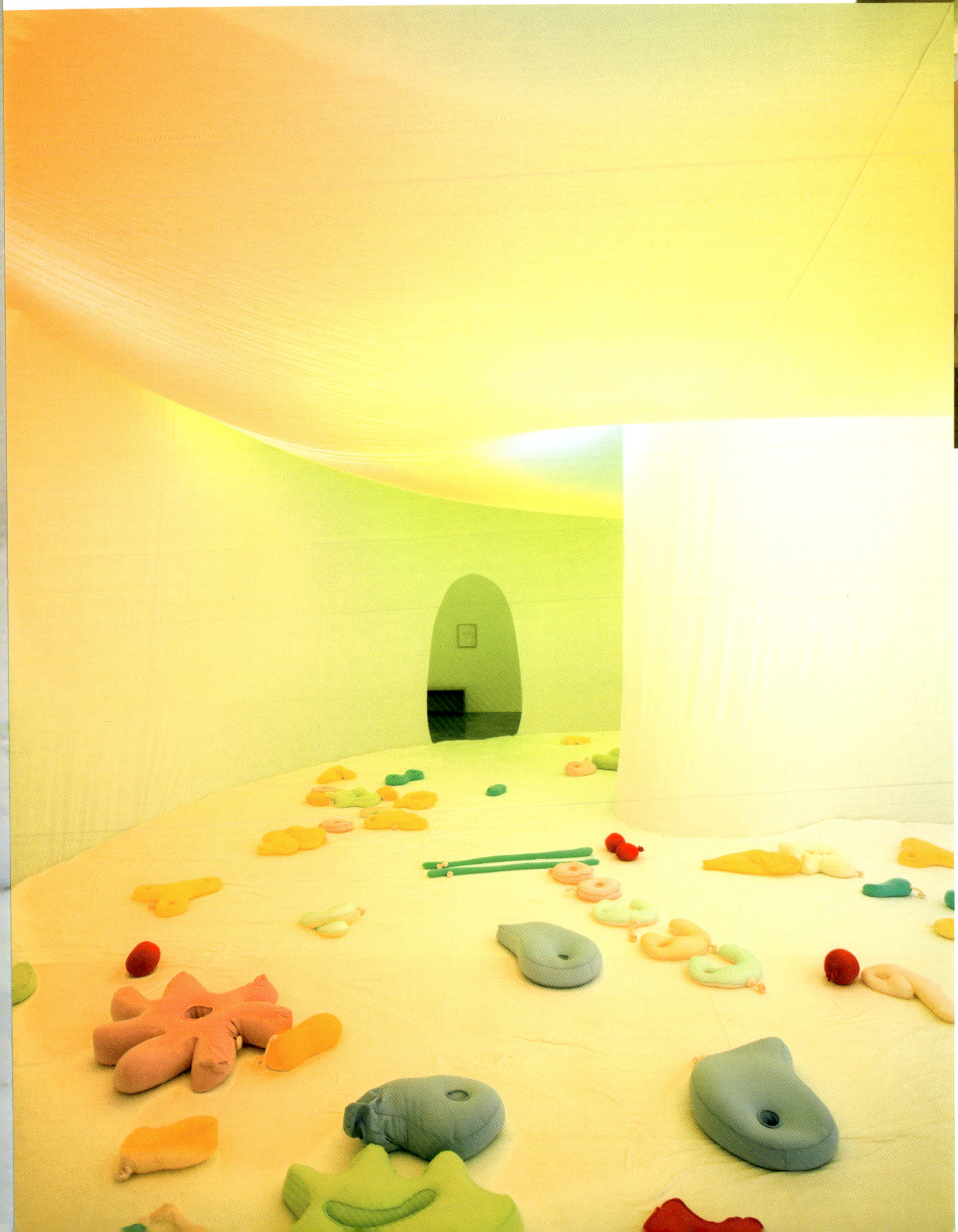

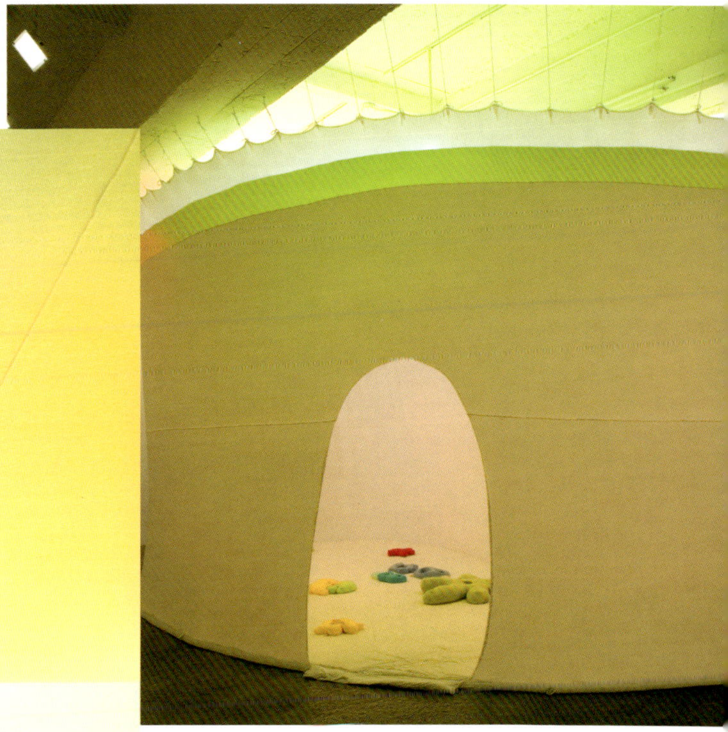

From What Are We Made, Made Of Of, **2006**

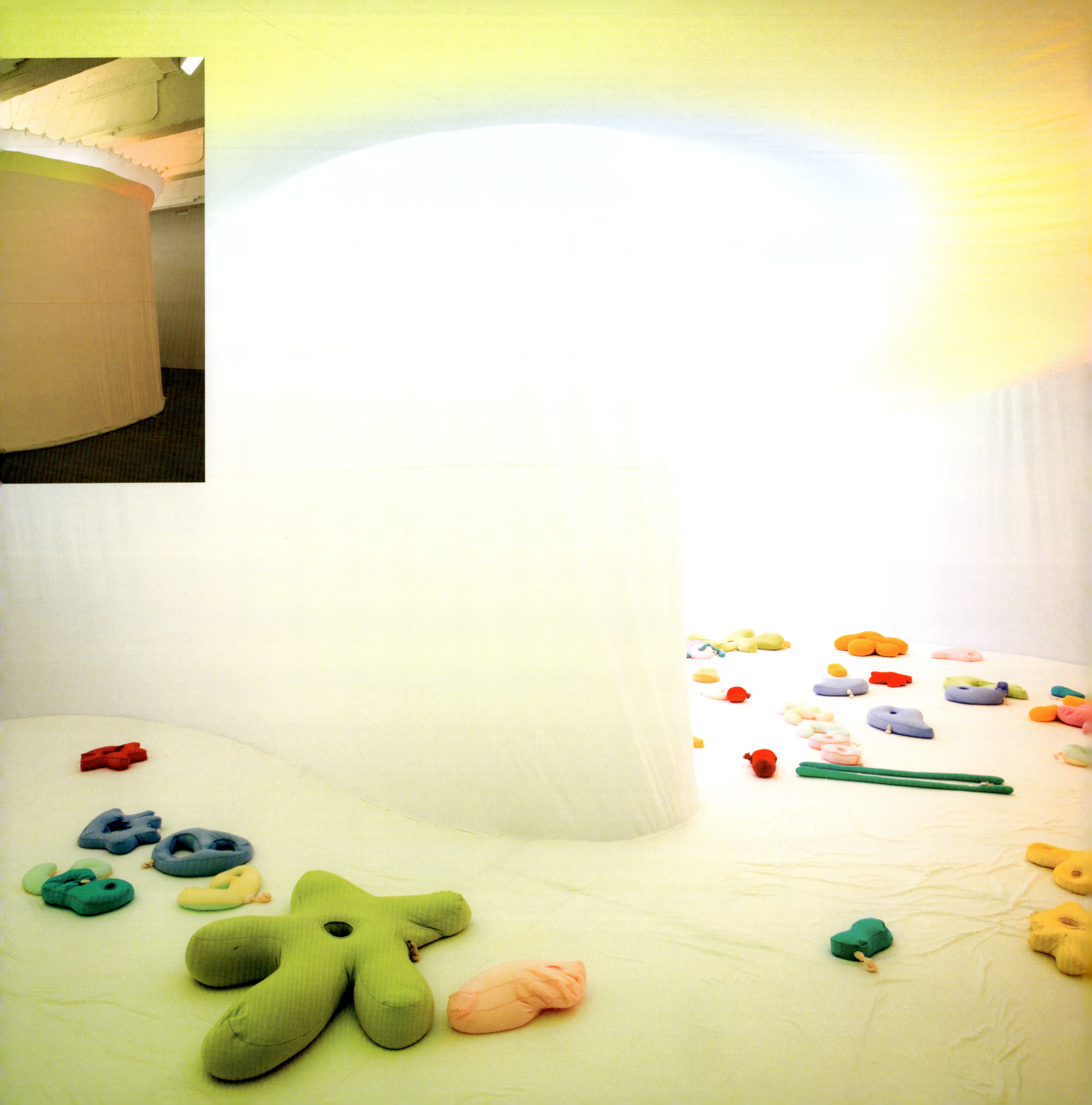

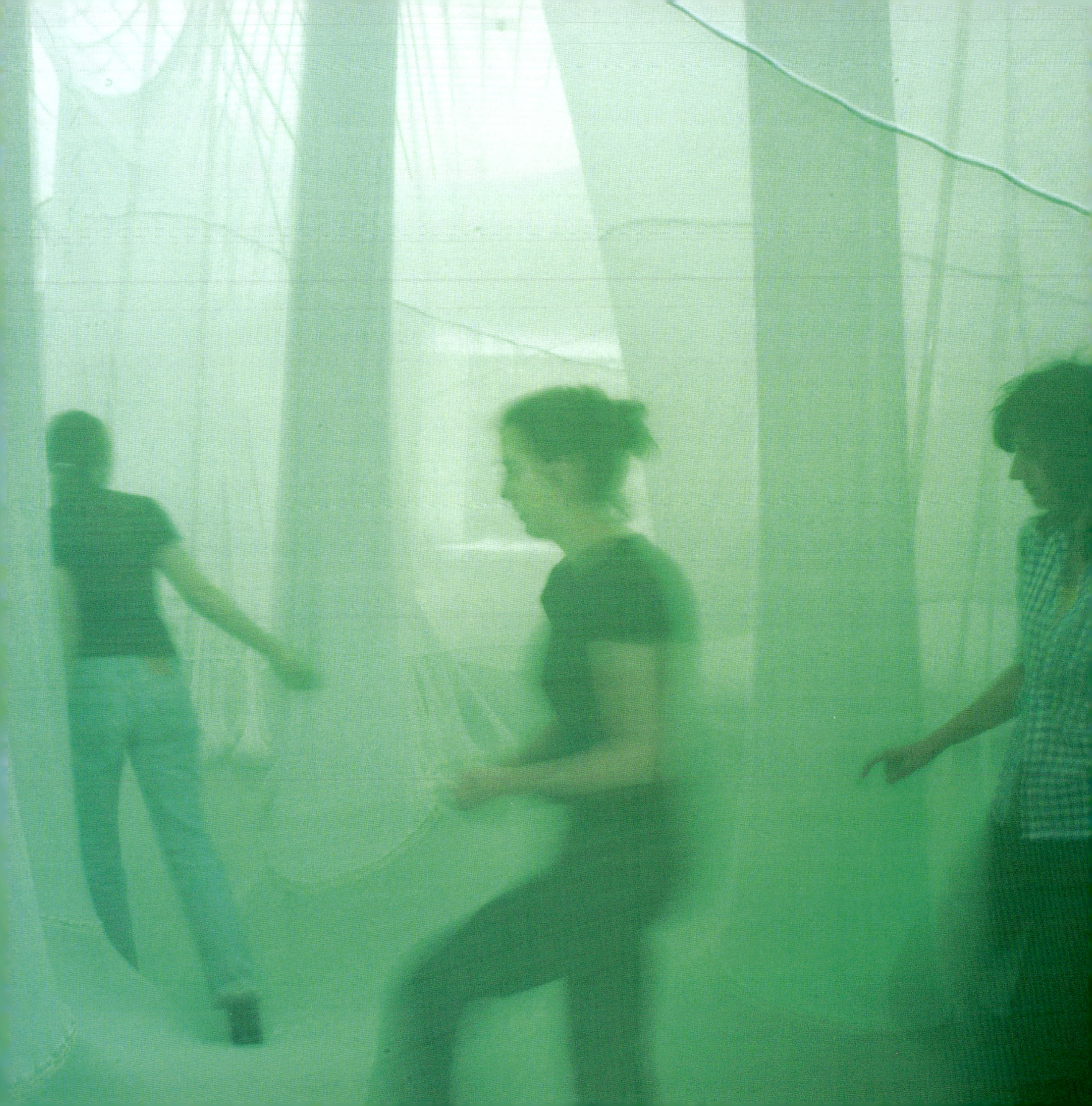

Cellula Nave. It happens in the body of time, where truth dances, **2004**

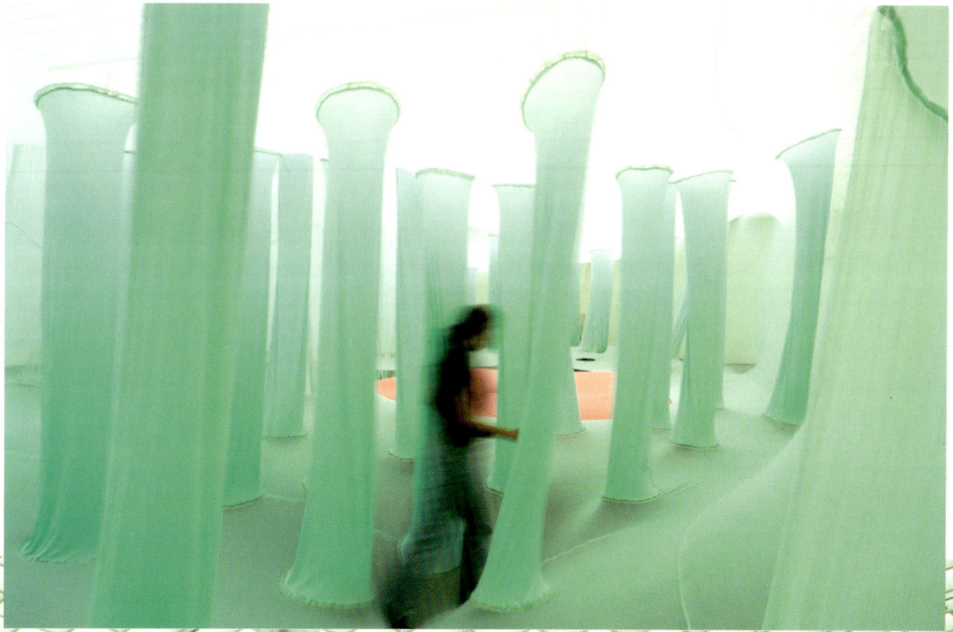

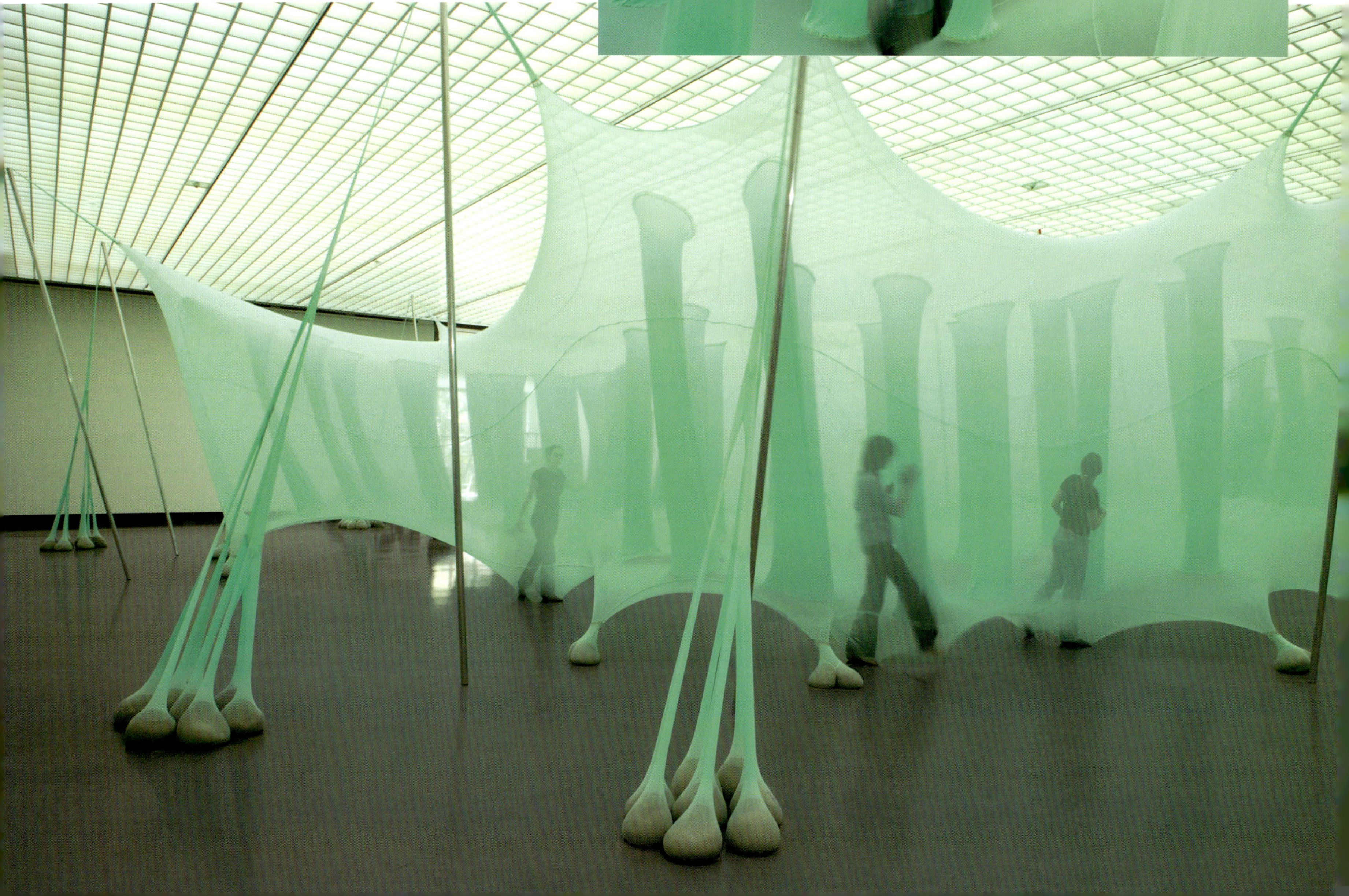

Walking in Venus Blue Cave, **2001**

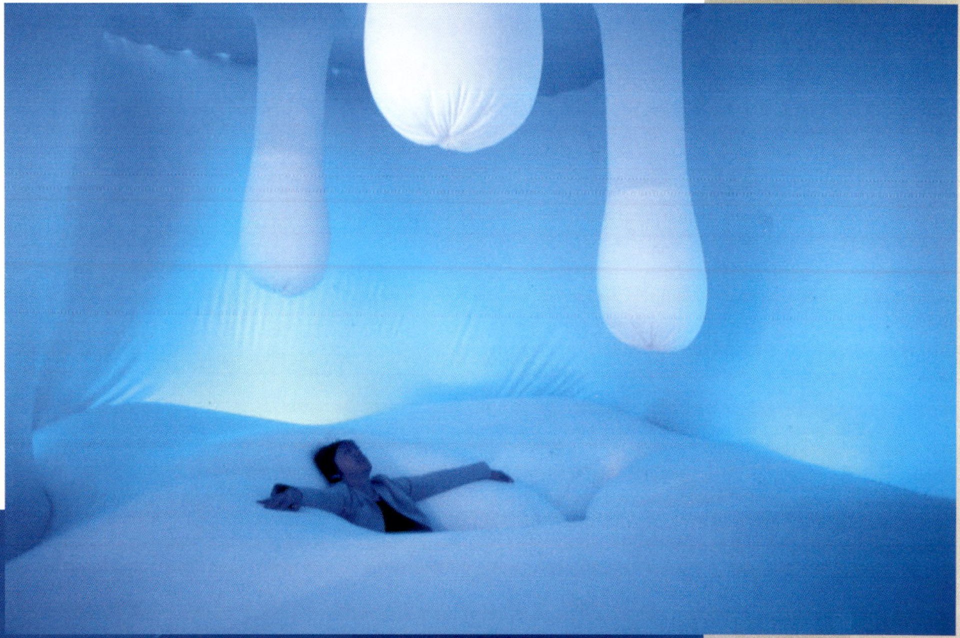

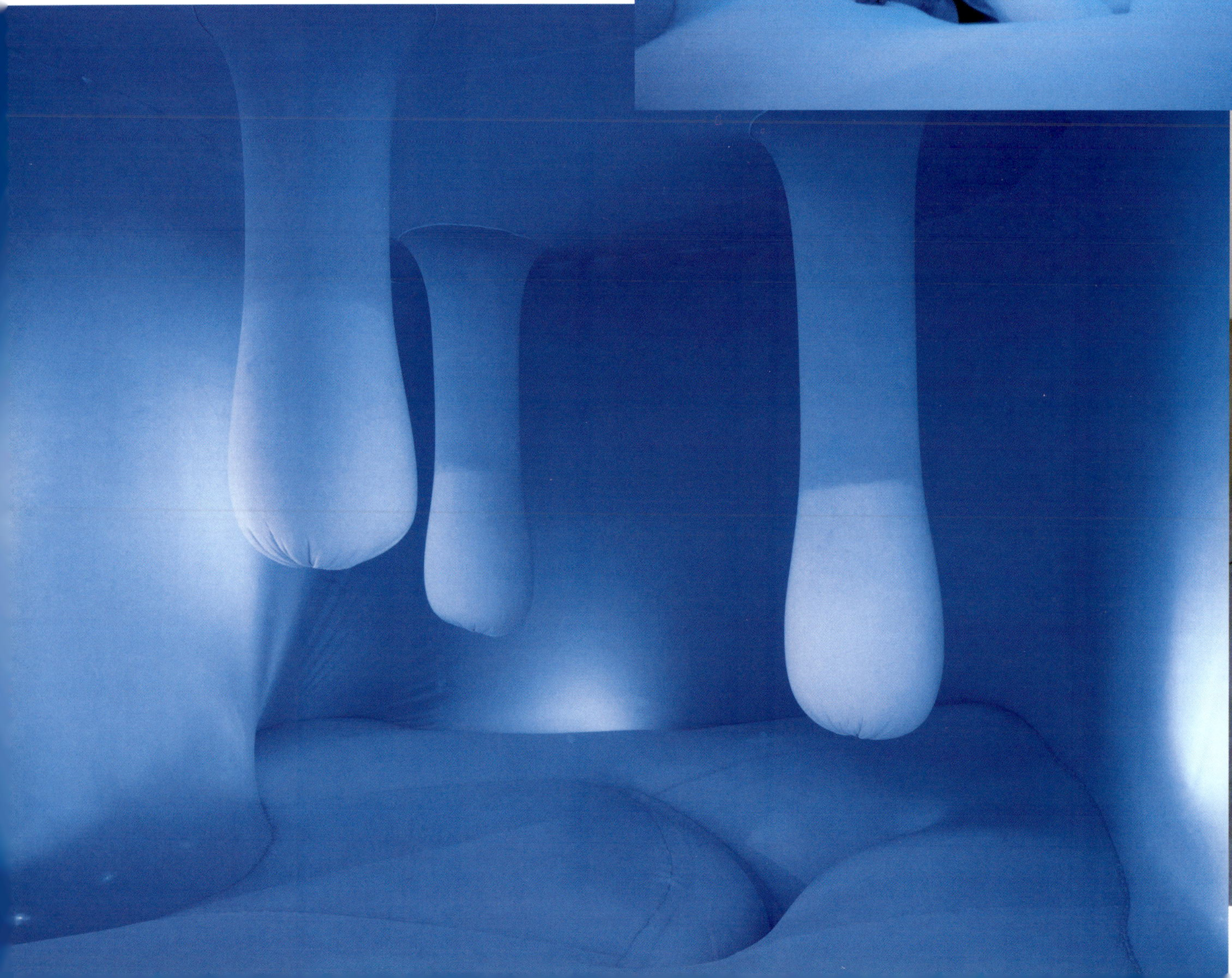

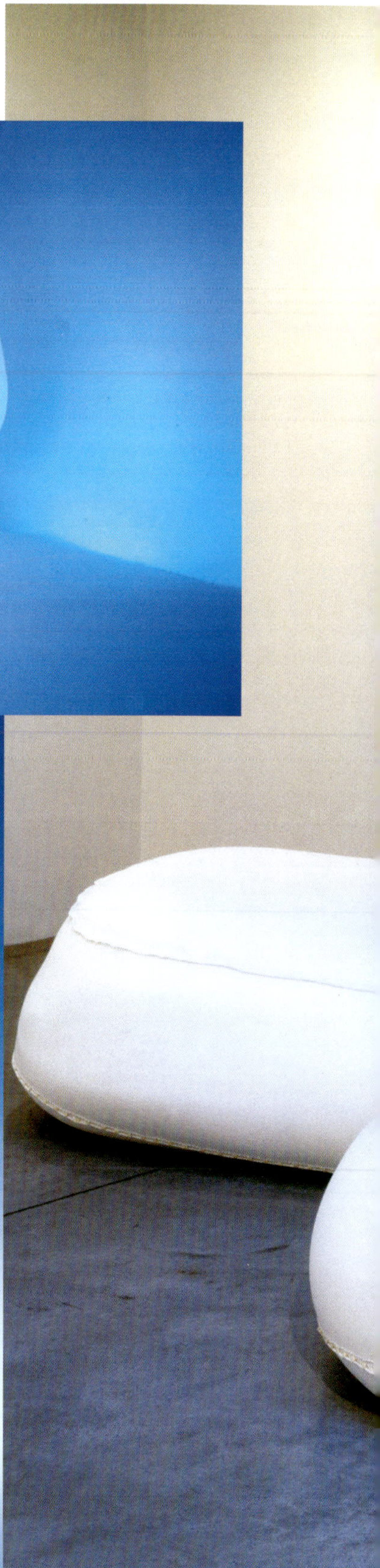

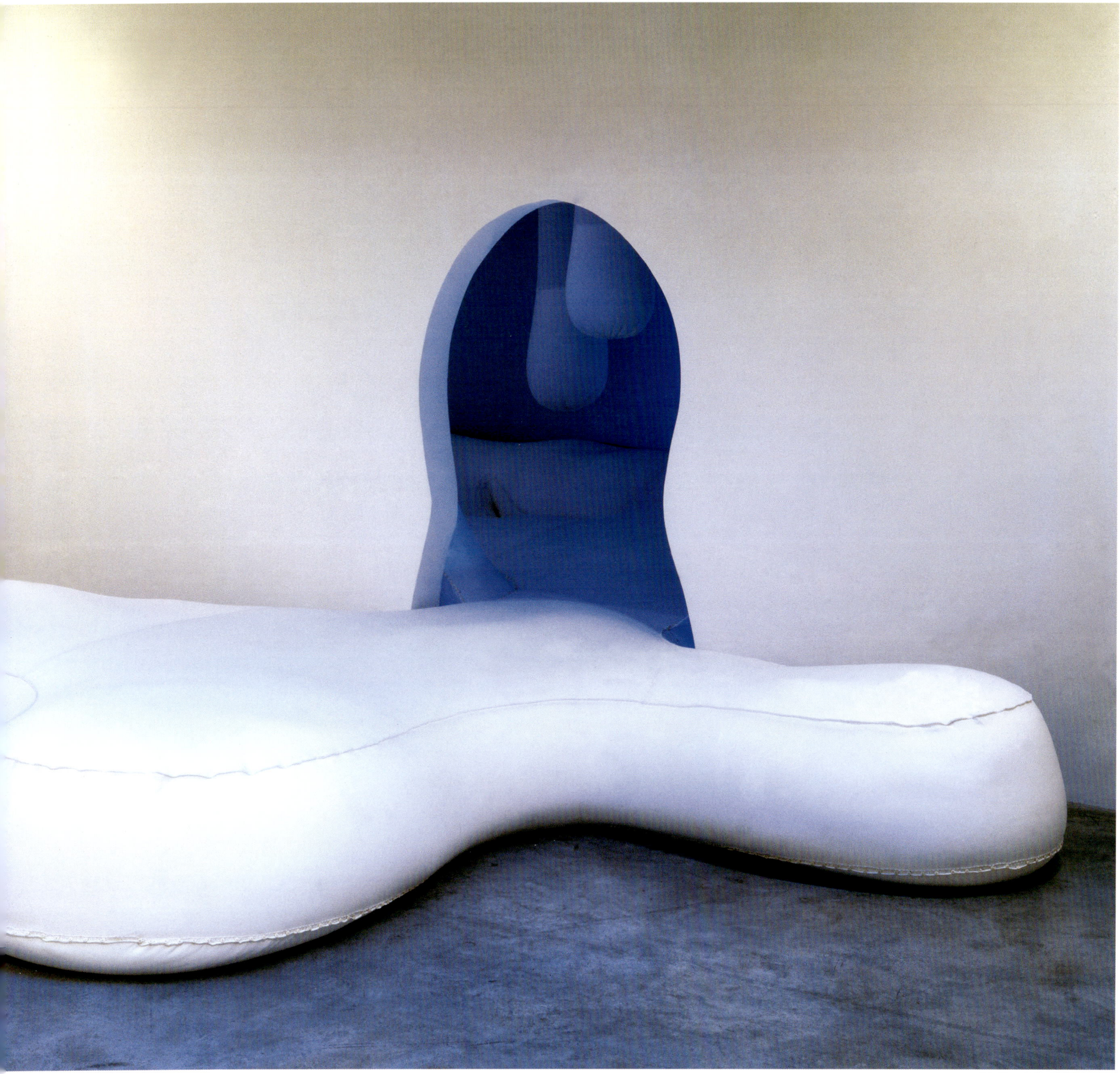

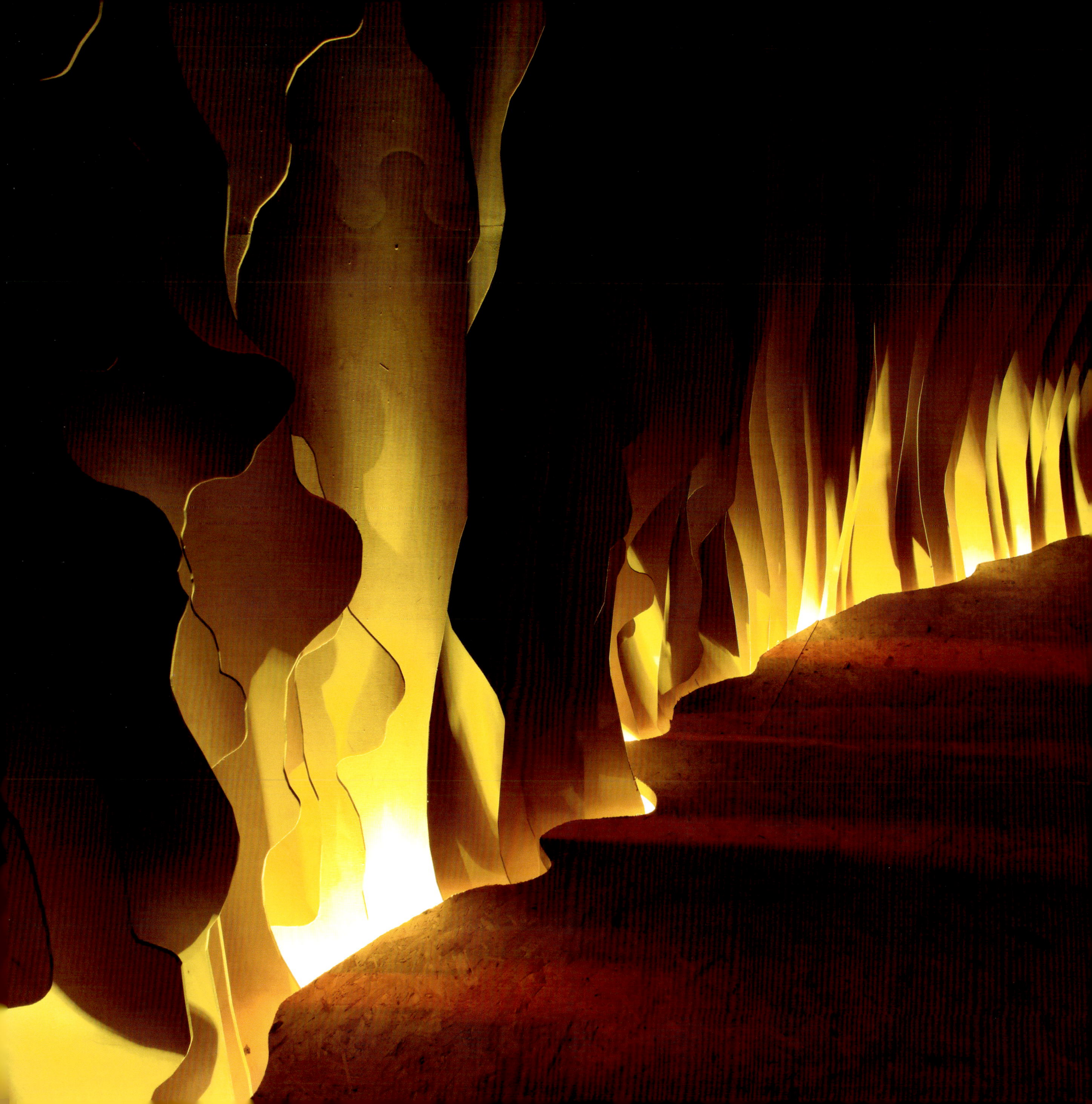

TOBIAS PUTRIH

FRANCESCO MANACORDA

Tobias Putrih's practice occupies the slippery territory between architectural planning and surrealist prototype. His interest focuses on movie theatres conceived as complex machines that facilitate the access to alternative realities. Putrih has produced scale models of cinemas, preparatory drawings of their interiors, and sculptures testing different construction materials. This ongoing artistic and quasi-scientific research sometimes leads to full-scale functioning prototypes, such as the artist's work *Venetian, Atmospheric* (2007). Putrih's work can be situated in the tradition of architectural experiments with expanded cinema and the cinematic apparatus inaugurated by Buckminster Fuller and Frederick Kiesler, later carried out by experimental artists and filmmakers such as Chris Marker, Stan Vanderbeeck and Anthony McCall.

Similar to the filmic experience, Putrih's prototypes swing between desire and reality, idea and function, existing and imagined situations. His sculptures often employ materials that belong to the vernacular of model-making: cardboard, foam, tape and plywood. The artist links the negotiation between present reality and future possibilities that takes place in architectural planning to a similar combination of real and imaginary operating in the movie theatre. For example, in *Movie Tales* (2001), he custom-built models of cinemas dedicated to Robert Smithson, Frederick Kiesler, Herbert Beyer and Chris Marker. While in the sculpture *Roxy vs. Capitol* (2003), Putrih compared the different ratios of European and American movie screens, and with *Anthology (How to Make Cinema Invisible)* (2005) he built a curved screen meant to envelop the viewer entirely.

Initially conceived as the Slovenian pavilion for the 2007 Venice Biennale, *Venetian, Atmospheric* is a real-scale prototype, a fully-functioning cinema used to screen other artist's films. The project was inspired by the work of the architect John Eberson, the original inventor of the 'atmospheric cinema'. These were movie theatres, popular in the 1920s, built to generate the illusion of sitting outdoors in an exotic location while watching a film — thus doubling the confusion between reality and fiction. Their ceilings were white domes onto which special lights projected a canopy of moving clouds in the nocturnal sky, and in-built small twinkling lights simulated constellations. The sidewalls were theatre-like sets faking traditional buildings overlooking a public square. In more than 100 cinemas, Eberson constructed a variety of fantasy scenarios, including an Andalusian village, a Persian palace with a real fountain, and a Venetian *campo* — as in the Paradise Theatre, in The Bronx, New York, which was the inspiration for Putrih's monumental sculpture.

Putrih's *Venetian, Atmospheric* restages the transitions between degrees of illusion obtained by Eberson's atmospheric dream machines. Its exterior is a forest of scaffolding holding a white curtain that can be opened to reveal the inside. The exterior structure and skin are reminiscent of a theatre's backstage, while the inner structure is similar to an elegant biomorphic rococo cave. Its walls are composed of a sequence of horizontal wooden strips oriented toward the screen, similar to an oval-shaped Venetian blind turned on its side. The artist traced the outlines of every strip on the chiaroscuro produced by the baroque features depicted in an original photograph of the Paradise Theatre's interior. His ceiling also functions as an additional screen onto which stars and clouds are projected. When the curtain is open, the spectators can see the outer world filtering through the Venetian blind strips. Visitors are invited to sit in this 'starting mode' and, before the film projection starts, they experience a sequence of events — the fading of the lights, the clouds projected onto the ceiling turning into twilight and then into a starred sky leading to total obscurity — that carefully stages their transition from reality into the world of film.

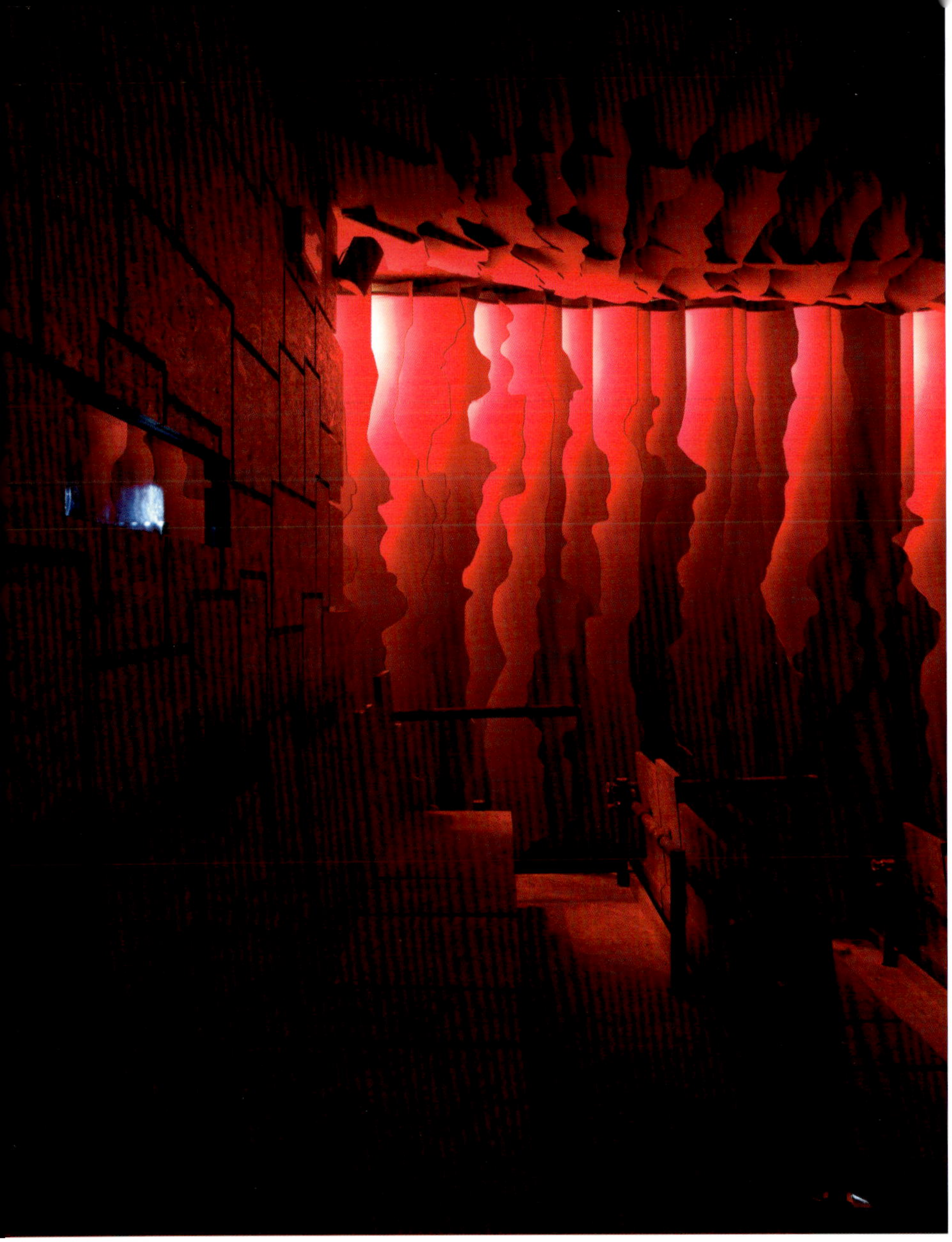

Venetian, Atmospheric, **2007**

In London, *Venetian, Atmospheric* will be installed on The Hayward sculpture terrace, facing Waterloo Bridge. Visitors will be able to make use of it as a normal screening room, a satellite extension of The Hayward's exhibition space specially conceived to show artists' films and videos. This is the third occasion in which Putrih has built an architectural environment to host films by other artists. In 2005, he turned Thomas Dane Gallery in London into a biomorphic-shaped viewing room, entirely built in cardboard, where a small artist's film festival was held. In 2007, he designed a futuristic room exclusively to screen *La Jetée* (1962) by Chris Marker, a key influence for his practice and thinking. Like a science fiction movie, *Venetian, Atmospheric* transports the spectators into a different reality, translating cinematic techniques into the core of cinema architecture.

In Putrih's view, movie theatres are designed to hermetically block outer reality from interfering with the film's constructed universe. In atmospheric cinemas, even the situation in which the spectator sits is artificial and fictionalised, thereby lending degrees of veracity to the fiction on screen. Putrih's works facilitate the cross-fading between real and not-yet-real. They are thresholds connecting reality and the shadow world of artifice. Similar to Dan Graham's pavilions, the theatres and their screens operate as two-way mirrors lending and borrowing the status of reality from one side to the other. Rather than mere buildings, they are sophisticated machines, conceived to shift and reveal at once degrees of psychological illusion.

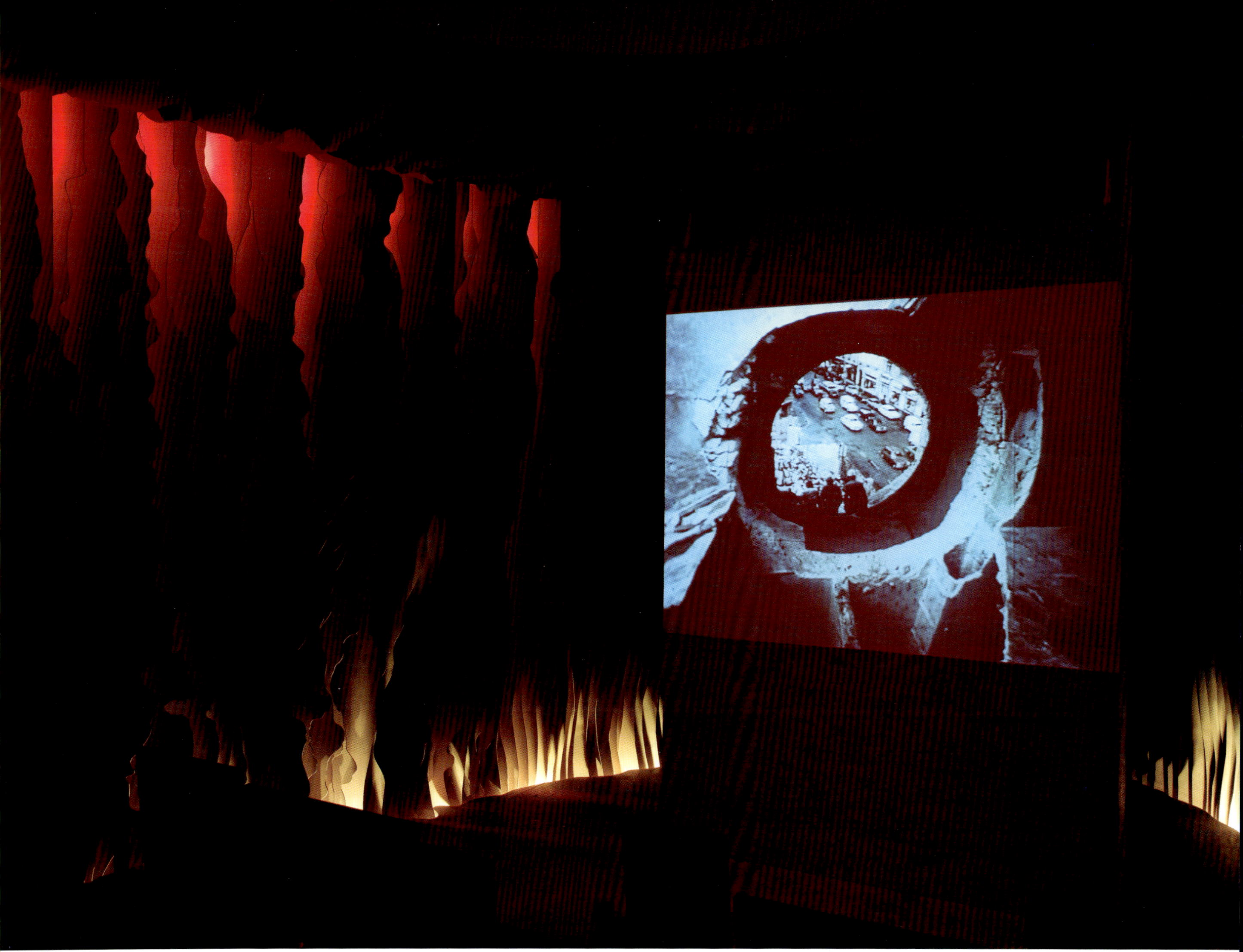

overleaf
Runa Islam and Tobias Putrih: Lost Cinema Lost, **2008**

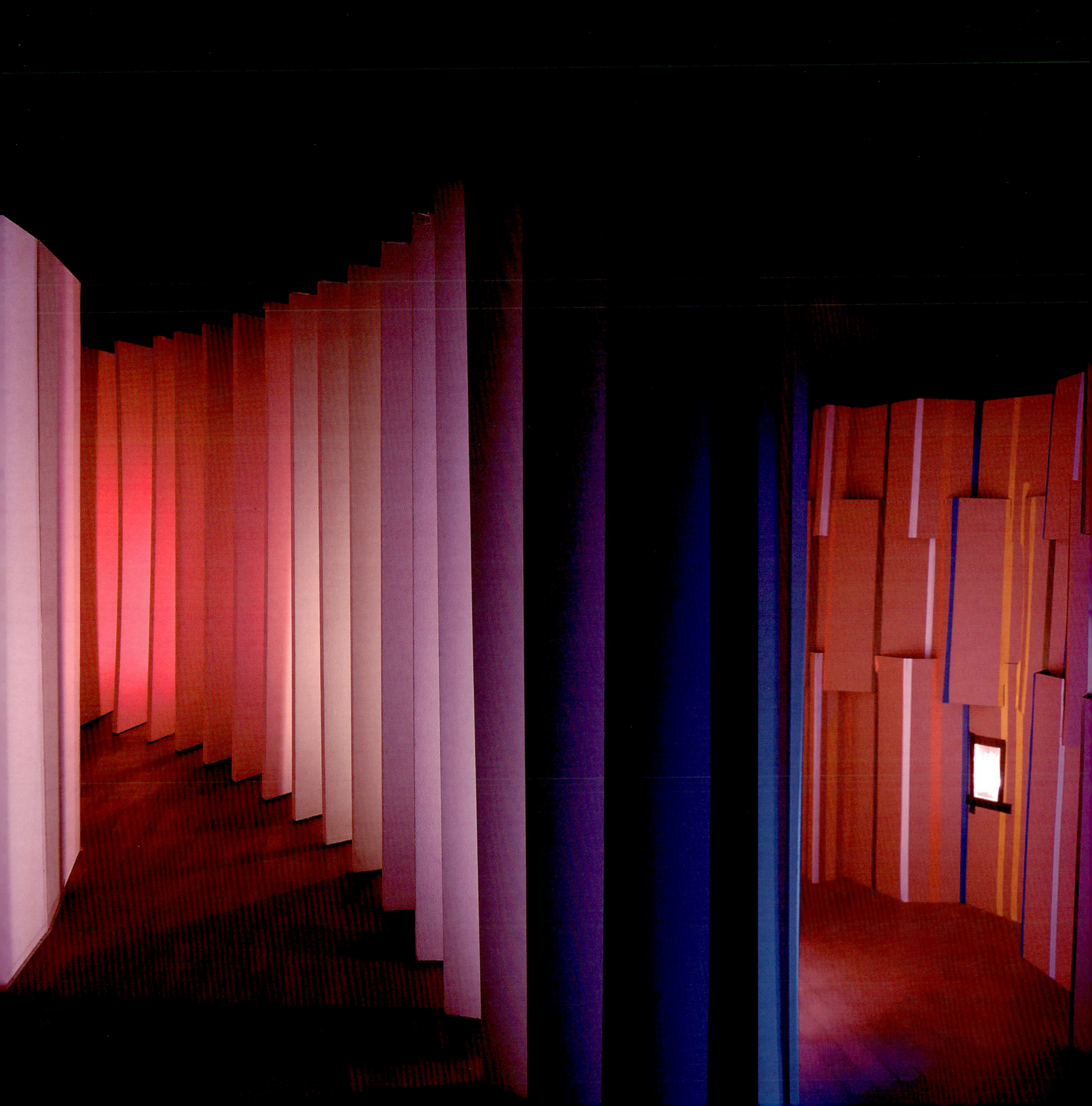

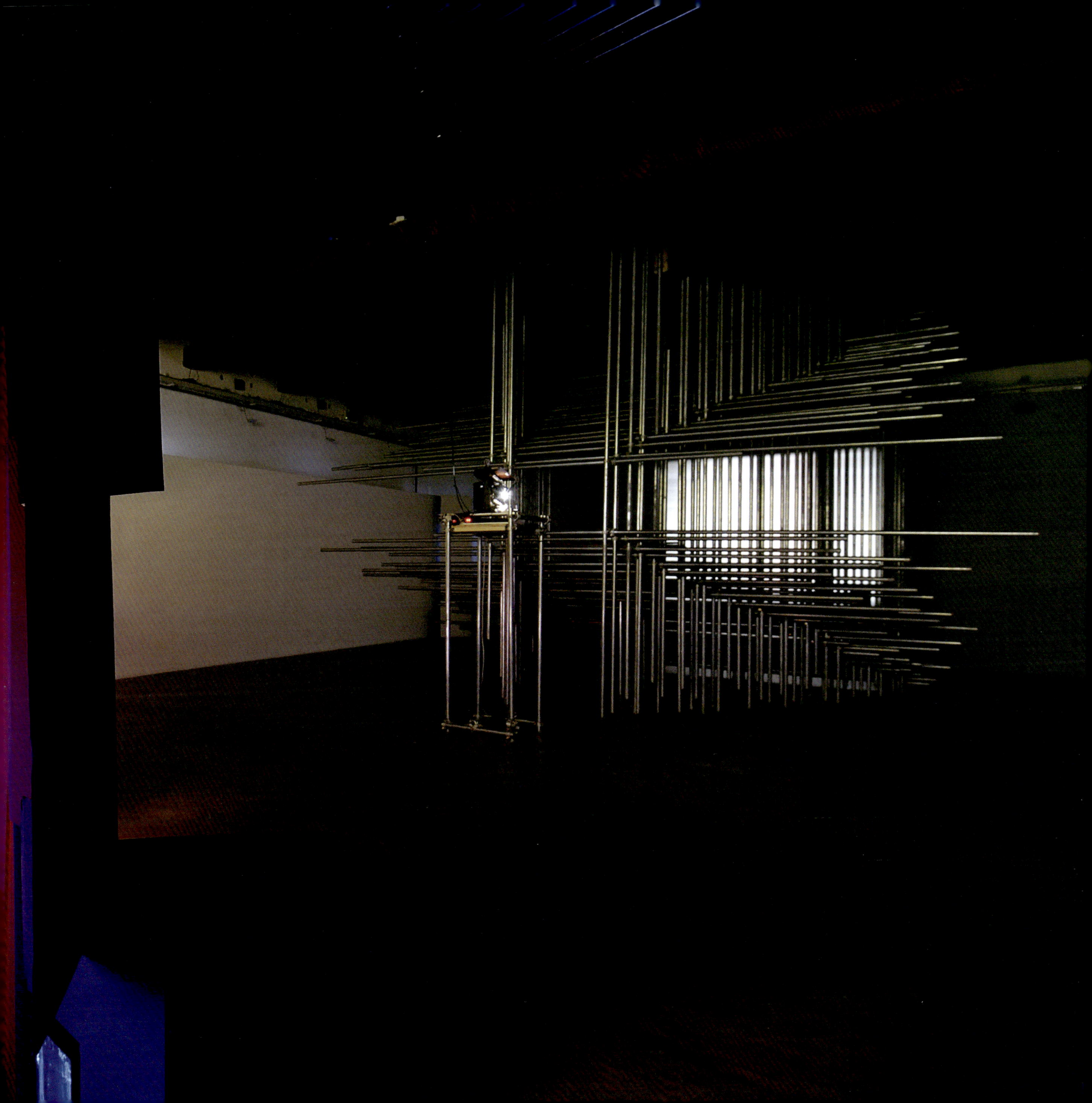

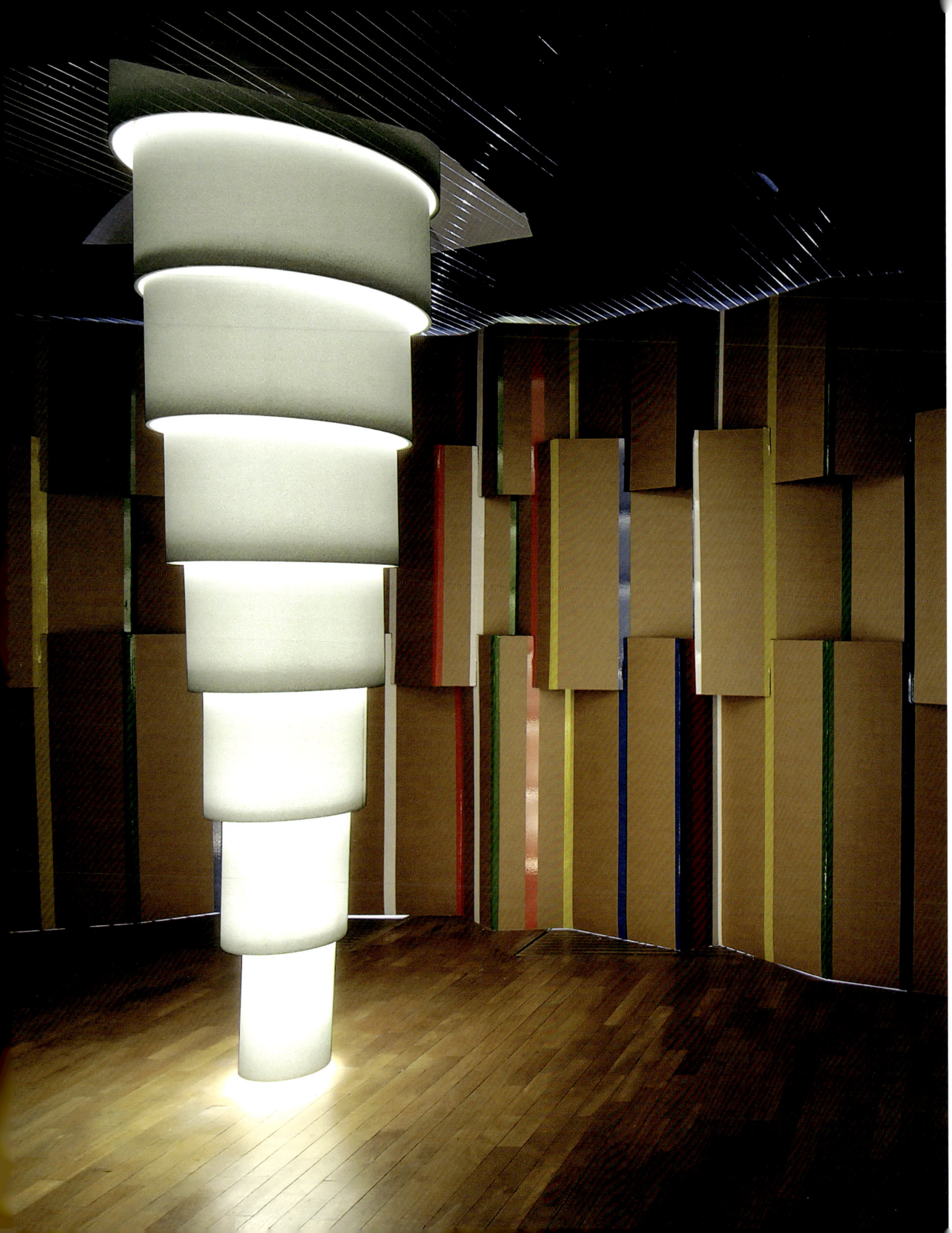

left
Lost Cinema Lost, **2008**
right
Cylinder, **2007**
overleaf
Studio at the Mudam, **2006**

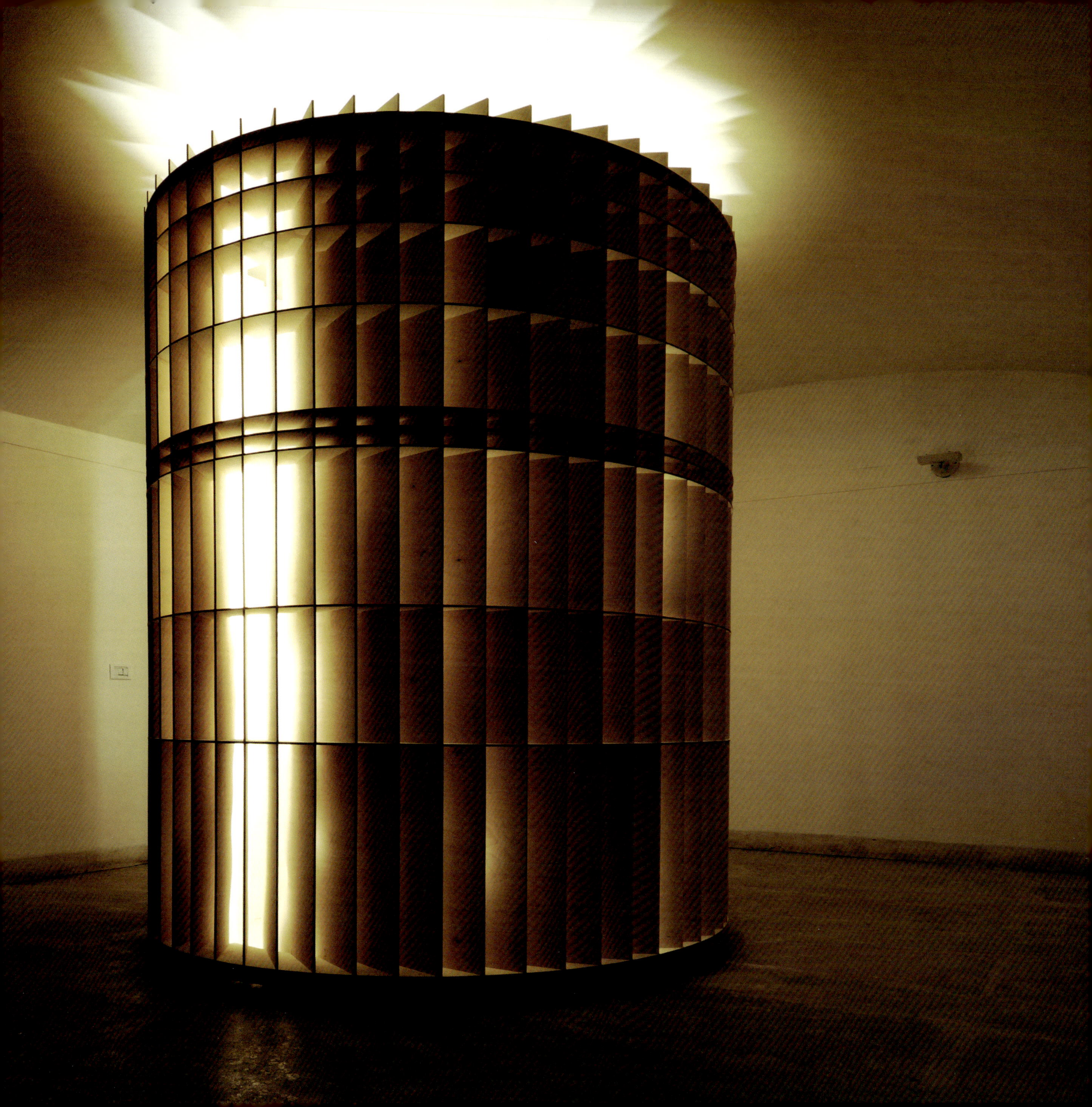

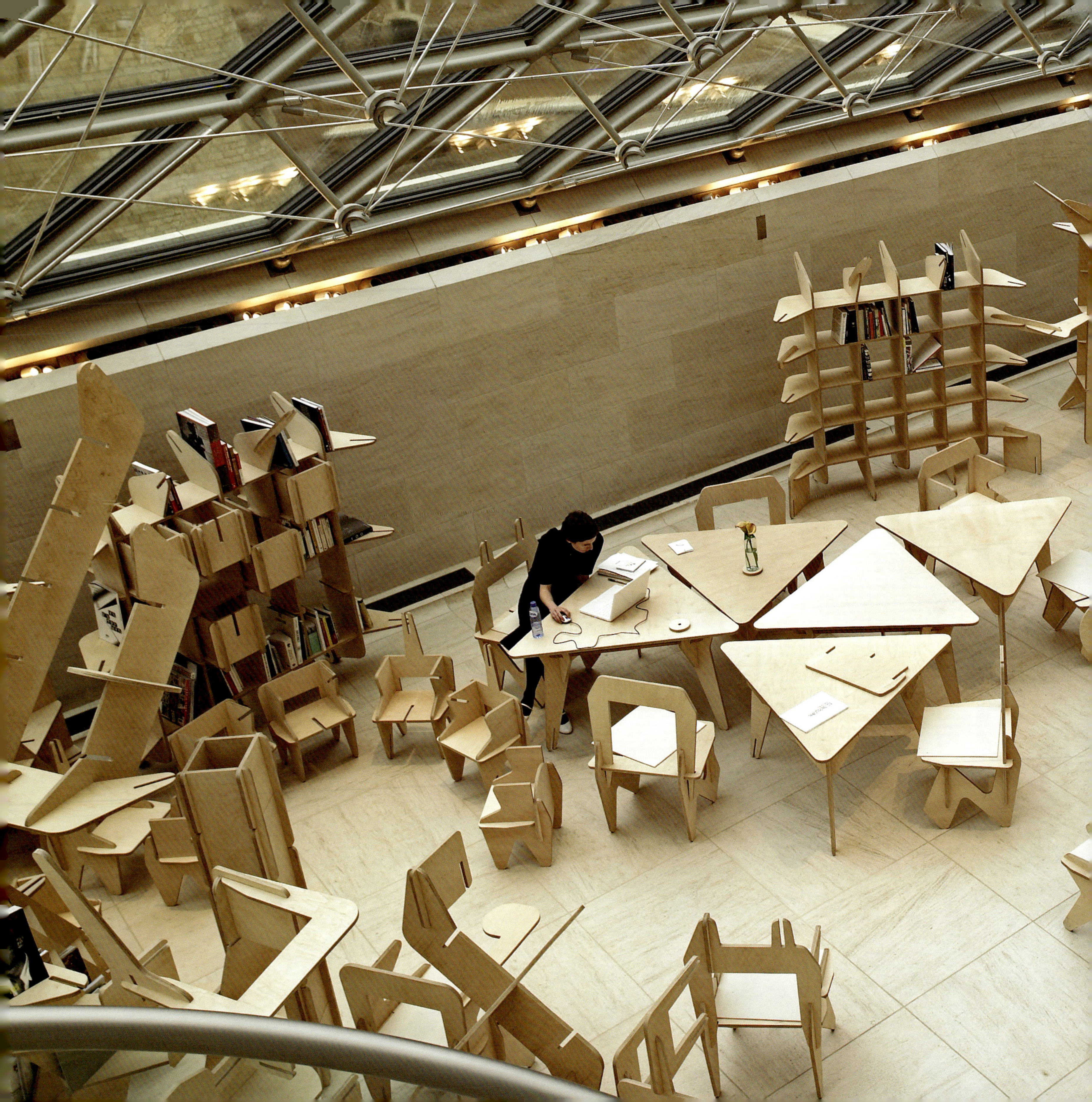

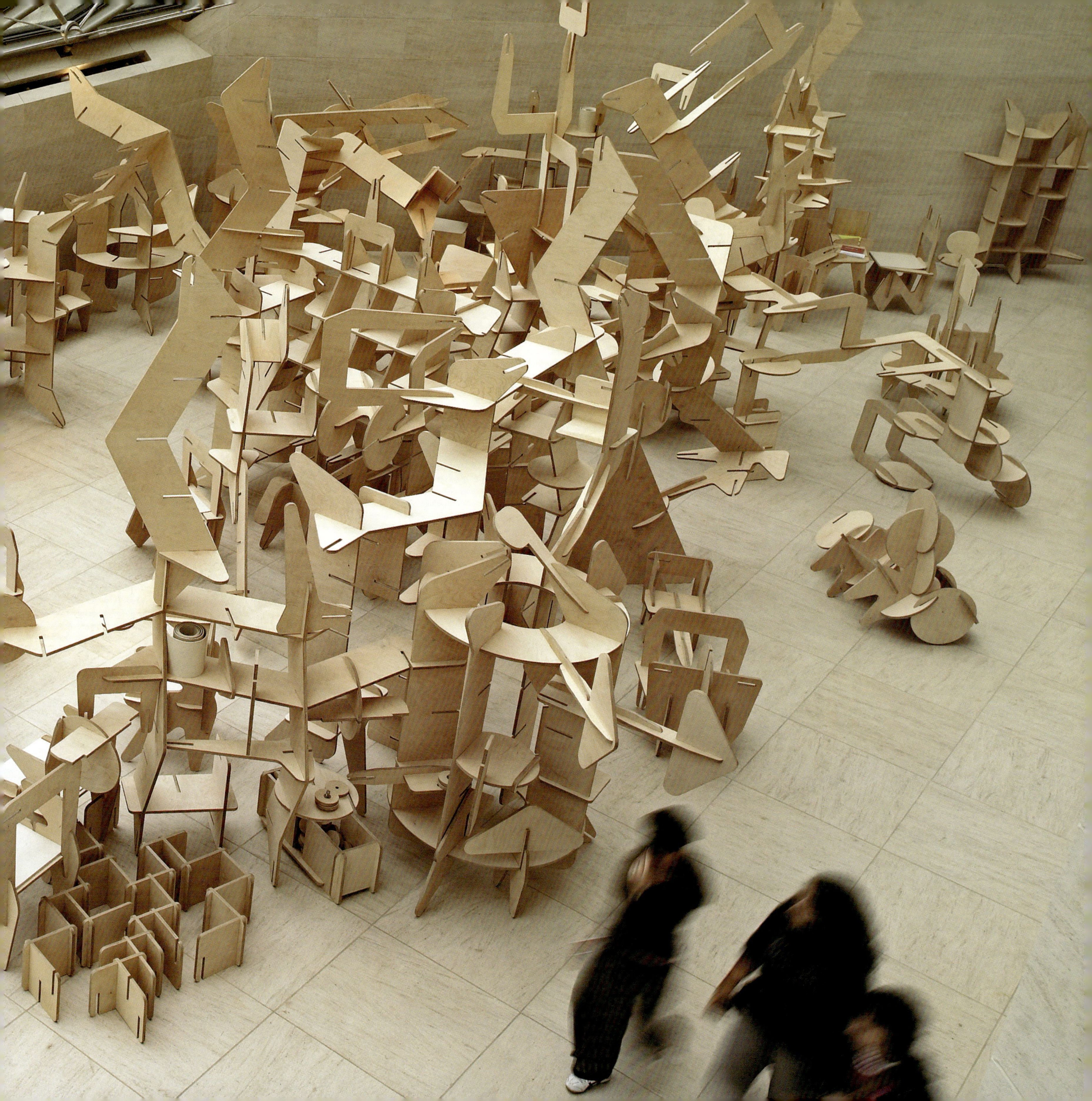

Anthology/Courthouse, **2005**

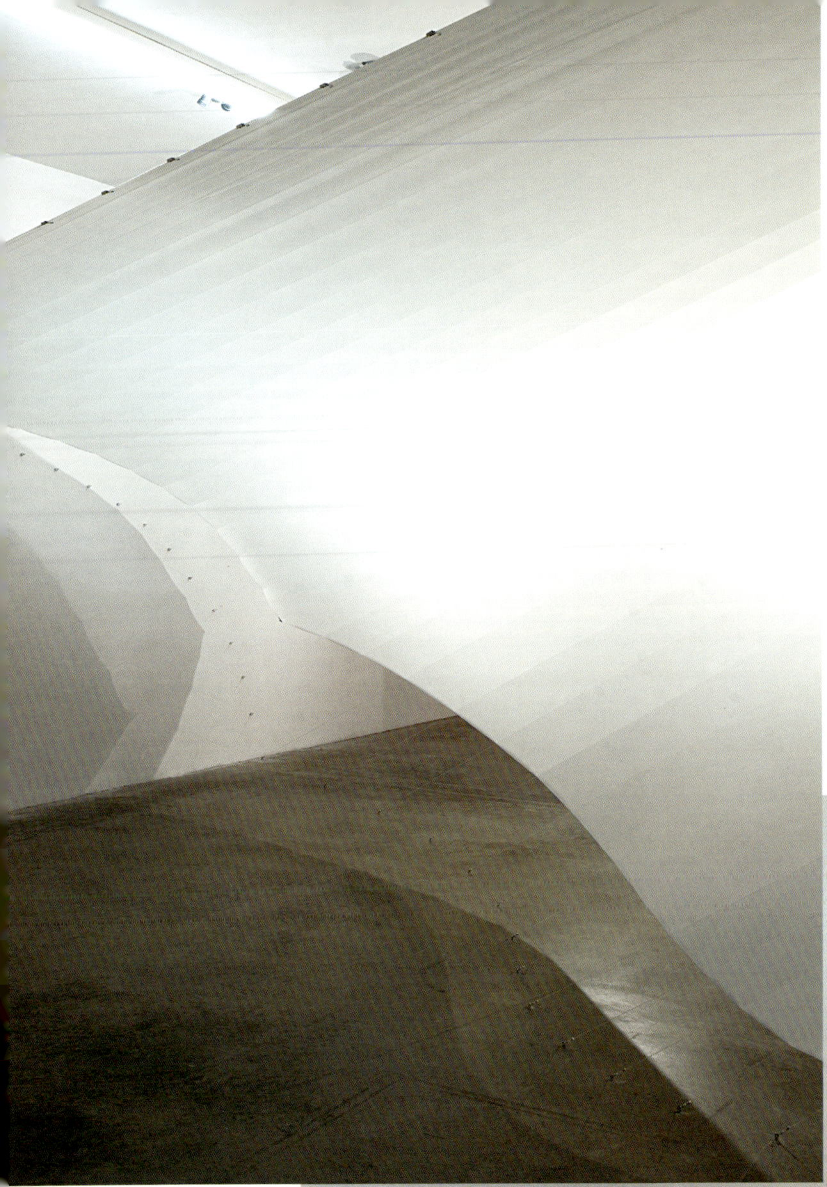

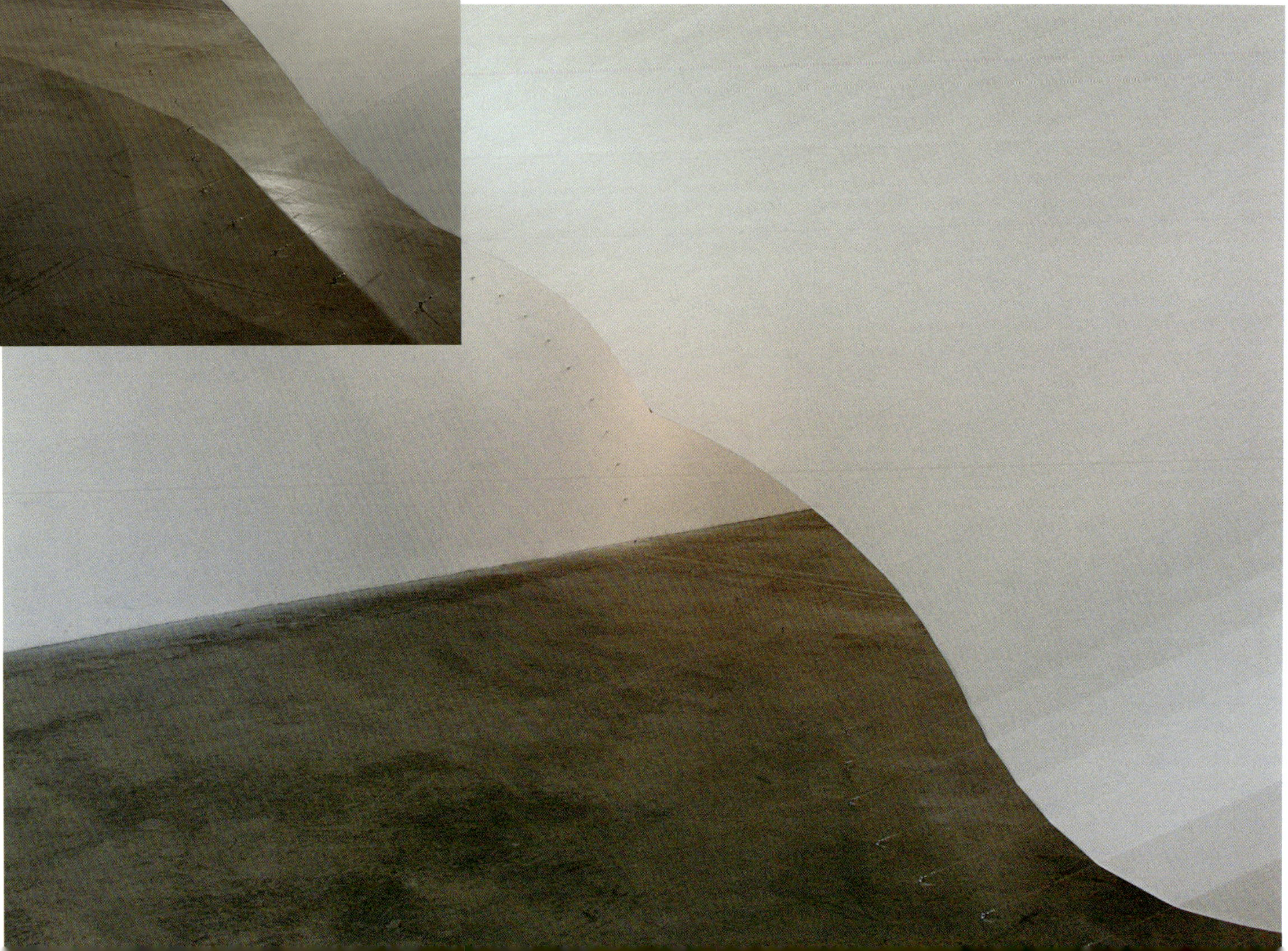

43,3 m, **2002**

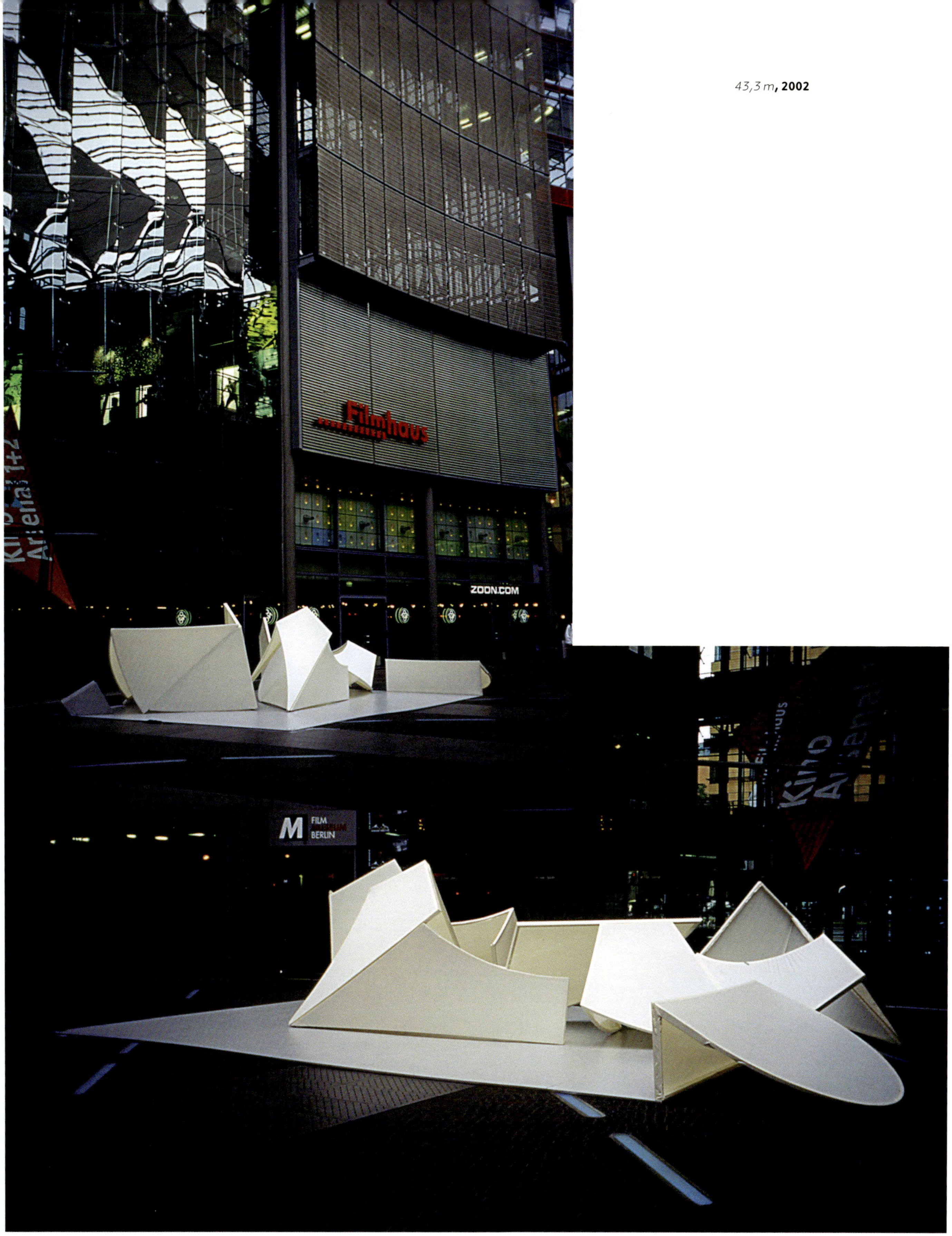

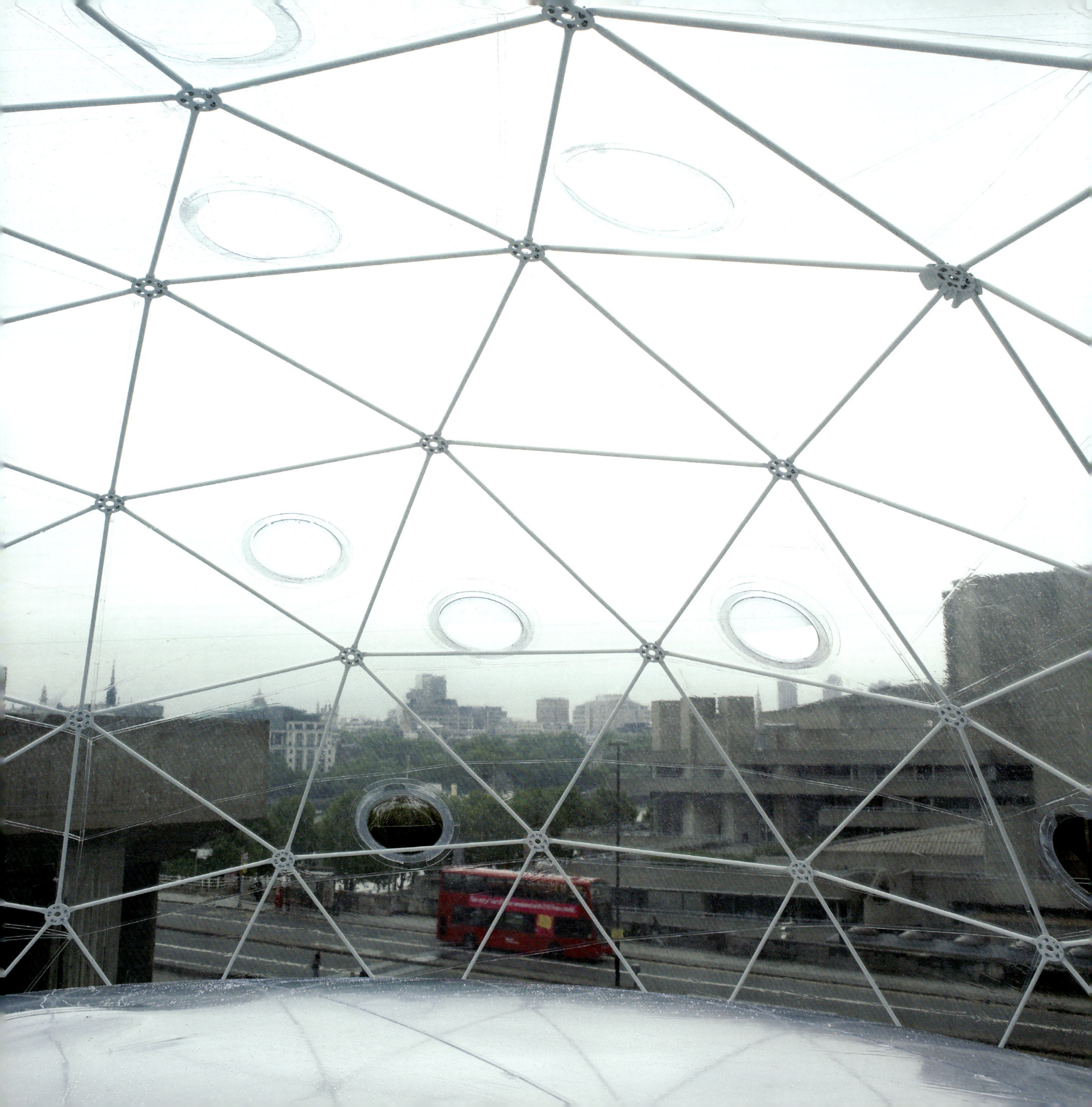

Observatory, Air-Port-City,
2008

TOMAS SARACENO

TOM MORTON

Trained as an architect, the Frankfurt-based Argentine artist Tomas Saraceno plans on leaving terra firma behind. His ongoing project *Air-Port-City* envisions networks of habitable cells that float in the air; combining and recombining like clouds into endlessly mutating, Utopian analogues of our earthly urban settlements. These supra-national cities (which draw on the legacy of visionary architects such as Buckminster Fuller and the Archigram group) will, the artist has said, 'search for their positions in the air in order to find their place in the universe', flying 'through the atmosphere pushed by winds, both local and global, in an attempt to equalise the (social) temperature and difference in pressure.'[1] Governed, like the airports from which the project takes it name, by International Law (a rare example of real-life planetary agreement), they defy entrenched notions of territory, and point towards a possible future in which the ownership of space, and the uneasy inclusions and exclusions it gives rise to, might be replaced by an equitable sci-fi nomadism. As Saraceno has it, 'this structure seeks to challenge today's political, social, cultural and military restrictions in an attempt to re-establish new concepts of synergy.'[2]

Air-Port-City might easily be dismissed as an unusually well-developed futurological fantasy (many of us, as children, sketched castles in the air, and nearly all of us have indulged idle thoughts of weightlessness and flight), but for the fact that, in addition to alluding to this airborne habitat in a series of works that veer between sculptures and architectural structures, Saraceno seems to be seriously engaged in the business of bringing it into being. The artist has invented and patented a new application for a material named Aerogel which points towards the possibility of solar powered flight on a grand scale, and thus a environmentally neutral colonization of the sky (anticipating this new reality, he has, since his 2001 project *Solar Balloon*, already succeeded in launching several dirigibles that have borne passengers aloft purely through the energy provided by the sun's rays). Similarly, his models for *Flying Gardens* (2006) shown at Tanya Bonakder Gallery, New York, in 2006 employ Spanish moss, a plant of the genus Tillandsia which lives on nothing more than rainwater and air-born nutrients. Hanging in green fronds from clusters of floating transparent balloons, these thriving life forms suggest a post-terrestrial tomorrow for other earth based species, including our own.

The baby steps Saraceno makes towards his Utopian vision remain, however, ambiguous, and it might be argued that they illustrate not our proximity to a better future, but our distance from it. It's also perhaps important to consider that, for all the emancipatory potential of *Air-Port-City*, its realisation would almost certainly depend, at the very least, on collaboration with governments and multi-national corporations — agencies that have been historically unwilling to let their own power interests slide in the pursuit of a perfect world. Saraceno's cloud cities may promise shifts in political and economic thinking, but such shifts would in all likelihood have to take place on our problematic earth before we abandon it for the skies.

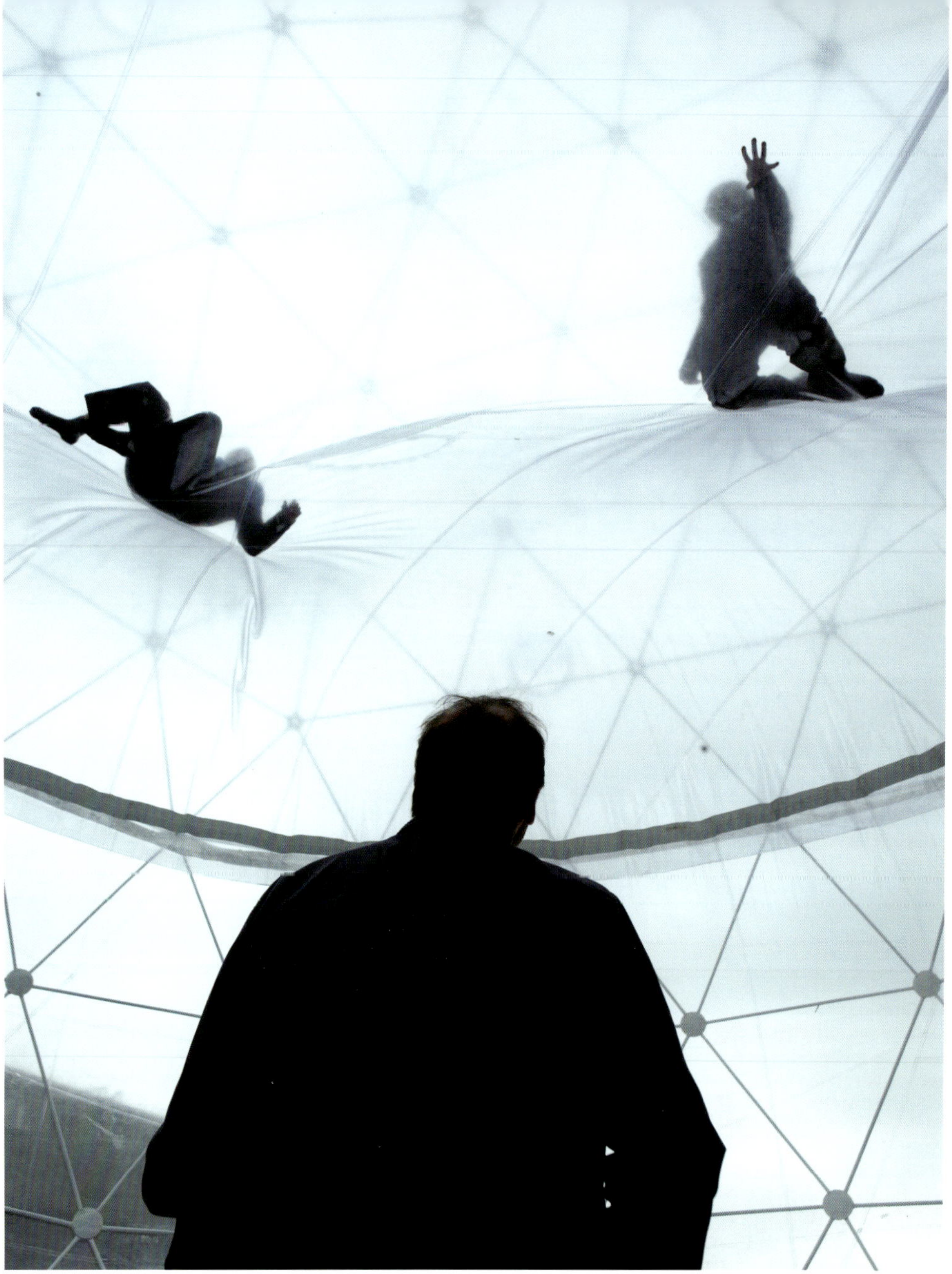

In 2004, at Pinksummer, Genoa, Saraceno installed a clear PVC 'room', divided by a vertical membrane into one lower and one upper chamber, accessed by two separate entrances. If you stood in the lower chamber and looked up, you could see other gallery goers 'floating' above you like putti on a frescoed ceiling. If you laid on the membrane in the upper chamber and looked down, you would experience something close to flight. In many ways, this work anticipated *Observatory, Air-Port-City* (2008), the artist's project for *Psycho Buildings*. Taking the form of a Buckminster Fuller-influenced, steel-framed, clear PVC clad geodesic dome, the work sits high on one of The Hayward's sculpture terraces, commanding views of both the city of London and of the hopeful skies above it. Ephemeral, low-weight, and permeated by light, it sits in marked contrast to the dark, almost impenetrable masses of the architecture that surrounds it. Inside the dome, a thick, air-filled clear PVC 'pillow' bisects the space, creating — as in the Genoa piece — a lower and upper chamber. Held in place entirely by air pressure, this 'pillow' might be thought of as a proxy cloud on which visitors to the upper chamber might recline and watch the passing of other clouds high above. If these visitors roll onto their bellies, however, they will see themselves reflected in the mirrored foil floor of the lower chamber, the sky apparently both at their backs and stretching before them in all its blue infinity. Just as a telescope allows us to see faraway worlds, so Saraceno's *Observatory, Air-Port-City* provides us with a glimpse of his mooted aerial Utopia. A huge lens, it demands that we look — both at our proximity to the heavens and to difficult ground beneath our feet.

1 'Tomas Saraceno in Conversation with Hans Ulrich Obrist and Stefano Boeri', http://www.barbican.org.uk/artgallery/event-detail.asp?id=4107&pg=296.

2 Ibid.

Observatory, Air-Port-City,
2008

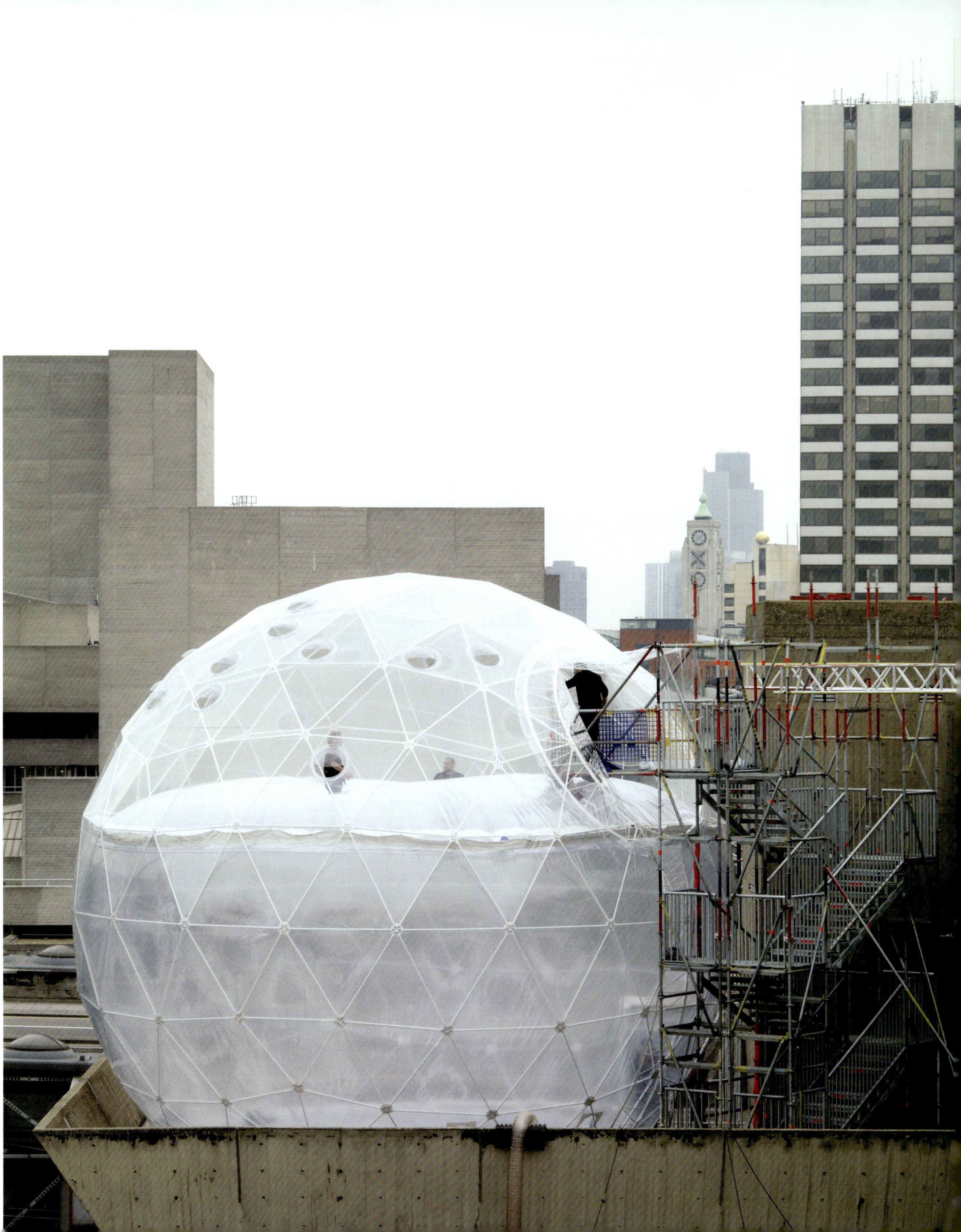

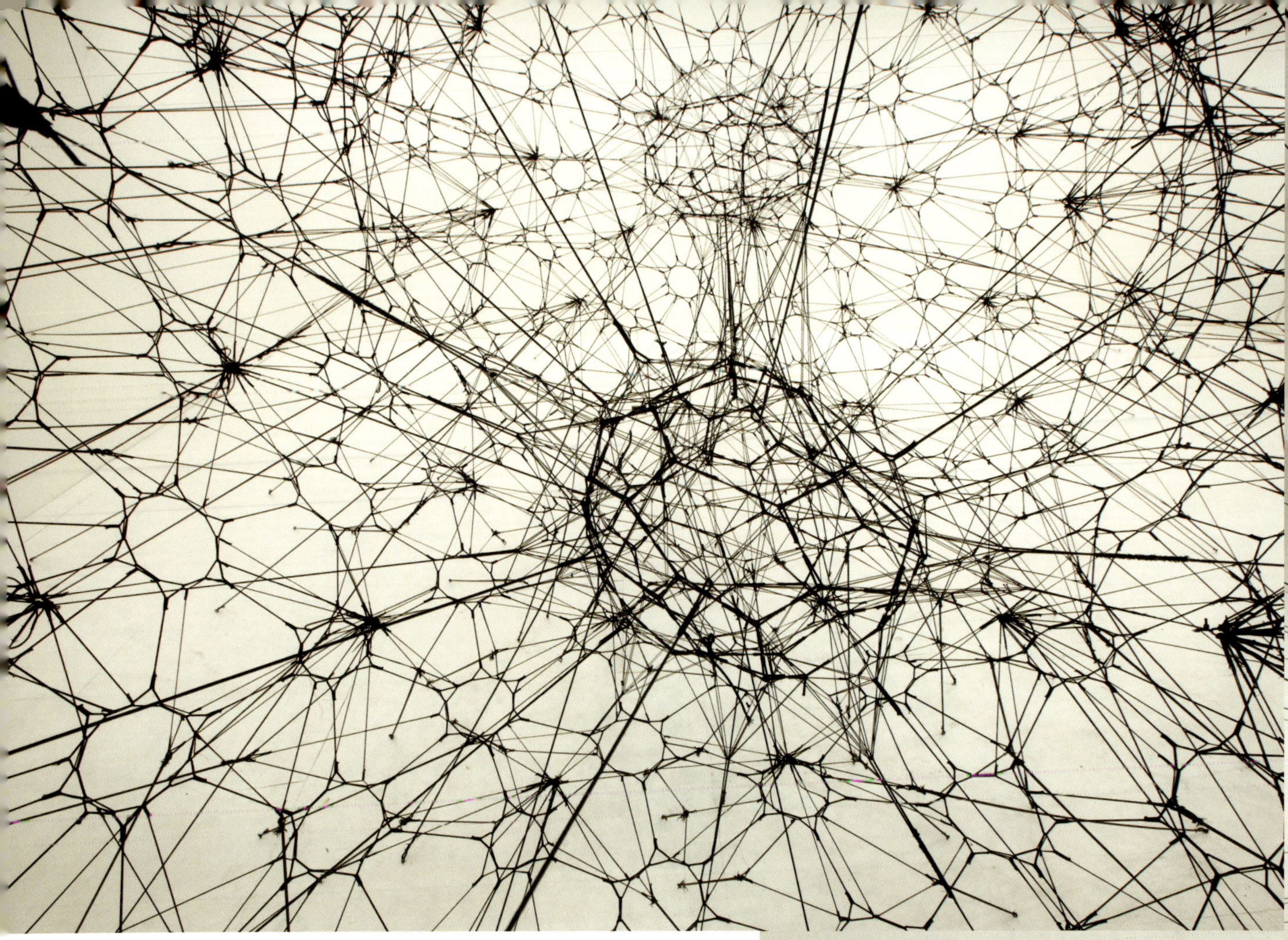

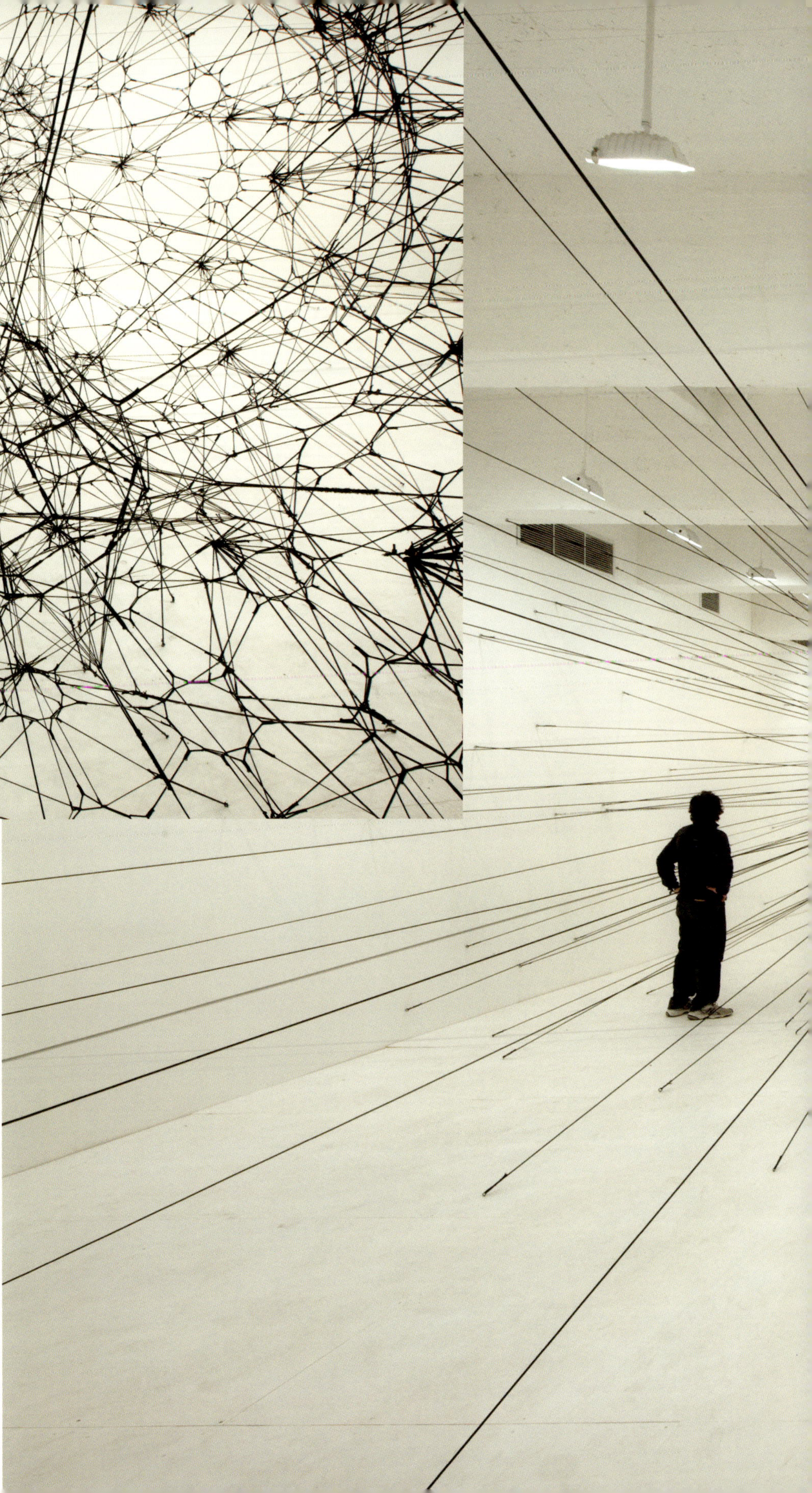

Galaxies Forming Along Filaments,
Like Droplets Along the Strands
of a Spider's Web, **2008**

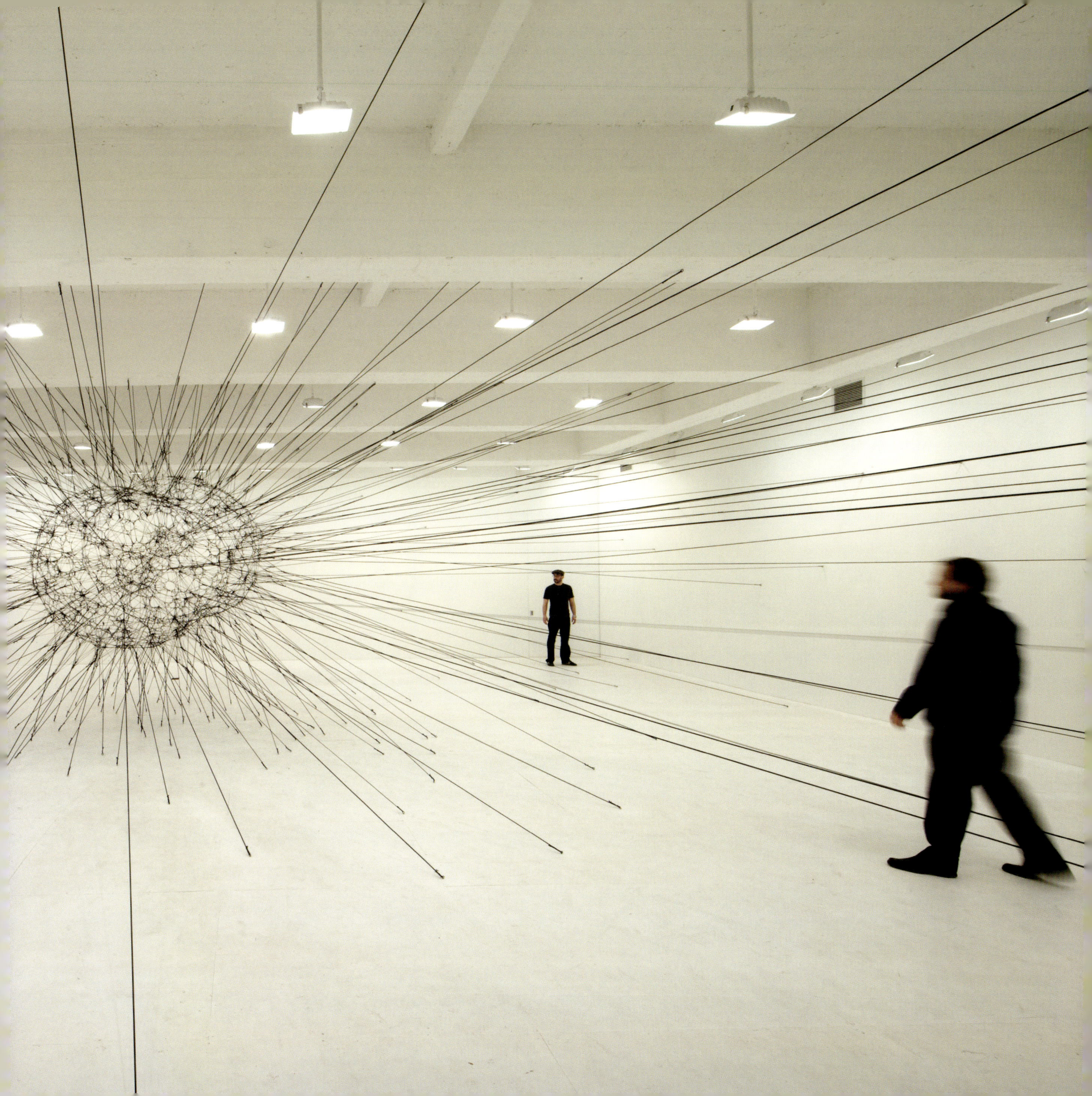

Biosphere MW 32, **2007**

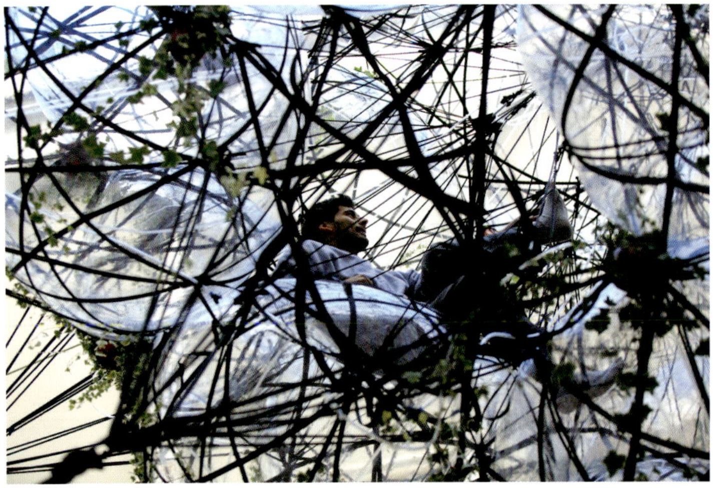

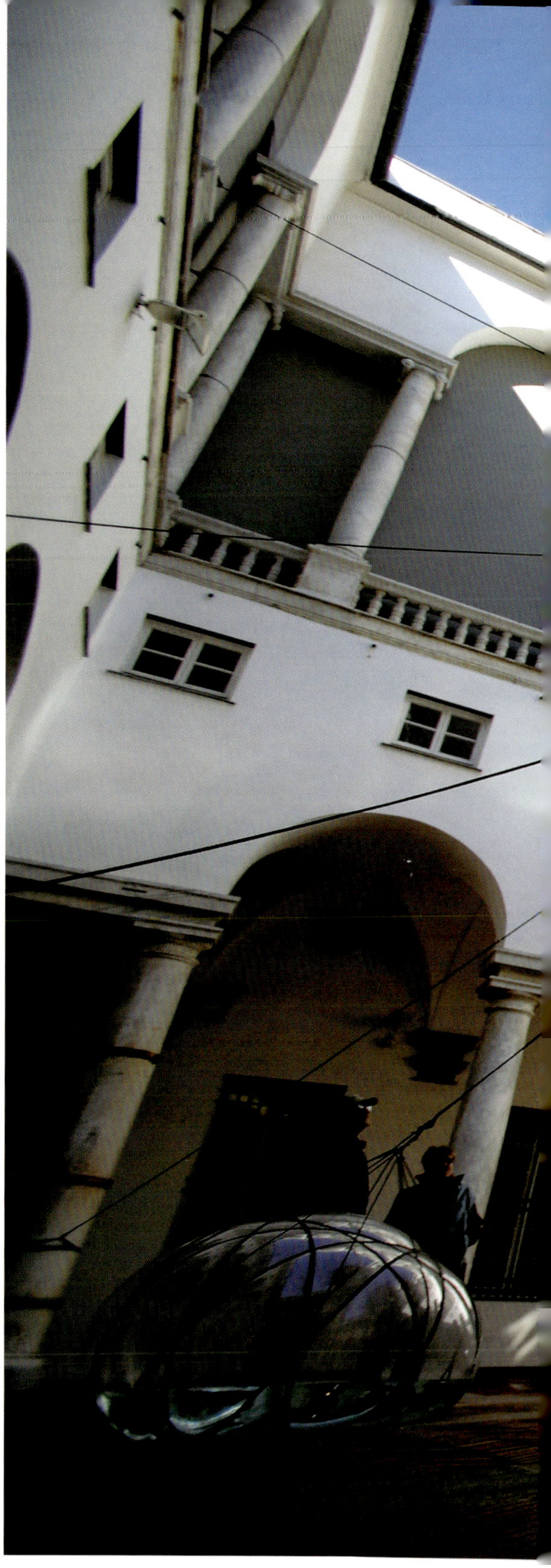

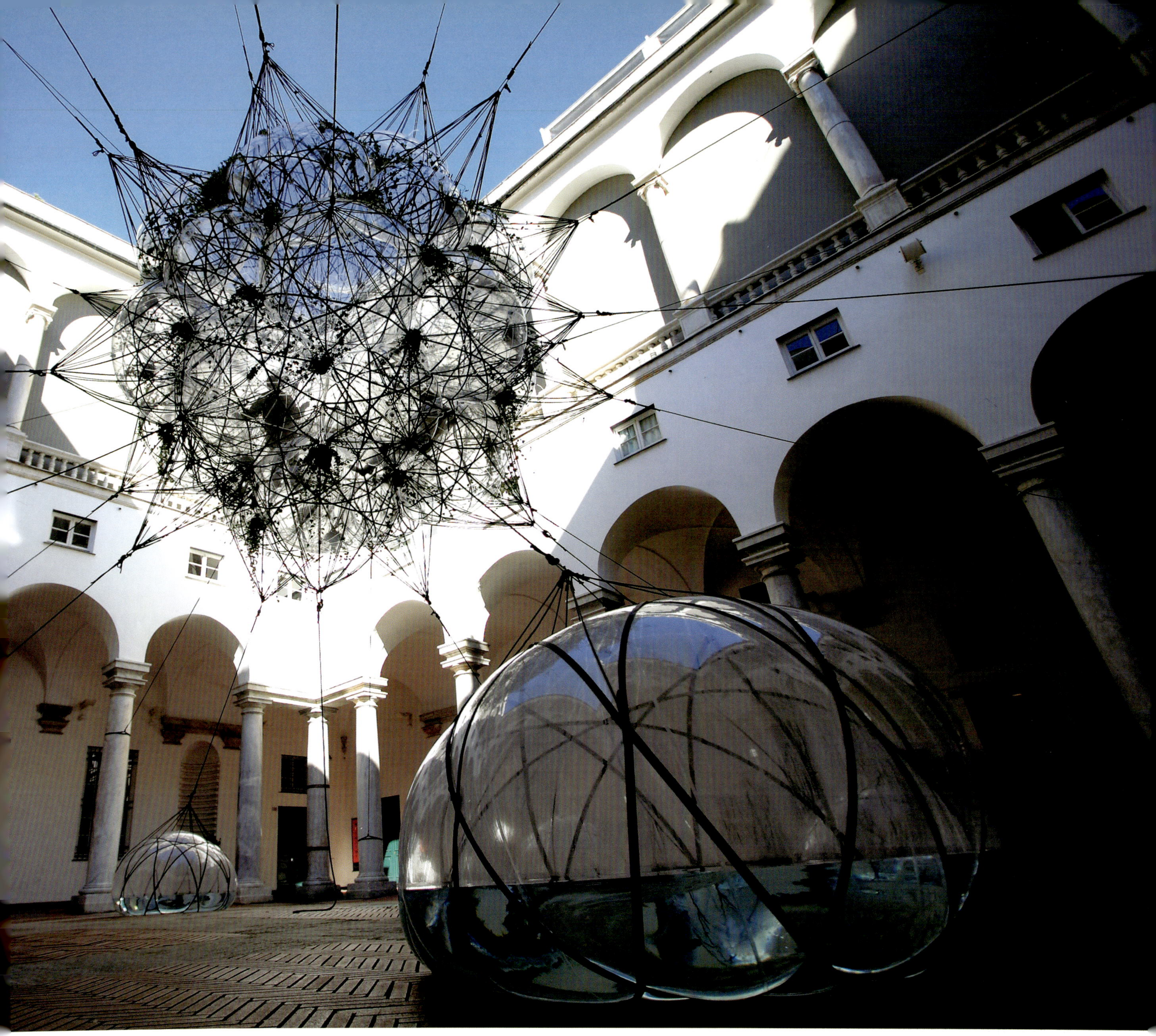

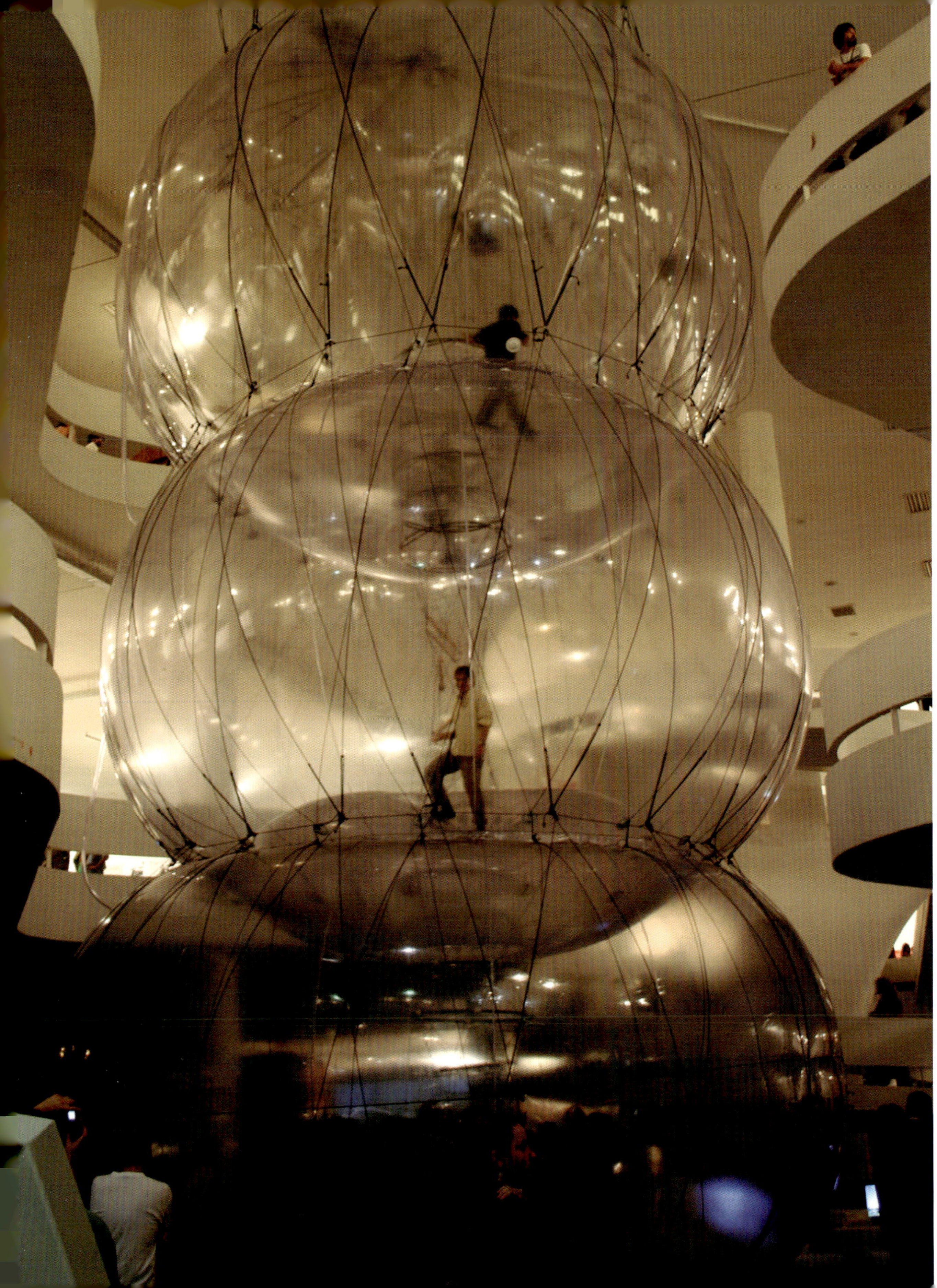

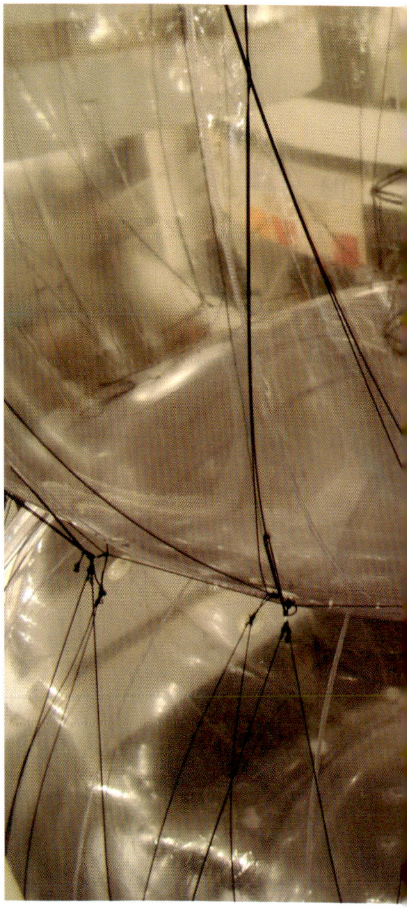

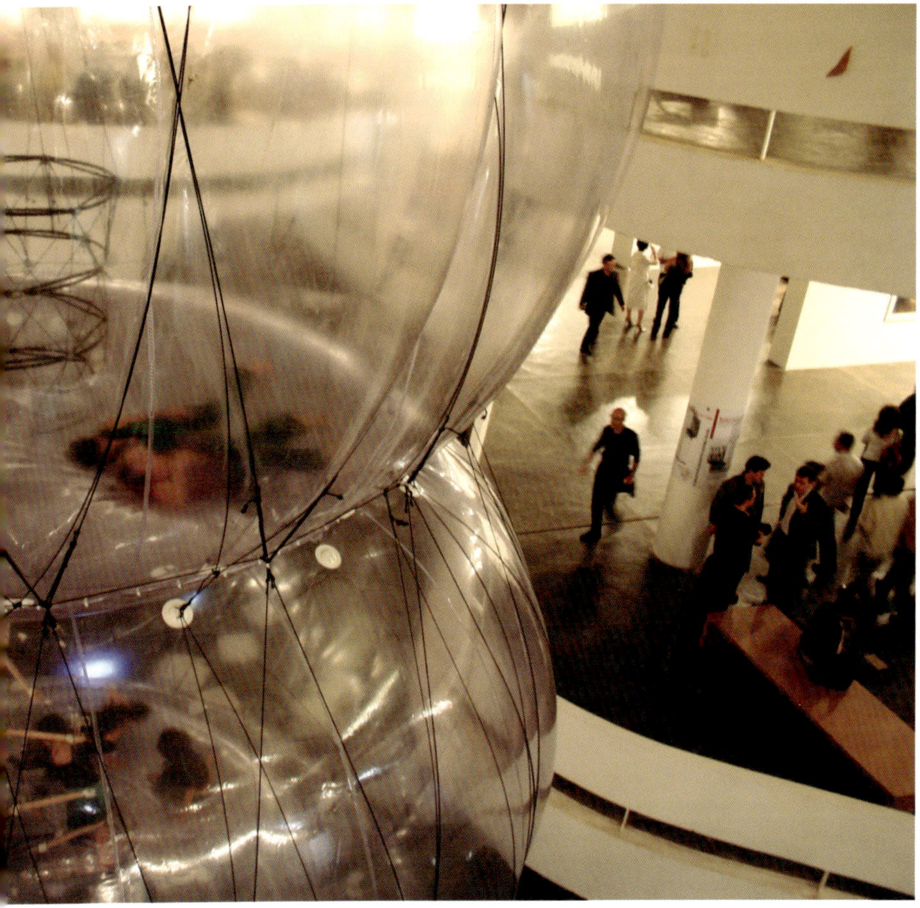

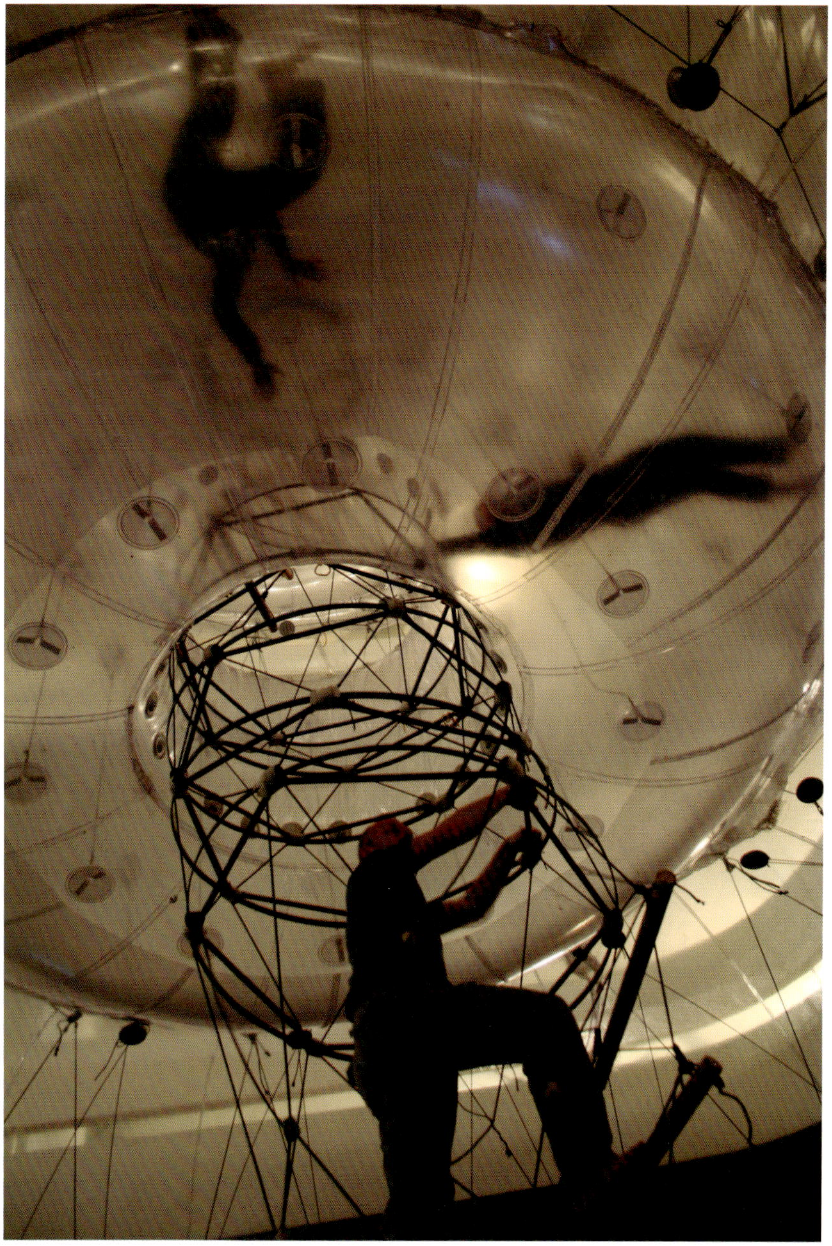

On Air, **2004**

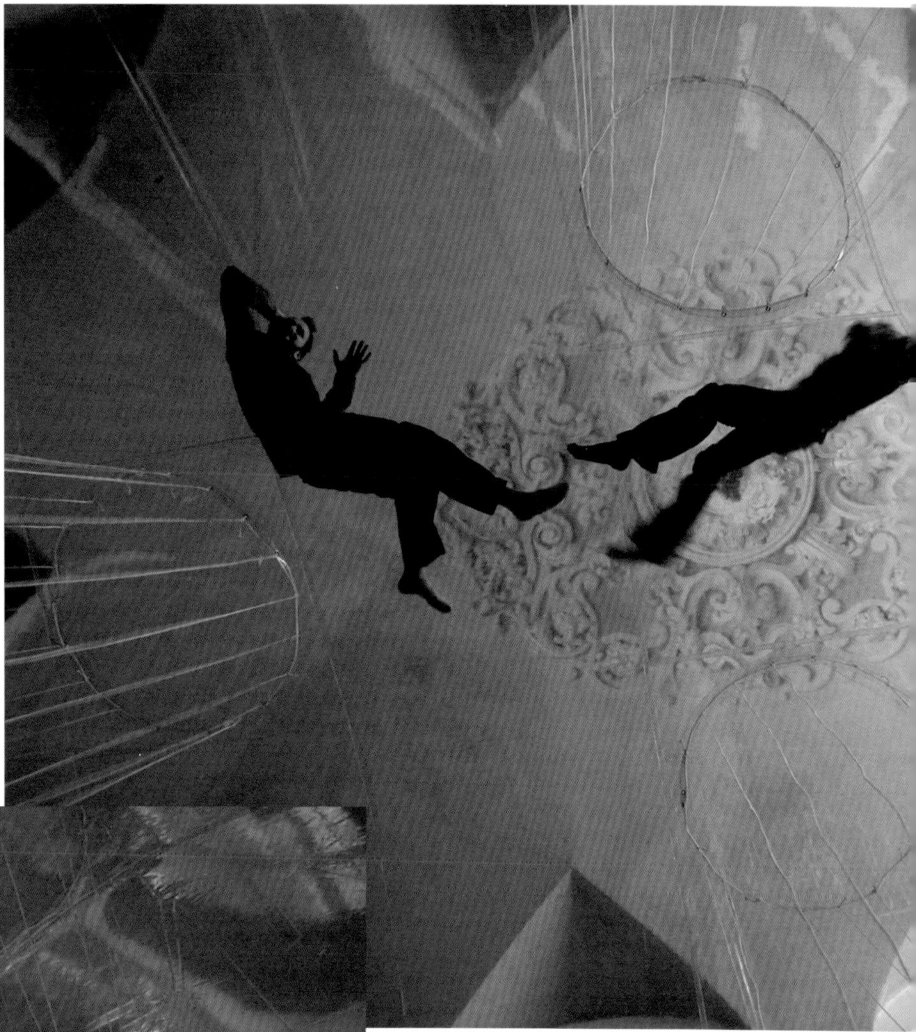

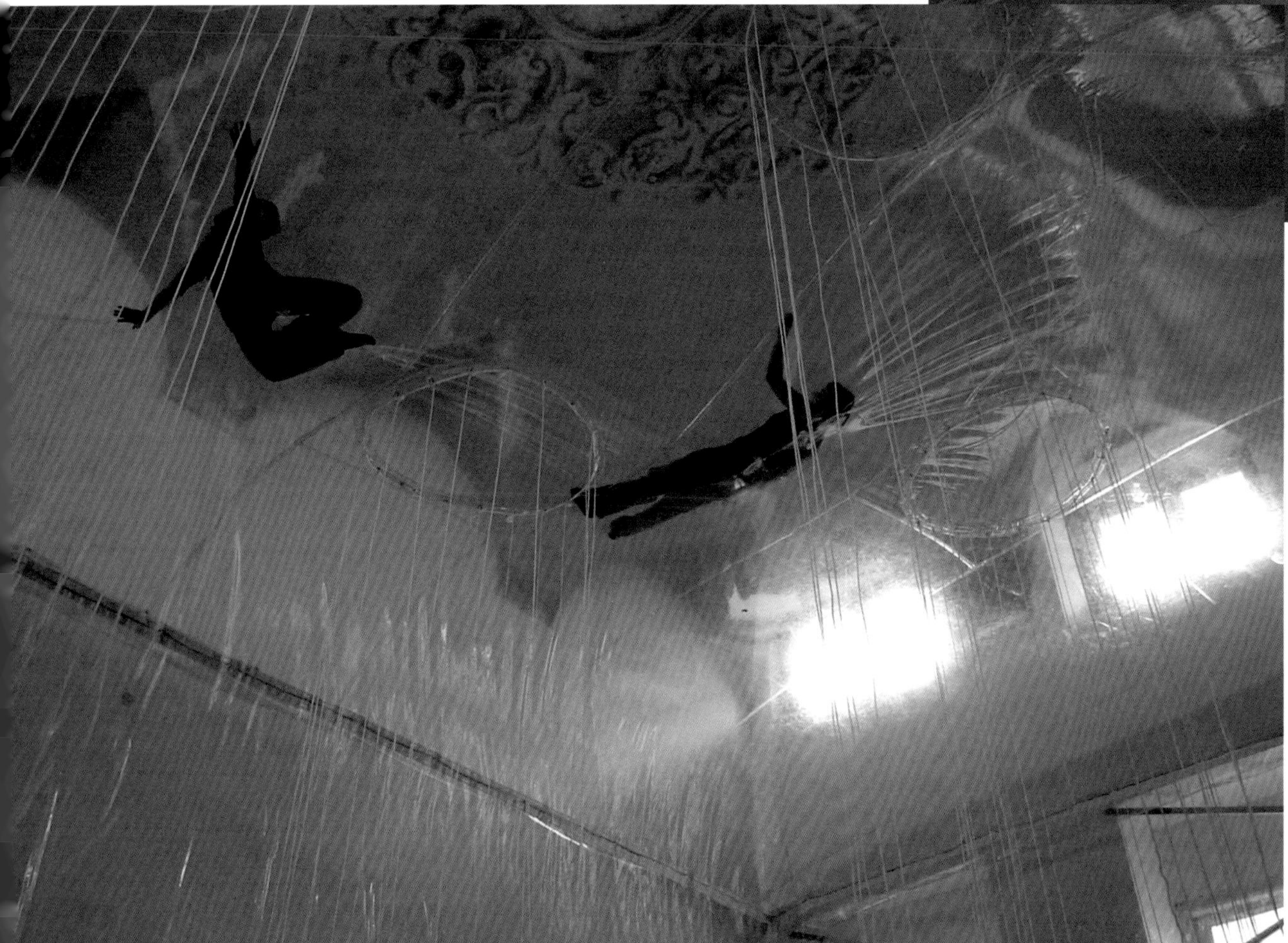

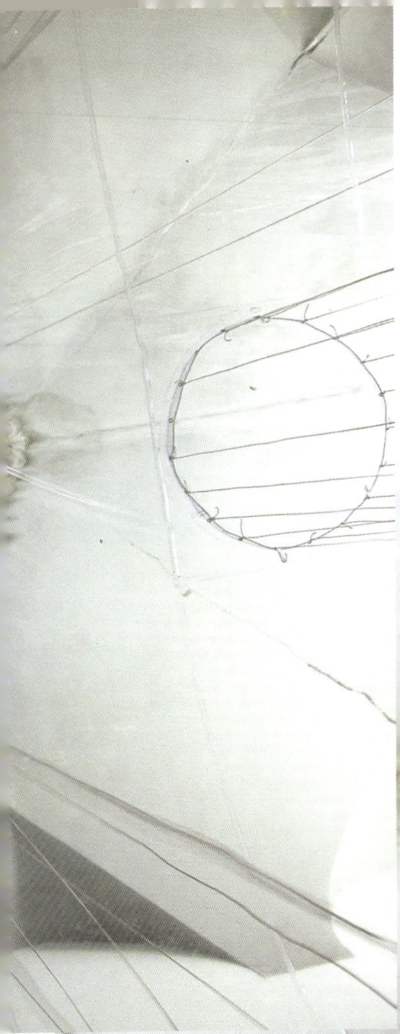

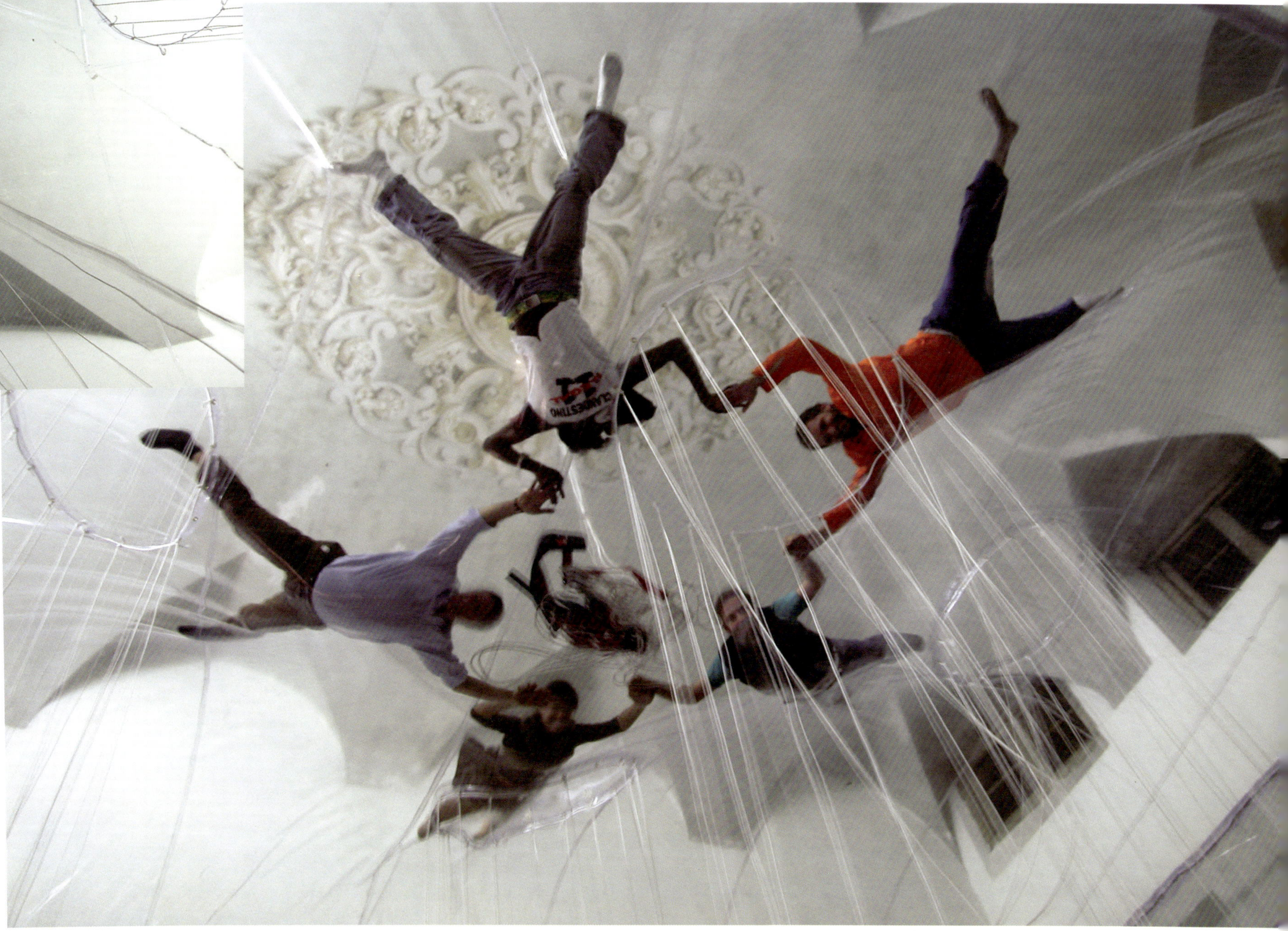

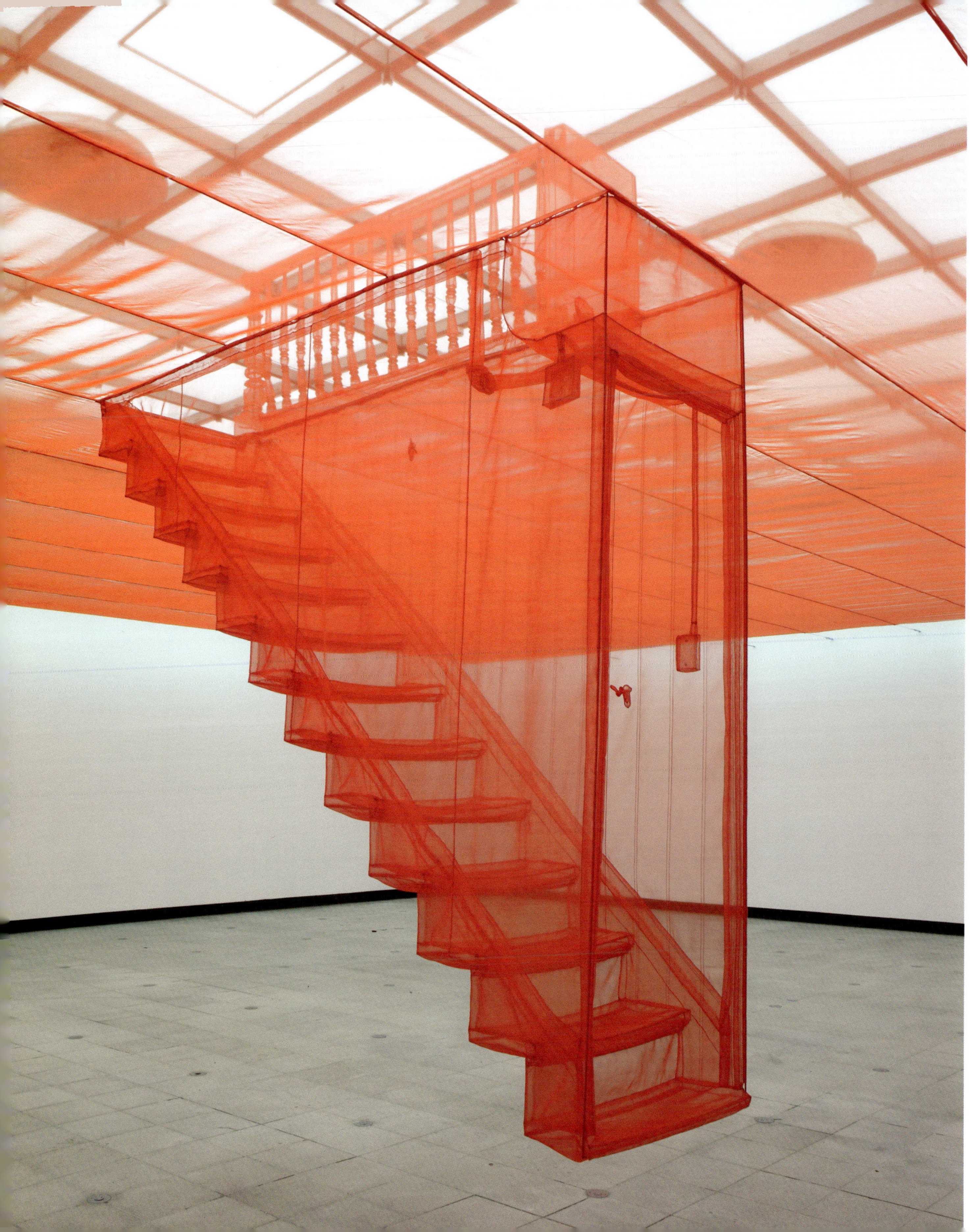

Staircase—V, **2003/04/08**

DO HO SUH

MIWON KWON

Architecture has been a central point of reference for Do Ho Suh's sculptural work since the mid-1990s. Even when the imagery of his installations happens to be human bodies rather than buildings, the figures have often taken on a scale and presence not unlike architectural structures (as in his *High School Uni-Form* **(1996) or** *Some/One* **(2002), for instance), organising the viewer's spatial experiences of containment and openness, interiority and exteriority, and transparency and opacity. Some of his other installations, such as** *Seoul Home/L.A. Home/New York Home/Baltimore Home/London Home/Seattle Home/L.A. Home* **(1999) and** *Perfect Home* **(2002), have been more explicit and literal architectural constructions. These are full-scale fabric replications of specific spaces or buildings integral to the artist's life. The physically enveloping quality of such works also produces resonant psychological impact for viewers.The sensorial experience of Suh's meticulously manufactured environments, especially when coupled with knowledge of the biographical references of the rendered spaces, prompt feelings of delight, nostalgia, longing, awe and, at times, anxiety in the audience.**

Suh's ongoing engagement with architecture over the past decade can be divided into three distinct bodies of work, each manifesting an attitude or methodology that proposes a different possibility for sculpture and architecture, or sculpture as architecture. The first set of works, not represented in *Psycho Buildings***, involves modifications to given exhibition spaces, done in a manner that is barely perceptible. For example, Suh's** *Floor* **(1997–2000), an expansive platform comprised of tiny plastic figures compressed together beneath thick glass plates, does not register as an art object in the gallery so much as continuous with it. It is installed in such a way as to seamlessly blend into the existing space; the viewers find themselves stepping upon it, traversing across it, before they realise that they are treading on an artwork. Similarly,** *Who Am We?* **(1996–2000), an installation of artist-designed wallpaper, transforms gallery walls into a field of barely discernible faces – 37,000 of them collected from the artist's high school yearbooks. What looks to be an empty room at first glance turns out to be haunted by the unsettling presence of countless strangers.**

Somewhat reminiscent of Institutional Critique and gestures that direct viewers' attention to normative exhibition display conventions, *Floor* **and** *Who Am We?* **both explore the thematic of collectivity versus individuality, and foreground the architectural condition of the gallery. But contrary to the critical aspirations of Institutional Critique, which often denies the viewer the visual pleasure or perceptual stimulation expected in exhibition spaces, Suh's works offer a delayed aesthetic satisfaction. In calling attention to the gallery as an architectural container, the artist fuses the artwork into it, embedding or hiding the art** *in* **the architecture while overtaking it at the same time.**

The second group of Suh's works, proposing another kind of sculptural/architectural possibility, involves expert sewing. *Seoul Home/L.A. Home...* **and** *Perfect Home***, as mentioned already, are architectural structures rendered in diaphanous fabric such as silk or nylon that produce an ethereal effect.** *Staircase – V* **(2003/04/08), included in The Hayward exhibition, belongs to this group of works that meticulously translate hard surfaces, erect volumes and solid materials into soft screens, drooping planes and fragile forms. The fact that these ghostly husks are one-to-one doubles of existing spaces – the artist's childhood home in Korea, his New York city apartment, and the passageway between the floor of the artist's apartment and his landlord's one floor above, respectively – renders them photographic in logic. They are indexical, in other words, emphasising displacement, fragmentation and discontinuity of space and time in contemporary life. Architecture emerges in these works as a dream-image, immaterial and impermanent, a site of desire, memory and longing.**

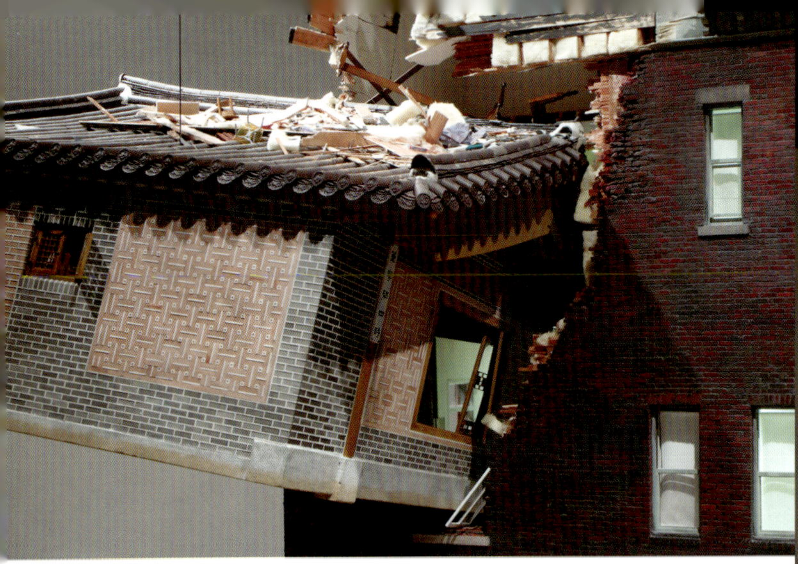

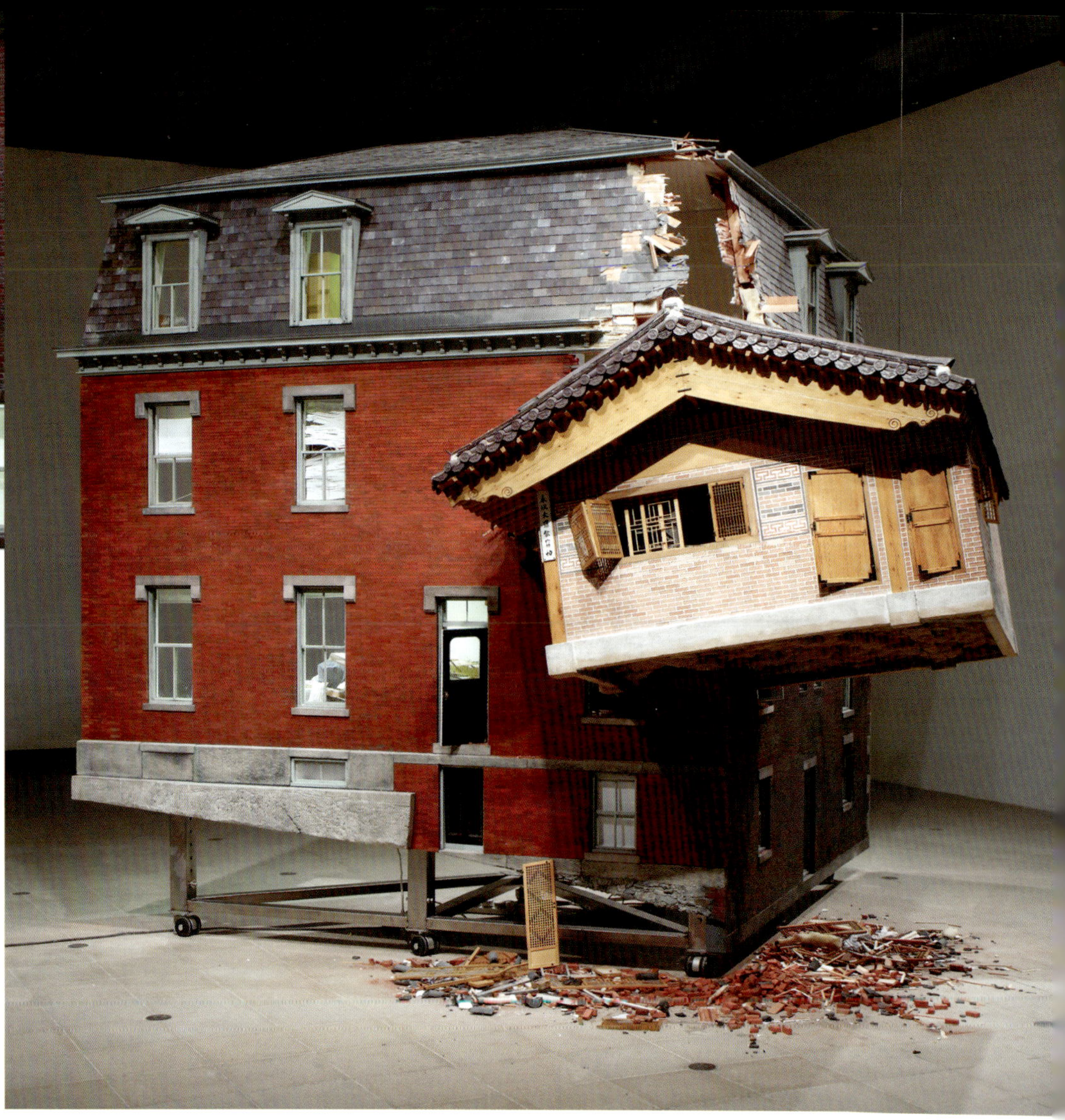

In Suh's most recent work, *Fallen Star 1/5* (2008), yet another approach to architecture is manifest, which could be best described as scenographic. Here, we have a 1/5 scale model/tableau in which the artist's Korean childhood home has crashed into the side of a four-storey apartment building in Providence, Rhode Island — the artist's first home in the United States. In this fantastical scene, architecture is no longer a phenomenal or structural condition framing aesthetic experience but objectified, and it functions like a character in a story (as almost a surrogate for the artist, in fact). The depiction of the physical and stylistic collision of the two buildings, at once comic and tragic, may be taken as a metaphor for the psychological impact of the artist's experience of moving to America, conjuring violence, shock, destruction and trauma, even as it also provokes laughter and a sense of playfulness. The sectional cut through the apartment building (itself as violent an act as the crash, a violence that is perhaps endemic to the architectural imagination) exposes lives lived on the various floors of the apartment building. Rendered like an oversized dollhouse, uncannily frozen, *Fallen Star 1/5* positions the viewer as an omniscient voyeur rather than encompassing him or her in a dynamic phenomenological situation as in Suh's prior works.[1]

The most immediate reference for this crash scene, in fact, is less architectural than filmic. Not only does Suh's flying house recall the Hollywood rendition of Dorothy's airborne house in the *Wizard of Oz*, the work looks like a film set whose artificiality and unreal-reality is waiting to 'come to life' as a new simulacral reality through the mediation of a camera. It is perhaps no coincidence that the artist has become more interested in storytelling as the driving force behind the making of such elaborate and spectacular constructions (I can no longer say sculptures), which are now conceptualised almost like props for a grand narrative.[2]

Throughout the past decade, much of Suh's engagement with architecture has been motivated by his personal experience of cultural displacement and its profound impact on his sense of identity and home. As his exploration continues with this new body of work, one cannot help but wonder about the turn toward architecture as an image (even weapon?) of disaster, because I am reminded of other houses in flight, ripped off the ground by tornadoes or washed away by floods. Perhaps Suh's work and *Psycho Buildings* can help us to reflect on architecture not only as a material, formal, perceptual and psychological phenomenon but in social and political terms as well.

1 According to the artist, *Fallen Star 1/5*, while a 'finished piece', is still a model. He envisions and hopes to be able to produce a 1:1 construction of the scene at some point in the future. Email communication with artist, 3 March 2008.

2 See Sunjung Kim's essay, 'Do Ho Suh', in *The 19th Sun Award Artist: Do Ho Suh*, Sun Contemporary, Seoul, 2006.

Fallen Star 1/5, **2008**

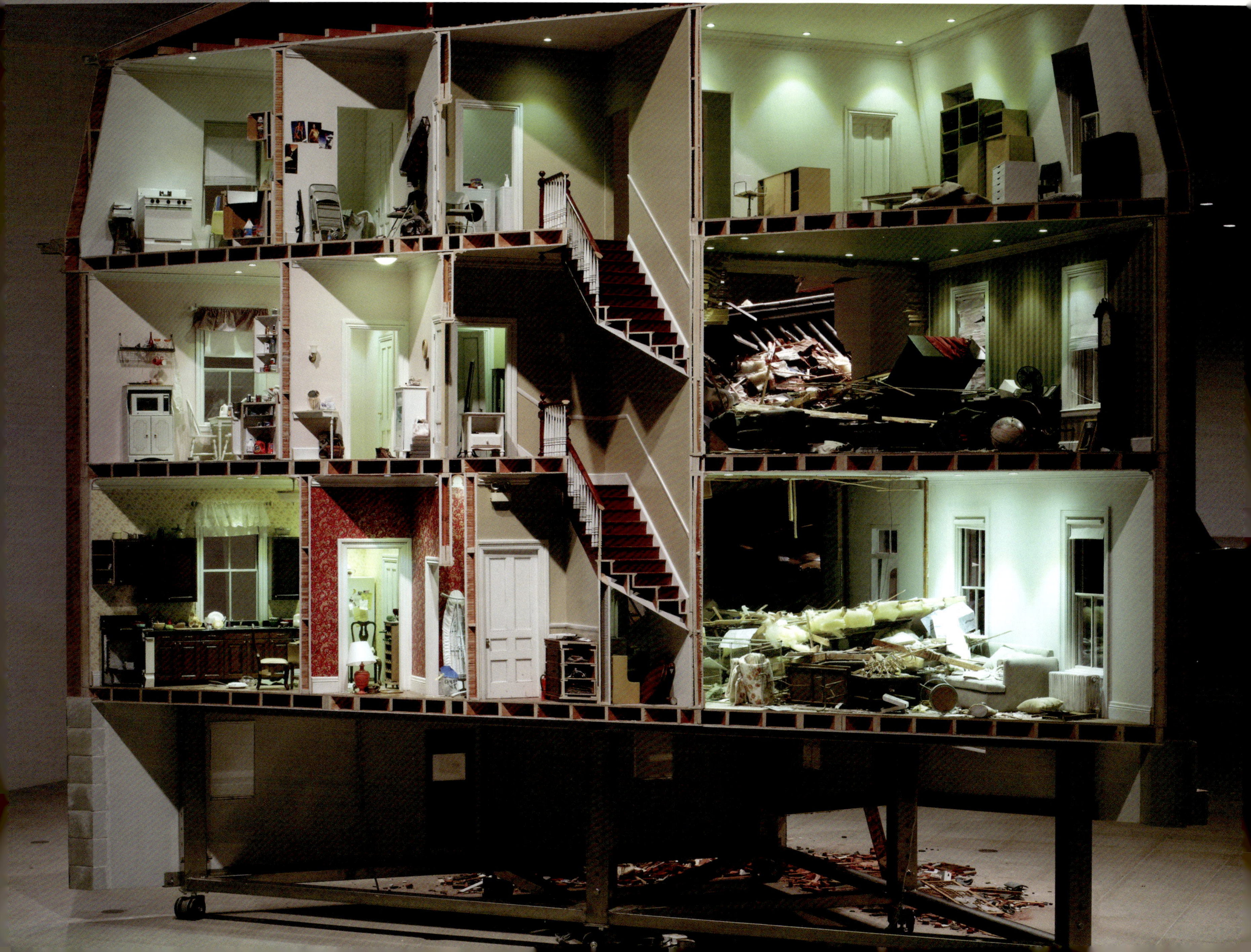

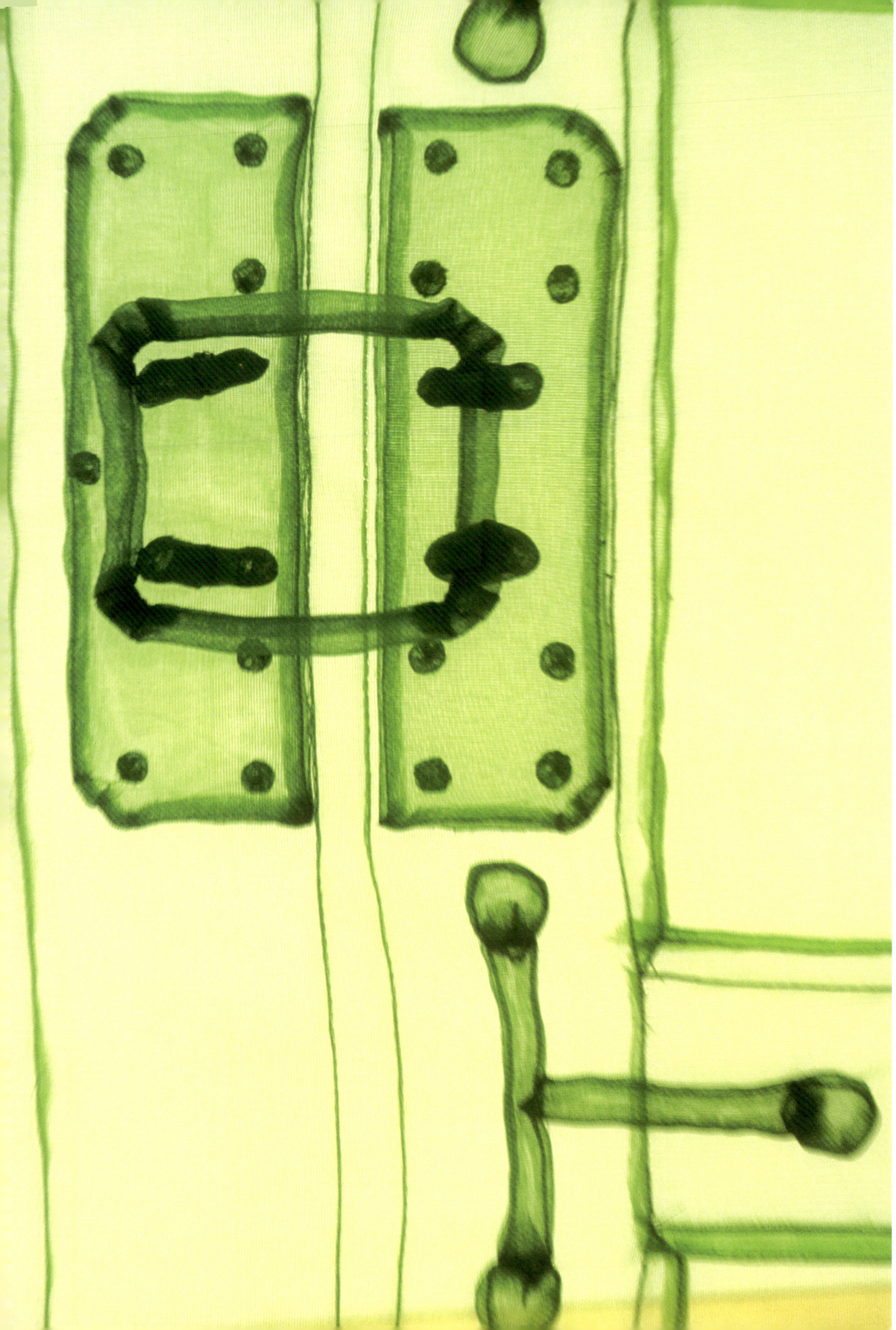

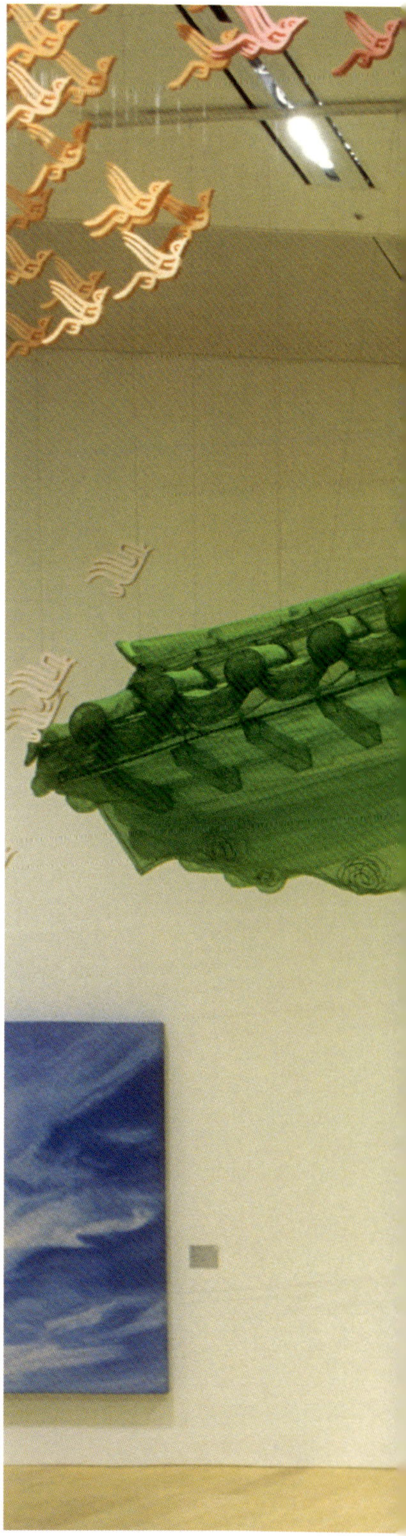

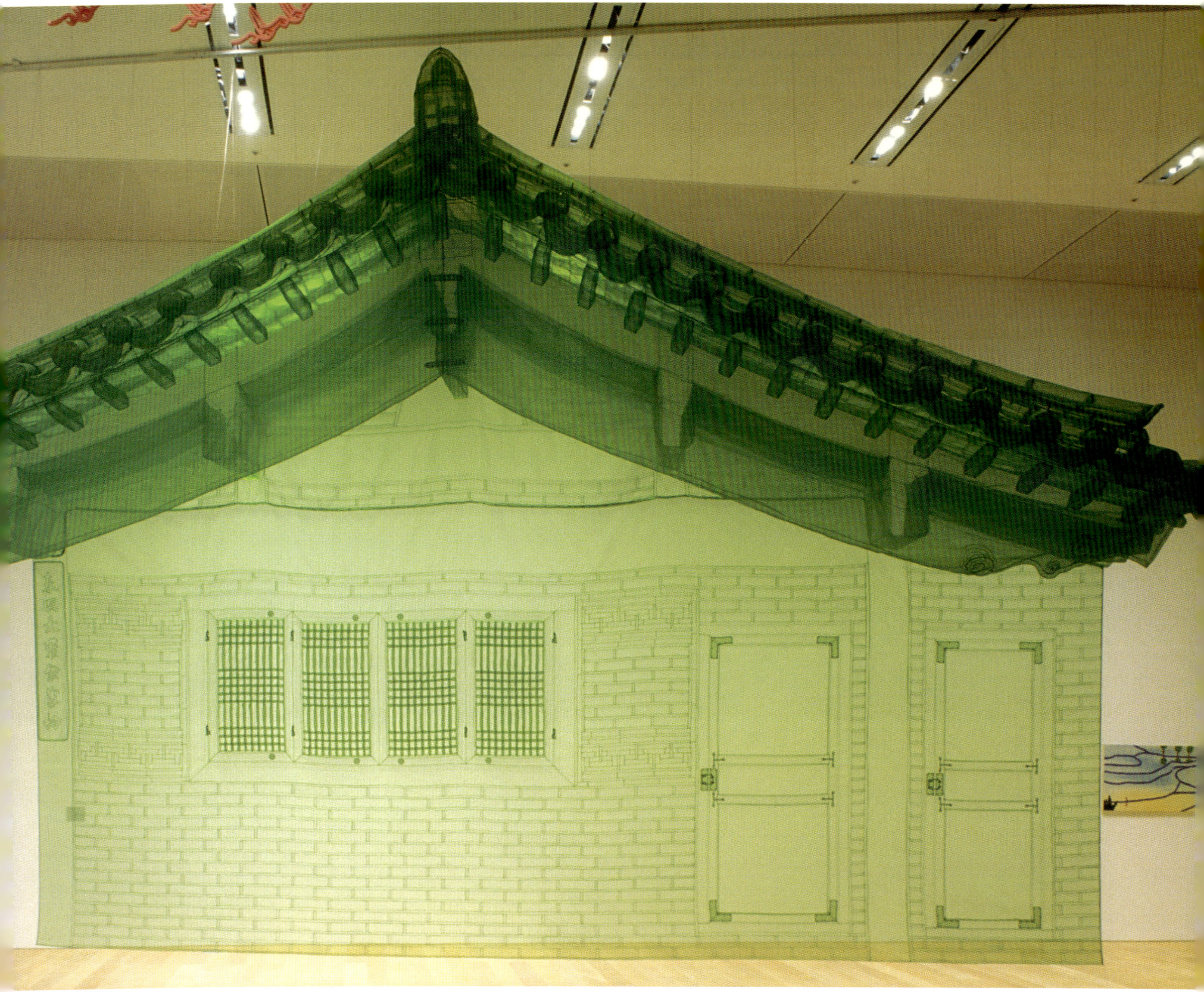

North Wall, **2005**

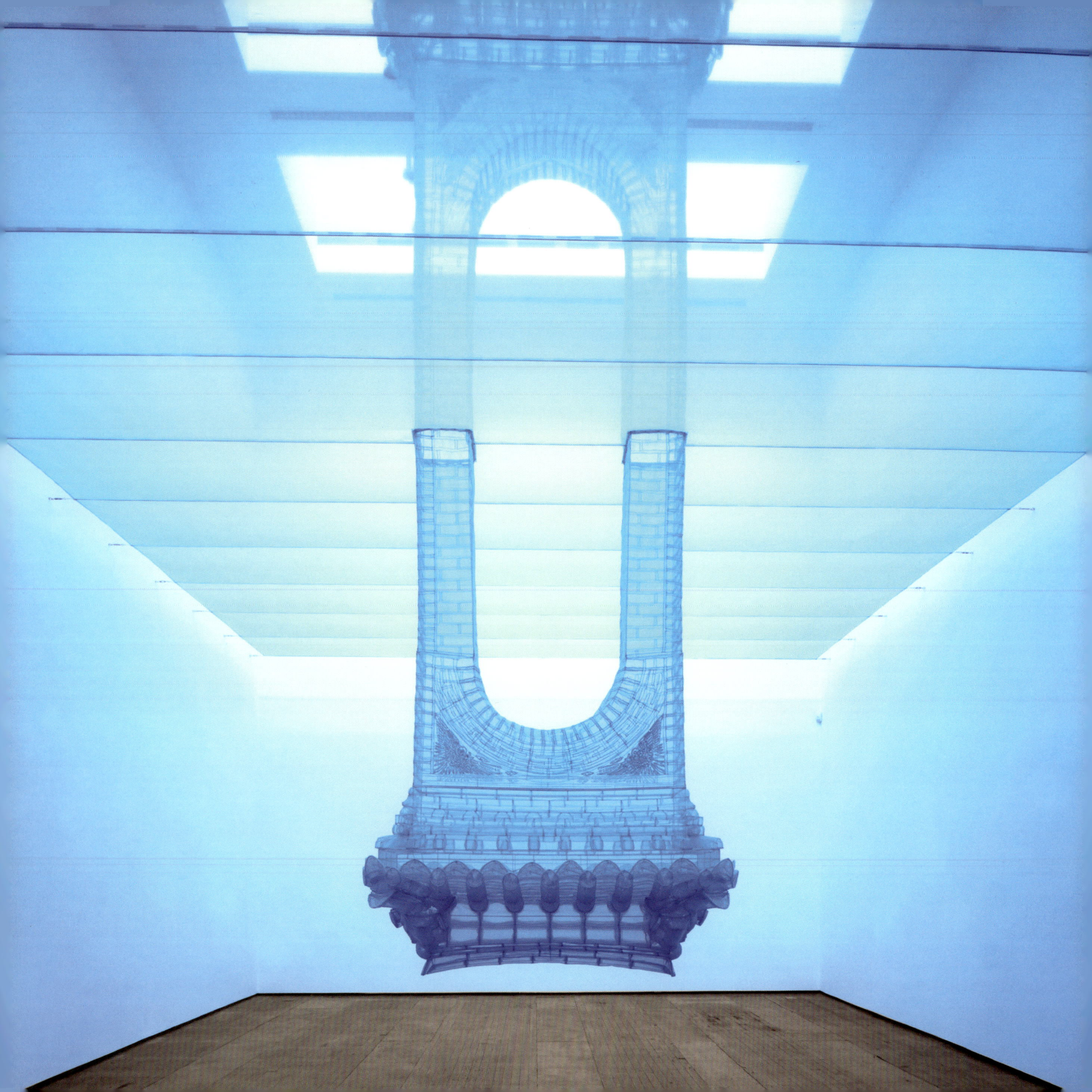

Reflection, **2004**

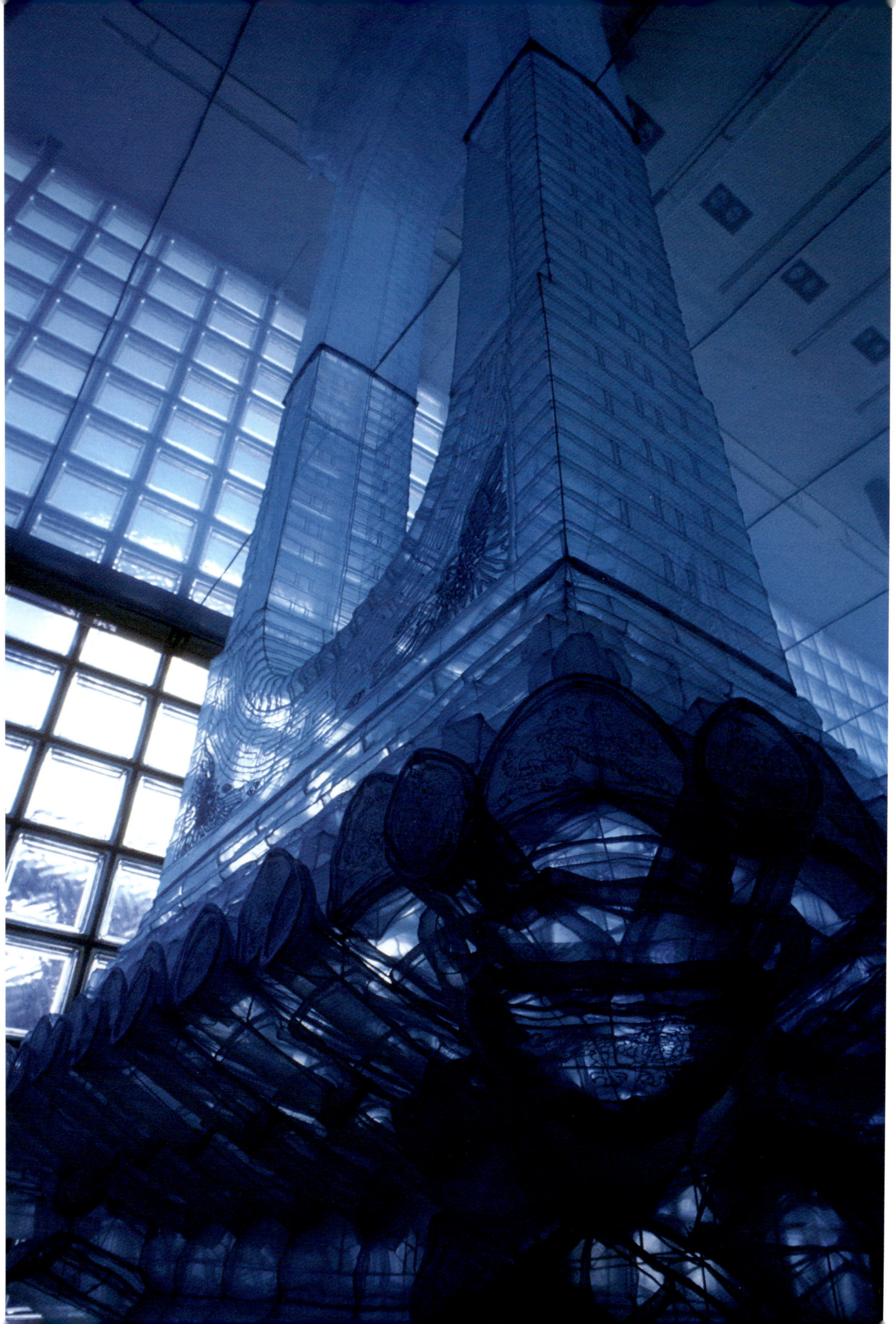

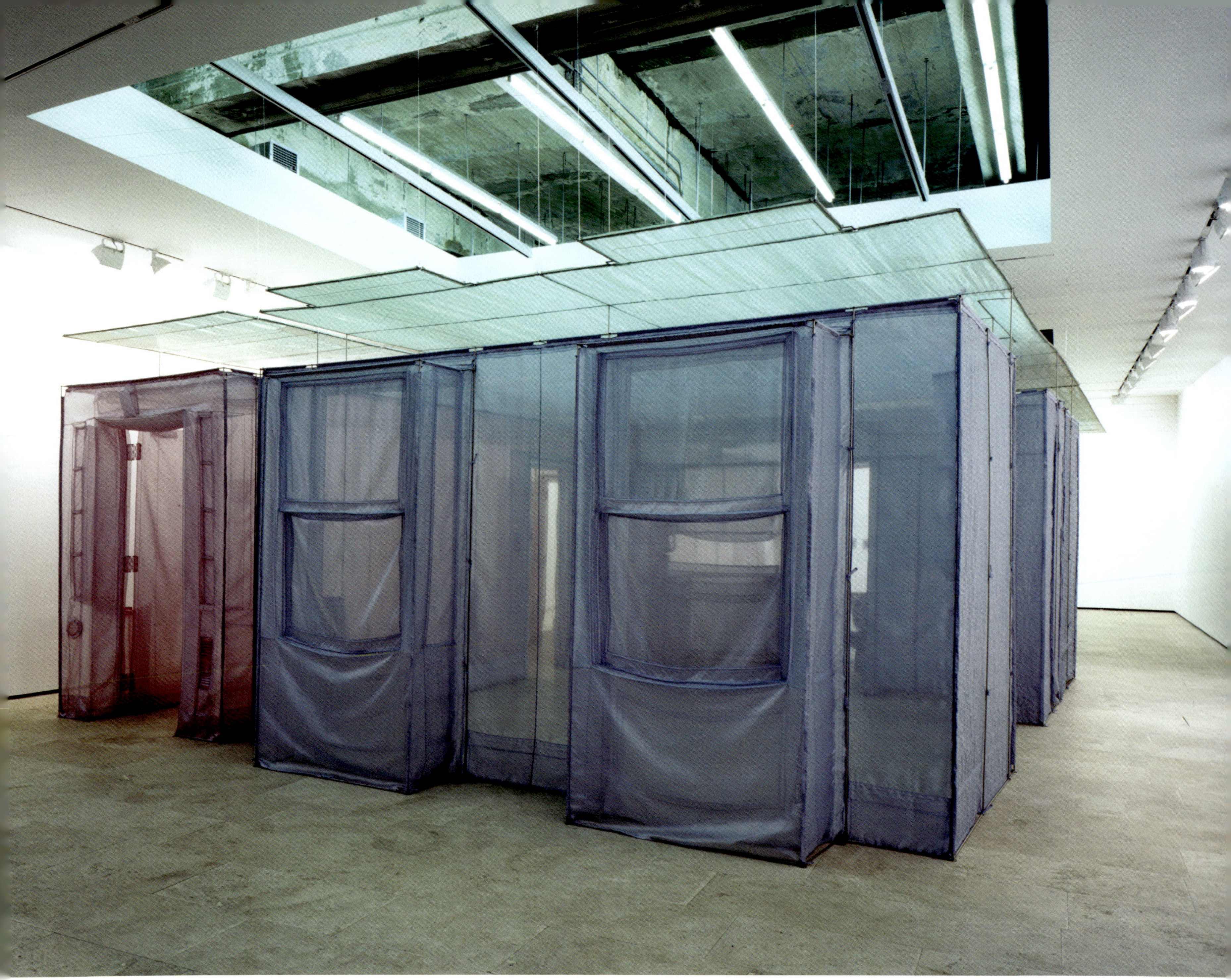

The Perfect Home II, **2003**

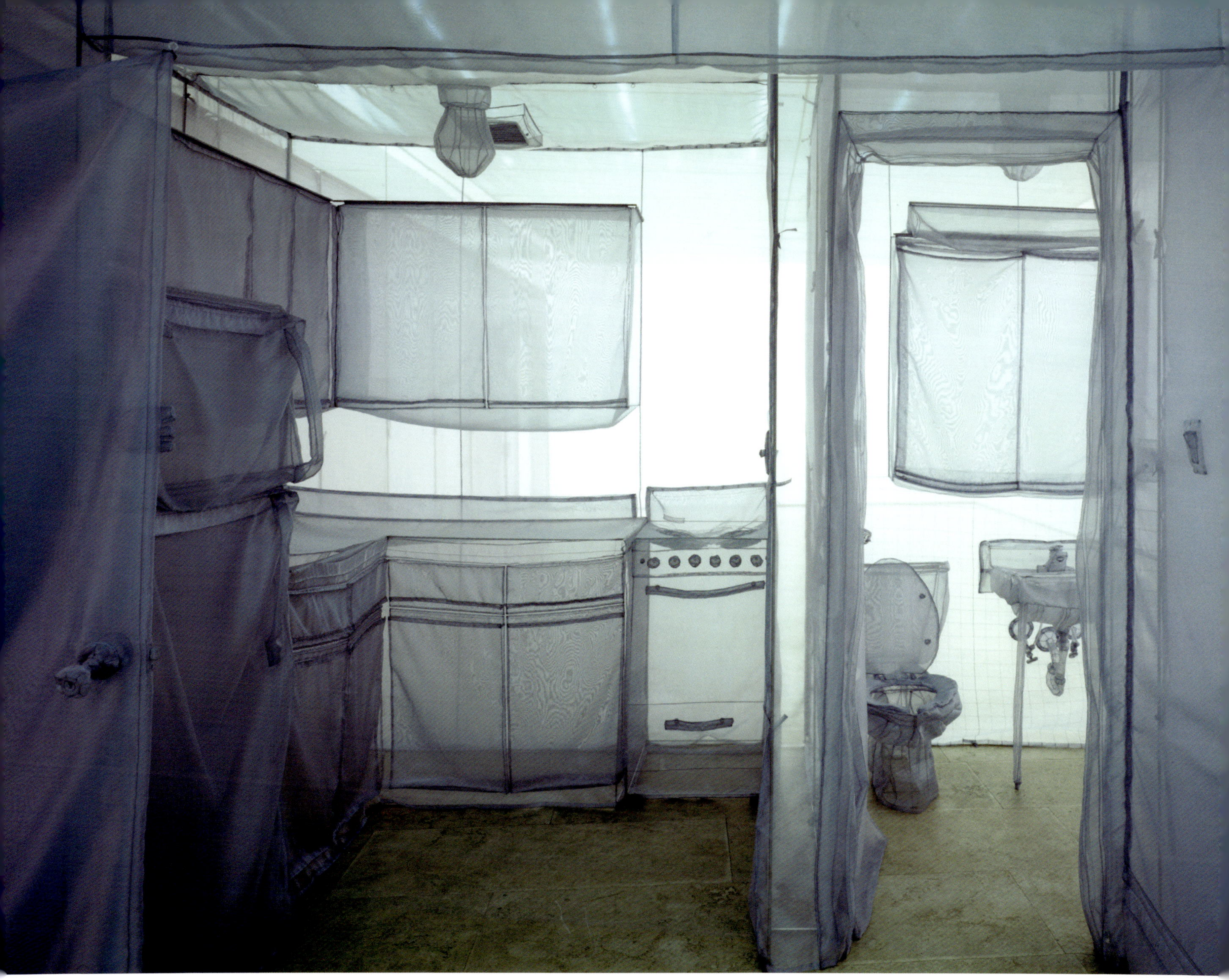

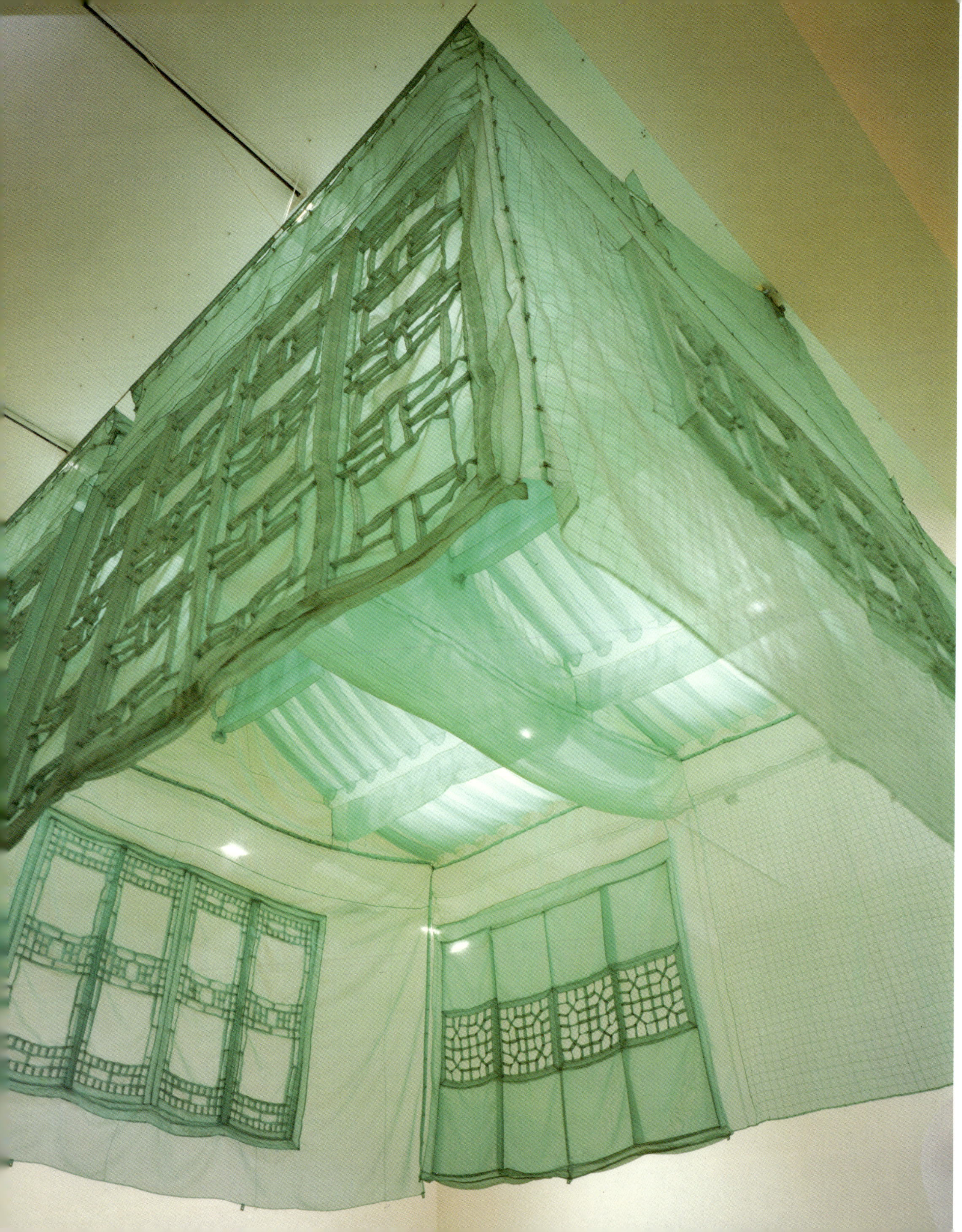

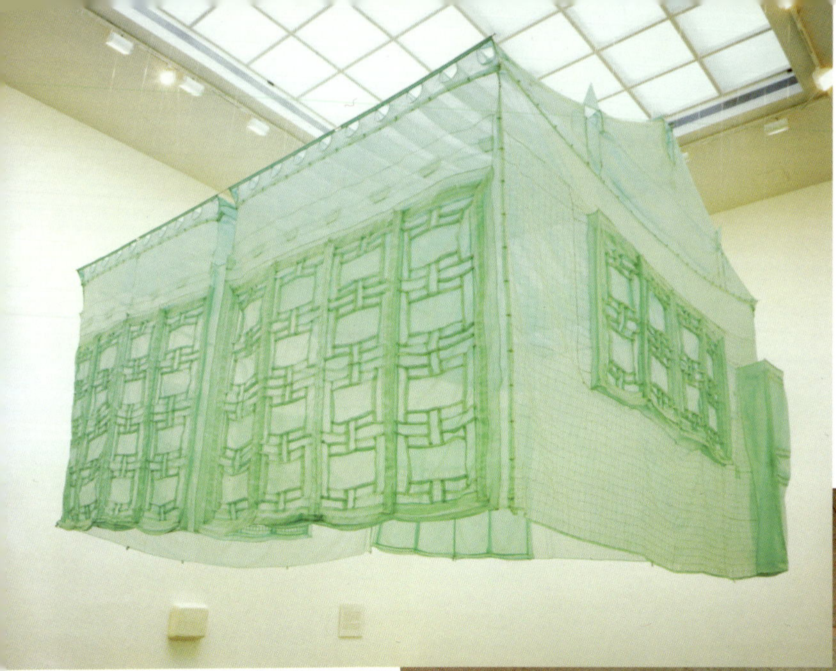

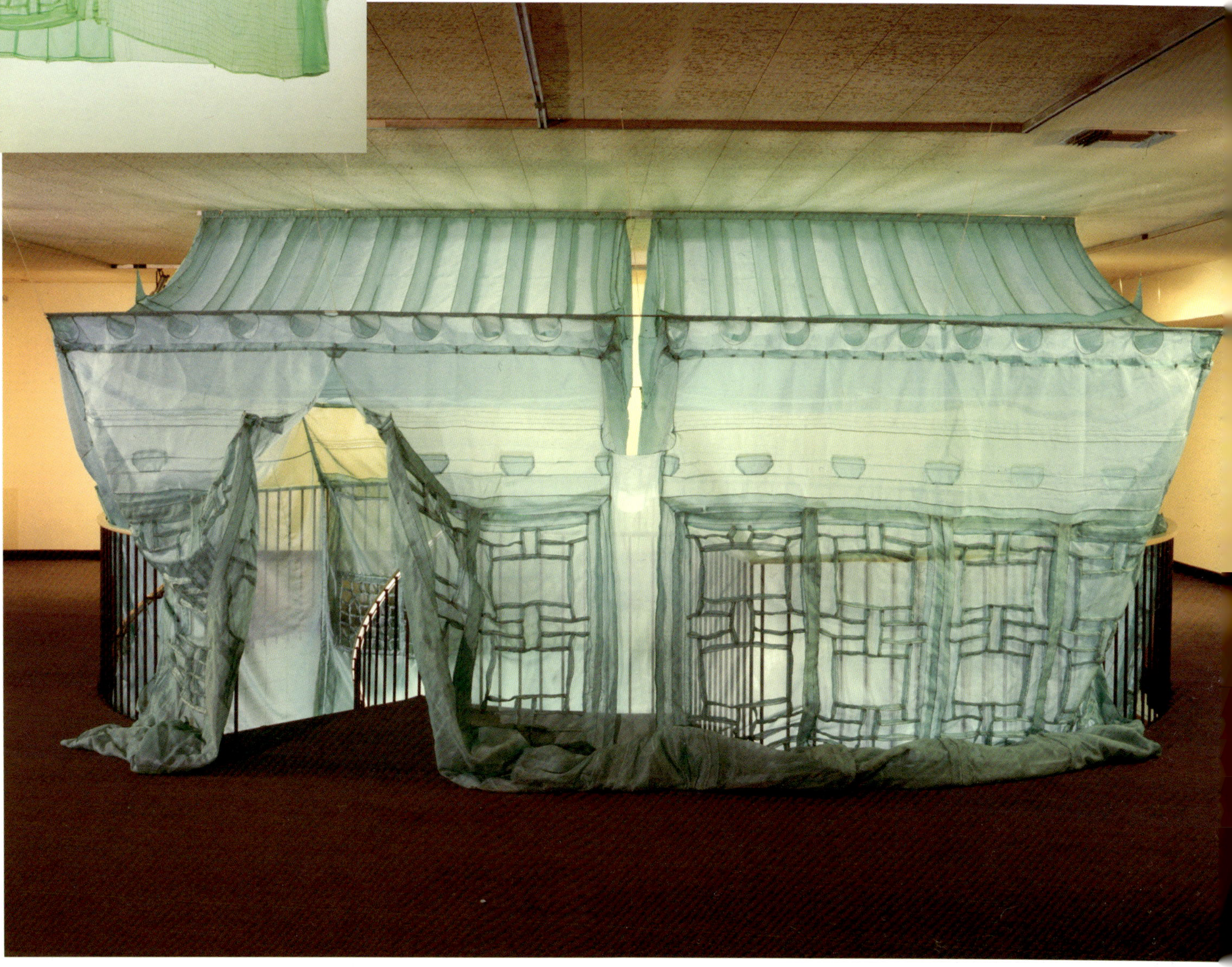

Seoul Home/L.A. Home/ New York Home/Baltimore Home/London Home/ Seattle Home/L.A. Home, **1999**

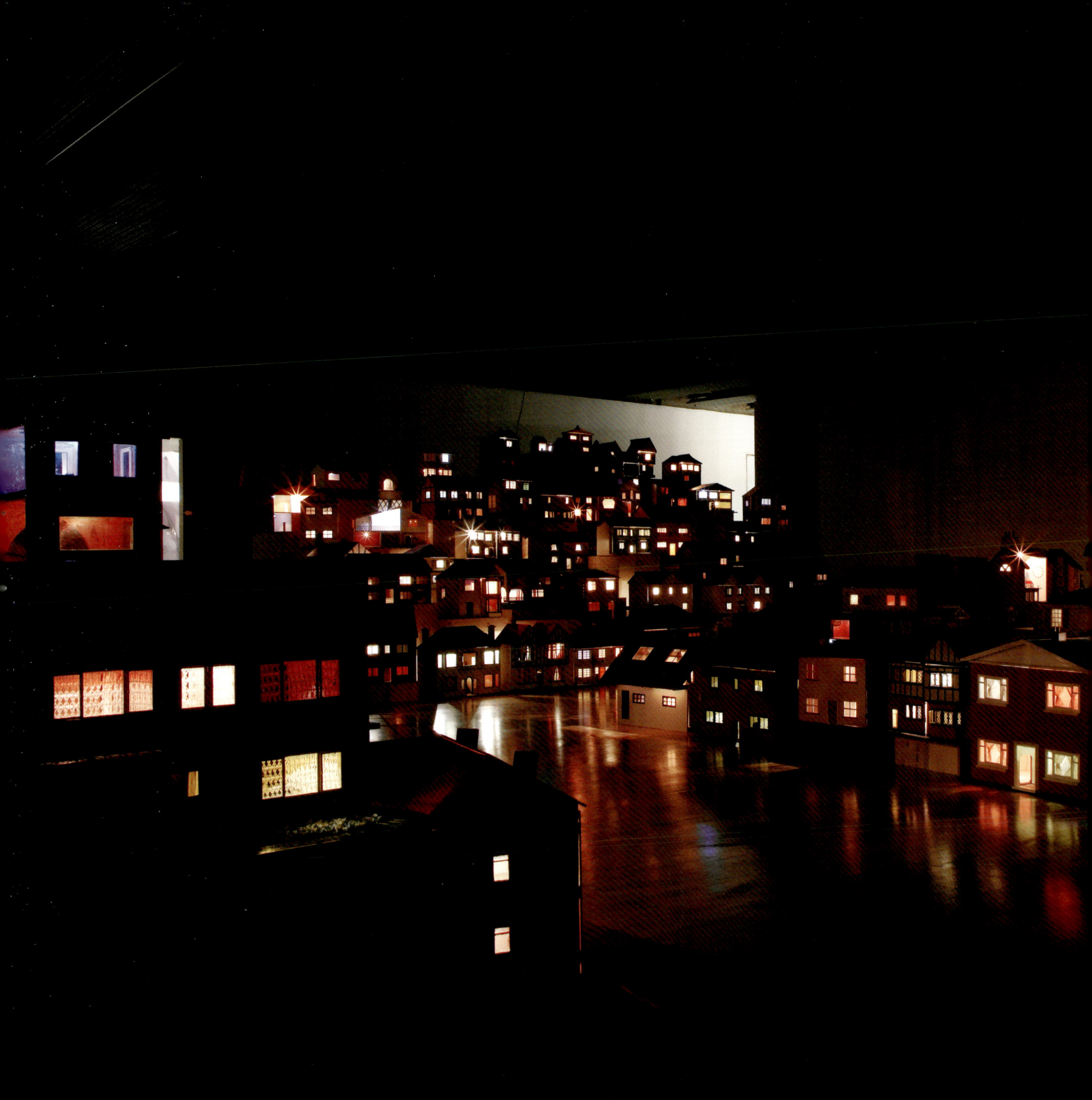

Place, 2008

RACHEL WHITEREAD

IAIN SINCLAIR

All the lights are on in the stacked town. There is an enforced hierarchy of size in a place condemned to perpetual night, the largest and most important dwellings front the harbour (or river) that isn't there. There are no sirens, no surveillance helicopters, no shrieks from rutting foxes. *Where have they gone, the humans?* Nuclear families with their tiny chairs and unyielding beds. And the dogs who refuse to bark in the night. Why have they vanished, leaving a conglomerated settlement of over 200 houses open to the darkened skies, every window blazing? A very quiet catastrophe. A civilisation that has disappeared into the huge boxes that once contained it. The deserted set, so alien in its Englishness, is like one of those fake settlements the SAS use to practice anti-terrorist tactics. Or a hamlet built to be bombed on the Isle of Grain.

Rachel Whiteread's *Place* (2008) is, by its unadorned title, a linear descendant of the celebrated *House* (1993) and the earlier *Ghost* (1990), a negative-space casting of an Archway Road room in an unfashionable quarter of north London. The germ of her artistic practice, as the artist understands it, flows back to a child-self hiding away within the comforting darkness of a mother's wardrobe, among clothes and shoes, particular smells. There is no C.S. Lewis trapdoor to another world, no theology to impose, just a heightened perception of space, a hunger for physical memorials to transient textures. The fossils of deep-time. Human heat is recovered through considered geometric arrangements, sharp edges, no curves. Sentiment is neutralised by a sequence of workmanlike procedures that must arrive at some intimate construction, probably white and cold-blooded, offered up to the public gaze.

If the long journey towards *Place* begins with the casting of a cupboard, then an abandoned room, those sites could be managed with discretion. The *House* project on Grove Road, an area caught between the old London of squat terraced streets and the evolving Docklands corridor, was a much more troubling exposure: to the furious realpolitik of a borderland borough where every visible manifestation of art was an incendiary act. Whiteread took the last survivor of a row of houses damaged by wartime bombing raids and cast its interior, by a complex industrial process, to create a paradoxical structure that defied easy interpretation. The icy block, with spectral traces of stairs and fireplaces, seemed to have been turned inside out. The skin of the work was no sooner revealed than it was decorated by hot graffiti. Practices that honour personal obsession must, directly or indirectly, respond to the politics of place. Grove Road was on the border of everything: new money leaking out of Docklands, a local tradition of communal living in crumbling properties, eco parks running down to the river Thames. The achievement of this built-to-vanish monument was to become, very quickly, a place of pilgrimage that anticipated a cultural drift to the east of the city, the computer-generated playground of the Olympic Park in the Lower Lea Valley.

Spending long hours, forensically masked and covered, inside the sole survivor of a Grove Road terrace, Whiteread came to admire the eccentric DIY interventions of the house's previous occupier, Mr Gale. She relished clashing migraine colours, palimpsests of bad wallpaper decisions, scratched floorboards and trailing wires. In those memories, she locates the germ of the *Place* project.

Over a period of 20 years, Whiteread accumulated a collection of dollhouses, chosen for their nakedness and lack of sophistication: small thick squares of carpet like discarded psychedelic wigs. The implication being that the houses would, one day, be cast, processed and metamorphosed into the artist's catalogue. When she lived close to Kingsland Road in Hackney, Whitread was a familiar at the Waste Market; she combed beaches of errant and accidental rubbish. London's chartered markets, under threat from civic busybodies, factor a lowlife Surrealism: odd keys, tools, straw hats perched on stuffed goats. The market taught Whiteread how to build a speculative topography from boards and trestles. The hillside on which *Place* has been constructed evolves from the customised coffin-boxes in which individual dollhouses have been packed away or prepared for transport. Supporting ladders look like pylons in a liminal landscape, some brownfield site waiting for its development package.

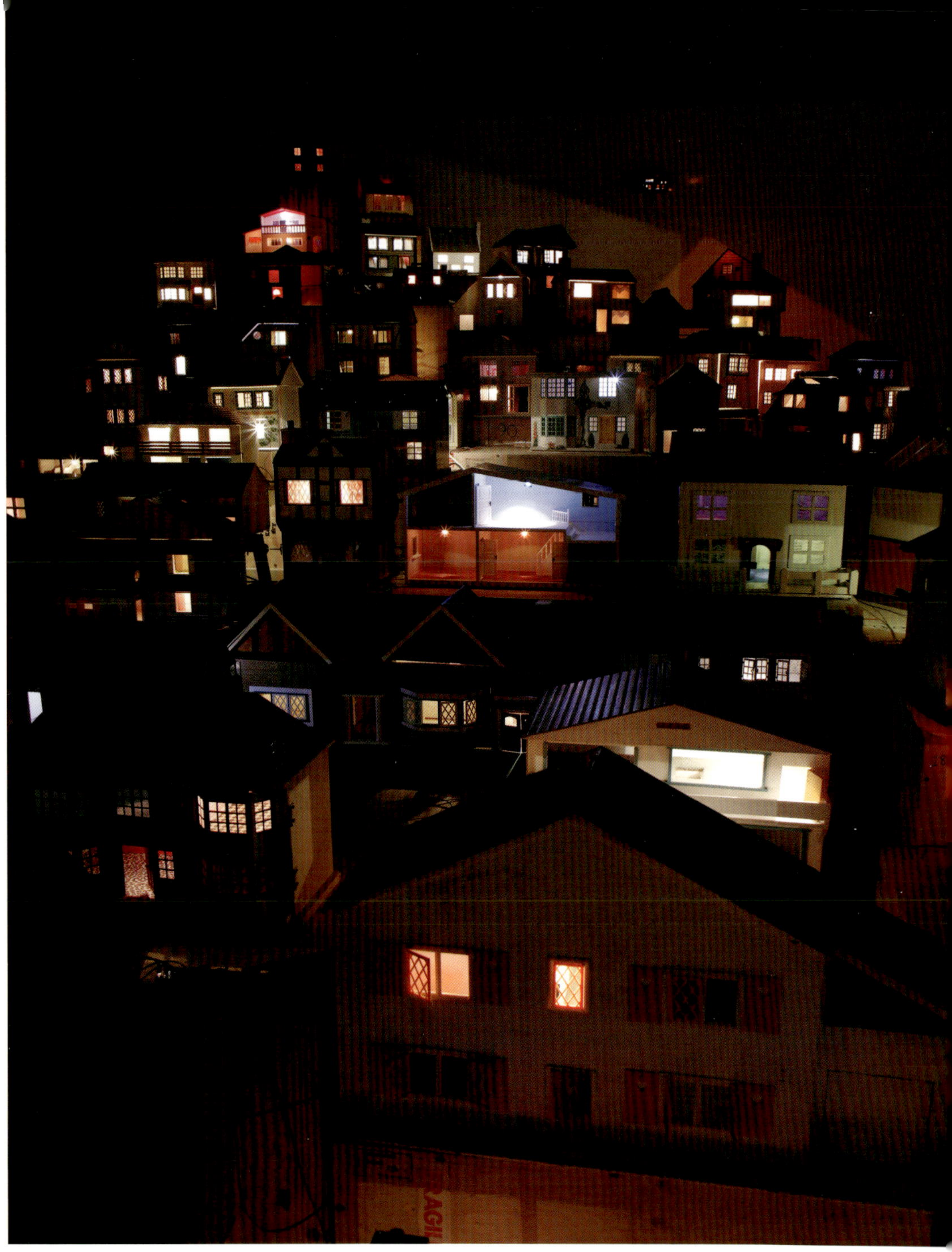

The dollhouses, stored within the artist's studio, have such presence, so ripe a past history, that they resist casting. Here are individual histories of dirt and cobwebs, plywood kennels spurning display. Whiteread loves her Tudorbethan hutches, the Arts and Crafts villas with Metroland ambitions. She is both architect and sole developer of an enigma: the migrated suburb that looks like an Ackroydian model of London, all historical periods co-existing. Soliciting the next Great Fire.

Place, initially a gathering of 52 houses, was first shown at MADRE in Naples: a setting that reminded Whiteread of the Hackney of 20 years ago. The miniaturised future estate is a contemporary icon: ghost towers on long tables, sites marked for demolition. In an age preoccupied with shoehorning uniform developments onto the flood plains of the Thames Estuary, it's an intriguing perversion to bring one of them inside the brutalist hulk of The Hayward. The beauty of *Place* is that is doesn't have to be built. It isn't a model of some compulsory future. It's wonderful that a nightmare version of Prince Charles' little England village of Poundbury should be exhibited in a building that gave him the vapours as he drifted down the Thames, sounding off about the iniquities of late-modernist architects.

Place, **2008**

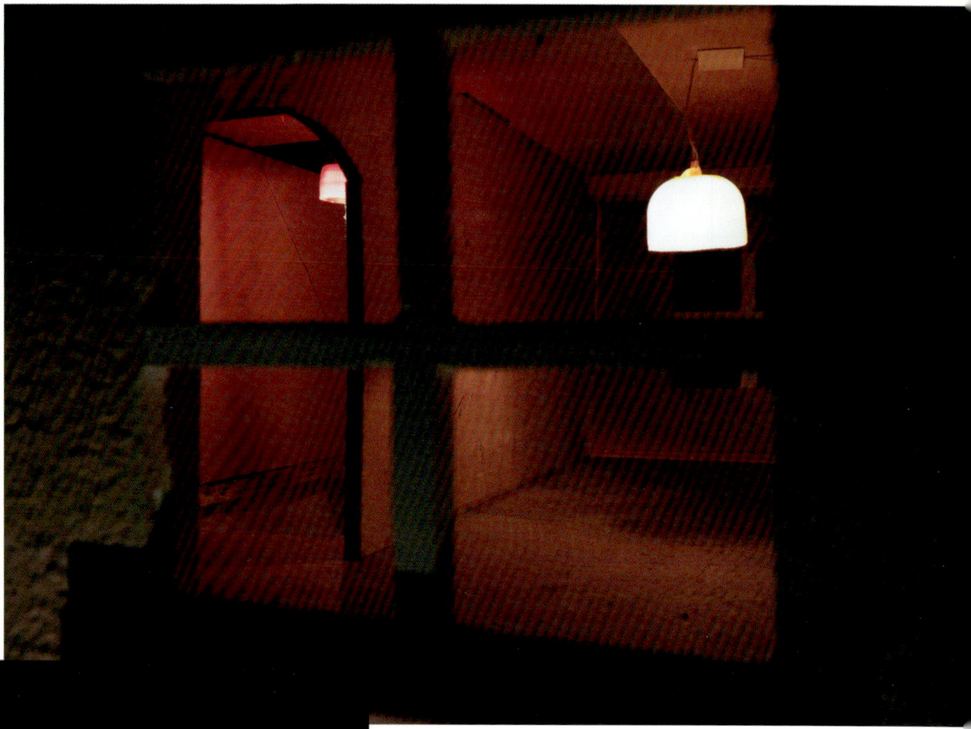

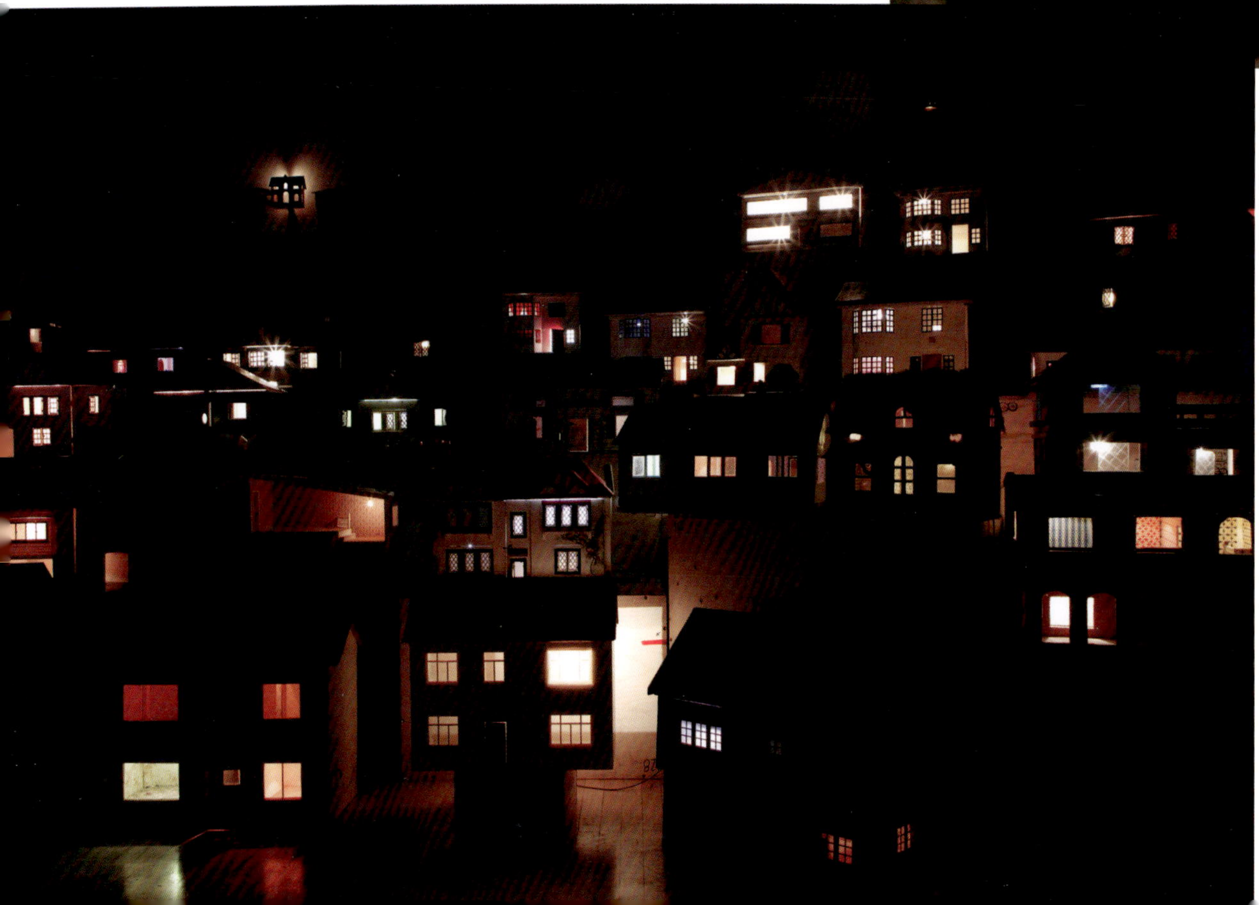

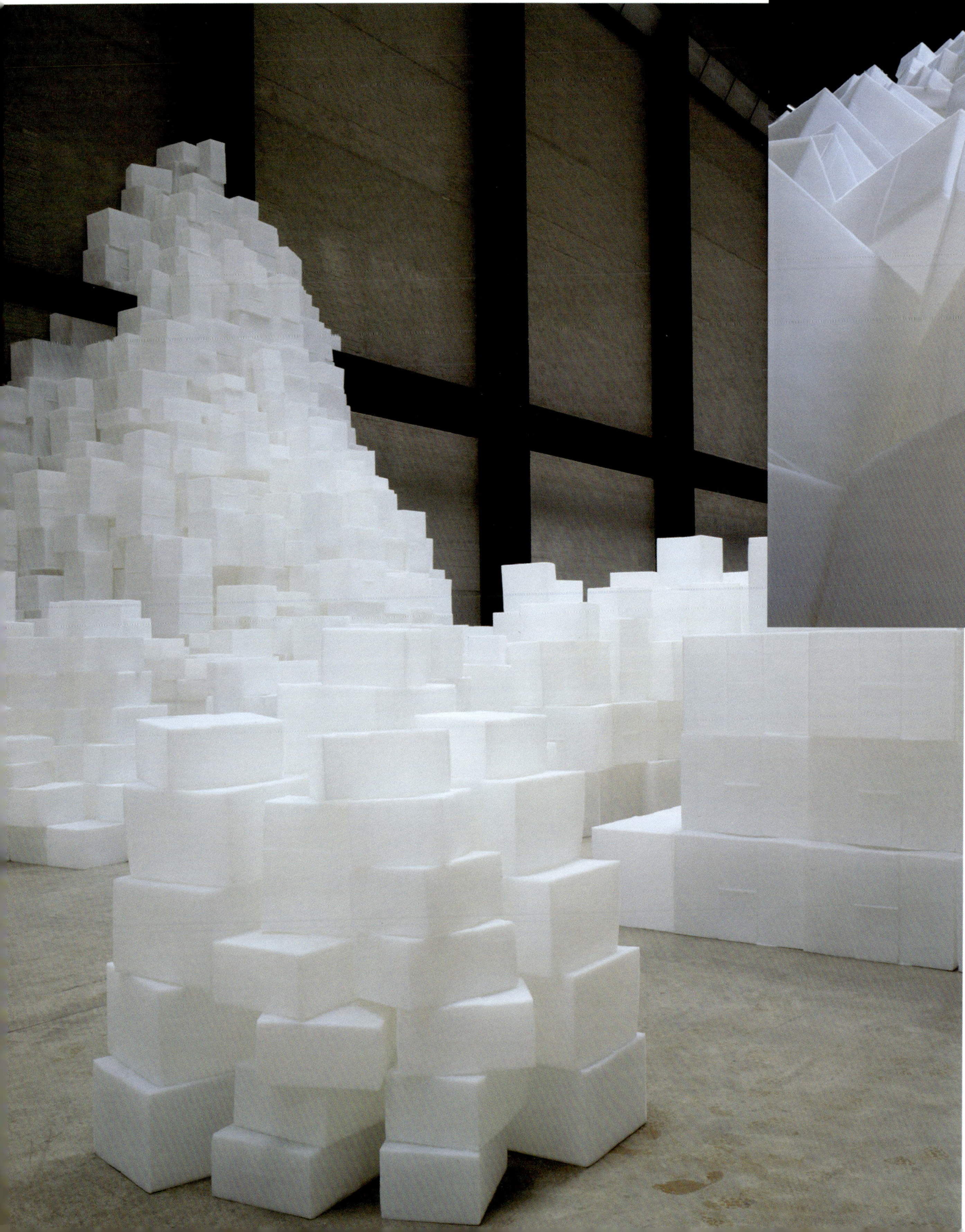
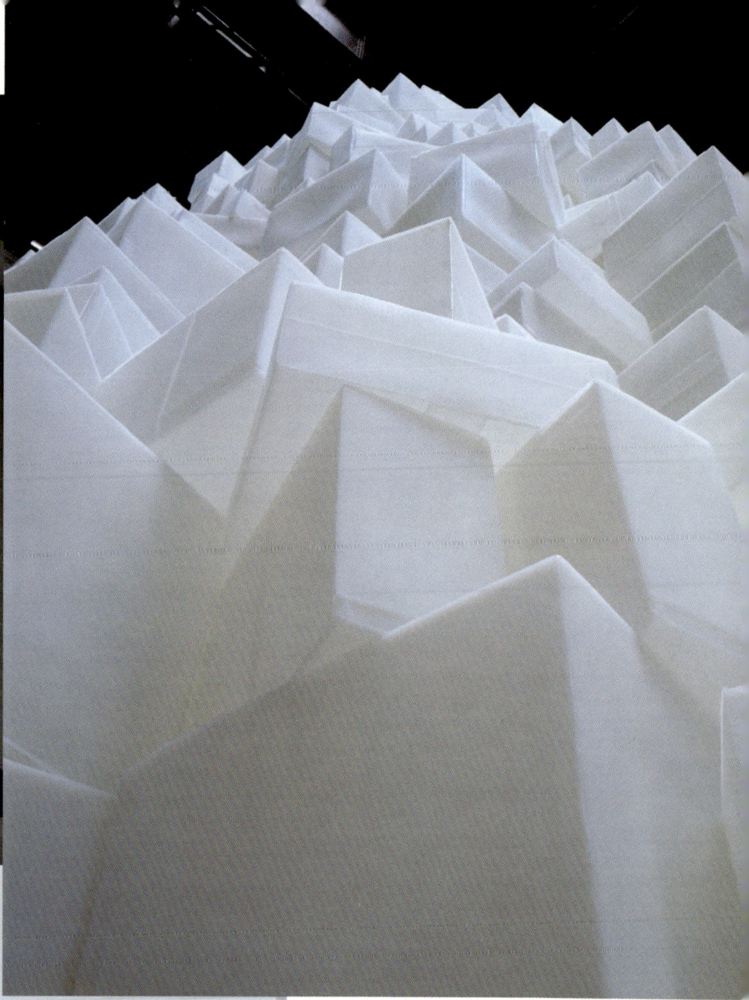

Embankment, **2005**

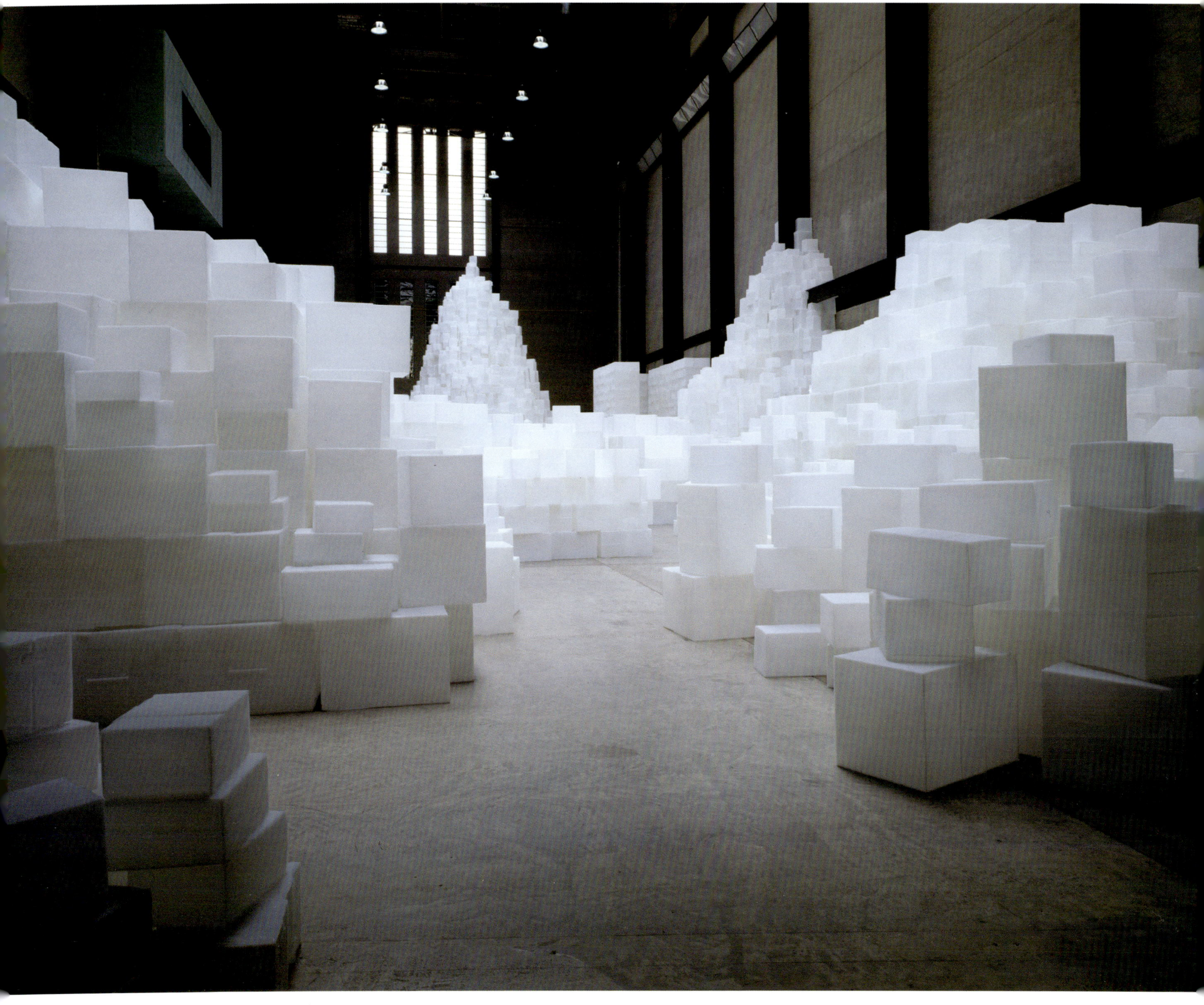

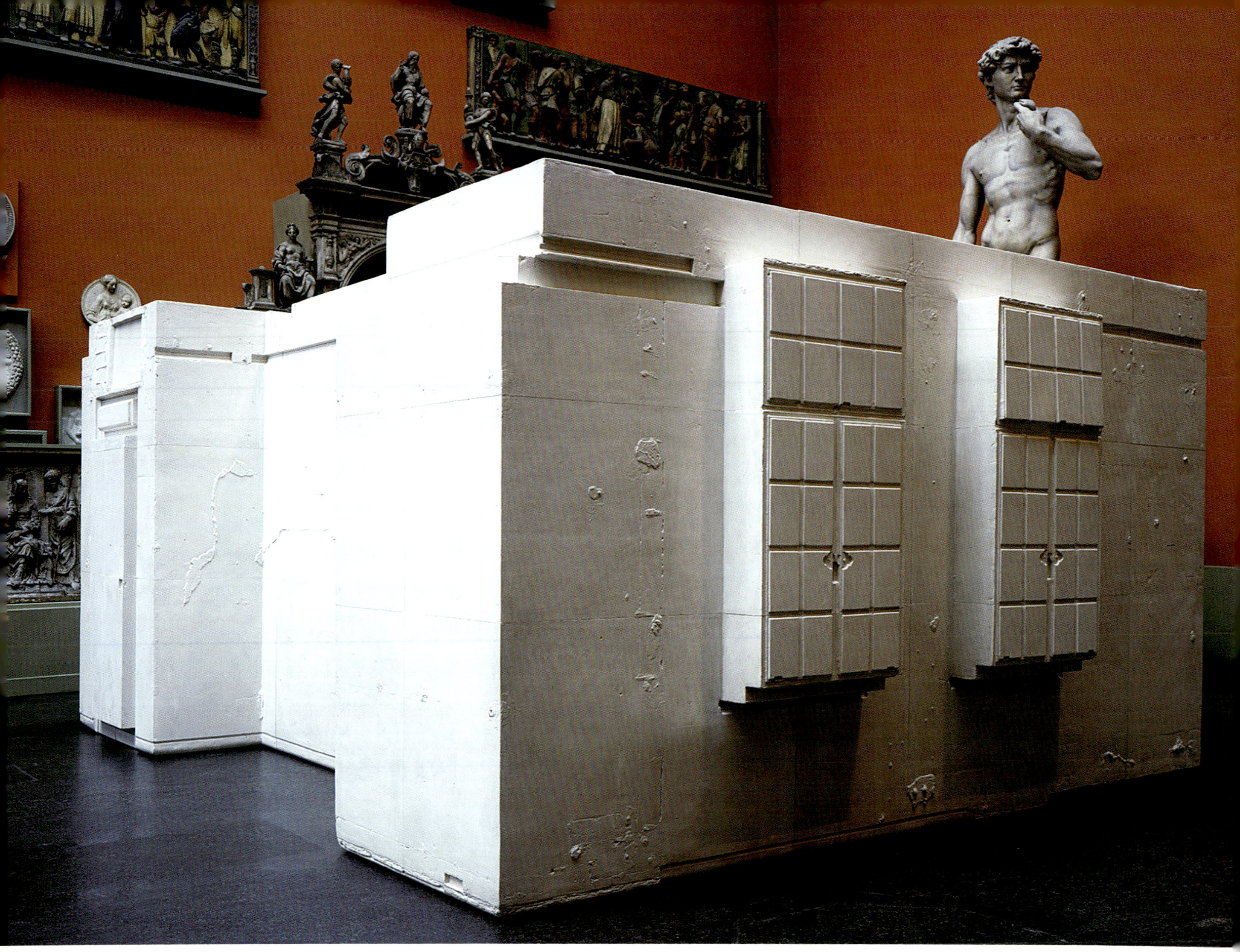

Untitled (Room 101), **2003**

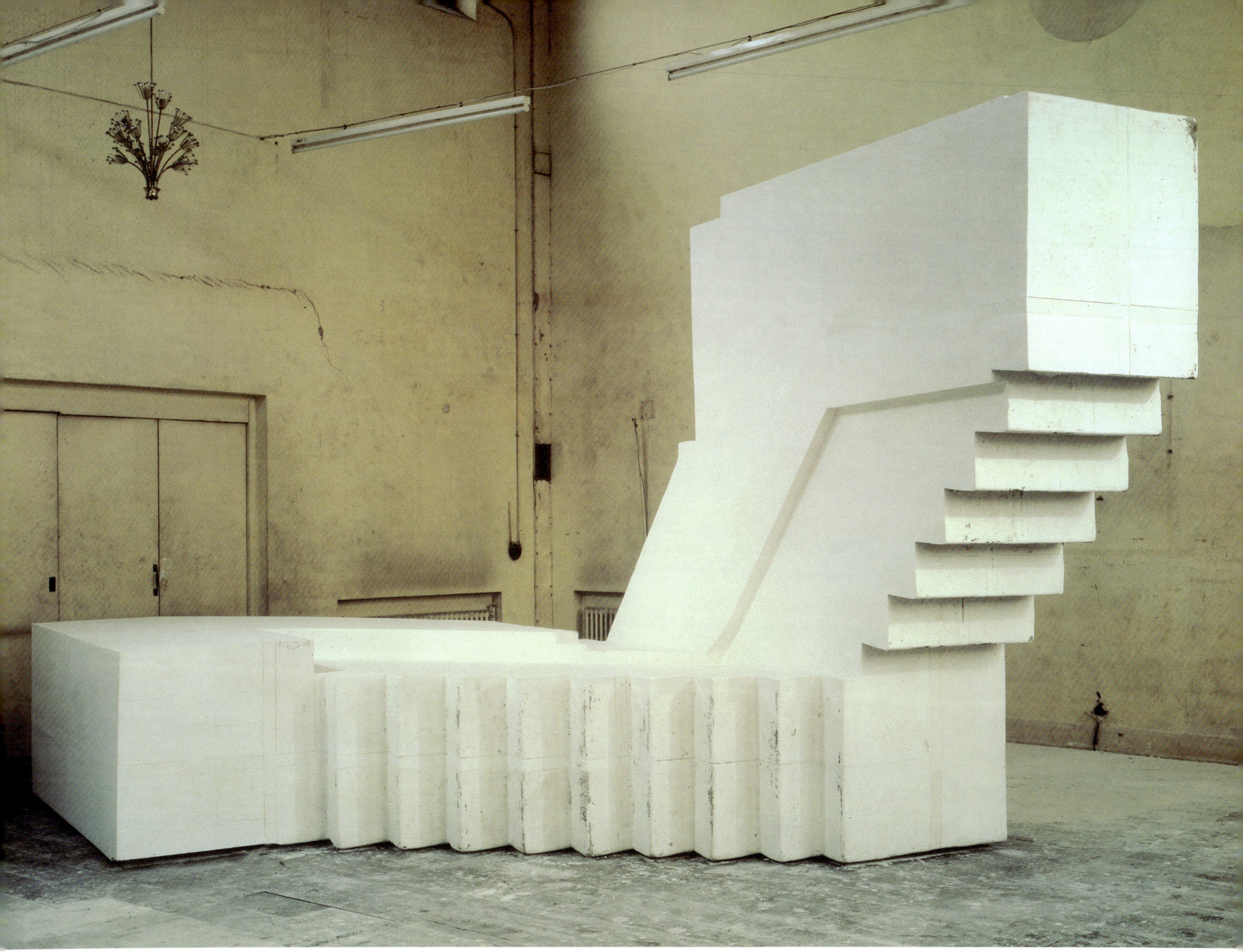

Untitled (Basement), **2000–01**

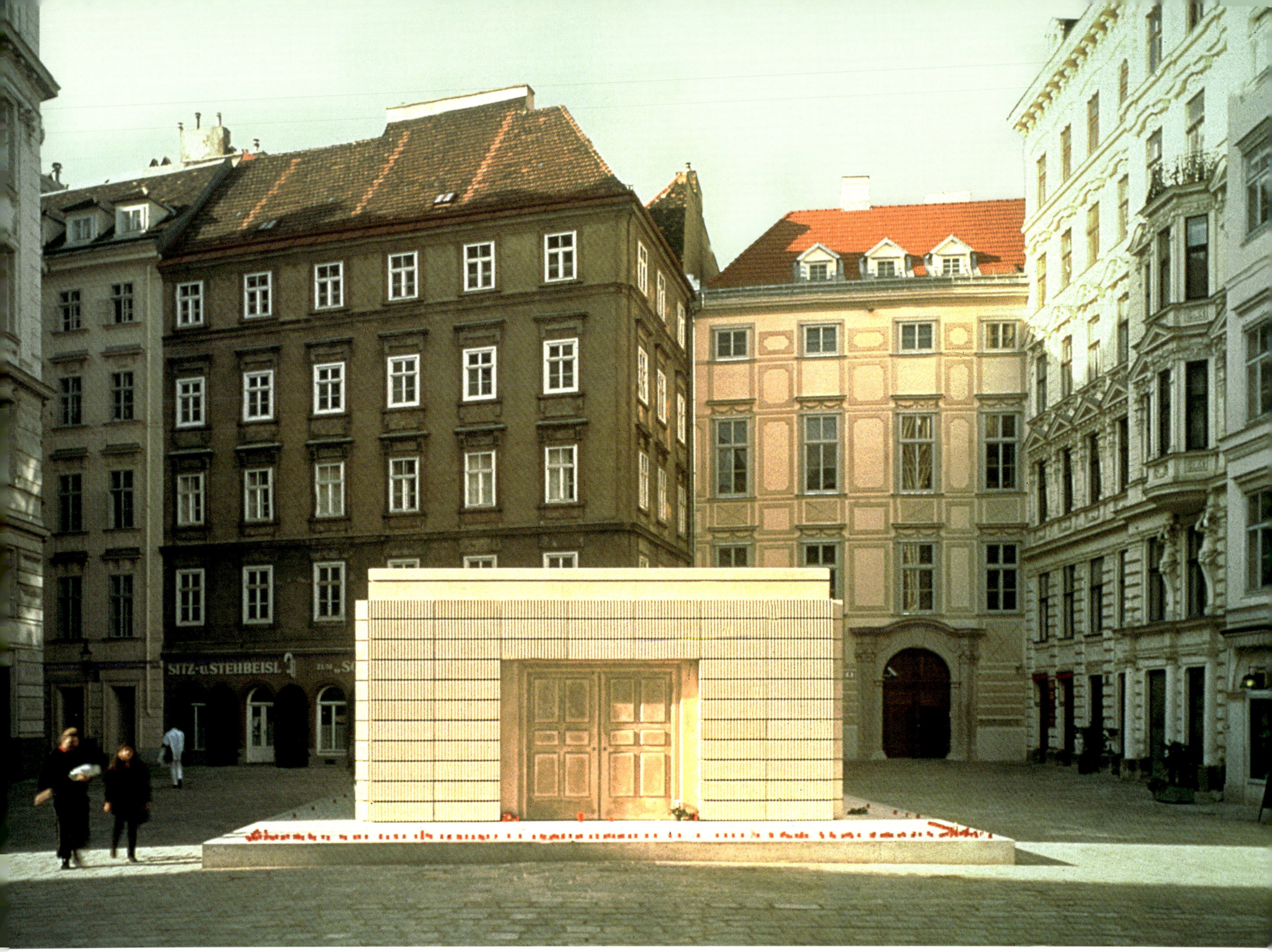

Holocaust Memorial,
Judenplatz, Vienna, **2000**

Water Tower, **1998**

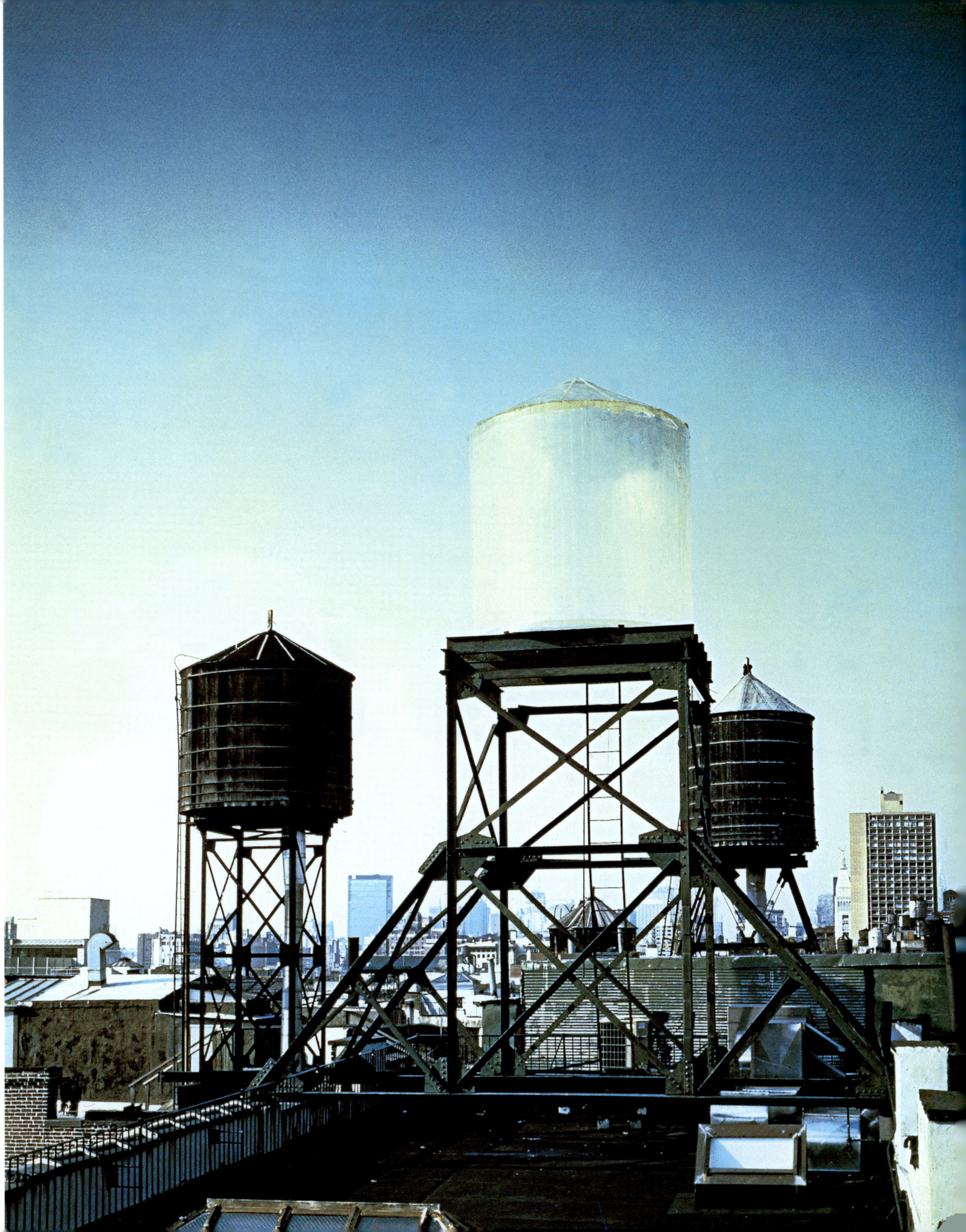

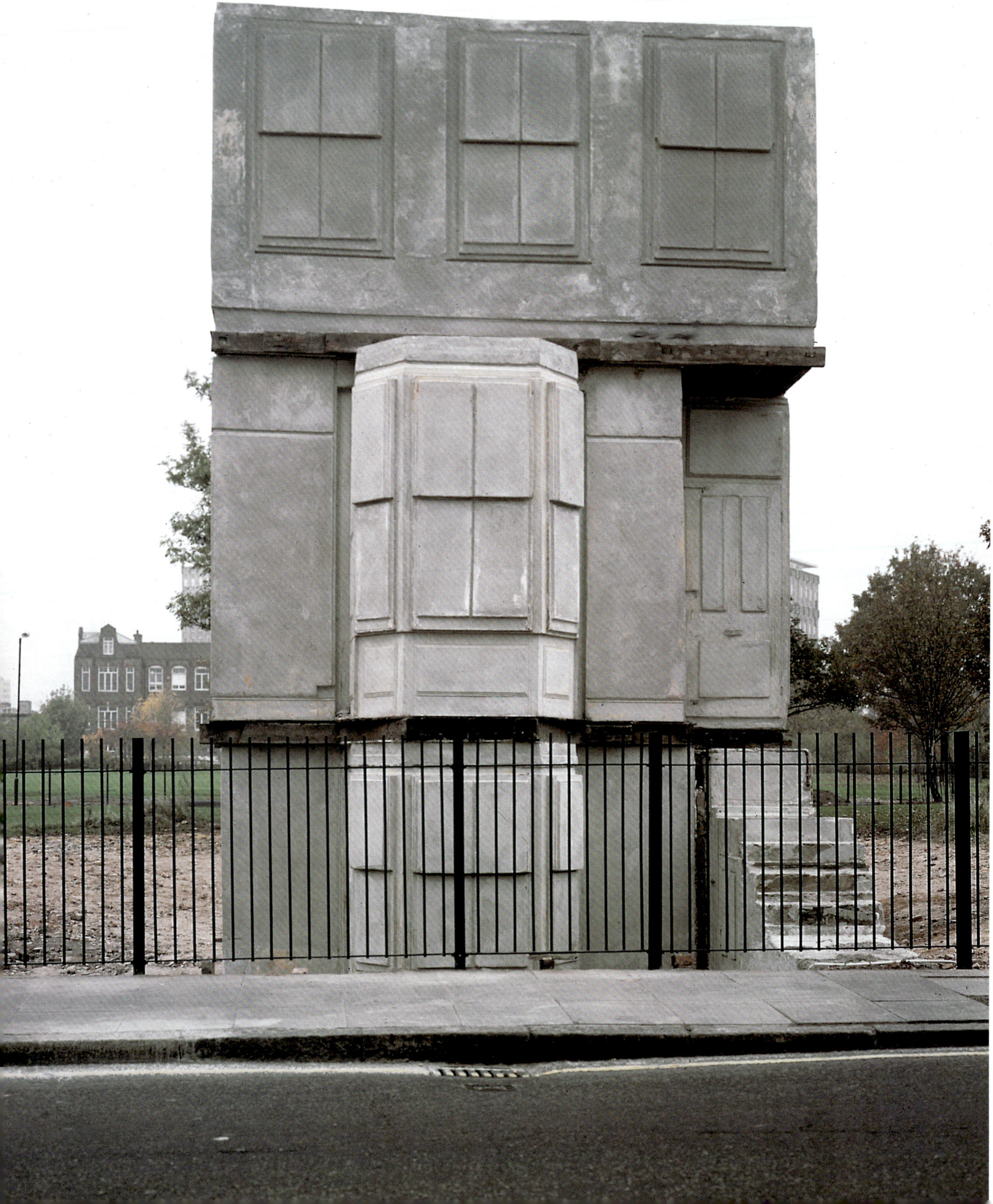

House, **1993**

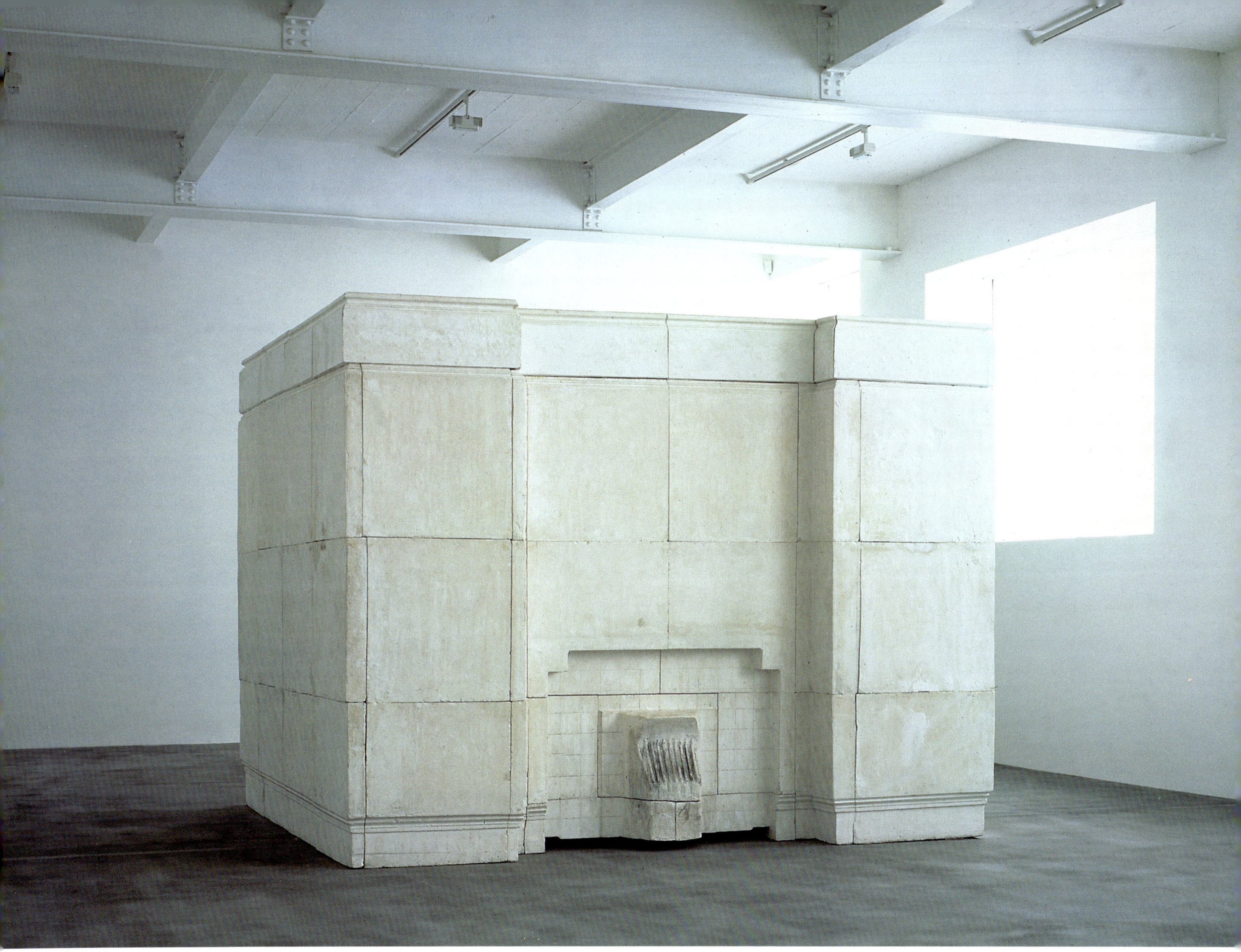

Ghost, **1990**

PSYCHO BUILDINGS
AN ILLUSTRATED HISTORY

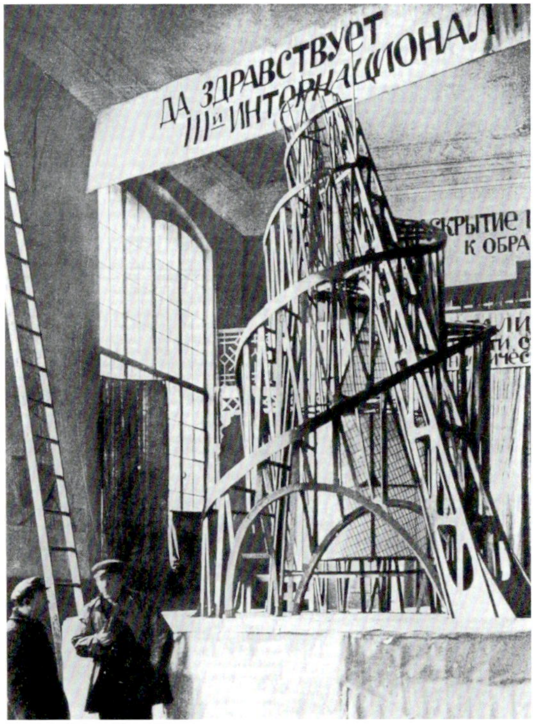

Vladimir Tatlin with his model of the *Monument to the Third International*, **1919/20**

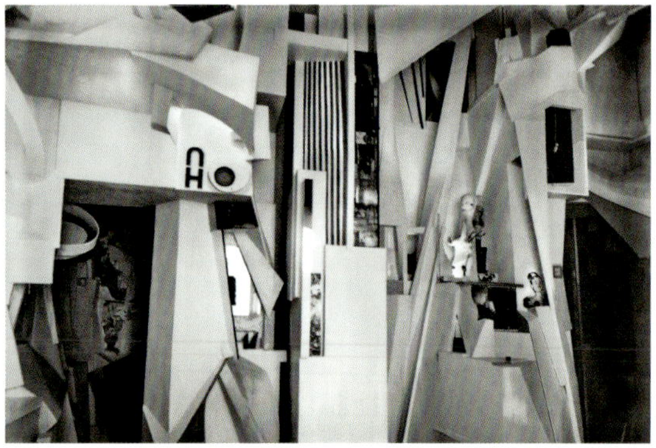

Kurt Schwitters
Merzbau, **c.1932**

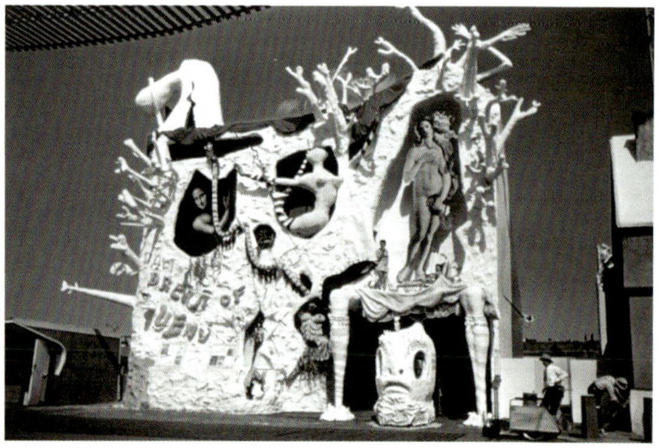

Salvador Dalí
Facade of the *Dream of Venus* **pavilion, 1939**

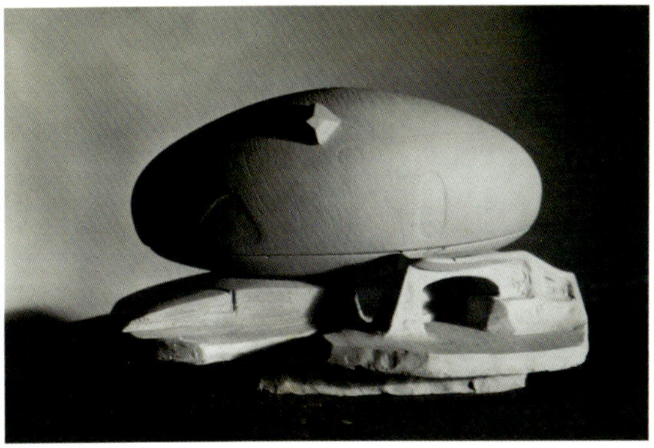

Frederick Kiesler
View of the Model of the Endless House, **1959**

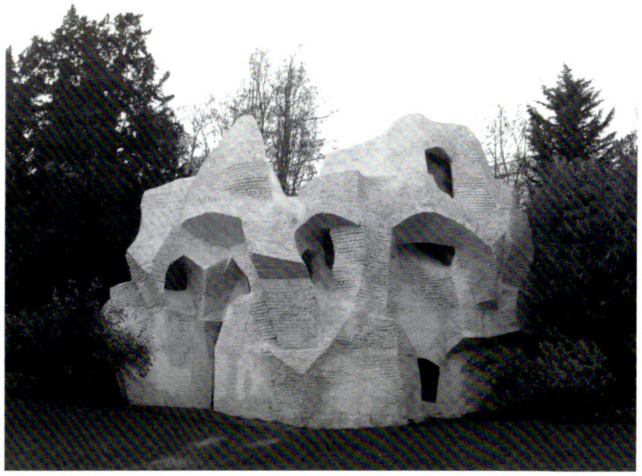

André Bloc
Sculptures-Habitacle, **1964**

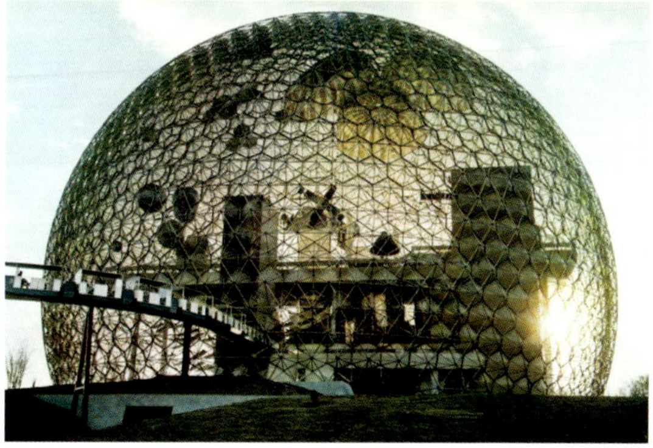

Buckminster Fuller
Geodesic Dome, Expo 67, **Montreal, 1967**

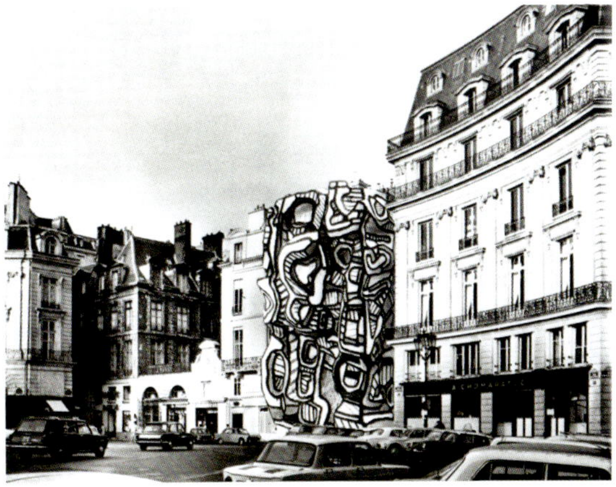

Jean Dubuffet
Photomontage of *Pavillon à deux étages*, **from** *Edifices*, **1968**

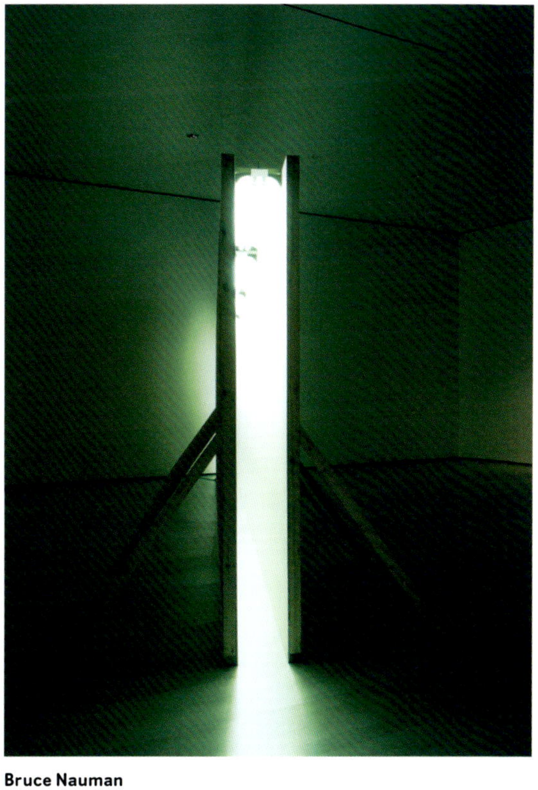

Bruce Nauman
Green Light Corridor, **1970**

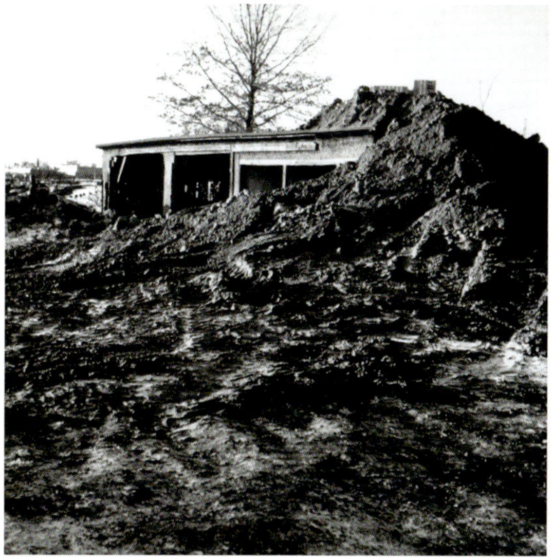

Robert Smithson
Partially Buried Woodshed, **1970**

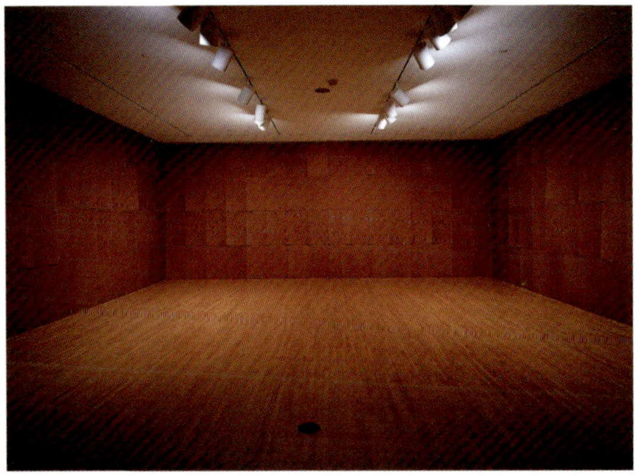

Ed Ruscha
Chocolate Room, **1970/2004**

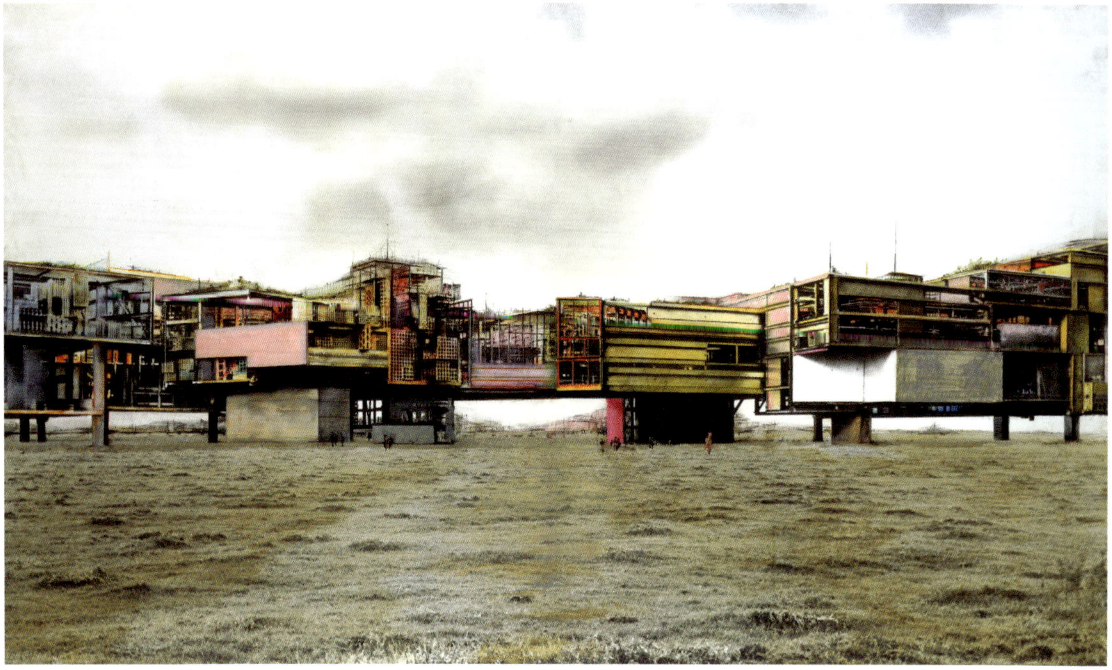

Constant A. Nieuwenhuys
View of New Babylonian Sectors, **1971**

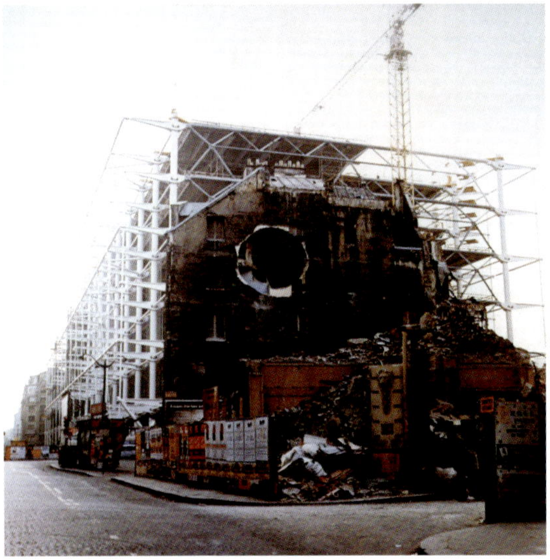

Gordon Matta-Clark
Conical Intersect, **1975**

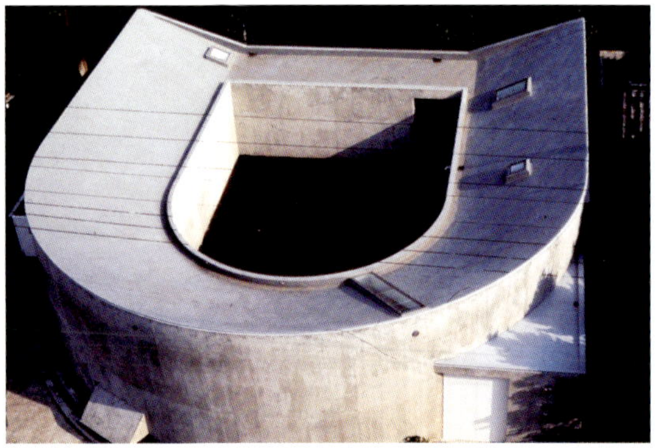

Toyo Ito
White-U, **1976**

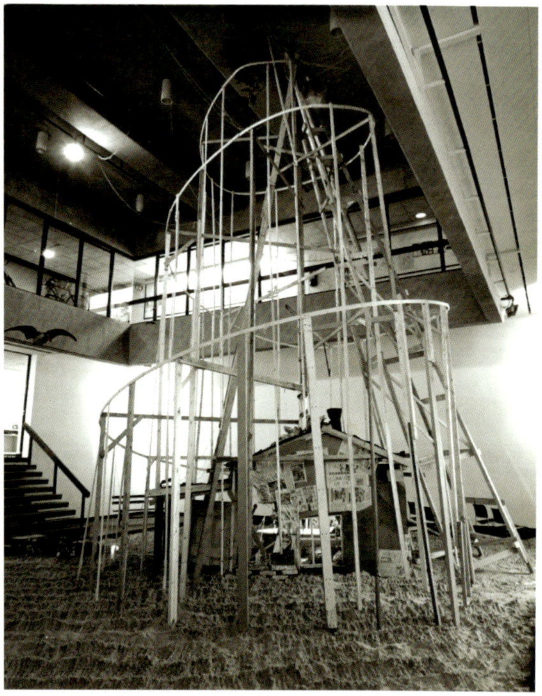

Paul Thek
Processions, **1977**

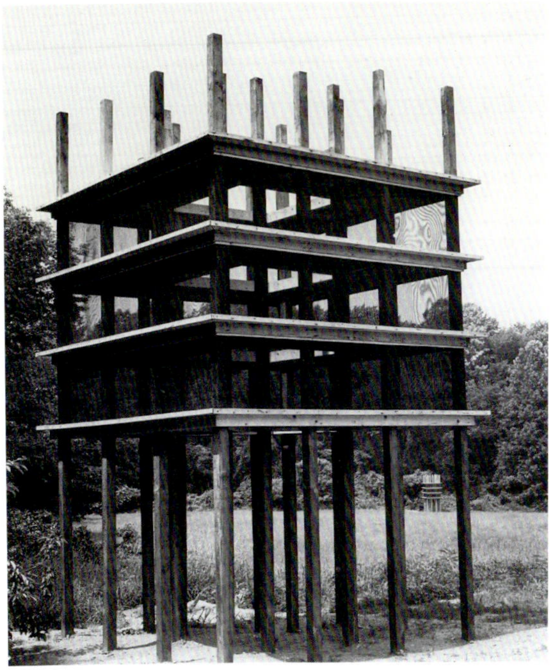

Mary Miss
Perimeters/ Pavilions/ Decoys, **1977–79**

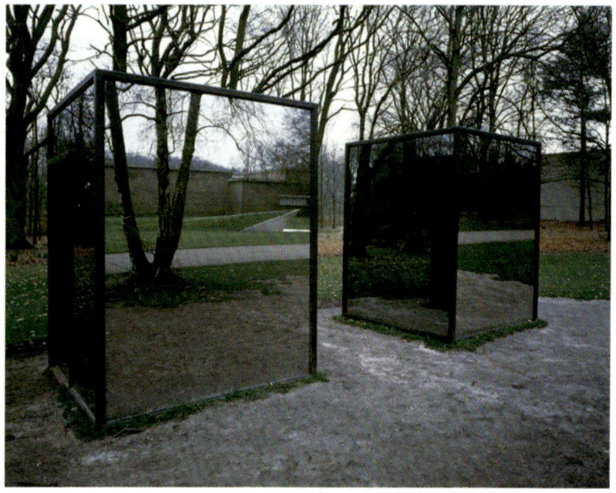

Dan Graham
Two Adjacent Pavilions, **1978–81**

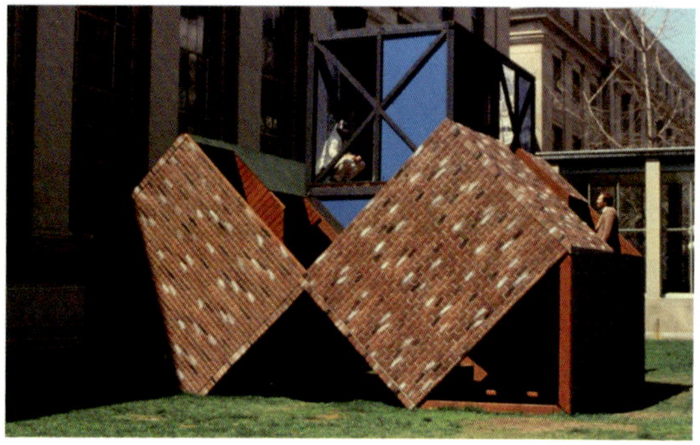

Vito Acconci
Bad Dream House, **1984**

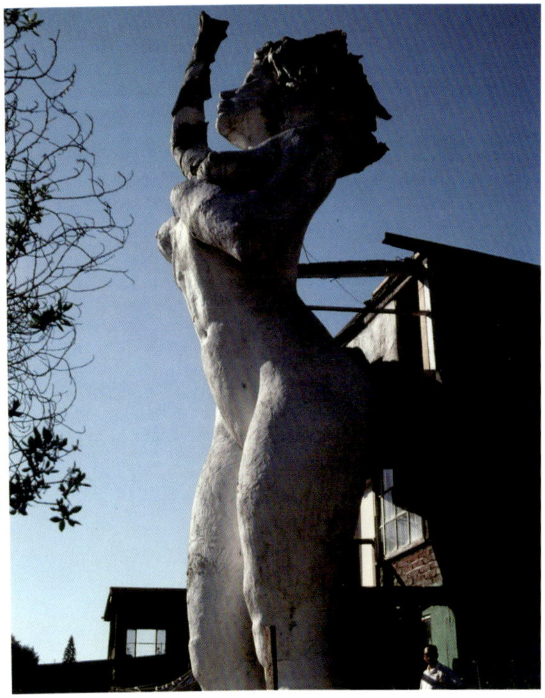

Armando Munoz-Garcia
La Mona, **1985–90**

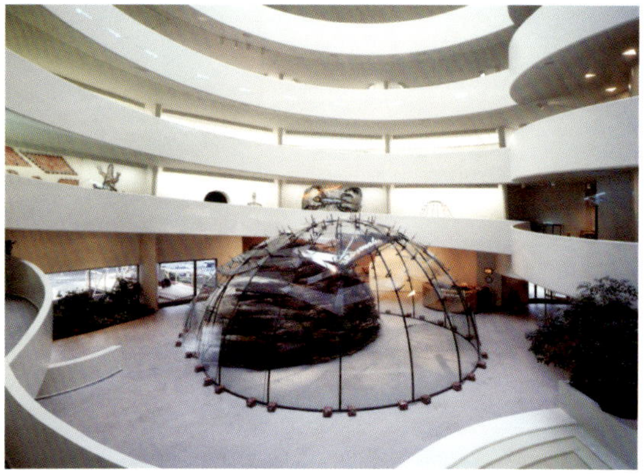

Mario Merz
Unreal City, Nineteen Hundred Eighty-Nine, **1989**

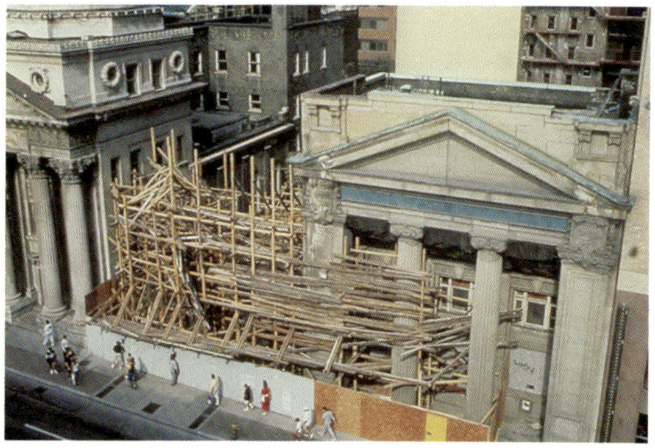

Tadashi Kawamata
Toronto Project, **1989**

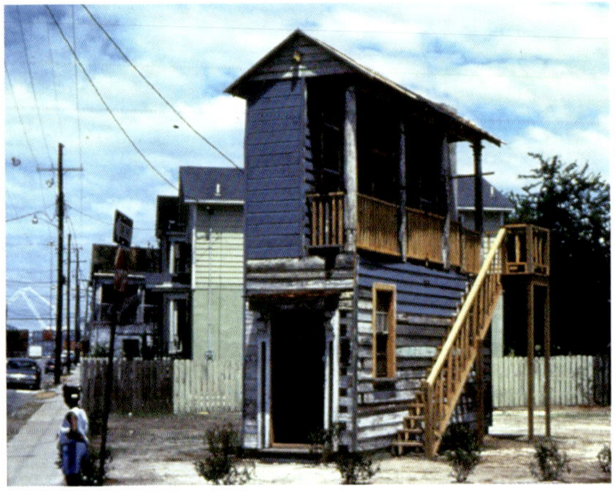

David Hammons
House of the Future, **1991**

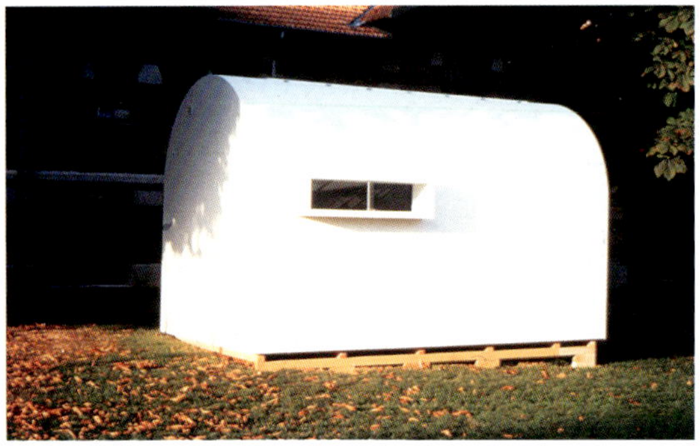

Absalon
Cellule n°1 (Prototype), **1992**

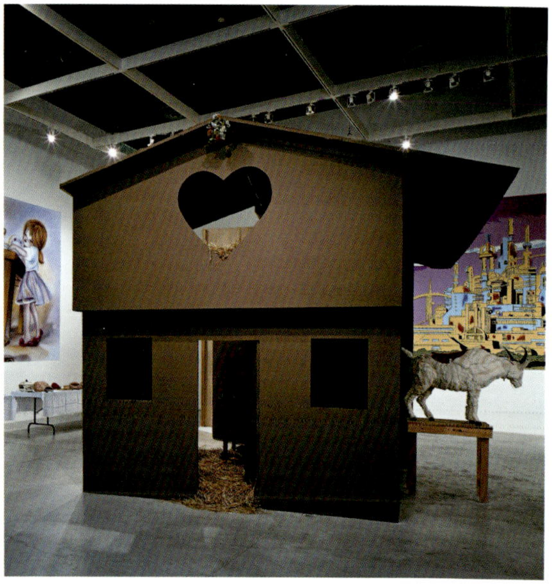

Paul McCarthy and Mike Kelley
Heidi, Midlife Crisis Trauma Center and Negative Media Engram Abreaction Release Zone, **1992**

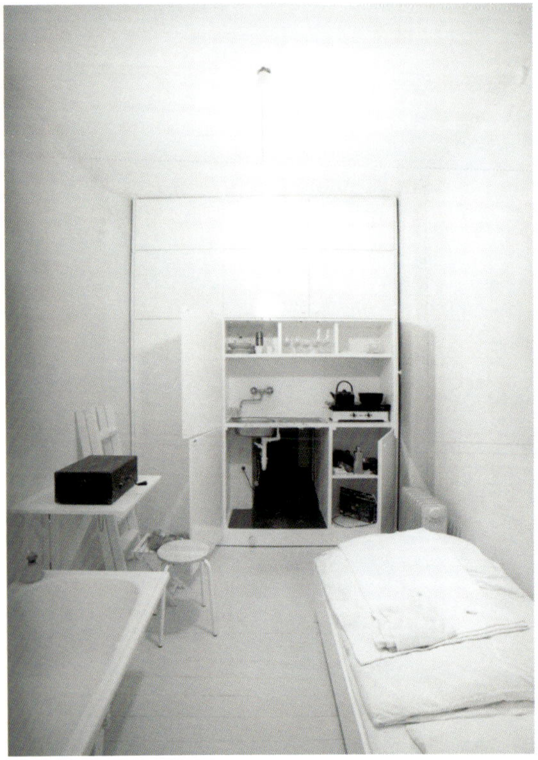

Gregor Schneider
Haus u r, **(1985–) 1995**

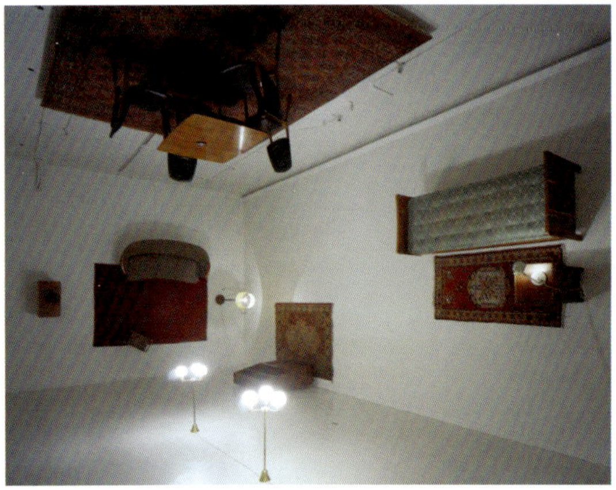

Jaroslaw Kozlowski
Gravity Room, **1995**

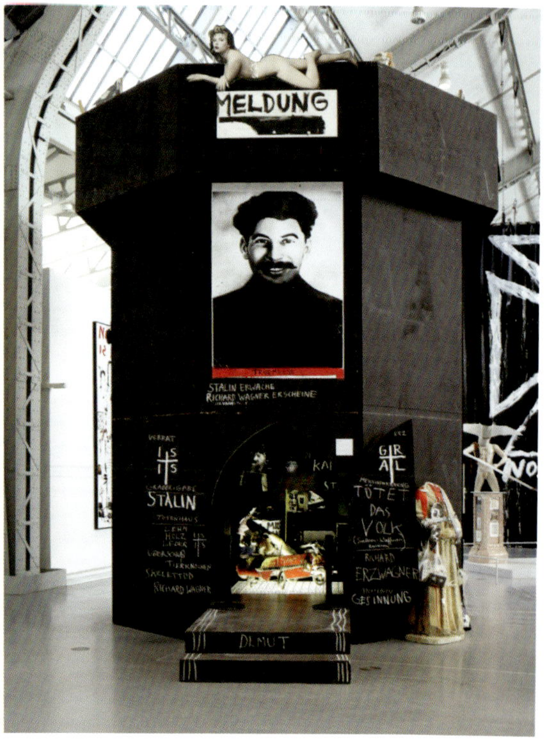

Jonathan Meese
The Third Man in the Round House/ MALDORORTURM, **1998**

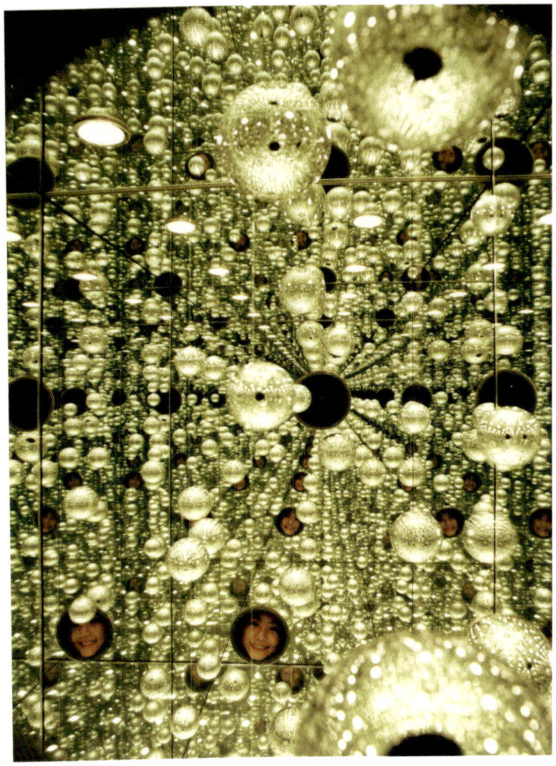

Yayoi Kusama
Infinity Mirrored Room, Rain in Early Spring, **2002**

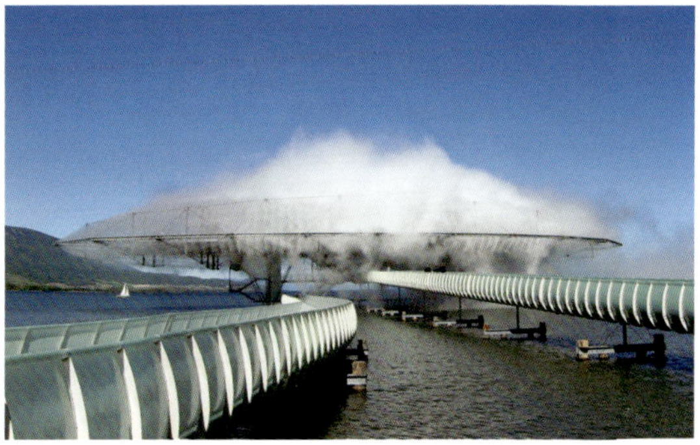

Diller+Scofidio
Blur Building, View from Shore, **2002**

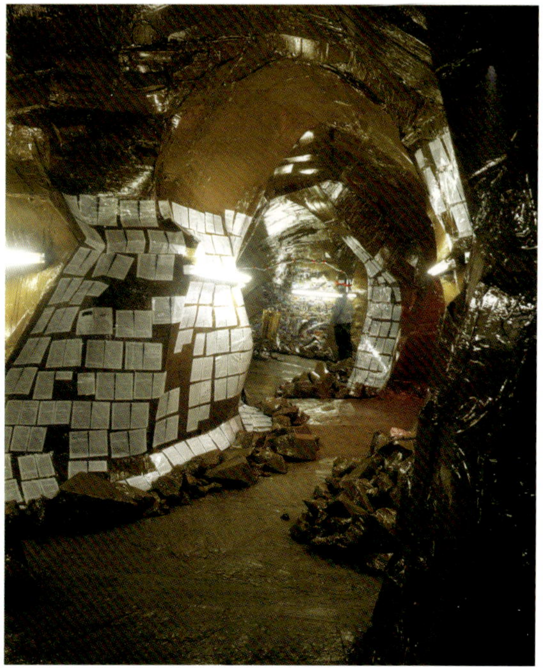

Thomas Hirschhorn
Cavemanman, **2002**

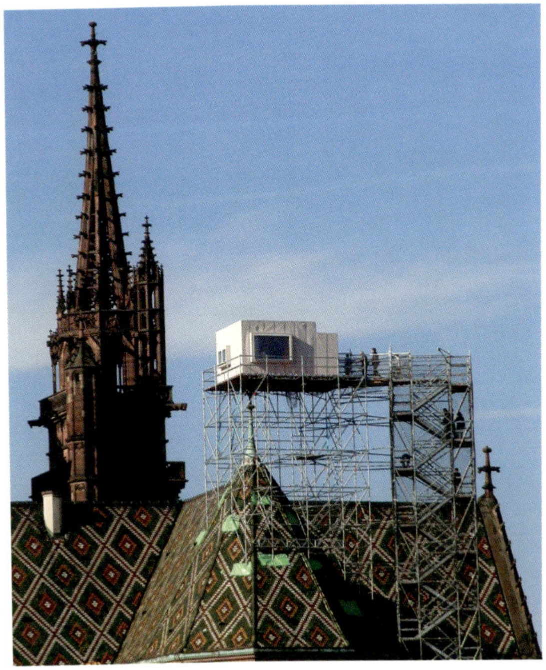

Tatzu Nishi
Engel, **2002**

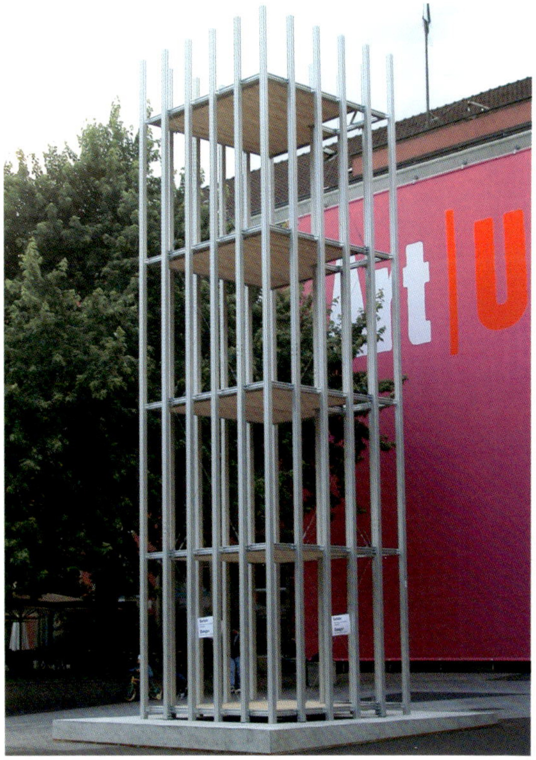

Chris Burden
Small Skyscraper, **2003**

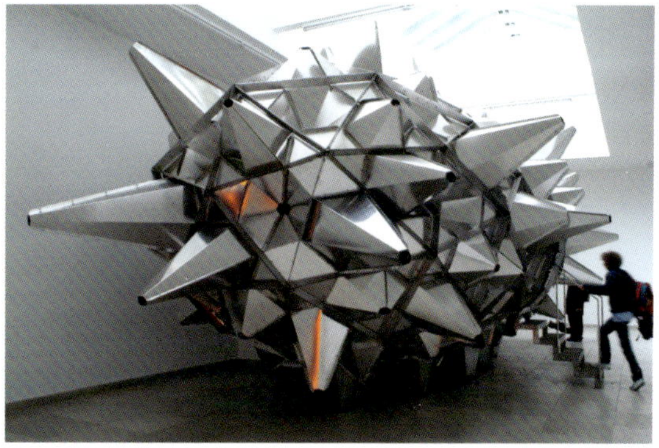

Olafur Eliasson
The antispective situation, **2003**

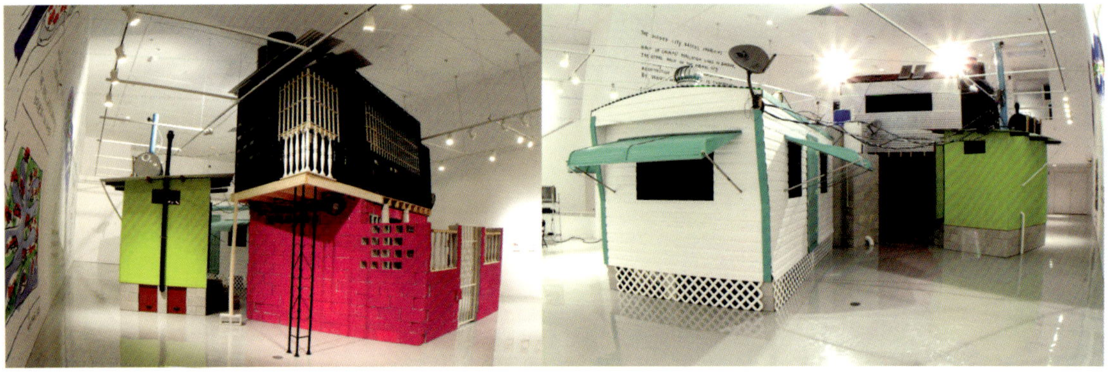

Marjetica Potrč
Hybrid House: Caracas, West Bank, West Palm Beach, **2003**

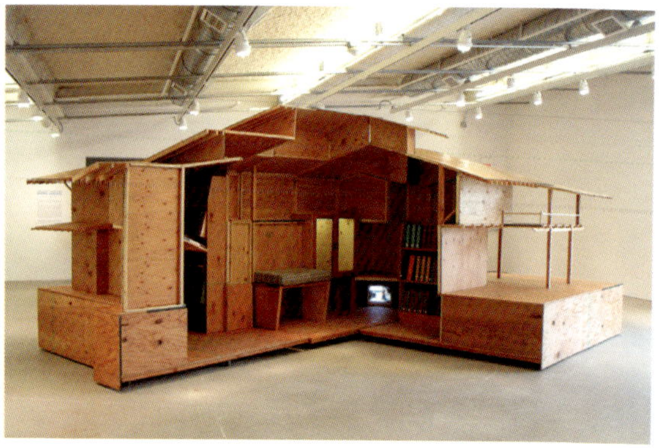

Brian Jungen
Arts and Crafts Book Depository/ Capp Street Project, **2004**

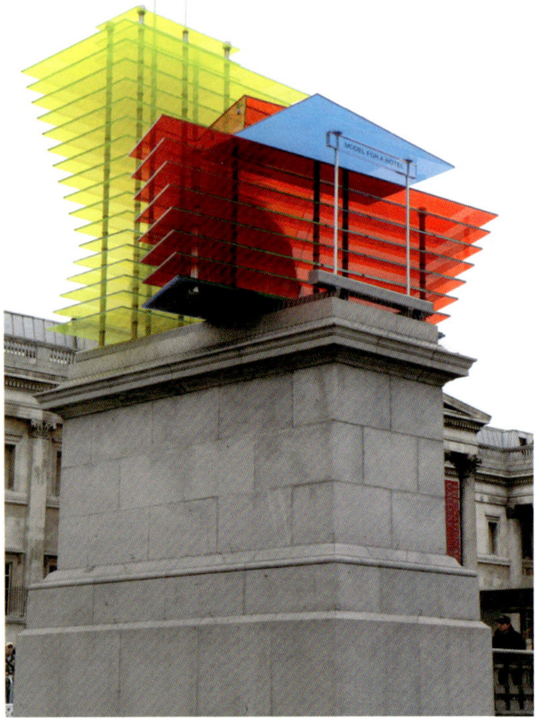

Thomas Schutte
Model for a Hotel, **2007**

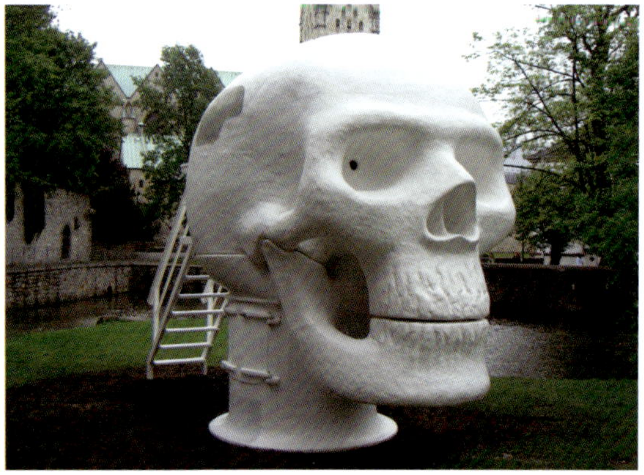

Atelier Van Lieshout
Wellness Skull, **2007**

RELATED EXHIBITIONS

1995 *Archisculpture*, **Musee d'art Contemporain, Geneva**
1999 *Anarchitecture*, **Stichting De Appel, Amsterdam**
2000 *Against Design*, **Institute of Contemporary Art, University of Pennsylvania, Philadelphia**
Wonderland, **Saint Louis Art Museum, St Louis, Missouri**
HausShau: The House in Art, **Deichtorhallen, Hamburg**
2002 *Out of Site: A Group Show of Fictional Architectural Space*, **The New Museum, New York**
2004 *The Snow Show*, **Rovaniemen Taidemuseo, Rovaniemi, Finland**
2005 *Archilab: new experiments in Architecture, Art and the City, 1950—2005*, **Mori Art Museum, Tokyo**
Art & Architecture: A Century of creative projects in building, design, cinema, painting, sculpture, **Palazzo Ducale, Genoa, Italy**
2006 *How to Live Together*, **Sao Paulo Biennale, Brazil**
2007 *Megastructure Reloaded*, **Berlin Mitte, Germany**

BIOGRAPHIES AND SELECTED EXHIBITIONS

ATELIER BOW-WOW

Yoshiharu Tsukamoto: b. 1965, Kanagawa, Japan
Momoyo Kaijima: b. 1969, Tokyo, Japan
Live and work in Tokyo

Recent solo exhibitions

Mediapod, **TITLE, Bungeishunju (2005);** *Snoopy Life Design*, **Tokyo International Forum (2005);** *Pet Architecture Guide Book Museum*, **Venice Biennale (2003);** *Les Plus Petites Maisons per Atelier Bow-Wow*, **IFA, Paris (2001);** *Pet Architecture*, **Gallery MA, Tokyo (2000)**

Recent group exhibitions

Monkey Way, **Sao Paulo Biennale (2006); Yokohama Triennale, Yamashita Pier, Yokohama, Kanagawa (2005);** *How latitudes becomes forms: Art in a Global Age*, **Walker Art Center, Minneapolis (2003); Fukuoka Asian Art Triennale (2002); Gwangju Biennale (2002)**

For more information
www.bow-wow.jp

MICHAEL BEUTLER

b. 1976, Oldenburg, Germany
Lives and works in Berlin, Germany

Recent solo exhibitions

Portikus, Frankfurt (2007); *Aluminium Pagode*, **Lufthansa Aviation Center, Frankfurt (2006);** *Manin City*, **Villa Manin (2006); Kunstverein Braunschweig (2004); Wiener Secession, Vienna (2002)**

Recent group exhibitions

Kunstmaschinen Maschinenkunst, **Schirn Kunsthalle, Frankfurt (2007);** *Dialectics of hope*, **Moscow Biennale (2005);** *Whitecubeponderosa*, **Griesinger Schule, permanent installation, Frankfurt (2002);** *New Heimat*, **Frankfurter Kunstverein, Frankfurt (2001)**

For more information
www.galerie-nagel.de

GELITIN

Wolfgang Gantner: b. 1968
Ali Janka: b. 1970
Florian Reither: b. 1970
Tobias Urban: b. 1971
Live and work in Vienna, Austria

Recent solo exhibitions

La Louvre Paris, **Musée d'Art moderne de la Ville de Paris (2008);** *The Dig Cunt*, **Six Actions for New York City, Creative Time, New York (2007);** *Chinese Synthese Leberkäse*, **Kunsthaus Bregenz (2006);** *Nasser Klumpatsch*, **Institute of Contemporary Art Sofia, Bulgaria (2004);** *Die totale Osmose*, **Venedig, Austrian Pavilion with Granular Synthesis, Venice Biennale (2001);** *The B-Thing*, **Lower Manhattan Cultural Council, World Trade Center, New York (2000)**

Recent group exhibitions

Hamsterwheel, **Venice Biennale, and tour (2007);** *Dionysiac*, **Centre Pompidou, Paris (2005);** *Armpit*, **Liverpool Biennial (2002);** *Furball, Playing amongst the ruins*, **Royal College of Art, London (2001)**

For more information
www.gelitin.net

LOS CARPINTEROS

Marco Antonio Castillo Valdés: b. 1971, Camagüey, Cuba
Dagoberto Rodríguez Sánchez: b. 1969, Caibarién, Las Villas, Cuba
Live and work in Havana, Cuba

Recent solo exhibitions

Los Carpinteros: Inventing the World / Inventar el mundo, **USF Contemporary Art Center, University of South Florida, Tampa, and tour (2005–06);** *Fluido*, **Museo Nacional de Bellas Artes, Havana (2003);** *Los Carpinteros' intervention at B. Opening*, **BALTIC, Gateshead (2002);** *Túneles Populares*, **Palacio de Abrahante, Salamanca, Spain (2001);** *Ciudad Transportable*, **PS1, New York, and tour (2001)**

Recent group exhibitions

Cuba, Art and History. From 1868 to today, **Musée des Beaux Arts, Montreal (2008);** *Manipulations on Economies of Deceit*, **Prague Biennale of Contemporary Art, and tour (2005);** *Art and Architecture 1900–2000*, **Palazzo Ducale, Padua (2004); Sao Paulo Biennale (2002); Havana Biennale, Fortaleza de la Cabaña (2000)**

For more information
www.loscarpinteros.net

MIKE NELSON

b. 1967, Loughborough, UK
Lives and works in London, UK

Recent solo exhibitions

A Psychic Vacuum, **Creative Time, New York (2007);** *Lonely Planet*, **ACCA, Melbourne (2006);** *Spanning Fort Road and Mansion Street – Between a formula and a code*, **Turner Contemporary, Margate (2005);** *Triple Bluff Canyon*, **Modern Art Oxford (2004);** *Nothing is True. Everything is Permitted*, **Institute of Contemporary Art, London (2001);** *The Deliverance and The Patience*, **Peer Commission for the 2001 Venice Biennale, off-site project at The Old Brewery, Giudecca (2001)**

Recent group exhibitions

AMNESIAC SHRINE or The misplacement (a futurological fable): mirrored cubes – inverted – with the reflection of an inner psyche as represented by a metaphorical landscape, **Turner Prize, Tate Liverpool (2007);** *Poetic Justice*, **International Istanbul Biennale (2003); Biennale of Sydney, New Commission:** *42a Orwell St* **(2002);** *Intentional Communities*, **Rooseum – Center for Contemporary Art, Malmo (2001);** *Another Place*, **Tramway, Glasgow (New Commission:** *The Resurrection of Captain Mission*) **(2000)**

For more information
www.mattsgallery.org

ERNESTO NETO

b. 1964, Rio de Janeiro, Brazil
Lives and works in Rio de Janeiro

Recent solo exhibitions

Ernesto Neto, **Museum of Contemporary Art San Diego (2007);** *Leviathan Thot*, **Panthéon, Paris. Part of 35th Festival d'Automne (2006);** *Ernesto Neto-The Malmo Experience*, **Malmo Konsthall, Sweden (2006);** *Ernesto Neto*, **The Fabric Workshop and Museum, Philadelphia (2004);** *Ernesto Neto*, **Museum of Contemporary Art, Sydney (2002)**

Recent group exhibitions

Tropicália uma revolução na cultura brasileira, **Museu de Arte Moderna, Rio de Janeiro (2007); Reykjavik Triennial (2007);** *Perception of Space*, **Museum Boijmans van Beuningen, Rotterdam (2004);** *Shape*, **21st Century Museum of Contemporary Art, Kanazawa (2002);** *Bodyspace*, **The Baltimore Museum of Art (2001); Brazilian Pavilion and the Arsenale, Venice Biennale (2001)**

For more information
www.tanyabonakdargallery.com

TOBIAS PUTRIH

b. 1972, Kranj, Slovenia
Lives and works in New York, USA

Recent solo exhibitions

Quasi-Random, **Neuberger Museum of Art, Purchase, New York (2007); Slovenian Pavilion, Venice Biennale (2007); Laumeier Sculpture Park, St. Louis, Missouri (2006); Grazer Kunstverein, Graz, Austria (with Toby Paterson) (2005); Mala galerija, Museum of Modern Art, Ljubljana, Slovenia (2003)**

Recent group exhibitions

Megastructure Reloaded, **Berlin (2008);** *Eldorado*, **Musée d'Art Moderne Grand-Duc Jean, Luxembourg (2006);** *Downtime: Constructing Leisure*, **New Langton Arts, San Francisco (2005);** *Collective Effort*, **Baltimore Museum of Art (2004);** *Manifesta 4*, **Frankfurt (2002)**

For more information
www.maxprotetch.com

TOMAS SARACENO

b. 1973, Tucuman, Argentina
Lives and works in Frankfurt, Germany

Recent solo exhibitions

Air-Port-City, **De Vleeshal, Netherlands (2007);** *Tomas Saraceno*, **Centre d'Art Santa Monica, Barcelona (2006);** *Tomas Saraceno*, **The Curve, Barbican Art Gallery, London (2006);** *Personal States/Infinite Actives*, **Portikus, Frankfurt (with Marjetica Potrč) (2006);** *in-migration*, **Universität Kaiserslautern, Germany (2003)**

Recent group exhibitions

Megastructure Reloaded, **Berlin (2008); The Sharjah Biennial 8 (2007);** *Dialectic of Hope*, **Moscow Biennale of Contemporary Art (2005);** *Un-build cities*, **Kunstverein, Bonn (2003);** *Real Presence*, **Tito Museum, Belgrade (2001)**

For more information
www.tanyabonakdargallery.com

DO HO SUH

b. 1962, Seoul, South Korea
Lives and works in New York, USA

Recent solo exhibitions

Sun Gallery, Sun Art Center, Seoul (2006); The Fabric Workshop and Museum, Philadelphia (2005); *The Perfect Home*, **Kemper Museum of Contemporary Art, Kansas City (2002); Serpentine Gallery, London (2002);** *Some/One*, **Whitney Museum of American Art at Philip Morris, New York (2001);** *Seoul Home/L.A. Home*, **Korean Cultural Center, Los Angeles (2000)**

Recent group exhibitions

To the Human Future: Flight From The Dark Side, **Contemporary Art Gallery, Art Tower Mito, Japan (2006);** *Living Inside the Grid*, **The New Museum of Contemporary Art, New York (2004); Biennale of Sydney (2002);** *Korean Pavilion*, **Venice Biennale (2001);** *BodySpace*, **The Baltimore Museum of Art (2001)**

For more information
www.lehmannmaupin.com

RACHEL WHITEREAD

b. 1963, London, UK
Lives and works in London

Recent solo exhibitions

Rachel Whiteread, **Donna Regina Museum of Contemporary Art (MADRE), Naples (2007);** *Embankment*, **Unilever Series, Turbine Hall, Tate Modern, London (2005);** *Walls, Doors, Floors and Stairs*, **Kunsthaus Bregenz, Austria (2005);** *Rachel Whiteread in Brazil*, **Museu de Arte Moderna, Rio de Janeiro**

Recent group exhibitions

Part Object Part Sculpture, **Wexner Center for the Arts, Ohio State University, Colombus (2005);** *Design ≠ Art: Functional Objects from Donald Judd to Rachel Whiteread*, **Cooper-Hewitt National Design Museum, New York, and tour (2004);** *Century City*, **Tate Modern, London (2001);** *Public Offerings*, **Museum of Contemporary Art, Los Angeles (2001);** *Open Ends: 11 Exhibitions of Contemporary Art from 1960 to Now*, **Museum of Modern Art, New York (2000)**

For more information
www.gagosian.com

LIST OF WORKS

This list was accurate at the time of publication. There may have been subsequent changes to works in the exhibition.

Atelier Bow-Wow
Life Tunnel, **2008**
Steel plate
Courtesy Atelier Bow-Wow

Michael Beutler
Sandwiches, Dobbels and Burgers, **2008**
Paper and mesh
Courtesy the artist and Galerie Christian Nagel

Gelitin
normally, proceeding and unrestricted with without title, **2008**
Mixed media
Courtesy the artists

Los Carpinteros
Show Room, **2008**
Cinder blocks, fishing nylon, Ikea and B&Q furniture
Courtesy Sean Kelly Gallery, New York

Mike Nelson
To the Memory of H.P. Lovecraft, **1999, 2008**
Mixed media
Courtesy the artist, Matt's Gallery, London and Galleria Franco Noero, Torino

Ernesto Neto
Life fog frog...Fog frog, **2008**
Polyamide textiles, digital cut plywood, spices, pellets and hooks
Courtesy the artist, Fortes Vilaça SP and Tanya Bonakdar Gallery, New York

Tobias Putrih
Venetian, Atmospheric, **2007**
Plywood, OSB plates, scaffolding, PVC curtain, digital projectors
Courtesy the artist and Max Protetch Gallery, New York

Tomas Saraceno
Observatory, Air-Port-City, **2008**
Mixed media
Courtesy the artist and Tanya Bonakdar Gallery, New York

Do Ho Suh
Fallen Star 1/5, **2008**
ABS, basswood, beech, ceramic, enamel paint, glass, honeycomb board, laquer paint, latex paint, LED lights, pinewood, plywood, resin, spruce, styrene, polycarbonate sheets, PVC sheets
Courtesy the artist and Lehmann Maupin Gallery, New York

Do Ho Suh
Staircase – V, **2003/04/08**
Polyester and stainless steel tubes
Courtesy the artist and Lehmann Maupin Gallery, New York

Rachel Whiteread
Place, **2008**
Mixed media: doll's houses, crates, boxes, wood, electrical fittings and fixtures, electricity
Courtesy Rachel Whiteread

Films

Gordon Matta-Clark
Conical Intersect, **1975**
16 mm film transferred to DVD, colour
Running time: 18 minutes, 40 seconds
Courtesy Electronic Arts Intermix (EAI), New York

Chris Burden
Beam Drop, **1984**
16mm film transferred to DVD, black and white
Running time: approx. 6 minutes
Courtesy the artist

Gregor Schneider
Nacht-Video Haus ur, Rheydt, Oktober 1996, **1999**
Colour video transferred to DVD
Running time: 26 minutes, 14 seconds
Rubell Family Collection, Miami

Andrea Fraser
Little Frank and his Carp, **2001**
Colour video transferred to DVD
Running time: approx. 6 minutes
Courtesy of the artist and Friedrich Petzel Gallery

Jane Crawford (director)
Jane Crawford and Robert Fiore (producers)
Sheds, **2004**
Colour
Running time: 22 minutes
Courtesy Electronic Arts Intermix (EAI), New York

Victor Nieuwenhuijs and Maartje Seyferth
New Babylon de Constant, **2005**
Digi-betacam
Running time: approx. 13 minutes
Courtesy Victor Nieuwenhuijs and Maartje Seyferth

PICTURE CREDITS

Psycho Hayward

Atelier Bow-Wow
Courtesy Atelier Bow-Wow

Gelitin
Courtesy the artists

Los Carpinteros
Watercolour on paper
Courtesy the artists and Sean Kelly Gallery, New York

Ernesto Neto
Courtesy the artist, Fortes Vilaça SP and Tanya Bonakdar Gallery, New York

Tobias Putrih
Includes NASA and STScI image, *A Perfect Storm of Turbulent Gases in the Omega/Swan Nebula*
Courtesy the artist and Max Protetch Gallery, New York

Tomas Saraceno
Courtesy the artist and Tanya Bonakdar Gallery, New York

Do Ho Suh
Courtesy the artist and Lehmann Maupin Gallery, New York

Rachel Whiteread
Psycho Building, **2008**
Collage on paper
Courtesy Rachel Whiteread

ESSAYS

Psycho Buildings

Martin Kippenberger
Images from *Psychobuildings*, **1988**
Walther Konig, Cologne
Small paperback book consisting of black-and-white photographs (some appropriated) of various buildings
© Estate of Martin Kippenberger
Photo: Courtesy private collection, Switzerland

Gordon Matta-Clark
Splitting, **1974**
Colour photograph
© ARS, NY and DACS, London 2008
Photo: Courtesy Estate of Gordon Matta-Clark and David Zwirner, New York

Los Carpinteros
Cold Study of Disaster, **2005**
Thyssen-Bornemisza Art Contemporary
Photo: Courtesy Sean Kelly Gallery, New York

Do Ho Suh
Staircase, **2003**
Installation view at *Poetic Justice*: **8th International Istanbul Biennial, Turkey**
Translucent nylon
Photo: Courtesy the artist and Lehmann Maupin Gallery, New York

Ernesto Neto
Leviathan Thot, **2006**
Installation view at *Le Festival d'Automne*, **Panthéon, Paris**
Photo: Courtesy the artist; Tanya Bonakdar Gallery, New York; and Galeria Fortes Vilaça, Sao Paulo

Tobias Putrih
Venetian, Atmospheric, **2007**
Plywood, OSB plates, scaffolding, PVC curtain, 16mm projectors and digital projectors
Courtesy the artist and Max Protetch Gallery, New York

Species of Spaces: Art, Architecture and Environment

Joseph Paxton
Crystal Palace, **London, 1851**
(pictured in Sydenham)
Photo: © F. R. Yerbury/Architectural Association

El Lissitzky
Photomontage of the Wolkenbugel (Cloud-Iron), **Nikitskii Square, 1925**
© DACS 2008
Photo: Courtesy Research Library, The Getty Research Institute, Los Angeles, California (950076)

Constantin Brancusi
The Endless Column, **Târgu Jiu, Romania, *c.*1938**
Cast iron and steel
© ADAGP, Paris and DACS, London 2008
Photo: © CNAC/MNAM, Dist. RMN © Georges Meguerditchian

Yves Klein
Drawing for *Air Architecture* **project:** *Urbanisme de l'air architecture de l'air décorations-Intégrations architecturales et urbaines, l'eau et le feu, principe du toit d'air. Gelsenkirchen*, ***c.*1959**
Charcoal on paper mounted on canvas
© ADAGP, Paris and DACS, London 2008
Photo: Courtesy Yves Klein Archive

Buckminster Fuller
Proposal for an airborne habitat: *Cloud Nine*, **1958**
Photo: Courtesy The Estate of R. Buckminster Fuller

Kurt Schwitters
Merzbau, ***c.*1932**
Vintage photographic print
Sprengel Museum and Kurt und Ernst Schwitters Stiftung, Hannover
© DACS 2008
Photo: Wilhelm Redemann, Hannover

Art's Use of Architecture: Place, Site and Setting

Dan Graham
Two Adjacent Pavilions, **1978–81**
© Dan Graham 2008
Photo: Courtesy the artist and Lisson Gallery

Robert Smithson
Partially Buried Woodshed, **Kent State University, Kent, Ohio, 1970**
1 woodshed, 20 truckloads of raw earth
© Estate of Robert Smithson/DACS, London/VAGA, New York 2008
Photo: Robert Smithson. Courtesy James Cohan Gallery, New York

Gordon Matta-Clark
Window Blowout, **Bronx, New York, 1976**
© ARS, NY and DACS, London 2008
Photo: Courtesy Estate of Gordon Matta-Clark and David Zwirner, New York

Gordon Matta-Clark
Conical Intersect, **1975**
© ARS, NY and DACS, London 2008
Photo: Courtesy Estate of Gordon Matta-Clark and David Zwirner, New York

Robert Morris
Untitled (Box for Standing), **1961**
© ARS, NY and DACS, London 2008
Photo: Courtesy Sonnabend Gallery

ARTISTS

ATELIER BOW-WOW

Monkey Way, **2006**
Installation view at the Sao Paulo Biennale
Wood
Photo: Courtesy the artists

White Limousine Yatai, **2003**
Installation view at Echigo-Tsumaari Art Triennale
Steel
Photo: Courtesy the artists

Jumbo Origamic Arch Orange, **2005**
Installation view at Kobe Arts Village Centre, Hyogo, Japan
Paper
Photo: Courtesy the artists

Pet Architecture TAS, **2003**
Installation view at Walker Arts Center, Minneapolis
Wood
Photo: Courtesy the artists

Furnicycle, **2002**
Installation view at Shanghai Biennale
Steel
Photo: Courtesy the artists

Manga Pod, **2002**
Installation view at Gwangju Biennale
Wood
Photo: Courtesy the artists

MICHAEL BEUTLER

A-Frame, **2007**
Installation view at Gallery Christian Nagel, Berlin
Paper, cardboard, glue, chipboard, iron profiles, cable ties, tape, nails
Photo: Courtesy Collection Grässlin, St. Georgen

Aluminium Pagode, **2006**
Permanent installation at Lufthansa Aviation Center (LAC)
Aluminium
Photo: Michael Beutler. Courtesy Collection Lufthansa AG, Frankfurt am Main

Manin City, **2006**
Installation view at Villa Manin, Italy
Pecafil, cable ties, bamboo
Photo: Michael Beutler. Courtesy the artist, Gallery Christian Nagel, Berlin

Outdoor-yellow 9, **2004**
Installation view, Frankfurt, Germany
Pecafil, cable ties
Photo: Sabine Reitmaier. Courtesy the artist, Gallery Christian Nagel, Berlin

Glashaus, **2002**
Installation view at Secession, Vienna
Glass, band iron, cable bindings, laths, chipboard, paper, wire
Photo: Matthias Herrmann. Courtesy the artist, Gallery Christian Nagel, Berlin

GELITIN

Stellungswechsel 500, **2007**
Top left: Installation view at *Festival Printemps de Septembre*
Mixed media
Photo: Courtesy the artists

Stephan With PH Please!, **2002**
Mixed media
Photo: Courtesy the artists

Kinosaal, **2006**
Mixed media
Photo: Courtesy the artists

Kacksaal, **2006**
Mixed media
Photo: Courtesy the artists

Sweatwat, **2005**
Installation view at Gagosian Gallery
Mixed media
Photo: Courtesy the artists. Bottom left photo: © Thomas Sandbichler

Coliseum, **2001**
Installation view at Leo Koenig Inc
Mixed media
Photo: Courtesy Leo Koenig Inc

LOS CARPINTEROS

La Montaña Rusa, **2008**
Installation view at Sean Kelly Gallery, New York
Mixed media
Photo: Steven P. Harris, New York. Courtesy Sean Kelly Gallery, New York

Felled Lighthouse, **2006**
Mixed media
Photo: Courtesy the Latin American Acquisitions Committee 2006. Lent by the American Fund for the Tate Gallery

Watch Towers, **2002**
Aluminium and polycarbonate
Courtesy: Galeria Fortes Vilaça, São Paulo

Transportable City, **2000**
Aluminium and cloth
Photo: Eileen Costa. University of South Florida Collection, Tampa. Gift of the Artists. Courtesy Sean Kelly Gallery, New York

MIKE NELSON

Triple Bluff Canyon, **2004**
Installation view at Modern Art, Oxford
Mixed media
Photo: Courtesy the artist, Matt's Gallery, London and Galleria Franco Noero, Torino

Magazin: Büyük Valide Han, **2003**
Commissioned for *Poetic Justice*, **8th International Istanbul Biennial**
Photo: Courtesy the artist, Matt's Gallery, London and Galleria Franco Noero, Torino

The Coral Reef, **2000**
Installation view at Matt's Gallery, London
Photo: Courtesy the artist, Matt's Gallery, London and Galleria Franco Noero, Torino

To the Memory of H.P. Lovecraft, **1999**
Installation view at the Collective Gallery, Edinburgh
Mixed media
Photo: Courtesy the artist, Matt's Gallery, London and Galleria Franco Noero, Torino

Barker Ranch, **1996**
Installation view at W139, Amsterdam
Mixed media
Photo: Courtesy the artist, Matt's Gallery, London and Galleria Franco Noero, Torino

ERNESTO NETO

The Creature, **2006**
Installation view at *Ernesto Neto: The Malmo Experience*, **Malmo Konsthall, Sweden**
Photo: Courtesy the artist; Tanya Bonakdar Gallery, New York; and Galeria Fortes Vilaça, Sao Paulo

From What Are We Made, Made Of Of, **2006**
Installation view at *From Sebastian to Olivia*, **Max Hetzler Gallery, 2007**
Cotton, polypropylene, lycra, buckwheat shells, lavender and foam
Photo: Courtesy the artist; Max Hetzler Gallery, Berlin; and Tanya Bonakdar Gallery, New York

Cellula Nave. It happens in the body of time, where truth dances, **2004**
Installation view at Museum Boijmans van Beuningen, Rotterdam
Lycra, aluminium tubes, sand, styrofoam
Photo: © Bob Goedewaagen. Courtesy the artist; Tanya Bonakdar Gallery, New York; and Galeria Fortes Vilaça, Sao Paulo

Walking in Venus Blue Cave, **2001**
Installation view at *From Sebastian to Olivia*, **Max Hetzler Gallery, Berlin 2007**
Photo: Courtesy the artist; Max Hetzler Gallery, Berlin; and Tanya Bonakdar Gallery, New York

TOBIAS PUTRIH

Runa Islam and Tobias Putrih: Lost Cinema Lost, **2008**
Installation view at Pallazzo Santa Margherita, Galleria Civica del Comune di Modena
Photo: Paolo Terzi. Courtesy the artist and Galleria Civica del Comune di Modena

Lost Cinema Lost, **2008**
Installation view at Pallazzo Santa Margherita, Galleria Civica del Comune di Modena
Photo: Courtesy the artists and Galleria Civica del Comune di Modena. Photographer: Paolo Terzi

Cylinder, **2007**
Installation view at the Slovenian Pavilion at the Venice Biennale
Wood, neon lights, cable
Photo: Courtesy the artist and Max Protetch Gallery, New York. Photographer: Michele Lamanna

Studio at the Mudam, **2006**
Collection Mudam Luxembourg, Musée d'Art Moderne Grand-Duc Jean
Photo: Rémi Villaggi, 2006. Courtesy the artist and Max Protetch Gallery, New York

Anthology/Courthouse, **2005**
Monofilament, rear projections screen and clamps
Photo: Courtesy the artist and Max Protetch Gallery, New York. Top left photo: Christopher Burke

43,3 m, **2002**
Installation view at Sony Center Plaza at Postdamer Platz, Berlin, Germany
Project screen fabric, wooden frames
Photo: Courtesy the artist and Max Protetch Gallery, New York

TOMAS SARACENO

Galaxies Forming Along Filaments, Like Droplets Along the Strands of a Spider's Web, **2008**
Installation view at Tanya Bonakdar Gallery, New York
Elastic, rope
Photo: Fabian Birgfeld Photo TECTONICS. Courtesy the artist and Tanya Bonakdar Gallery New York

Biosphere MW 32, **2007**
Installation view at Pinksummer, Italy
Photo: © Marco Rokma. Courtesy the artist; Tanya Bonakdar Gallery, New York; Pinksummer, Genova; and ANDERSEN_S Contemporary, Copenhagen

How to Live Together, **2006**
Installation view at the Sao Paulo Biennale, Brazil
Photo: Courtesy the artist; Tanya Bonakdar Gallery, New York; Pinksummer, Genova; and ANDER-SEN_S Contemporary, Copenhagen

On Air, **2004**
Installation view at Pinksummer, Italy
Photo: Courtesy the artist; Tanya Bonakdar Gallery, New York; Pinksummer, Genova; and ANDERSEN_S Contemporary, Copenhagen

DO HO SUH

North Wall, **2005**
Polyester, stainless steel armature and cable
Photo: Courtesy the artist and Lehmann Maupin Gallery

Reflection, **2004**
Left: edition 2 of 2
Right: edition 1 of 2. Installation view at Maison Hermes in Tokyo, 2005
Nylon and stainless steel tube
Photo: Courtesy the artist and Lehmann Maupin Gallery

The Perfect Home II, **2003**
Translucent nylon
Photo: Courtesy the artist and Lehmann Maupin Gallery

Seoul Home/L.A. Home/New York Home/Baltimore Home/London Home/Seattle Home/L.A. Home, **1999**
Silk
Photo: Courtesy Museum of Contemporary Art, Los Angeles. Purchased with funds provided by an anonymous donor and a gift of the artist

RACHEL WHITEREAD

Embankment, **2005**
Unilever Series, Turbine Hall, Tate Modern, London
Photo: Marcus Leith and Marcella Leith. © Tate, London 2008

Untitled (Room 101), **2003**
Mixed media
Photo: Mike Bruce

Untitled (Basement), **2000–01**
Mixed media
Photo: Courtesy the artist and Luhring Augustine

Holocaust Memorial, **Judenplatz, Vienna, 2000**
Concrete
Photo: Courtesy Gagosian Gallery

Water Tower, **1998**
Resin cast of the interior of a wooden water tank, June 1998–99
Photo: Marion Harder. Courtesy Gagosian Gallery

House, **1993**
Mixed media
Photo: Sue Ormerod. Commissioned by Artangel. Sponsored by Becks. Courtesy Gagosian Gallery

Ghost, **1990**
Plaster and steel frame
Photo: Courtesy Gagosian Gallery

Psycho Buildings: An Illustrated History

Vladimir Tatlin with his model of the *Monument to the Third International*, **1919/20**
Photo: G. Costakis Collection

Kurt Schwitters
Merzbau, **c.1932**
Vintage photographic print
Sprengel Museum and Kurt und Ernst Schwitters Stiftung, Hannover
© DACS 2008
Photo: Ernst Schwitters

Salvador Dalí
Facade of the *Dream of Venus* **pavilion, 1939**
© Salvador Dali, Gala-Salvador Dali Foundation, DACS, London 2008
Photo: Eric Schaal. Courtesy Fundació Gala-Salvador Dalí

Frederick Kiesler
View of the Model of the Endless House, **1959**
Clay
© 2008, Austrian Frederick and Lillian Kiesler Private Foundation, Vienna. Source: Archive of the Kiesler Foundation Vienna
Photo: New York 1950, Collection of Museum of Modern Art, New York. Photographer unknown

André Bloc
Sculptures-Habitacle, **1964**
Photo: Courtesy Ernesto Neto

Buckminster Fuller
Geodesic Dome, Expo 67, **Montreal, 1967**
Photo: Courtesy The Estate of R. Buckminster Fuller

Jean Dubuffet
Pavillon à deux étages, **from** *Edifices*, **1968**
Photomontage
© ADAGP, Paris and DACS, London 2008
Photo: © Archives Fondation Dubuffet, Paris

Bruce Nauman
Green Light Corridor, **1970**
Painted wallboard and fluorescent light fixtures with green lamps
Solomon R. Guggenheim Museum, New York. Panza Collection, Gift, 1992. 92.4171
© ARS, NY and DACS, London 2008
Photo: Erika Ede Barahona © The Solomon R. Guggenheim Foundation, New York

Robert Smithson
Partially Buried Woodshed, **Kent State University, Kent, Ohio, 1970**
1 woodshed, 20 truckloads of raw earth
© Estate of Robert Smithson/DACS, London/VAGA, New York 2008
Photo: Robert Smithson. Courtesy James Cohan Gallery, New York

Ed Ruscha
Chocolate Room, **1970/2004**
Installation view at the Museum of Contemporary Art, Los Angeles
Chocolate on paper
© Ed Ruscha
Photo: Courtesy Ed Ruscha Studio / Museum of Contemporary Art, Los Angeles

Constant A. Nieuwenhuys
View of New Babylonian Sectors, **1971**
Inkjet print from original
© DACS 2008
Photo: Courtesy Municipal Museum, The Hague

Gordon Matta-Clark
Conical Intersect, **1975**
© ARS, NY and DACS, London 2008
Photo: Courtesy Estate of Gordon Matta-Clark and David Zwirner, New York

Toyo Ito
White-U, **1976**
© Toyo Ito & Associates, Architects
Photo: Courtesy Toyo Ito & Associates, Architects

Paul Thek
Processions, **1977**
Installation view at Institute of Contemporary Art, University of Pennsylvania, Philadelphia
© Estate of Paul Thek, courtesy Alexander and Bonin, New York
Photo: © Will Brown

Mary Miss
Perimeters/ Pavilions/ Decoys, **1977–79**
Wood, metal screening, wooden ladder
Photo: Courtesy Mary Miss Studio

Dan Graham
Two Adjacent Pavilions, **1978–81**
© Dan Graham 2008
Photo: Courtesy the artist and Lisson Gallery

Vito Acconci
Bad Dream House, **1984**
Wood, brick-face, shingles, Plexiglas, screen
© Acconci Studio
Photo: Courtesy Acconci Studio

Armando Munoz-Garcia
La Mona, **1985–90**
Concrete, steel rods, wire mesh
© the artist/David Covey 2001
Photo: David Covey 2001

Mario Merz
Unreal City, Nineteen Hundred Eighty-Nine, **1989**
Glass, mirror, metal pipes, twigs, rubber, clay and clamps
Solomon R. Guggenheim Museum, New York. Gift of the artist, 1989. 89.3631
Photo: David Heald. © The Solomon R. Guggenheim Foundation, New York

Tadashi Kawamata
Toronto Project, **1989**
Photo: Courtesy Mercer Union

David Hammons
House of the Future, **1991**
Charleston, SC and at the Spoleto Festival, 1991
Photo: Courtesy Tilton Gallery, NY. Photographer: H. Mark Weidman

Absalon
Cellule n°1 (Prototype), **1992**
Wood, cardboard, white paint
Photo: Courtesy Galerie Chantal Crousel

Paul McCarthy and Mike Kelley
Heidi, Midlife Crisis Trauma Center and Negative Media Engram Abreaction Release Zone, **1992**
Installation view at Galerie Krinziger, Vienna/AT
Performance, video, installation
© Paul McCarthy and Mike Kelley
Photo: Courtesy the artists and Hauser & Wirth Zürich London

Gregor Schneider
Haus u r, **(1985–) 1995**
© DACS 2008/Gregor Schneider
Photo: Courtesy Sadie Coles HQ, London

Jaroslaw Kozlowski
Gravity Room, **1995**
Installation view at Museet for Samtidskunst, Oslo
© Museet for Samtidskunst and Jaroslaw Kozlowski
Photo: Courtesy Emerson Gallery Berlin. Photographer: Morten Thorkildsen

Jonathan Meese
The Third Man in the Round House/ MALDORORTURM, **1998**
Mixed media
Photo: Courtesy Contemporary Fine Arts

Yayoi Kusama
Infinity Mirror Room, Rain in Early Spring, **2002**
Mixed media
© Yayoi Kusama
Photo: Courtesy Victoria Miro Gallery / Ota Fine Arts, Tokyo. Collection of Contemporary Art Museum Kumamoto

Diller+Scofidio
Blur Building, View from Shore, **2002**
Photo: Courtesy Diller Scofidio + Renfro

Thomas Hirschhorn
Cavemanman, **2002**
Installation view at Gladstone Gallery, New York
Wood, cardboard, tape, aluminium foil, books, posters, videos of Lascaux 2, dolls cans, shelves, fluorescent light fixtures
© Thomas Hirschhorn
Photo: Courtesy Gladstone Gallery, New York

Tatzu Nishi
Engel, **2002**
In collaboration with Littmann Kulturprojekt, Basel Switzerland
Photo: Courtesy the artist and Blum & Poe, Los Angeles, CA

Chris Burden
Small Skyscraper, **2003**
Photo: Courtesy Galerie Krinzinger

Olafur Eliasson
The antispective situation, **2003**
Stainless-steel mirrors
© Olafur Eliasson 2003
Photo: Giorgio Boato 2003. 21st Century Museum of Contemporary Art, Kanazawa, Japan

Marjetica Potrč
Hybrid House: Caracas, West Bank, West Palm Beach, **2003**
Palm Beach Institute of Contemporary Art, Lake Worth, Florida, 2003
Massachusetts Institute of Technology, List Visual Arts Center, Cambridge, Massachusetts, 2004
Building materials, energy and communication infrastructure
Photo: Michael Price

Brian Jungen
Arts and Crafts Book Depository/ Capp Street Project, **2004**
Architectural model; mixed media
Photo: Courtesy Catriona Jeffries Gallery, Vancouver / Collection of Pamela and Richard Kramlich, San Francisco

Thomas Schutte
Model for a Hotel, **2007**
Trafalgar Square's fourth plinth, London
© DACS 2008
Photo: © James O Jenkins. Courtesy Mayor of London's Office/Thomas Schutte/Frith Street Gallery

Atelier Van Lieshout
Wellness Skull, **2007**
© Atelier Van Lieshout
Photo: Courtesy Atelier Van Lieshout

NOTES ON THE AUTHORS

BRIAN DILLON is the author of a memoir, *In the Dark Room* **(2005), and UK editor of** *Cabinet*. **His writing appears regularly in** *frieze*, *Art Review*, *Modern Painters*, *The London Review of Books*, *The Times Literary Supplement* **and** *Sight & Sound*.

DAVID GREENE founded Archigram with Sir Peter Cook. He is Visiting Professor at the School of Architecture and the Built Environment, University of Westminster, London; a first year tutor at the Architectural Association; and teaches the Diploma in Architecture course and Masters course in Advanced Architectural Design at Oxford Brookes University.

PAULO HERKENHOFF is an art critic and independent curator living in Rio de Janeiro. His career includes Chief Curator of the XXIV Sao Paulo Biennale (1998) and Adjunct Curator of the Department of Painting and Sculpture of the Museum of Modern Art, New York.

MIWON KWON is Associate Professor of contemporary art history at University of California Los Angeles. She is the author of *One Place After Another: Site-Specific Art and Locational Identity* **(2002).**

FRANCESCO MANACORDA is Curator at the Barbican Art Gallery, London, and Visiting Lecturer in Curatorial Studies at the Royal College of Art, London.

MIDORI MATSUI is a Tokyo-based art critic, whose writing on Japanese and American contemporary art has been published extensively. Associate Professor at Tohoku University between 1990 and 2001, she now teaches contemporary art and theory at Musashino Art University and Tama Art University.

FRANCIS MCKEE is Director of CCA Glasgow and Director of the 2008 Glasgow International Festival.

TOM MORTON is a curator, writer and Contributing Editor of *frieze* **magazine. Formerly the Curator of Cubitt Gallery, London (2006—07), his recent curatorial projects include** *How to Endure*, **at the 2007 Athens Biennale.**

TUMELO MOSAKA is Associate Curator of Exhibitions at the Brooklyn Museum, New York. Recent exhibitions and projects include *Infinite Island: Contemporary Caribbean Art* **(2007),** *Open House: Working in Brooklyn* **(2004),** *Passing/Posing: Kehinde Wiley* **(2005) and** *Alexis Rockman: Manifest Destiny* **(2004).**

JANE RENDELL is Director of Architectural Research at the Bartlett, UCL. An architectural designer and historian, art critic and writer, she is author of *Art and Architecture* **(2006),** *The Pursuit of Pleasure* **(2002) and co-editor of** *Pattern* **(2007),** *Critical Architecture* **(2007),** *Spatial Imagination* **(2005),** *The Unknown City* **(2001),** *Intersections* **(2000),** *Gender Space Architecture* **(1999) and** *Strangely Familiar* **(1995).**

RALPH RUGOFF is Director of The Hayward, London.

IAIN SINCLAIR has lived in (and written about) Hackney, East London, since 1969. His novels include *Downriver*, *Radon Daughters*, *Landor's Tower* **and** *Dining on Stones*. **Non-fiction books, exploring the myth and matter of London, include** *Lights Out for the Territory*, *London Orbital*, *Edge of the Orison* **and** *London: City of Disappearances*.